THE
ROAD
TO
PEACE

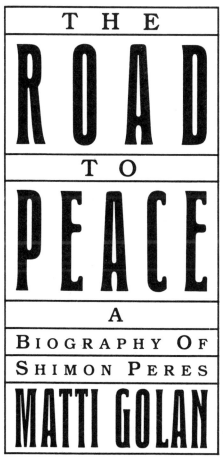

THE
ROAD
TO
PEACE

A
BIOGRAPHY OF
SHIMON PERES

MATTI GOLAN

TRANSLATED BY
AKIVA RON

WARNER BOOKS

A Warner Communications Company

Warner Books, Inc., 666 Fifth Avenue, New York, NY 10103

 A Warner Communications Company

Printed in the United States of America

First Printing: November 1989

10 9 8 7 6 5 4 3 2 1

Book Design by Nick Mazzella

Library of Congress Cataloging-in-Publication Data

Golan, Matti.
    The road to peace.

    1. Peres, Shimon, 1923–   .   2. Statesmen—Israel
—Biography.   3. Israel—Politics and government.
I. Title.
DS126.6.P47G63 1989   956.9465'092 [B]   89-40047
ISBN 0-446-51425-X

To Tamar,
my beloved daughter

ACKNOWLEDGMENTS

A great deal of the material for the period starting in 1981 was gathered by Akiva Eldar, the diplomatic correspondent and columnist for the newspaper *Ha'aretz*.

CONTENTS

PROLOGUE

No POLITICAL PERSONALITY reflects the reality of today's Israel in his actions and achievements as much as Shimon Peres. Yet, no other personality has so often reached the spring but been prevented from drinking. Even on the one occasion he was allowed to, he was permitted only a brief taste before being sent back to the starting gate by the Israeli people.

This is the strange story of a man who served the people all his life with talent and loyalty, but never really won their trust or love. The Israeli public seems to have great respect for Peres's abilities but a lack of confidence in his character.

Few Israelis, including Peres's political opponents, will deny that he fulfilled all his tasks with vision and got things done in a manner that brought benefits to the nation he served. But far fewer have been prepared to crown him as their leader. There is no practical reason for this. After hesitating, stuttering, and groping for the right words, people are liable to say that he is not worthy, not credible— that something about him is false.

Peres himself frequently says that nothing in his life has come to him easily. In fact, this is only partly true. At the start of his political career, things came to him very easily. In his early twenties, he was appointed to senior positions in the Haganah, the prestate Jewish defense force. In his late twenties, he was appointed deputy director general of the Israel Defense Ministry by Prime Minister David Ben-Gurion, and immediately afterward to director general. At that time he had everything necessary for success in public and political

1

life: the trust and confidence of Ben-Gurion, the strong man and undisputed leader.

There is no doubt that he earned the trust. Ben-Gurion was busy with all the matters on the agenda of the young nation he was creating, and naturally, could not devote too much time to the Defense Ministry. In effect, Peres set up the defense establishment of Israel, with Ben-Gurion providing the political umbrella that enabled him to operate. He worked unceasingly, with talent and loyalty. During this period his vision and ability to get things done were seen to their best advantage.

He resolved to establish an aircraft industry, which in time was to produce a combat airplane, when there was scarcely enough to eat and when the Israel Defense Forces, the IDF, had only a few pathetic cannons and tanks. He created a military industry that was to supply all the needs of the IDF, when the national budget was less than that of a medium-sized American factory.

But his greatest achievement, which possibly guaranteed the future of the State of Israel, was to build the atomic reactor in Dimona. Peres understood in the 1950s that the day would come when Israel would no longer be able to compete in an arms race with Arab states, when their treasuries were swollen with petrodollars. He convinced Ben-Gurion to anticipate this danger by acquiring the capacity to deter the Arab states from attacking Israel or even destroying it.

The few who were in on the secret strenuously opposed the project, because of its dangerous nature and its dizzying cost. Also, it seemed at the time that it was an impractical goal, for who would give Israel an atomic reactor at a time when the great powers were firmly opposed to building them in other countries?

Peres found the nation prepared to do it. At a time when the prevailing opinion in Jerusalem was that Israel should strive to become close to the United States, Peres looked toward France. He did this not for love of France, but out of a cool calculation that "the enemy of my enemy is my friend." France was then fighting to retain control over Algeria against an underground that was armed and supported by the Arab states; Israel was in a state of war with the Arab nations. Here was fertile ground for close cooperation. Peres's calculation proved correct beyond what he anticipated.

Acting entirely on his own, disregarding the Foreign Ministry,

Peres forged close ties with the French ruling establishment—in particular, those in defense. The direct result was the acquisition of massive supplies of all types of weapons, including the most sophisticated, at a time when most of the world (including the United States) was imposing an embargo on arms shipments to Israel. Peres's French orientation, which was built up in back rooms and by unconventional methods, created the basis for the Israel Defense Forces and guaranteed the future of the state.

Those were Peres's glorious years—years during which he was able to dream and implement, protected from all harm by Ben-Gurion's mantle. Then he was at his best. His personal tragedy—the period when things started to come with difficulty—began when Ben-Gurion was no longer there to protect him.

Peres took the step from the civil service into political life when he was elected to the Knesset in December 1959. Ben-Gurion was now able to appoint him deputy defense minister. (According to Israeli law, a deputy minister must be a member of the Knesset.) To all appearances, Peres was continuing on the same path in the same field; but, in fact, there was a genuine change in his status and career. As a political figure, he could play a greater part in public life, but the price was greater exposure to criticism. This is when his problem with the public started to manifest itself. It became even more evident against the background of his close political and personal relations with Moshe Dayan.

Peres and Dayan were the political twins of Israel, but they were not identical. Dayan was dashing, macho, very independent in thought and deed, direct and crude, a rebel against accepted norms—he behaved as he wished. In contrast Peres was much more inhibited, introverted, and sophisticated. He calculated his steps with care and strove to make a favorable impression, wanting to be popular. As so often happens, the less Dayan wooed the public, the more the public ran after him. With Peres, the opposite was true.

Both of them were adopted and nurtured by Ben-Gurion; both operated in the realm of defense and reached the summit. Dayan became defense minister via the IDF, after he had been chief of staff; Peres reached the post via the Defense Ministry itself. They were political allies and personal friends because Peres accepted (sometimes with humiliation) Dayan's leadership, which was the only possible basis for their relationship. Peres's acceptance of this situation was manifested in the respective roles of the two men: Peres was the one who did the dirty work; Dayan was the one who reaped the rewards. In other words, Peres built the political power that Dayan wielded.

The Yom Kippur War of 1973 changed Peres's situation. Dayan was blamed by the public for the failures of the war and was forced to resign his public offices. It seemed as if the time had come for Peres to unfold his independent wings and rise to the top. And, in fact, just before the general election of May 1977, he appeared about to reap the reward of his continuous efforts.

Prime Minister Yitzhak Rabin was forced to resign the leadership of the ruling Labor party because of a scandal concerning his wife's foreign bank account, and Peres became Labor's candidate for the premiership. The elections were only a few weeks off and Labor, the party Peres now led, had always won in the past. This was the first time he had come so near the spring, and it seemed as if no force in the world would be able to prevent him from drinking.

When the fog of the elections had dispersed, it became clear that, for the first time in Israel's history, the public had taken power away from the Labor party and given it to the Likud. Instead of being prime minister, Peres found himself at the head of a wounded and bitter party that had lost its way—and was in opposition. Despite this shattering personal blow, Peres quickly recovered and devoted the next years to rehabilitating the party.

In the general election of 1981, it again seemed that Peres had reached the spring. The Likud mobilized for the elections with its leader, Menachem Begin, in low spirits, and with the economy in a bad state. When the votes were counted, it was found that the Labor party had indeed increased its strength significantly, but not enough to oust Begin from power. Peres and his party returned to opposition.

In the Labor party and the public at large, people started saying that Peres was an able man but unelectable. At the same time, the Likud government was going from bad to worse. Under the orchestration of Defense Minister Ariel Sharon, the nation had become involved in a brutal, costly, and pointless war in Lebanon. The country was suffering from an annual inflation rate of several hundred percent. The government fell before its four years were up, and a new general election was called in 1984.

It now seemed that Peres was not simply close, but actually at the spring. The Likud was responsible for the disastrous mistakes of the government, and it was led, not by the charismatic Menachem Begin, but by Yitzhak Shamir, a drab and virtually unknown figure. The Labor party anticipated an overwhelming victory.

But once again it didn't happen: the public did not give either party the strength to set up a government. The outcome was a government of national unity with Shimon Peres and Yitzhak Shamir taking turns as prime minister.

Peres headed the government for the first two years. He brought the IDF out of Lebanon. He performed an economic miracle by bringing inflation down to reasonable levels without causing either large-scale unemployment or significantly reducing the standard of living. He took diplomatic initiatives that restored Israel's reputation as a peace-loving nation. His popularity and that of his party were at an all-time high.

After two years Peres transferred the premiership to Shamir, according to the coalition agreement, and went to the Foreign Ministry. After two years as prime minister, during which he rightly felt he had achieved a great deal, it was a difficult move for him. But he hoped that in another two years the public would remember his achievements as prime minister: the fact that after receiving from the Likud a country entangled in Lebanon and on the verge of economic collapse, he had given back a stable and peaceful nation.

However, during the next two years, the qualities that had harmed him all his political life reemerged. He was unable to sit quietly, carry out his work faithfully, and wait for his day to dawn. He went on acting as if he were prime minister, at least on the diplomatic front. He initiated talks in the world's capitals about having an international, Middle East peace conference, despite the opposing view of the prime minister and the official policy of the government.

Thus the impossible situation arose whereby Israel spoke with two voices: the foreign minister in favor of an international conference, the prime minister against it. Peres justified his conduct with the argument that the possibility of peace was more important to him than formality or official positions. Shamir claimed that the forces driving Peres were his unwillingness to accept the loss of the premiership and his inability to take the straight path.

Thus they again went to the people in November 1988, and the

Israeli public was asked to decide between Peres's achievements and
his character. Shamir won forty Knesset seats; Peres thirty-nine.
The balance was held by the religious parties, whom the two leaders
began to woo. During this period, Peres proved to whoever needed
proof that the public's lack of confidence in him was based on genuine
considerations.

The religious parties utilized the power that the election results
had given them to make far-reaching demands, both in the field of
religious legislation and in the financial sphere, as the price for
forming a coalition government with one of the large parties. Public
morale was low in the face of the danger that the extremist religious
parties, some of which were even anti-Zionist, would dictate the
nation's life-style in the coming years.

From both left and right voices were heard demanding the
formation of a national unity government by the two large parties, in
order to take the bargaining chips away from the religious parties. It
was Peres's opportunity to cross the line from party politician to
national leader.

Many people thought that he would announce that, whatever
happened, he would not go into a narrow coalition with the religious
parties, and that he would issue a call to the Likud to form a joint
government. The people thought that Peres would be the one to do
this because he had nothing to lose, as it was clear to everyone that
the religious parties could not and did not want to go into a coalition
with Labor's allies on the left, which were hostile to them.

It was clear to everyone—except Peres. He continued negotiating with the religious parties, even after it was explained to him, in
newspaper articles and private conversations, that they were using
him as a bargaining chip in their talks with the Likud.

He continued the negotiations after he had announced on
television that he would not do so and even after the president had
charged Yitzhak Shamir with forming the government.

And Peres paid a heavy price. The religious parties, as anticipated, kicked him in the face and preferred Shamir, whereupon
Shamir kicked the religious parties in the face and brought in the
Labor party, which was forced to come crawling and agree to its
leader being finance minister with no say in diplomatic matters.

As a bonus Shamir won great popularity, whereas Peres merely confirmed his reputation as one who preferred the crooked path to the straight.

Why? Possibly because in his great days, during the time of the relationship with France, he learned to achieve things in unconventional ways. Or possibly because over the years he lost the self-confidence needed to take steps inspired by noble motives, as opposed to political wheeling and dealing. Or maybe it is simply his nature.

Anyway, it is certain that, had he worked for a national unity government from the outset, he could have entered it on a basis of equality with Shamir and rotation of the premiership. However, to do that, he would have had to take the straight path—something he seemed unable to do.

CHAPTER ONE

THE BEGINNING OF THE ROAD

SHIMON PERES'S PARENTS belonged to that minority who did not need Adolf Hitler to convince them of their Zionist beliefs. Possibly this was because they lived in the small Polish town of Vishneva, where the 170 families had two prominent characteristics: poverty and Judaism. Unlike other, similar towns, their Judaism was not expressed through religion. Like most of the families in Vishneva, Shimon's was not Orthodox, and their religious observance was limited to eating kosher food and attending synagogue on festivals.

Jewishness in the town was expressed through Zionism, and Shimon's parents sent him and his elder brother, Gershon, to a secular school instead of a religious cheder. The school served as a breeding ground for the Zionist ideas that were starting to strike deep roots in Eastern Europe.

Shimon was eight years old when his father went to Palestine in 1931 to prepare for the family's immigration. Two years later Shimon and Gershon helped their mother pack their belongings, and the three of them traveled on a dilapidated boat to join the head of the family in Palestine.

His parents registered Shimon at the Balfour primary school, but his heart was not in his studies. When he finished, with grades of the sort that parents do not boast about, his father resolved that he should learn a useful trade, so he found himself in a commercial high school. At this time he joined Hanoar Ha'oved, the youth movement of the Histadrut Labor Federation, where the emphasis was on training members of the movement for kibbutz life.

"I was excited by the kibbutzim, the farming, the blue shirts, the encounter with Yemenite youth and working youth," Peres wrote many years later in his memoirs.

Within a short time, Shimon stood out for his rhetorical and organizational abilities, and his youth leader, Elhanan Yishai, persuaded the Ben Shemen Youth Village to award him a scholarship covering tuition and accommodation at the village boarding school.

By then Shimon was a plump young man. He hated sports, so in contrast to the other, tanned youngsters, his face was always pale. Possibly, during this period, he developed a "suntanned-look complex," and in later years would never lose an opportunity to sit in the sun. In a chauffeur-driven car, he would sit on the sunny side; in a room, he would take up a position by the open window with the sun streaming in; and in his rare leisure hours, he would sit on the beach in a deck chair. Few people—if any—can claim to have seen him in swimming trunks, but his face was always tanned.

Shimon stood out for his writing talent and even more for his compulsion to write. He wrote regularly for *Bama'aleh*, the journal of Hanoar Ha'oved. He also earned a reputation as a gifted lecturer and public speaker, and as a superb organizer. However, in those days, status in that society was determined by the ability to perform physical labor. Other talents could add to it, but not serve as a substitute. Shimon's desire to prove himself in his field bordered on masochism. During this period he learned to manage on five, sometimes even four, hours of sleep a night, which became a habit in his adulthood.

It was in Ben Shemen that Peres met Sonia Gelman, the daughter of the carpentry teacher. She was a thin girl, with long, black plaits, cheerful and good-natured. Her modesty stood out even in the modest atmosphere of those days, and she has remained self-effacing. Their courtship was typical of the times—Sonia would accompany Shimon on guard duty when it was their turn, and in a distant position, by the light of a flickering candle, he would read her poetry and selections from Marx's *Das Kapital*. Because he also loved music, Shimon began to play the guitar with Sonia. However, the peak of musical achievement attained by the couple was a joint rendering of "Hatikva," the national anthem.

Although he did not lack vision, and his analytical talent was probably superior to that of many of his fellows, these were not the qualities that propelled Peres to the top. He reached the summit, essentially, because of his ability to get things done, which was the result of determination, boundless ambition, and an almost inhuman capacity for hard work.

When these qualities came to the fore in his activities in the group at Ben Shemen, it was even then clear to Peres, and became clear to those who knew him, that the youth village environment was too small for him. The opportunity to give expression to his talents came when Peres left Ben Shemen in August 1941, and went with his group for training to Kibbutz Geva in Lower Galilee.

On the surface, he had every reason to be content, at least for a time. He was able to enjoy Galilee—to drink in the beauty of the green hills and the scent of the yellow wildflowers, to take a young lady to the barn and whisper words of love on enchanted moonlit nights, when the rolling hills in the pale light were so beautiful as to be unreal.

Peres never was able to rest and relax. While working as a dairyman, with all that it entailed, including rising early and doing physical labor that left people stronger than he without the energy for other activities, Peres actively sought out extra responsibility. He found it in the branches of Hanoar Ha'oved, first in the area around Ein Harod and, after a few months, in the entire Jezreel Valley, from Kiryat Amal in the west to the Beisan valley in the east.

He took on himself the task of revitalizing the movement. Every week—in fact, almost every day—he traveled to the branches, which were far away and dangerous. Hitchhiking on a horse-drawn wagon, traveling in a creaking, battered bus, or most often, on foot, he would arrive at the shacks that accommodated the movement groups. He organized seminars, lectures, debates, parties, and sing-alongs, converting the lifeless huts into centers that attracted the young members.

Even then no one thanked him, either for his efforts or his

success. In fact, as would be the case throughout his life, it was not just that he received no gratitude, but that he drew enmity and dislike. What was it then that turned them, and later, other comrades, against him? Possibly Peres himself had the best explanation, when he wrote, many years afterward: "I have to accept the fact that many people think I am the type who pushes to the front of the queue."

The thing people could not stand, and that turned them against him, was his insistence upon doing more, doing it faster and without being asked, striving for the top position.

Peres says that he accepts the fact that "many *think* that I am the type who pushes to the front." He does not accept that this claim is justified; not then, not later. "I am convinced, deep in my heart, that I am incorrigibly shy," he was to write later. This is the source of a feeling that was to develop and grow: "Nobody likes me. Even my good actions and positive qualities are distorted."

Others might examine themselves, change their style, or fight against such an image. But Peres accepts it, preferring to see himself as unjustly assessed and to build a wall against those who hold that opinion.

The ideas that Peres espoused certainly did nothing to increase his popularity. Here again he had a problem of "more and faster"— thinking more, as well as doing more. He lived among young people for whom farming was not a way of advancement but the fulfillment of a romantic dream of arduous physical labor. They were pure socialists, who believed in modesty and simplicity, in earning their bread from the soil. This also was not enough for Peres. Milking cows and growing vegetables was fine, but not everything. The future, he would say, lay in modern industry, science, and technology; and if the kibbutzim wanted to survive, they had to enter this field also. In the conservative-socialist society of Kibbutz Geva, these ideas were heresy, and the person who put them forward was an unbeliever. Worse, he was regarded as almost a capitalist.

In fact, Peres's main fault was that he was ahead of his time. He foresaw the future more clearly than others and did not know how to wait for the right moment to put forward his ideas.

Years later, when he became minister of transport and communications, this experience was to cause him a certain satisfaction. One of the innovations he tried to introduce was the use of magnetic cards for public telephones, instead of tokens or coins. He investigated and found that these cards were used in the Paris subway. He asked the French if it was possible to use them in public telephones and received a positive answer. When he inquired where the cards were manufactured, he was told that they were made at Kibbutz Geva in Israel.

Traveling to Geva, he discovered that the cow shed where he had once labored had been converted into a factory for electronic devices and magnetic cards. The same people who had been intensely irritated by his youthful ideas were now operating the sophisticated modern equipment.

He was seen as a pusher in those early days, both in the field of action and in the realm of ideas. To add insult to injury, Peres made an ideology out of his pushiness, which was the exact opposite of the accepted moral code of the kibbutz movement. This code determined that it was bad form to want public office, and that it should not be given to somebody who strove for it. Even today, kibbutz leaders fight with all their energy for a public position, and when they attain it, talk of "bowing to the movement's decision," as if they are accepting the post with reluctance, only out of a sense of duty.

In those days, this attitude was even stronger, and Peres found it hard to accept. He loved public affairs, felt driven to achievement, and sought positions which enabled him to implement his ideas. He did not see why he should conceal this. In the evening discussions in the communal dining hall, which were the main source of entertainment of the members and which he made use of to air his ideas, he would argue forcefully that "ambition is not a dirty word, and I admire ambitious people who don't try to disguise it."

This message, and the hint that there were others in the group who took care to hide their ambitions, caused a great sensation. Of course, his words were absolutely true, but then, even more than now, self-righteousness prevailed over truth in the kibbutz movement.

In September 1942, Peres and his comrades completed their training at Kibbutz Geva and went out to found a new settlement, Kibbutz Alumot, overlooking the marvelous view of Lake Kinneret (the Sea of Galilee).

Here, Peres had to learn the new skills of field hand and shepherd. Here, too, he married his girlfriend Sonia, who was to follow him faithfully over the years and to become his main support during his turbulent political career. The routine of laboring on the kibbutz and running the youth movement branches was brought to an end on an exceptionally hot summer day.

On that day the members of Kibbutz Alumot had to sweep out their tents, straighten the lines of stones bordering their footpaths, and put on their best clothes, because they were to receive a visit from the head of the Jewish Agency's settlement department.

At the time, when the Jewish Agency executive was in effect the government of the Jewish community and when settlement of the land was top priority, the head of the department dealing with settlement seemed like God, or, as David Ben-Gurion already had that role, at least like His deputy.

A black Buick arrived at noon with white smoke pouring from it as if the engine were begging for a rest. His wet white shirt clinging to his body, and mopping his face with a handkerchief, Levi Eshkol emerged from the vehicle, exclaiming in Yiddish: "My children, it is very hot." After again wiping his smiling face, he asked: "Where is the coolest place here?"

The members searched, until their eyes focused on a nearby spot.

"What is the problem?" asked Eshkol, following their gazes.

"Are you prepared to climb down?"

"To get out of this heat, I am prepared to climb down to the bottom of the world."

So Eshkol led them, wearing their best Sabbath clothes, down into an ancient well no longer in use. He spread his handkerchief on the ground and sat on it. The four members who had descended with him, all of them senior kibbutz office-holders, did the same. After satisfying their curiosity with the latest news of developments in the Zionist movement, Eshkol came to the point: "*Kinderlach*, I need Shimon at the Hanoar Ha'oved secretariat."

Eshkol went on to explain, in his pleasant voice, that the leaders of Hanoar Ha'oved wanted Peres to duplicate all over this country the job he had done in Galilee.

The kibbutz secretary was not impressed. He did not see how the kibbutz could agree to Comrade Eshkol's request. In a small community, he noted, every pair of working hands was precious, and Shimon was one of the good workers. Someone else, just as good as

Shimon, could be found for the Hanoar Ha'oved secretariat in Tel Aviv.

Eshkol explained that Shimon Peres was experienced and had already proven himself, and that the matter was also important to the party. As he continued speaking—a little Hebrew and a lot of Yiddish—he felt that the members were weakening. His experience had taught him that one more argument would make them give way. "*Kinderlach*," said the member of nearby Kibbutz Degania, "we are neighbors, after all. Are you going to refuse a neighbor's request?"

The kibbutz leaders could not resist such an appeal, and so it was that, at the bottom of a dry well, from considerations of good neighborliness, Peres was launched on a path, the destination of which nobody—except possibly Peres himself—could have foreseen.

In the first stage it led him to several dozen buildings on the main streets of Tel Aviv: Ha'aliya, Allenby, Hayarkon, the beginning of Dizengoff. Peres was amazed to see how much the town had grown and developed in so short a time.

Even if he was not fully conscious of the fact, he was ready for town life and all it had to offer, and it was ready for him. He could hear the noise of the vital industry of the large town. This was where the big and important things were happening, and that was why he belonged here.

A short while after he arrived in Tel Aviv, elections for the 22nd Zionist Congress in Basel, Switzerland, were due to be held. Levi Eshkol, head of the Mapai election staff, appointed Peres to the staff's organization branch. In the course of this work, Peres had to travel from Tel Aviv one day to visit the Haifa party branch—no easy matter in those uncertain times. Somebody who found out that Ben-Gurion was going that way arranged a lift for Peres.

His excitement at the prospect of meeting the Zionist leader was great. He looked forward to a lively discussion with Ben-Gurion on the long journey. To his great disappointment, "almost the entire journey passed without him opening his mouth. Just as we were approaching the outskirts of Haifa, he suddenly turned to me and said, 'You know, Trotsky was not a statesman.' To this day, I don't know why Ben-Gurion suddenly thought of Leon Trotsky, but as I was keen to continue the conversation, I asked him why. He became more enthusiastic and explained: 'What sort of a policy is no peace, no war? Either you decide for peace, and pay the heavy price it sometimes demands, or you decide on war, and accept the terrible danger it entails. Lenin understood that.'"

Peres got out of the car in Haifa. "I did not imagine that the day would come when I would see Ben-Gurion decide both on war and on steps toward peace," he said later. He certainly did not imagine that this man, more than any other, would determine his fate and his future.

It might have been expected that Shimon's work on the Mapai election staff for the 22nd Zionist Congress would have resulted in his organizational abilities being mobilized for the meeting, but in fact it took a clear directive from Ben-Gurion to Moshe Shertok, the head of the Jewish Agency's political department: "Don't send only tried and trusted activists, but young people who represent the movement." As a result, two youngsters attended the congress as observers: Shimon Peres, then twenty-three, and Moshe Dayan, thirty-one.

The congress was characterized by stormy clashes between the activists and those favoring a more moderate line. Ben-Gurion led the activist camp, which demanded disengagement from the British, and aimed at the establishment of a Jewish state. Against them the legendary leaders of the Zionist movement, Chaim Weizmann, Nahum Goldman, and Abba Hillel Silver, favored continuing cooperation with Britain, until independence could be gained by means of understanding and partnership.

Peres and Dayan found themselves in Ben-Gurion's camp and even went further than he. They proposed to the congress that the refugee camps the British had established on Cyprus for "illegal" Jewish immigrants be burned down, to force the authorities to bring the internees to Palestine. The suggestion so upset Avraham Harzfeld, the secretary of the agricultural center, that he broke down and cried. The proposal was not seriously considered, but its planning and formulation resulted in the first ties between Peres and Dayan—ties that would become deeper and stronger in the years ahead.

At the beginning of 1947, Shimon was invited to join the school for diplomats that had just been established by the political department of the Jewish Agency. He did not hesitate for long. He had a definite feeling that the niceties of diplomatic language were not appropriate to his burning desire to get things done. Shortly afterward, Levi Eshkol again made the trip to Kibbutz Alumot. As he had several years previously, he asked for the release of Comrade Shimon Peres—this time not to work in Hanoar Ha'oved, but to be head of manpower in the Haganah General Staff.

CHAPTER TWO

THE FRENCH ORIENTATION

He Says He Will Make a Jet

EARLY ONE MORNING in May 1947, Peres strode down Hayarkon Street in Tel Aviv, enjoying the view of the sea, which, after the winter's storms, was waiting for the quiet days of summer. It was a typical spring day—not yet hot, but warm enough for a few dozen impatient people to strip, lie on the soft, golden sand, and expose their bodies to the caressing rays of the sun. Although he liked the sun and the sea, Peres was not envious of them. There was work waiting to be done, and he loved work better than anything else. He felt great satisfaction at the fact that in a few minutes he would take his place in the building that was the nerve center of the Yishuv (Jewish community) in those days.

It was called the "Red House," although the color was actually closer to pink, because the wind from the sea had coated it with a generous layer of salt. Apart from its color, it was no different from the hundreds of other buildings constructed in Tel Aviv at the time. It had four floors, balconies facing the sea, simple lines: not at all luxurious, very functional. What distinguished it from the surrounding houses was the type of work that went on there twenty-four hours a day. Here in this building was the headquarters of the Haganah, the official underground of the Yishuv, which was responsible for defending the state as it developed, and would later be the foundation of the army.

Peres was assigned a small room on the second floor, which he had to share with a secretary. He was given a few days to learn his new job as head of manpower, and then was summoned by Ben-Gurion. The conversation lasted less than three minutes. Ben-Gurion expressed the hope that the young man was managing and, before turning his back on him, said forcefully, as if annoyed with him: "We have to prepare for war. We haven't much time, and we have to mobilize as large a force as possible."

Apparently Peres carried out his tasks very efficiently because he was gradually given extra jobs. When the naval section of the Haganah ran into difficulties, he was appointed to the post of head of naval services in the General Staff. Another job he was given—far more significant in terms of his future career—was with Teddy Kollek, who was in charge of arms procurement from the United States.

One day Kollek arrived back in Tel Aviv and complained to Levi Eshkol that there was no one to talk to at Haganah headquarters. If someone were not appointed to deal with American arms purchases at General Staff headquarters, he, Kollek, would not be prepared to continue at his post. On the spot, Eshkol summoned Peres and asked him, "What are you doing at the moment, young man?"

"Manpower," Peres said.

"Do you know English?"

"No."

"Have you been to America?"

"No."

"You are just the man I'm looking for. As of today, you are in charge of arms purchases from the United States."

After Peres left the room, Kollek exploded: "What do you think you are doing? You have appointed a completely inexperienced man."

Eshkol smiled. "Don't worry," he told Kollek. "I promise you, he is going to do it better than anyone."

Manpower, naval services, American arms purchases—the days

now seemed woefully short for Peres. A normal day's work started at five or six in the morning, and ended after midnight, for everything was new and problematic. Everything was in short supply, and each problem solved brought in its wake others. The only way of navigating without coming aground on one of the many sandbanks was by improvization. Peres could not have wished for a better school to acquire the faith that nothing was impossible. He learned this lesson well, and it became an integral part of his thought and personality.

Peres was still carrying out those jobs when, on May 15, 1948, the State of Israel was established. The next day a ceremony was arranged for the members of the Haganah General Staff, which had now become the Israel Defense Forces (IDF) General Staff, to swear loyalty to the new state.

Together with eleven other members of the General Staff, Peres ascended to the roof of the Red House, swore loyalty to the IDF, received mobilization card number 45546 and the rank of private. Peres went through the War of Independence with that rank and those tasks.

Twice during the war, Peres submitted requests to be posted to a field unit. Both times, Ben-Gurion turned him down on the ground that his work at General Staff headquarters was immeasurably more important than anything he could contribute in a combat unit.

Ben-Gurion did agree to another request, one that Peres made immediately after the war. Peres was twenty-six; and, although he had carried out important tasks and won the confidence of the leaders of the young state, he was upset by the fact that he lacked a formal education. He came to Ben-Gurion and asked to be allowed to study. Ben-Gurion reacted positively, but at once made it conditional on his accepting a new task. He agreed that Peres should go and study in the United States, but on condition that he head the Israeli purchasing mission instead of Teddy Kollek, who was about to finish his tour of duty in the post.

Peres left for the United States in January 1950, and it didn't take long for him to discover that political independence had not liberated Israel from the underground. The Washington embargo on arms to the Middle East meant that there was no chance of buying directly from the administration. He therefore concentrated his efforts on the huge market of surplus equipment from World War II.

For the most part it was scrap or outdated equipment that an established nation would not have thought of buying, but Israel was no normal state—certainly not with regard to weapons or money.

However, the U.S. government placed severe limits even on this low-grade weaponry, and Peres, like his predecessors, needed all his ingenuity to find ways around the regulations. Under the circumstances, he did not do so badly. Ben-Gurion's diary of Wednesday, September 13, 1950, provides an illustration: "Shimon Peres arrived. He is working for the Defense Ministry and studying in the evenings. So far we have spent $1.7 million on arms in the U.S., $1.1 million on the air force (80 planes and spare parts), $0.41 million on the navy (a frigate, 12 landing craft, three launches, spare parts), $0.09 million on the infantry (explosives, .22 ammunition, shells, etc.).

"Canada is being very friendly. Lester Pearson (the foreign minister) is being helpful. Young McNaughton (the son of Canada's chief of staff during World War II) is our agent there. The Canadians have sold us 5,000 armor-piercing shells, 200 used machine guns ($80 each, instead of $1,300; repairs will cost $20 apiece). We've got a license to buy Mosquitos (aircraft)."

In Ben-Gurion's diary, matters sounded much simpler than they were in reality. The problem was not only in forging appropriate ties with the administration, but in finding money to pay for the equipment. The matter of buying artillery from Canada was typical of the problems of those days, and of Peres's methods of solving them. Israel's entire artillery complement at that time consisted of four cannons. The country's chief arms agent was a Polish aristocrat called Stefan Czernski, who lived in France in a marble palace, called "Malle Mademoiselle," built by Napoleon. Czernski claimed that he could acquire cannons, in which Israel was very interested, in Canada.

The director general of the Defense Ministry, Pinhas Sapir, wrote about this to Peres, who replied that he had established his own contacts and was sure he would be able to get them directly from the supplier, thus saving the very large commission that Czernski would require. Sapir cabled back: "Wonderful, but we don't have any money." Peres started investigating how to raise the necessary sum. He was told that there was a Canadian Jew who could help—Sam

Bronfman, founder and president of Seagram, the giant liquor corporation.

Peres heard that the best way to approach Bronfman was through Dr. Nahum Goldmann, president of the World Jewish Congress. However, as the matter was secret, he decided to approach Bronfman directly. When he arrived at the gate of the Seagram plant, the guards would not let him in. Peres asked the guards to inform Bronfman that he was waiting for him by the gate. After a few minutes, Bronfman came out and personally escorted Peres to his office.

Peres told the Canadian millionaire about the cannons—the numbers involved and the price. Bronfman frowned and said, "They are asking too much money." On the spot, he phoned the minister of commerce and industry and asked for a meeting. The following day, the two of them set out for Ottowa in Bronfman's car. It was midwinter; the roads were covered with snow and the temperature was below zero. Bronfman did not like heating in his car, so they traveled wrapped in blankets, keeping themselves warm by drinking generous tots of whisky—Seagram, of course.

As soon as they entered the minister's office, Bronfman began bargaining. To Peres's great surprise, the Canadian official agreed, without much difficulty, to reduce the price by half a million dollars. He was in "seventh heaven," but was somewhat chastened on the return journey, when Bronfman asked him, "Where are you going to get the other one and a half million dollars?"

"From you," Peres replied without hesitating. Bronfman looked at him for a long minute and finally smiled. "In fact, you are right. Tomorrow evening I'll invite some people over and we'll raise the money." When they got out of the car, Bronfman saw that Peres was wearing light-colored socks. "You can't come to my house in the evening with socks like that," he said, and he told his driver to take Peres to a clothes store to buy dark ones. At the appointed time, the financial elite of the Montreal Jewish community assembled at Bronfman's home, and by the end of the evening, Peres had at his disposal one and a half million dollars—a huge sum in those days. When he reported the matter to Sapir, the latter refused to believe him. Thirty cannons that did not cost the State of Israel anything?! Only when he saw them with his own eyes, Sapir said, would he believe it. A few weeks later he saw them—all thirty cannons.

It was Peres's first contact with Sam Bronfman; it was a connection that would continue with Bronfman's sons. After the deal had been completed, Peres gave Bronfman a gift—a silver-bound Bible, which remained on Bronfman's desk to his dying day.

In the United States, Peres devoted a lot of time to the purchase of Mosquito aircraft. Ben-Gurion described them as "small, mobile bombers made of wood." They were flown to Israel by a number of routes, including over the North Pole. During one of these flights, a plane disappeared over Newfoundland. After some persuasion and the mobilization of Ben-Gurion, El Al agreed to lend its one and only plane, a Constellation, to carry out the search. The condition was that Peres personally join the search party to prevent the pilots, who would be eager to find their lost comrade, from acting rashly. The search operation was based at Goose Bay, a small village in Newfoundland. Every day they would fly long sorties over the blinding snow. In the evenings they would assemble, exchange impressions, and put forward new ideas for continuing the search.

On one of those evenings, Peres gave vent to thoughts that seemed fantastic to his listeners. The day would come, he said, talking as if in a midsummer night's dream, when Israel would no longer be dependent on secondhand planes from other countries. It would establish its own industry, which would manufacture sophisticated and reliable aircraft. The pilots looked at him pityingly. They, too, were affected by the cold, but not to that extent.

They never found the missing plane. The members of the search party returned to New York and went about their separate affairs, but even after he came in from the cold, Peres could not forget the experience, and he began looking for ways to fulfill his dream. As sometimes happens, he found the solution under his very nose.

The planes that Israel acquired in the United States were not complete and ready to fly at the time of purchase. The first stage was buying the parts, the second stage assembling them. They were assembled in Burbank, California, near Hollywood, in a small plant that was owned by Al Schwimmer, a young American Jew whom Peres described as "a man of forceful opinions and great vision— possibly the best technological leader I ever met."

As soon as the two met, the chemistry started working. The young American and the Israeli kibbutznik were both eager to get things done. The more daring and impossible the challenge, the more it fired their imagination. On one of Ben-Gurion's visits to the United States, Peres persuaded him to visit Schwimmer's plant in Burbank. When he saw the simple machinery and the small plant, the prime minister exclaimed: "What, with these few machines you can repair and assemble aircraft? Come to Israel at once." These were the words that Peres had hoped to hear.

The following week, Schwimmer and Peres started to plan the establishment of a plant for assembling and overhauling planes in Israel. On one of their joint visits to Israel, Peres took Schwimmer to Kibbutz Alumot for the weekend, where he introduced him to his close friend, Elhanan Yishai. It was the height of summer, and the three of them sat on the small porch of Yishai's small home, sipping cool drinks. Suddenly, Peres said to Yishai, "You know, this American says he will make a jet."

"How can he make a jet?" Yishai asked.

"Yes, I'll make a jet," Schwimmer said.

"Listen to me—you don't know this guy. If he says he'll make a jet, he'll make a jet," Peres said.

Although Yishai had doubts that this was possible, the vision excited his imagination. "You know what," he suggested, "let's go for a dip in the Kinneret. That way we'll remember his promise to make a jet." The three of them walked down to the lake, stripped off their clothes, and plunged in. The water cooled their bodies, but not their enthusiasm.

When Peres returned to Israel after completing his mission in the United States at the end of 1951, it seemed that his defense career had come to an end. Important people had different ideas about his future. Zalman Aranne, one of the leaders of Mapai, suggested to Ben-Gurion that he start Peres off in the party by appointing him secretary of the Tel Aviv branch. Ze'ev Schind, the director general of the Defense Ministry, offered him the post of his deputy, with the rank of chief assistant. Peres rejected the term "assistant."

Ben-Gurion hesitated, as he wrote in his diary on January 21, 1952: "I told Peres that I still want to think about where he will work—in the Defense Ministry, in my office, or he'll be charged with responsibility for manpower and youth, especially for the army. I'll decide finally after consultations."

At the same time, Al Schwimmer, Leo Gardiner, one of Israel's top pilots, and Danny Agron, who had been given the job of establishing Bedek, the plant for overhauling planes, met with Ben-Gurion. They told the premier and defense minister that "they had bought part of a maintenance base in Los Angeles, which they had transferred to New York and would bring here. They could begin work, they intimated, but they needed a man in the government who would be the 'father of the project,' to coordinate maintenance, flying, and so on. They suggested Peres."

Possibly it was this suggestion that tipped the balance. Ben-Gurion reached his final decision on Peres after the meeting. On February 1, he wrote to Kibbutz Alumot:

"I have appointed Comrade Shimon Peres deputy director general of the Defense Ministry, and hereby request that you permit him to take up this post. I know it is a difficult thing to ask. Your kibbutz does not have many members and Shimon has already been away a long time. If the job were not central and vital to the state's security, I wouldn't lay this difficult burden on you . . . consider Shimon's work for defense as one of the tasks of the kibbutz."

(Peres never returned to Kibbutz Alumot as an active member, although he took care to maintain formal membership.)

The director general of the Defense Ministry, Ze'ev Schind, was also the administrative head of the Transportation Ministry, with the result that he could not devote all his time to the former. This meant that Peres gradually became the acting director general. He found a Defense Ministry more appropriate to a state-on-the-way. The infrastructure was, in his view, unsuitable for an existing state. In a short while, he reorganized the entire ministry and took personal charge of purchasing, production, and administration. No one was surprised therefore when, after he had been deputy director general for nine months, Ben-Gurion announced, in a letter dated October 5, 1952: "Shimon Peres has been appointed acting director general of the Defense Ministry."

He was then twenty-eight. The first time he was invited to a meeting of Ben-Gurion's immediate defense staff, Chief of Staff Yigael Yadin could not stop himself from saying, in Peres's presence: "How can you appoint such a young and inexperienced man to a central position in the defense network?"

Ben-Gurion replied in a manner that reflected his behavior all his life: "To be young is not a defect." Then he added: "As to lack of experience, we will see."

Director General Peres and Chief of Staff Dayan

About the same time—November 1952—decisive changes were taking place in the senior ranks of the army. The second IDF chief of staff, Lieutenant General Yigael Yadin (the first had been Ya'acov Dori), decided to retire from his post and was replaced by Mordechai Makleff. Those were still days of uncertainty about methods of work, and in all departments they were searching for the best modus operandi. Among other things, the division of authority between the Defense Ministry and the Israel Defense Forces had still not been clearly delineated. Each chief of staff had his own idea, according to his talents and personality. Dori and Yadin had seen their task as army commanders, with matters of security being handled by the Defense Ministry. Not Makleff. He was convinced that the IDF was the body responsible for all the matters connected with security, starting with manpower and including purchase and production. The Defense Ministry should assist him and, in effect, be under his authority.

Peres saw it entirely differently. He believed that the IDF and the General Staff should deal exclusively with military matters; everything else should be under the authority and responsibility of the Defense Ministry. These differing conceptions resulted in a situation where everyone was pulling in his own direction.

As both bodies were dear to Ben-Gurion, he took extended leave from his post as defense minister in order to examine the problem and appointed as his replacement Pinhas Lavon, one of the leaders of Mapai, whom Peres had recommended.

Ben-Gurion took advantage of his leave to examine the defense establishment from top to bottom. He visited army camps, descended into the trenches, and examined all the departments of the Defense Ministry. His conclusions supported Peres's view. Ben-Gurion saw the defense establishment as a pyramid, with the defense minister at its head, and two assistants serving him. One, the chief of staff, would command the army alone; the second, the director general of the Defense Ministry, would be in charge of all branches that were not strictly combat-related.

It was clear to Ben-Gurion that the structure on which he had decided did not satisfy all the individuals operating within it, and, when Makleff tendered his resignation on October 11, he accepted it without hesitation.

Makleff was not the only one to depart. Ben-Gurion himself felt weary of political life. On November 2, he told the president of his decision to resign the premiership in order to retire to the simple wooden hut built for him at Sde Boker, a new kibbutz in the Negev. Before his departure on December 7, Ben-Gurion took steps to ensure that the two institutions that he thought were the most important in the state would be headed by people in whom he had absolute trust.

The first appointment was made at the initiative of Pinhas Lavon, who had noticed that in the correspondence of the Defense Ministry, Peres was still referred to as the "acting director general."

At the end of December 1953, Ze'ev Sharef, the cabinet secretary, announced: "Shimon Peres was formally appointed director general of the Defense Ministry, on the recommendation of Pinhas Lavon, acting defense minister, on December 27, 1953."

The second appointment was far more problematic—that of the IDF chief of staff to succeed Makleff. With all his heart, Peres recommended that Ben-Gurion appoint Moshe Dayan. Opposed were many of the party leaders, such as Moshe Sharett, Golda Meir, and Zalman Aranne, who described Dayan as a "partisan"— disorganized, impulsive, and undisciplined. Ben-Gurion also had doubts about Dayan's character and wondered whether he was ready to head the IDF.

In the end, Ben-Gurion overcame his hesitation and appointed Dayan chief of staff. Not many days had passed before something happened to make Peres wonder whether Dayan's critics had not been right after all. One morning he was sitting in Ben-Gurion's office at the Defense Ministry in Ramat Gan, when a panic-stricken officer burst in saying: "Chief of Staff Dayan is standing on his office porch, shooting in all directions."

Ben-Gurion flashed Peres a reproachful glance. "Look what your Moshe Dayan is doing." Peres rushed outside toward the neighboring two-story building, where the chief of staff had his office.

Approaching, he saw Dayan standing on the balcony with a smoking rifle in his hands.

"What's wrong with you?" demanded Peres. "What are you doing?"

Dayan smiled. "You were invited to dinner at my house tonight, weren't you?"

"Yes," Peres replied.

"Do you know why?"

"No."

"Today is my fortieth birthday. I have decided to invite forty guests and serve them forty pigeons, and I'm shooting them right now."

Peres was to tell this story many times, and he could never conceal his sense of wonder at Dayan the man, based on a feeling of admiration for his unbridled panache and his ability to do things that a reserved character like himself could never do. By his loyalty and support, and in the way he related to Dayan, Peres gave the impression that the one-eyed soldier was all he wanted to be, but could not.

Pinhas Lavon, the man Ben-Gurion appointed to succeed him as defense minister, was one of the brightest rising stars in the Mapai firmament. He was forty-nine, handsome, with silver hair that added dignity to his suntanned face. His mind was extremely sharp, his speeches carefully thought out. But his appearance and great intelligence disguised character traits known only to intimate colleagues. In his relations with others there was more than a trace of arrogance and a great deal of suspicion. As insensitive as he was to the feelings of others, he was vulnerable when it came to himself.

Even if Peres and Dayan had known about these traits, they would still have been pleased about Ben-Gurion's choice because Lavon's activist approach to foreign affairs and defense matters was similar to their own. They saw him as an important counterweight to the moderate positions of Moshe Sharett, who replaced Ben-Gurion as prime minister.

Despite this ideological compatibility, the first strains became apparent, more quickly than anyone had foreseen, in the relationship between the defense minister, his director general, and the chief of staff. Already, in February 1954, some two months after Ben-Gurion's resignation, Dayan and Peres paid him a visit at his new home in Sde Boker, with bitter complaints about Lavon. Dayan complained about his rash decisions and actions; Peres was annoyed about his defense budget cuts, notably in the fields of purchasing and production. Peres had learned the hard way that Lavon's sharp intellect was not evident when it came to getting things done and looking to the future. He was finding it difficult to agree with his superior on almost anything.

A typical example was the purchase of the French AMX tank. In the first six months of 1954, Egypt acquired large numbers of tanks from Britain. Iraq was about to receive tanks of American manufacture. The IDF had only ancient Sherman tanks. There was the possibility of buying a modern French tank, which, while not free of faults, was certainly much more sophisticated than the Sherman. Dayan and Peres strongly supported acquiring it; they saw it as vital to the strengthening of the armored corps. Lavon came out against the idea, accepting the views of a number of officers whom he had consulted behind Dayan's back. As a result, Dayan tendered his resignation as chief of staff June 16. Ben-Gurion invited Lavon to discuss "relations with the chief of staff and the director general of his ministry. Lavon promised that the relations would be rectified."

As a result of this intervention, Dayan withdrew his resignation. Lavon invited him to a reconciliation lunch. An interesting point emerging from their conversation is recorded in one sentence of Dayan's diary: "Lavon put all the blame for the misunderstanding on Shimon's shoulders." Nehemia Argov, Ben-Gurion's close aide, wrote: "The Old Man says that Lavon seems to have something against Shimon."

It is interesting to note that the main confrontation, which took on an unpleasantly personal character, was between Lavon and Dayan. However, when the two had a reconciliation (very temporary, as it turned out), Peres got the blame.

This pattern was to be repeated many times during the political careers of Dayan and Peres. Peres never liked to talk about the matter and would dismiss it with a wave of his hand, or say it was not true. However, on the few occasions he did speak about it, he explained that the attacks on him resulted from the fact that Dayan, as an army man and a national hero, was above criticism. Until the Yom Kippur War, he was an almost legendary figure. People were also reluctant to criticize Ben-Gurion. Therefore, whenever someone wanted to attack Dayan or Ben-Gurion, or both of them, the easiest and most effective way was to criticize Peres. He added that the element of envy also played an important part in the attacks on him, and that was the price he had to pay for Ben-Gurion's trust in him.

There is, no doubt, some truth in these allegations. The only flaw is the fact that there were other people close to Ben-Gurion, so why only Peres? Was it because he was the most active of the people close to the Old Man? Or because much of his work was confidential, and thereby aroused curiosity—or worse, suspicion? Possibly something in Peres's personality or behavior made him an easy target, almost asking to be attacked. There is no doubt that he deserved the criticism more than he is prepared to admit—maybe more than he realizes. In his drive to achieve a certain goal, he can be uncompromising and not too choosy about the means he uses. When he is accused he withdraws into himself; he casts his eyes down; his expression becomes sad and vulnerable—the embodiment of someone inviting his rivals to continue hitting him.

The attitudes of Ben-Gurion and Dayan to criticism of Peres—which intensified as his political career advanced—were not the same. Ben-Gurion understood and was annoyed when in many instances barbs aimed at himself were deflected to Peres. He often sprang to Peres's defense in letters to the press, from the Knesset rostrum, and in party discussions. The results were often the opposite of what Ben-Gurion intended. The more he defended Peres, the more his rivals realized that this was a very sensitive point with him, and they never stopped taking advantage of it.

Dayan's approach, which was completely different, stemmed from his overall attitude toward Peres and toward people in general. He considered it perfectly natural that Peres shielded him at every opportunity; it never occurred to him that this obligated him to a similar role. Only rarely did he come to Peres's defense, or have a good word to say about him. When Dayan did mention Peres, either verbally or in writing, he did so grudgingly, and only when the chronological order of events demanded it. For his part, Peres did not see any fault in this behavior on the part of his ally. Quite possibly he would have been amazed, even disappointed, if Dayan had conducted himself in a manner different from that which Peres so loved and admired.

My Enemy's Enemy Is My Friend

Judging by the fire and enthusiasm of Israel's internal quarrels, one might assume that everything else was quiet and calm. Anyone making such an assumption knows nothing about the character of the Israeli leadership. At that time everything was new: the state, the authority, the positions of power. Given the mercurial Jewish nature, the result was an almost unlimited capacity for angry confrontations, even though there was great security tension, particularly on the Egyptian border.

Suicide squads (fedayeen) were infiltrating Israeli territory almost every night, sowing death and destruction in the settlements near the border. From time to time, Israel retaliated with daring raids on Egyptian territory. Gradually, the conflagration spread to the Jordanian and Lebanese borders.

The hardest blow struck Israel in September 1955. After several months of negotiations, Czechoslovakia and Egypt signed an arms deal of unprecedented proportions. By the terms of the agreement, Egypt was to receive 200 MiG-15 and Ilyushin-28 jet fighter-bombers, 230 tanks, 200 armored personnel carriers, 100 self-propelled cannons, and some 500 other artillery pieces, as well as naval vessels, including torpedo boats, destroyers, and six submarines.

Clearly, this deal changed the regional balance of power to Israel's detriment. The Western powers were also aware of the new reality. Cairo was deluged with protests and demands that the agreement be canceled, but in vain. Israel knocked at the doors of Western capitals, but apart from lip service, did not receive anything. Most disappointing of all was the attitude of the United States, toward which the main Israeli efforts were directed. Secretary of State John Foster Dulles promised repeatedly that, in light of the Czech arms deal, Washington would reassess its stand regarding the supply of weapons to Israel. This reassessment ended with a message from Dulles saying that the United States was not opposed to other Western countries selling arms to Israel.

Despite the disappointment, the orientation toward the United

States and Britain continued in the prime minister's office and the Foreign Ministry in Jerusalem. Shimon Peres was almost alone in urging that efforts should be directed toward purchasing arms from France. The logic of Peres's "French orientation" was expressed in remarks he made at a closed meeting in the Defense Ministry on June 19, 1955, even before the Czech arms deal.

"Every Frenchman killed in Algeria, like every Egyptian killed in the Gaza Strip, is a step toward strengthening the ties between France and Israel," he declared. Although this statement was not pleasant to hear, it reflected the real situation.

There is no doubt that in France at that time there was a great deal of admiration and support for Israel and its struggle, particularly in military and defense circles. But Peres understood that genuine links between two states could not be based only on sentiment. There had to be a common interest, and he found it in France's efforts to maintain its control over Algeria. The Arab world, and Egypt in particular, supported the struggle of the Algerian rebels. Israel was the enemy of the Arabs and, according to the principle that "my enemy's enemy is my friend," Peres saw this situation as full of promise.

The first direct contact with France had been made at the end of 1953. Up to that point, Israel had purchased a small quantity of weapons through the agency of Stefan Czernski, who, apart from his commission of 15 percent, had been receiving extra funds for the purpose of what he described as "oiling the wheels." As soon as Peres was appointed director general of the Defense Ministry, he met with Czernski and told him that he wanted to know who was receiving the money—otherwise, he would stop paying. Czernski replied that the people concerned were "close to Paul Reynaud," the deputy premier. Peres said he wanted to meet Reynaud. There was no problem, replied Czernski, he would arrange it.

A few weeks went by and no meeting was arranged. Peres flew to Paris, phoned Reynaud, and asked for a meeting. He was received the following day. Peres described Israel's difficulties and needs to Reynaud and, almost at once, asked about the purchase of artillery. "I am your friend," replied Reynaud. "I'll arrange it." After the meeting, Peres phoned Czernski and asked him, "What about Reynaud?"

"He'll see you next week," the arms dealer replied. This

convinced Peres that the story about bribing Reynaud's aides was a fabrication, and he severed ties with Czernski. From then on, Israel purchased arms from France directly, although the amounts were small and the types of weapons limited. In order to strengthen the French connection, Peres needed a free hand—much freer than the defense minister, Lavon, was giving him. He received it when Ben-Gurion returned to the Defense Ministry.

On May 2, 1955, Ben-Gurion wrote in his diary: "Shimon Peres is going to England and France to deal with arms purchases. In his opinion, the time is ripe for buying from France, because of anger over Bandung [the Bandung Conference of Afro-Asian states, where Egypt's President Nasser was one of the stars] and the murder of the Syrian chief of staff. He suggests that Moshe Dayan write about this to General Koenig, who promised to treat Israel as if it were the French army. I agreed on condition that the prime minister [Sharett] gives his approval."

Equipped with Dayan's letter, Peres set out to meet French Defense Minister Pierre Koenig. In the conversation, Koenig made no effort to disguise his deep admiration for Israel, and in particular, for the IDF. After Peres had explained Israel's security needs, the French general asked him to prepare a memorandum for him with a list of purchases and the reason for each item.

"When do you want the memorandum?" asked Peres.

"On Sunday at 10:00 A.M.," replied Koenig.

"Do you work on Sunday?" asked Peres.

"Why not? Isn't it a day?" replied the general.

General Koenig did not disappoint Peres. He signed an agreement for the sale of light tanks and artillery, but the item in which Israel was most interested was combat planes. Peres found Koenig sympathetic in this field also. He agreed to sell Israel twenty-four Mystere-2 jet fighters. Although the quantity was small compared to its needs, Israel could not afford to be choosy. No other country was even prepared to sell it spare parts for planes. Despite the great warmth with which Peres had been received in Paris, the French government was manifestly hesitant about open, wide-ranging relations. At the time, Egypt and Syria were still regarded as allies of France against the states of the Baghdad Pact. Paris was concerned that supplying large quantities of arms to Israel would provoke the anger of those two Arab states and complicate her relations with them.

In September it became clear that the jubilation over the Mystere-2 deal had been premature. Senior officers in the French air force disclosed to their Israeli colleagues that the plane was riddled with defects. They suggested canceling the agreement and ordering the Mystere-4, which was then in the final stages of production.

Egypt's signing of the Czech arms deal made the acquisition of combat aircraft a matter of the highest importance. Prime Minister Moshe Sharett himself flew to Paris for a meeting with his French counterpart. It turned out to be an unnecessary meeting, because Peres had arrived in the French capital two days earlier, met with the heads of the French Defense Ministry, and had secured an agreement for Israel to receive twenty-four Mystere-4 planes. For this reason, the meeting of the two prime ministers lasted only ten minutes, during which the French premier ratified the accord already reached.

The agreement was, however, conditional on the approval of the United States because France had manufactured the aircraft for NATO at America's request. The U.S. government said one thing, then another, but never actually approved the deal. While Israel continued to urge the Americans to agree, there was a political upset in France that threatened to torpedo the deal altogether. Edgar Faure's government fell, and elections for a new National Assembly were set for the beginning of January 1956.

Peres came to two conclusions. First, there was no way the deal could be clinched by conventional methods. Second, a final commitment must be secured before the formation of a new government, the policies of which were unknown. He flew to Paris for a meeting with Defense Minister General Pierre Billotte (who had replaced Koenig). The main topic of discussion was the Mystere-4, the supply of which had been held up because of the need for American approval. Peres came to the discussion armed with the knowledge he had obtained from junior defense officials that the commander of the French air force would adamantly refuse to release any Mystere-2 planes from his stock. Thus he was able to say that Israel was prepared to purchase the Mystere-2, while secretly praying for the expected answer. He got it: Billotte jumped to his feet and said, "The Mystere-2 is out of the question. You will have to buy the Mystere-4.

I have spoken to Faure about it and it is all right, but I have to swear you to total secrecy because of the Americans and the British. If you can attack France in your newspapers, do so—it will help matters." Peres had the feeling that the only thing wrong with Billotte's words was that they were too good to be true.

"When do we sign?" he asked. Deputy Defense Minister Croisier pulled out a diary and they set a meeting for 5:00 P.M. the next day.

"At the appointed hour we arrived at Croisier's office in good spirits and wearing blue suits, ready to sign," wrote Peres in his diary. "Croisier smiled and asked: 'What is the weather like in Israel?' We spent five minutes talking about the weather, and there was no hint of a signing ceremony. Finally, I said, 'We have come to sign.' 'Ah,' he said, 'you have come to sign? But there are two problems here: the Americans and our own Foreign Ministry.'"

Back to square one: again the runaround with generals and officials. Two days later the signing took place: 155 cannons, Sherman tanks—everything but aircraft, and time was running out for the Faure government. In December, Peres again flew to France. When he met with Billotte, he found the French general angry. A few days earlier, Israel had carried out an extensive reprisal raid against the Syrians. Billotte maintained that such actions endangered French interests in Syria. He demanded that in future there should be coordination. Peres agreed. In the report he presented (December 28, 1955) he summed up: "The incident in Syria helped a bit, because at last we have something to offer the French."

Billotte promised Peres that the matter would be dealt with, but new problems came up, and Billotte was not available. Like his colleagues, he was busy with the election campaign. Peres drove to Billotte's constituency, some 350 kilometers from Paris, where he found the French general touring the streets of Dijon in a loudspeaker van.

Peres suggested to Billotte that they circumvent the American objections by sending dismantled planes to Israel. Billotte replied that Premier Faure preferred to wait for American approval because he had reason to believe it would be forthcoming. But Billotte reported that Faure agreed on the spot to order "the immediate signing of an agreement to sell twelve Mystere-4 planes. If the Americans give their approval, the planes will be sent at once. If the Dassault factory can manufacture twelve aircraft right away, without the Americans knowing about it, they will be supplied by July 1956."

At Peres's request, Billotte added a clause to the draft contract in his own handwriting, authorizing the transfer to Israel of "a reasonable number" of components, "so that, according to a gentlemen's agreement, we can assemble in Israel several other planes in addition to the twelve mentioned above."

The election results led to wide-ranging changes in the upper reaches of the French government. Socialist leader Guy Mollet was charged with forming the new government. He appointed Maurice Bourges-Maunoury, who had been interior minister in Faure's government, as his minister of defense.

Peres was ready for the changes. On visits to France before the elections, he had met with the people who were likely to occupy key positions in the new regime. In November, he had lunched with Guy Mollet in Paris. He had good reason to be apprehensive about the man and the meeting, for Israel had experienced disappointments with Socialist parties once they gained power. When Mollet expressed his friendship for Israel, Peres expressed his doubts. "Ernest Bevin was a friend of the Jews," he remarked. "But when he achieved power, he turned into an enemy." Mollet reacted decisively. "I won't be a Bevin."

The connection with Bourges-Maunoury had been established much earlier. It began with a meeting that the head of the defense mission in Paris, Yosef Nahmias, arranged with Abel Thomas, the director general of the Interior Ministry, which was headed by Bourges-Maunoury.

Although Peres did not know it then, this relationship would be decisive in determining Israel's future defense situation and its ties with France.

As soon as Guy Mollet was sworn in as premier of France, Peres came to him with a message from Ben-Gurion. Mollet said with a smile, "Now you will see that I am not a Bevin." He proved it at once by ordering that all the commitments made by previous governments be honored. The practical results of this order were seen on April 11, when Ben-Gurion arrived with a large party at a military airfield in northern Israel. Those who were present felt a shiver of excitement as the French Mystere-4 planes appeared on the horizon to touch down, one by one, on the runway.

There were, however, those among whom Peres's activities were causing concern. Finance Minister Levi Eshkol complained about the cost of the deals Peres had negotiated. Ben-Gurion replied (March 12, 1956): "To Eshkol, finance minister and citizen of Israel: I hope that Shimon will demand more for this purpose, but for the time being, you are requested to facilitate without delay the signing of those contracts that can be drawn up at once."

Moshe Sharett, who had returned to the Foreign Ministry when Ben-Gurion again became prime minister and defense minister, was even more displeased. His annoyance at Peres's independent activities in France had begun a long time before.

In April 1956 the confrontation became direct. Although it was a time of rising tension on the borders, and huge quantities of weapons were arriving in Egypt from the Eastern bloc, the United States turned down Israel's requests for military purchases. All Israel's efforts at persuasion—in fact, pleas—found their way to the desk of John Foster Dulles, whom Peres described after meeting him as "a strange combination of priest and lawyer; sometimes he uses attorneys' arguments, sometimes mysticism. He began by saying that the Jews murdered Muhammad, and ended with the statement that Russia is beginning to change its way of life because of America's success. Dulles has a Jewish complex. The only election he ever lost was in a constituency with a high proportion of Jews." Peres summed up: "Dulles has not, and will not, give us anything."

Ben-Gurion was infuriated by the American reply. He called a meeting in his bureau at which Chief of Staff Dayan, Sharett, Peres, and the director general of the Prime Minister's Office, Ya'acov Herzog, were present. Sharett continued to maintain that Dulles could be won over. Ben-Gurion ruled, "We must stop all intercession in the United States." During the discussion Dayan congratulated Peres on the success of the Mystere deal with France, while criticizing the Foreign Ministry's approach to arms acquisition.

Sharett was deeply offended by Dayan's remarks. Following the meeting, he sent Ben-Gurion a letter (April 3): "I am full of admiration for the energy and achievements of Shimon Peres, but this does not alter the fact that it was my conversation with Faure at the end of October (1954) which broke the deadlock that we had reached regarding the French arms deal and brought us out of a difficult situation."

The following day, April 4, Ben-Gurion sent his reply:

"I fail to see the problem, or the importance of who achieved more or first. I see all the ministries and all members of the government as envoys in the same cause. I am not in the least interested in the question of who deserves more credit. The chief of staff's attitude is, in my humble opinion, logical: the first approach should be made to the owner—to the factory or the army (if the army owns the weapons). Of course, the minister must be informed. If the owners turn to the Foreign Ministry, you should activate the minister, but if Shimon can also meet with [Foreign Minister Christian] Pineau, or another foreign minister or director general, I don't see any contradiction, provided that the approach is effective. All this departmental accounting seems rather strange to me. However, I am convinced that a man dealing with one matter is more likely to succeed than someone who deals with all the tasks, and that, I think, explains Shimon's success (when he does succeed)."

With this letter, Ben-Gurion effectively gave Peres a free hand for his independent style of operating. He understood that this system was necessary because a similar situation pertained in France; there differences in principle also existed between the Ministries of Foreign Affairs and Defense, which did not see eye to eye on the matter of aid to Israel. Bourges-Maunoury made it clear to Peres at their first meeting that he preferred direct cooperation, bypassing the diplomats.

Peres dealt with this situation when he lectured to senior Defense Ministry employees (April 30, 1956):

"The disagreements between the French Foreign Ministry and the Defense Ministry are not simply between two separate administrative frameworks, but between institutions that reflect two different approaches. The Foreign Ministry sees France as a central power in the Middle East—a power that can mediate between the United States and the Soviet Union. The Defense Ministry sees 1.6 million people in Israel, and 1.6 million Frenchmen in Algeria. They see Israel as a second front against Nasser, as against the more serious front in Algeria. Israel has to decide which orientation to choose. We must take advantage of any power that exists in any country in order to achieve results."

French arms purchases now became Peres's main occupation. When he was not in Paris—and he was there a great deal—he phoned

Yosef Nahmias, the head of the defense mission in Paris, several times a day. Anyone listening to them speak might have concluded that they were out of their minds. For example, this conversation occurred on May 1, 1956:

PERES: "Did Carmen Miranda get married or not?"
NAHMIAS: "Who?"
PERES: "Carmen."
NAHMIAS: "She left."
PERES: "Hasn't she found a bridegroom yet?"
NAHMIAS: "I still don't know whether the wedding is on or not."
PERES: "Okay."

It was not always clear whom the two of them managed to confuse more: the enemy or each other.

A War for a Reactor

Toward the end of 1956, President Nasser's Algerian policy was becoming more and more extremist. He was giving increasing assistance to the Algerian rebels, and in France's corridors of power, voices were heard demanding military action against Egypt.

In May 1956, Peres had first suggested to Ben-Gurion that Israel contract an unwritten alliance with France against Nasser. Ben-Gurion gave the idea his blessing, and Peres flew to Paris for a meeting with Bourges-Maunoury. Peres proposed to the French defense minister a package deal: a joint operation against Egypt, in return for massive arms supplies to Israel. Bourges-Maunoury liked the idea, and it was decided to convene a secret conference in France within a few days.

The idea, however, did not, at all appeal to Moshe Sharett, and this was the straw that broke the camel's back. Ben-Gurion came to the conclusion that he could not go on working with someone who disagreed with him on almost all matters of principle. On June 19, 1956, Sharett tendered his resignation from the Foreign Ministry. Ben-Gurion accepted it with sorrow, but also with relief. He appointed Labor Minister Golda Meir to the post.

At 9:00 P.M. on June 22, Chief of Staff Moshe Dayan, Chief of Military Intelligence General Yehoshafat Harkabi, and Shimon Peres boarded a French Nord aircraft at a small airfield near Tel Aviv. Twelve hours later the plane landed at an airfield outside Paris, where representatives of the French military were waiting to take them to the small town of Vermeuil, nearby. There they were accommodated in an ancient castle, surrounded by a large walled garden, which the owners had put at the disposal of the French government to ensure absolute secrecy.

That afternoon they began discussions with the French delegation, headed by Louis Mangine, the head of the defense minister's office, and including Generals Challe and Levaud and representatives of French intelligence. The exchange of views and assessments resulted in agreement about the need to topple President Nasser; and, without committing Israel, Dayan agreed in principle to cooperate with France toward this end. After a short break, the two delegations met again to discuss the other side of the coin—arms supplies to Israel. Peres put forward Israel's requests: 200 AMX tanks, 72 Mystere aircraft, 40,000 75-mm shells, 10,000 antitank missiles—in all, a deal worth $70 million. After Peres finished reading the list, the Israelis held their breaths, expecting the French representatives to stage an angry walkout, or at least to fall off their chairs.

Instead, Mangine asked quietly, "Are you prepared to sign?" Now it was the Israelis' turn to almost fall off their chairs. Peres was the first to recover. "Certainly, if you have the agreement prepared." Yosef Nahmias drew him aside and whispered in his ear, "You don't have authorization!"

Nahmias was absolutely right. The optimists in Israel, including Peres, had thought that the French might agree to half the list, at the very most, and that was the maximum to which Peres was authorized to agree.

Peres was well aware of this, but he was even more aware that this was a rare opportunity that might never recur. He did not hesitate to assume the heavy responsibility for carrying out an action for which he did not have the authority. This willingness to take the responsibility and make decisions won the heart of Ben-Gurion, who knew that, in the conditions pertaining at the time, it was the only way to operate. In wider circles, inside the party and out, however, Peres paid a heavy price, reinforcing his image as the unscrupulous man pushing to the front of the line, the politician in a hurry.

It is difficult to imagine what Israel's security situation would have been without Peres's daring, which bordered on presumption. Even one so unemotional as Moshe Dayan wrote in his diary, "The Paris talks were a special experience for me. They gave me hope, confidence, and pride. We will receive weapons, plenty of them, good weapons, and soon. Within a year we'll have a new air force and a new armored corps, offensive and defensive weapons; we will emerge from the crisis caused by the alliance between Egypt and the Soviet Union."

Apart from political matters, the visit, like many similar ones, included some other experiences. Although the whole operation had been carried out in absolute secrecy, on their last evening in the small, outlying town, the Israeli delegation decided that they had earned a night out in Paris.

They began in a cinema. "We entered the circle, and sat in the back row, in the certain knowledge that there were no Israelis in the vicinity," wrote Dayan. "However, Paris is small, and three seats away from us sat Paul Chomsky (an acquaintance). Fortunately for us, he was spellbound by the film. We got up in confusion and went down to the stalls, where we took new seats. As we sat here, I joked: 'I wouldn't be surprised if the woman two rows in front of us is Shoshana Damari (the well-known Israeli singer)—she looks just like her.' The woman turned around, and after all, why shouldn't Shoshana Damari resemble Shoshana Damari? We left quickly and unobtrusively."

When they returned to Israel, Ben-Gurion approved the deal. "It's rather a risky venture," he said, "but what can we do? Our entire existence is risky."

In July, the first thirty-six Mysteres arrived in Israel in complete secrecy. The tanks were brought in under similar conditions. The ship that brought them arrived at Haifa's Kishon Port late at night on July 24. Within an hour, thirty tanks and sixty tons of equipment had been unloaded. Ben-Gurion, who was present, wrote in his diary: "The coordination between our boys and the French sailors was amazing. The ship left Toulon as if for a journey to Algiers. At sea, the captain explained to the officers and crew that they were sailing to Israel." Nathan Alterman, the well-known Israeli poet, whose poems are rich with national feeling, was on hand to receive the consignment, and expressed his feelings in his weekly column in the *Davar* newspaper. The last verse ran:

Maybe it was a night that was, or will be,
On it the dusky sands and the whispering sea,
And the screech of metal, the secret conversation, and the
    salty wind,
And a feeling of a wonderful turning point and amazement:
If only the people knew the thanks they will eternally owe,
To the few who accomplished the task.

The feeling of elation did not last for long. Throughout that period the president of Egypt, Gamal Abdul Nasser, made frequent long and inflammatory speeches against the West and Israel, characterized by extremist nationalism. There was an oppressive feeling of danger and gloom in the air. The world waited tensely for the next step of the Egyptian president.

It came on July 26, 1956. Pouring ridicule on the Western nations to the roars of the crowd, President Nasser announced the nationalization of the Suez Canal.

The Western powers reacted in anger. France and Britain began consultations about military action against the Egyptian ruler, who had become the enemy of the Western world. They hoped that the United States would assist such an action, but Washington quickly poured cold water on this hope. Not only did the Americans have no intention of helping; they were completely opposed to the idea.

The seed from which the Sinai Campaign grew can be found in a cable that Peres sent Ben-Gurion and Dayan from Paris (July 27, 1956). In it he related that he had been urgently summoned by Louis Mangine, the head of the defense minister's bureau and Bourges-Maunoury's adviser on special operations. General Paul Ely, chief of staff of the French armed forces, and his air force chief, General Challe, were also present. "Without any preamble, they informed me that urgent consultations are to be held in London tomorrow between [British Prime Minister Anthony] Eden and [French Foreign Minister Christian] Pineau, concerning the steps to be taken in the wake of Nasser's announcement about the canal."

What did the French want from Israel? "The French foreign minister has promised to supply, by tomorrow, up-to-date information on the deployment and positions of the Egyptian army. He therefore wants to receive this from us before his trip to London," cabled Peres to Jerusalem. Nothing more for the present. Most interesting of all was the last paragraph of the cable: "They remarked with a smile that Israel will certainly be ready to play its part if asked to do so."

On August 1, Peres wrote to Ben-Gurion's personal aide, Nehemia Argov, "Although we are continuing to deal with the matter of purchases, money, and spare parts, it is impossible to begin a conversation in the [Defense] Ministry without mentioning the thing called Suez. The British and French have decided in principle on a joint military operation to take the canal; however, the British have made this conditional on Israel not participating at this stage, or even knowing about it. According to Abel Thomas, the British claimed that Israeli participation would unite the Arabs behind Nasser, and turn their operation into an Israeli-Arab war." Despite this, "the question of our taking part in the planning came up, and if necessary, more than that—for example, increasing tension on the southern border, or tying down Egyptian forces in the Gaza Strip."

At the end of the cable, Peres gave expression to his personal dilemma. "To Nehemia, confidential: I am worried about the situation in which I find myself. Bourges-Maunoury has asked me to stay a few more days so that he can give me full details. Please tell me if you think there is any value in this information and if the Old Man (Ben-Gurion) has any guidelines about what I should tell the French—if anything."

Before receiving the guidelines, Peres was summoned to another meeting with Bourges-Maunoury. "How much time do you estimate your army will require to cross Sinai and reach Suez?" asked the French defense minister. Peres replied that the accepted estimate in Israel was between five and seven days. Bourges-Maunoury was astounded and rather incredulous. In France, he said, an operation of that kind would be allotted three weeks. He also asked whether Israel did intend one day to act on its southern border, and if so, when? Peres replied, "Eilat is our Suez. We will never agree to its being blockaded, and that would be a reason for Israel to act, if it does."

Another French representative put all the cards on the table. "If France goes to war with Egypt, will Israel be prepared to go with us?" Peres replied at once: "Yes!" As they left the meeting, Yosef Nahmias, who had also been present, turned to Peres: "You should be hanged for a statement like that. How can you say such a thing? On what authority?"

"If I had said no," said Peres, "that would have been the end of our French connection. On the other hand, it is clear that an operation of that sort needs government authorization. We can always change our mind."

The ties with France, which Peres wanted to preserve whatever the cost, were by now not limited to arms sales. In meetings with senior officials of the French Defense Ministry, he put forward another request for an atomic reactor. In the mood of the time this was presumption bordering on insolence, and that was the way most Israeli leaders who knew about the proposal regarded it. Finance Minister Levi Eshkol described the idea as madness, both in itself and because of the enormous financial cost. The only one who liked the idea—at first hesitantly, but soon enthusiastically—was Ben-Gurion, and that was all that was required.

Initial French reaction was similar to that in Israel. The French hesitated, stammered, and found it very difficult to decide. Although Peres had talked about a reactor for peaceful purposes, some of the French suspected that he intended more than that. Peres came to the conclusion that the French would only be able to overcome their scruples if Israel offered something equal or similar in return, such as active military cooperation. From then on, the reactor became an inseparable part of the process that led to the Sinai Campaign—possibly, even its catalyst. The fact is that the fate of the Sinai Campaign was decided together with that of the reactor.

At the beginning of September 1956, Peres met with Bourges-Maunoury in Paris and heard from him that the British were having second thoughts. They had started talking of a military operation in two months' time; in the interval, diplomatic efforts would continue. The Americans were against military action and thought it was possible to topple Nasser by means of continuing covert action. But the French were in a hurry. Bourges-Maunoury said he was in favor of an immediate operation because of the imminent fall of the French government, although he admitted that, in the circumstances, mounting such an operation did not seem realistic.

From Israel's point of view, the British plan was more convenient, as the IDF had not yet absorbed all the French equipment that it had been receiving. Peres understood, however, that the new situation gave Israel the opportunity to offer France a quid pro quo, substituting for Britain in a military operation at a time suitable to the French. He cabled his recommendation to Ben-Gurion and received the answer he had expected (September 21): "Regarding the three possible options, we in fact prefer the timing proposed by the partners (the French). If they act at a time convenient to them, we will support them to the best of our ability." The beginning of the cable discloses the other side of the deal: "Congratulations. I am delighted at the agreement on the other matter."

"The other matter" was the atomic reactor. The agreement to construct it in Israel was signed on September 21, and immediately afterward, Peres set out for the United States. When he arrived in New York, he received a cable from Yosef Nahmias, telling him that Bourges-Maunoury wanted to see him urgently. Peres turned around and flew back to Paris. He arrived the following morning and drove, with Nahmias, straight from the airport to the Defense Ministry in the Rue Saint Dominique, only to find it closed and empty because it was Sunday.

"We looked for the duty officer, but he could not help us a great deal. Eventually he got hold of Abel Thomas, who told us the whereabouts of Bourges-Maunoury. The defense minister was spending the weekend at a hunting lodge near a small village several hours' drive from Paris. We phoned the lodge and were invited to lunch. Some three hours later, we arrived at the village, about two hundred kilometers north of Paris, only to find that Bourges-Maunoury was at another village of the same name, two hundred kilometers south of the capital. We turned back on our tracks and only with the help of a local police inspector did we find the village, the lodge, and our host—eight hours late. Bourges-Maunoury received us at the entrance of the lodge with the words, "Don't apologize or explain anything. First, I'm delighted to see you safe and sound. Second, if you had been half an hour late, I might have doubted your punctuality, but eight hours late—there has to be a good reason."

On September 25, Peres returned to Israel, to be met at the airport by Ben-Gurion and Dayan. Ben-Gurion wrote in his diary concerning Peres's report: "What he told us may be fateful. At a meeting with the defense minister, Bourges-Maunoury told him that, after the London conference, the (French) government decided it could not accept that plan, and is prepared to strike at Nasser with the knowledge and consent of the British. They want Israeli participation—that, also, with British agreement."

On October 20, the French captured an Egyptian ship smuggling arms to the Algerian rebels, and as a result, the French government decided to recall its ambassador from Cairo. The elections to the Jordanian parliament resulted in a victory for those identified as pro-Egyptian. The Russians were occupied with Poland, where Wladyslaw Gomulka was struggling against the Stalinists, and with Hungary, which was on the verge of a revolution against its Communist government.

All these factors made London and Paris realize that there was no time to waste. The two countries had a series of meetings, which resulted in a plan that called for Israel to initiate war, conquer the Sinai Peninsula, and reach the Suez Canal, at which point Britain and France would demand that both sides withdraw from the canal.

If the Egyptians refused, as anticipated, French and British forces would intervene to guarantee the orderly operation of the canal. It was also resolved to hold a French-Israeli summit, to which the British would also send a representative, to coordinate procedures. This was the first time that the British had agreed to coordinate action with Israel—and in writing.

Ben-Gurion learned about the agreement on October 17, when Peres brought him a cable from Nahmias. After consultations, in which Golda Meir, Levi Eshkol, Dayan, and Peres took part, he totally rejected the Anglo-French plan. "He is absolutely opposed to a situation where Israel would appear in the world—or before the bar of history—as an aggressive nation," Peres wrote in his diary. However, his complete lack of trust in British intentions, which bordered on hostility, was no less vehement. He saw in the proposal "the height of British hypocrisy, in which the desire to harm Israel was stronger than enmity toward the Egyptian dictator."

Ben-Gurion instructed Peres to inform the French of his position, but emphasized that if, in the circumstances, Guy Mollet's invitation still stood, he would come to Paris.

On the night of Thursday, October 18, Nahmias cabled Peres with Guy Mollet's reply: "He reiterates his invitation to Ben-Gurion, although he is aware of his opposition to the British plan." Mollet proposed Sunday, October 21, for a meeting. On the spot, Ben-Gurion instructed that Paris be informed that he accepted the invitation.

To bring Ben-Gurion to the meeting, the French dispatched an official plane, with Louis Mangine and General Challe on board. It was clear to Peres and Dayan, who met them at the airport, that they had been sent to Israel so that they could take advantage of the long flight to attempt to soften Ben-Gurion's uncompromising stand against the British plan.

In addition to the French representatives, Ben-Gurion; his military aide, Nehemia Argov; Peres; Dayan; and Dayan's adjutant, Mordechai Bar-On, were on the plane back to France. The plane landed in Paris after an exhausting flight of seventeen hours, and the guests were smuggled out of the airport through a side entrance. In order to ensure that Ben-Gurion would not be identified, he wore a low-brimmed hat which covered the white wings of hair for which he was famous. Moshe Dayan wore glasses to conceal his eyepatch.

The French cars sped the party to a luxurious villa in the Paris suburb of Sevres. Ben-Gurion and Argov were accommodated there; the other Israelis stayed at the Reynolds Hotel in Paris. The talks began the following morning.

The Sevres Conference lasted for three days. It was charged with tension as each side tried to shift responsibility onto the other. By the second day, failure seemed inevitable; but on the third and last day there was a breakthrough when the British approved an Israeli compromise.

The agreement resolved that on Monday, October 29, an Israeli force would parachute into the region of the Mitla Pass, near the Suez Canal. On the following day, Israel and Egypt would be asked to agree to a cease-fire and a withdrawal of forces ten miles back from the canal within twelve hours. If either of the states refused to agree to the ultimatum (and there was no doubt that Egypt would refuse), French and British forces would move on October 31.

Ben-Gurion thereby waived his demand that Israel not be the one to initiate hostilities, but this was not because of the French and British. He gave in to the pressure of Dayan and Peres, who did not see in the issue of who started it sufficient reason to miss the opportunity to get rid of Nasser and strengthen the alliance with

France. On Wednesday, October 24, 1956, at 7:00 P.M., the representatives of Israel, France, and Britain signed the Sevres Accords. After the signing had been completed, Bourges-Maunoury strode across the room to Peres. The two men who had conceived the operation, and had not given up even in the most difficult moments, shook hands with emotion.

At the appointed time, on October 29, Israeli soldiers parachuted into the Mitla Pass. Simultaneously, the IDF moved across the border, occupying the Gaza Strip and driving deep into the Sinai. On the following day, a little late, but according to plan, France and Britain issued their call for a cease-fire and a withdrawal of forces from the canal. Israel at once answered in the affirmative. As anticipated, Egypt refused.

From that point, nothing went as planned. The British, who were supposed to start bombing the Canal Zone, announced a twelve-hour delay. As a result, the French also postponed their entry into the fray. The bombing started only after a nerve-racking wait. Throughout this time, the IDF continued to advance. The United Nations Security Council was convened and resolved on the cease-fire. The United States began to pressure Israel to withdraw behind its borders. The IDF continued its race against the clock, with the aim of conquering the Sinai Peninsula before the cease-fire resolution went into force.

According to the plan, British and French forces were supposed to invade the Canal Zone on November 6. All French efforts to persuade the British to bring forward the operation were in vain. In view of this, France departed from the original plan and asked Israel to send its forces to take control of the canal. When the British commander of the joint force heard this, he shouted, "No Israeli soldier is to cross the ten-mile limit!"

On November 5, Israel completed the conquest of the Sinai Peninsula. On the same day, the French and British forces went in. After taking Port Said, these forces advanced south down the length of the canal, but then the Soviet Union intervened. The Soviets had completed the suppression of the Hungarian revolt the day before and now could turn their attention to the Middle East conflict.

Soviet Prime Minister Nikolai Bulganin dispatched messages to France, Britain, and Israel with an implied threat that nuclear rockets would be used against them if they did not stop firing at once. In the capitals of the world, fear of a third world war caused considerable panic.

The first to break—and this was certainly not a surprise to the Israelis—was British Prime Minister Anthony Eden, who told the French he intended to order his troops to cease fire. Paris followed suit immediately, which also did not surprise Jerusalem.

By now it made little difference to Israel. On the day Britain and France announced they were observing a cease-fire, the Israeli flag was flying at Sharm el-Sheikh on the southern tip of the Sinai Peninsula. The IDF held a line some ten miles from the Suez Canal. A wave of joy and pride swept the State of Israel. The military achievements of the IDF were impressive, almost incredible. Without any real help from its partners, Israel had succeeded in taking the Sinai Peninsula in only eight days from an Egypt armed to the teeth with Soviet weapons.

Summing up the achievements of the campaign to senior Defense Ministry staff (November 9), Peres said: "If what is written in the papers is true, and there were three partners (the three countries were still denying any collusion between them), only one of them achieved its aims 100 percent, and that is Israel. The other partners came out of it damaged. The French wanted to destroy Nasser, but because of British hesitancy, they did not succeed. The British wanted to occupy Suez; instead, they are being forced to evacuate for the second time. Israel wanted to eliminate the danger of an Egyptian attack, and that succeeded."

The summary accurately described the situation of the British and French, but with regard to Israel, it was overoptimistic. The basic aim of destroying the bases of the Egyptian army and the fedayeen in Sinai was achieved completely; but afterward, when the size of the victory became clear, Ben-Gurion, and to a lesser extent Peres, began to think in terms of annexing Sinai to the State of Israel. This was not achieved.

As soon as the fighting stopped, the United States, the Soviet Union and the United Nations began to exert heavy pressure on Israel, accompanied by threats, to withdraw from the Sinai Peninsula completely. Some three months after the campaign was launched, Israel completed its withdrawal. In return, the "Union of Maritime Nations" guaranteed free shipping for all nations, including Israel, through the Straits of Tiran. It would later become clear that this guarantee was not worth the paper on which it was written.

Although Peres's brain understood the logic of the need to withdraw from Sinai, his heart found it difficult to accept the harsh verdict. He gave expression to his feelings in a poem:

The Withdrawal from Sinai

You have tracks
But no road
Mighty wrecks
Still kneel before you
Blackened armor looks
On your shining morn;
And cannon will grow in you
In the treeless wastes;
On the humps of camels
Your borders again wander;
And your patient sands.
Cliffs thrust out of you
Like an orphan, an arrow is shot from a bow.
And from the strings of your mountains
As always the shape indistinct (suffused with light)
The melancholy echoes.
From a violin is given the Law.
Your sun hangs opposite
And your moon ambushes the other side.
Your uncombed mop of hair
Continues to breathe the cool air.
Are you wounded? Have you calmed?
Land of wandering ancestors
We are withdrawing from you
But you are not [withdrawn] from our heart.

Israel's military success opened a new era in its international relations. It was no longer a small, weak state whose very existence was in doubt. Now the world looked in wonder at the small country, without natural resources, that in eight difficult years of existence had become a global military power.

Despite the close cooperation with Paris, all attempts to secure a written alliance with France ended in failure. In reality, however, the developments were far in excess of Peres's most optimistic forecasts.

The friendship between the two countries reached heights that Israel would not have dared to dream about. Political leaders, journalists, poets, all sang praises to the unwritten alliance.

Peres used to fly to Paris several times a month; he always came with a purchasing list, and left with all that Israel wanted. "Assistance to Israel has become a key clause in French politics," he reported on returning from one of his trips. "Every politician is measured by his aid to Israel."

On the morning of May 27, 1957, a gray Chevrolet entered the gates of the Bedek Aircraft Plant adjoining Lod International Airport. The car drove onto the runway and stopped beside a DC-4 aircraft, the engines of which were already running. It was the same official French plane that had taken Ben-Gurion to the Sevres Conference. This time it swallowed up the top officials of the Israeli defense establishment, headed by Peres and Dayan.

It was the start of another breakthrough in Israel's relations with France. Its first stop was Istress Airport near Marseilles, where the Israeli party transferred to another plane which took them to their final destination—Colomb-Bechar in the Sahara Desert, France's testing ground for guided missiles. During their stay there, the Israeli delegation witnessed the firing of ground-to-ground guided missiles of the 1000- and 1100-type; air-to-air 103-type missiles (standard equipment on the Vautour aircraft) and ground-to-ground of the 4500-type. After the demonstration, there were talks on the spot with Generals Challe, Levaud, and Martin.

On their return home, the Israelis hurried to report to Ben-Gurion (August 1, 1957). Summing up his report, Peres remarked that "the French are not marking time. In two to three years, they will be making guided missiles that we don't know about. They won't want to sell them to us. We have to start building a plant that will manufacture missiles."

"I don't want to start talking about an electronics industry now," replied Dayan impatiently.

"I'm putting it forward to complete the picture."

"I don't know what it will be based on. If it will push us into subsidies, I'm against it."

Peres refused to give up his idea. Money and subsidies were important, but he believed then, and throughout his public life, that these considerations should not stand in the way of projects vital to the future security of the state. No country had yet gone to jail for failing to pay its debts, or even for becoming bankrupt; however, there were countries who had lost wars because of lack of suitable weapons. Peres did not argue with Dayan and the others about budgets and subsidies. Instead, he introduced the production of missiles into the aircraft industry, which became the IDF's main supplier. When the special relationship with France came to an end, Peres's foresight had a decisive influence on the IDF's military might.

The Large Reactor

Although he took seriously the matter of planes, tanks, and missiles, Peres was mainly occupied with the atomic reactor, the construction of which had begun near Dimona. Now that this aim had been achieved, he came to the conclusion that the time was ripe for a further step—one that he had envisioned from the start: a large, 24-megawatt reactor.

This plan had been raised in a special cabinet meeting, in conditions of great secrecy. There was a great deal of hesitation, with most ministers voicing negative opinions for political or financial reasons, or for both.

Ben-Gurion's uncompromising stand once again overcame the hesitation of his colleagues, and Peres set out for France, where he met with Bourges-Maunoury. Now prime minister after the fall of Mollet's government, he was ready to sign on the condition that the socialist party also agree. Socialist leader Guy Mollet had grave doubts, but in the end gave his assent. Peres returned to Israel before the agreements were signed. Foreign Minister Golda Meir, on a visit to France after Peres had left, was summoned to Pineau, who said he was against "this thing," because it involved great dangers. Meir returned to Jerusalem and reported on the French stand.

Quite a few in the government were relieved and suggested that the matter be forgotten. Peres was not inclined to accept the decision because it would mean giving up Israel's chances for becoming independent in the field of nuclear power. He was not prepared for this concession until he was sure that he had done all that was possible—and impossible—to see the process to its completion. So he set out for Paris without delay.

It is difficult to imagine worse political conditions for such delicate negotiations than those existing in France at that time. Aware that Bourges-Maunoury's government was about to fall, Peres entered a mad race against the political clock. He arrived in the French capital on Sunday, to discover that the government was expected to fall on Monday night. It was clear that "if anything can be achieved, it must be wrapped up by Monday—afterward, there will be no one to talk to."

Peres's first meeting was also his most difficult. Foreign Minister Christian Pineau had written to Peres even before he had left for France that, despite his basically warm attitude to Israel, he was opposed. He set out his reasons:

• There is no precedent in history for the sort of assistance that Israel is requesting.

• If the Americans find out, they will stop giving support to France in the realm of atomic energy.

• If France assists Israel in this matter, the Russians are likely to introduce atomic weapons into Egypt, with the result that, far from helping Israel, the French will be helping the Russians to arm Egypt with atomic weapons.

"All these points were difficult to refute," Peres admitted later, but this did not stop him from trying, and he began as soon as he met Pineau. "Possibly some of us are young," he told his host, "but we are not children. We have no intention of introducing this thing into the Middle East at this time. But do you know what the situation in the Middle East is going to be in another three or four years? Maybe by then the Americans will want us to do it. Maybe it will be America that you, Pineau, won't want us to consult."

Peres agreed with Pineau about the Russian danger, but he

stood the argument on its head. "It is true that the Russians might give Egypt the same thing, but what will happen if the Russians give it to Egypt and we are left with nothing? Will you sell it to us? Will the Americans give it to us?"

At that point, Pineau interrupted Peres's rush of eloquence. "That is a very serious point," he said. "You are right. I didn't think of that." He asked whether Israel was prepared to guarantee that, in three to four years' time, when the reactor was finally ready to start operating, Israel would be ready to consult with France. Peres agreed without hesitation. After some thought, Pineau replied that he "had been convinced by the points raised."

Peres was now burning to conclude the accord he had attained. "The French government is in the throes of a crisis. If it falls, what good will your agreement do us? Are you prepared to phone Bourges-Maunoury and tell him that you agree?" "Certainly," replied Pineau, and lifted the receiver, but Bourges-Maunoury was not at his office. Peres did not let up. "Give me your agreement in writing, and I will deliver it to Bourges-Maunoury," he suggested. Again Pineau obliged.

With Pineau's letter in his pocket, Peres went to look for Bourges-Maunoury. He was still away from his bureau, but there was a message waiting for Peres, saying that he was in the National Assembly, making desperate attempts to save his government. The note said that "he would try to recess the debate in order to meet with Peres at 6:30 P.M. to sign the agreement."

When Peres returned at the appointed hour, there was still no sign of Bourges-Maunoury. The clock moved on. To steady his nerves, Peres drank vast quantities of the whiskey that was offered him. With every minute that passed, the fall of the government drew closer. Eventually, he decided not to wait any longer but to drive to the National Assembly. Bourges-Maunoury emerged from the cabinet room and apologized. The debate had continued longer than expected. An attempt to bring down the government was in full swing, and he was sorry but he could not be available for anything else.

Peres's brain worked feverishly. He had the depressing feeling that it was now or never. He realized that the fate of the matter on which he had worked so hard depended on his finding a formula that would be effective. Speaking confidently, even casually, as if he was suggesting something absolutely normal, he remarked that he did not object "to postponing the business to tomorrow morning, provided Bourges-Maunoury agreed that, if the government fell during the night, he would sign the agreement in the morning but predate it to the previous day, before the fall of the government."

If Bourges-Maunoury had ordered the guards to throw him out, Peres would not have been surprised. Instead Bourges-Maunoury frowned, looked at Peres for a long time with a doubtful smile on his lips, and finally said, "Come to my office tomorrow morning at nine," and turned on his heel.

At the appointed hour Bourges-Maunoury arrived "after a sleepless night, red-eyed, and without a government, which he had lost during the night. He at once pulled out a pen, saying, 'I understand that my friend the Socialist (Pineau) agreed.' He wrote a letter to the energy minister (Guillaumat) stating that the French government had decided at its meeting on the previous day to approve the agreement for the construction of the installation in Israel. Accordingly, the minister was requested to implement the decision."

Peres left Bourges-Maunoury's office with a light heart. His first inclination was to report to Jerusalem on the great achievement, but "something in the sky told me not to cable home before all the documents were in my possession." His fears were not unwarranted. When Peres gave Bourges-Maunoury's letter to Guillaumat, the energy minister was astounded. He had never imagined that the matter would be completed. "You are suitable for war," he chided Peres, "but not for peace. I wish France had some people like you, but only in time of war. The pressure you exerted has turned the Foreign Ministry against you."

"What has this got to do with the Foreign Ministry?"

"The agreement has some political clauses. It is not a matter for signature between atomic energy authorities, but between foreign ministries. I am not prepared to sign."

Peres quickly returned to Bourges-Maunoury and reported on the conversation. Bourges-Maunoury at once summoned Pineau and Louis Joxe (Pineau's assistant for energy matters), and ordered them to implement the government decision.

The following morning Peres met with Joxe, and the two of them agreed that the two atomic energy commissions would sign a technical agreement saying that France would undertake to give Israel all the plans, technical assistance, and materials needed for building a large reactor.

Peres now felt able to go to the Israeli embassy in Paris and cable Ben-Gurion (October 3), "We signed the agreement this afternoon." Ben-Gurion cabled back, "Congratulations on your important achievement." Nehemia Argov sent Peres a cable. "We just passed your cable to the Old Man in Sde Boker. I have no doubt that you couldn't have given him a better gift for Yom Kippur. Be strong and of good courage."

What exactly was this agreement that made the prime minister so happy? In *The Nuclear Barons*, by Peter Pringle and James Spigelman (1982), the authors write, "The French government supplied Israel at the end of the 1950s, by means of a company called St. Gerain, a plant for producing plutonium." This fact is confirmed in the autobiography of Bourges-Maunoury.

It seemed that the "sky" of Israeli-French friendship had never been so "blue," although, in fact, ominous clouds had started to appear. All the manifestations of friendship and closeness could not disguise the fact that the happy, fruitful days of the French connection were coming to an end.

Worrisome Days for the Atomic Project

During the early months of 1958, the internal position in France began to deteriorate. Governments fell one after another, and each new administration was no more stable than the one preceding it. The army, under the influence of the right-wing parties, began to intervene in politics, particularly with regard to the Algerian situation. The French public yearned for an authoritative figure who would restore some sort of order. Everyone looked toward Colombey les deux Eglises, where General Charles de Gaulle, the hero of World War II, lived in splendid isolation. On May 31, 1958, de Gaulle was sworn in as prime minister, and shortly afterward, under a new constitution, he became president.

Israel was very worried by this development. The previous leadership was known and trusted, and links of friendship and strong cooperation had been forged with most of its elements. De Gaulle was, to a certain extent, an unknown quantity. Peres had met him once, following the Sinai Campaign. After hearing about the fighting, De Gaulle had remarked he was surprised that the Jews "were good farmers as well as good soldiers." Now the question of de Gaulle's attitude toward Israel was raised in Jerusalem, where there was concern as to whether he would continue the policy of his predecessors.

Immediately after the upheaval Peres flew to Paris to "take the pulse" of the new administration. On his return he presented Ben-Gurion with a memorandum on "Relations with de Gaulle's France (June 29, 1958)." On the basis of his talks with members of the new government, he calculated that, although de Gaulle would strive to restore France's position in the world—including the Arab world—he would continue the policy of friendship with Israel, "because de Gaulle is an honest man, who genuinely admires Israel as a political, military, and social dynamo."

De Gaulle, however, brought with him a new policy directed toward a pullout from Algeria, which meant that Israel's value to France was considerably diminished. It was not long before this situation had its effect on the atomic reactor project.

In a closed meeting, Peres described it as "one of the most important scientific projects that Israel had ever taken on itself, and an impressive scientific advance."

It would have been unnatural for so large-scale a project not to draw attention to itself. In fact, there were many who were interested in what was happening near the small town of Dimona.

Somebody announced that a textile plant was being built there, and people accepted the story for many years.

To divert scrutiny from the project, a small reactor was established at Nahal Sorek. Anyone who had awkward questions to ask was taken there. The small reactor was open to the media and the public, and to a large extent distracted attention from its bigger brother.

Even in Israeli ruling circles, only a few knew what was going on at the "textile plant." The members of the Israel Atomic Energy Authority knew and, of course, those who were working on it. Of the cabinet ministers, only those whose task necessitated it were informed.

On one of his visits to Eilat, perhaps on vacation, Peres was accompanied by Elhanan Yishai, his friend from Kibbutz Alumot, who was also working with him. Yishai brought along his eight-year-old son, Dudu. On the flight back to Tel Aviv in a light aircraft, Peres and Yishai fell asleep. Suddenly young Dudu woke up his father and asked him, "Where are we?" Yishai looked at his watch and muttered, "Above Avdat." The boy did not give up. "Where are the lights of Sde Boker?" he asked. Yishai sat up in his seat and looked outside. The boy was right. There were no lights—only white sands reminiscent of the Judean desert.

"What has happened?" Yishai asked.

"I've lost my way and I do not have radio contact," the pilot confessed.

Meanwhile, Peres woke up and told the pilot to continue flying by instinct. After some tense minutes, the pilot managed to make contact with Lod Airport and the control tower directed him to Sde Dov Airport in Tel Aviv.

When they descended from the plane, they were met by Air Force Commander Ezer Weizman, and his deputy, Mordechai Hod, with a bottle of brandy and glasses. Roaring with laughter, Weizman asked them, "Do you realize you were in Jordan, and we saw you on the radar and couldn't do anything?" Peres felt dizzy. He looked at the attaché case, which he had held on to even while he slept.

The unprecedented security precautions proved useless in the face of unrestrained gossip. One day a French priest arrived in Beersheba and met the mayor by chance. "How are things?" he asked. "How is the Negev developing?" The mayor was delighted with the opportunity to talk, and within a matter of minutes had told the priest about the atomic reactor being built near Dimona. Fortunately, the "priest" was a French intelligence agent, who had come to Israel to check the security of the reactor. "His report was extremely negative," noted Peres at a confidential briefing. After the priest's report, security precautions at the reactor were improved.

During the same briefing (November 1960), Peres laid emphasis on French insistence upon secrecy. If the fact of the establishment of the reactor is published, he said, "the French will deny that they gave any assistance to the project." A turnabout in French policy on this occurred three months later. Peres wrote in his diary (May 16, 1960): "Worrying news from France. Couve de Murville (the foreign

minister) summoned Walter Eytan (Israel's ambassador) on Saturday, and informed him—first orally, later in writing—about the
French government's decisions on the reactor. First, the time has
come to make the Dimona matter public. They appreciate the fact
that we have kept it secret, but the time has come for disclosure.
Second, the plant must have foreign (possibly international) supervision. Third, until then, they cannot supply the uranium that they
promised."

In his memoirs, de Gaulle explained France's reasons for lifting
the secrecy. "We stopped the assistance to the construction near
Beersheba of a facility for converting uranium into plutonium, from
which one bright day atomic bombs might emerge."

Ben-Gurion considered the matter sufficiently serious to ask for
a meeting with the French president. The Israeli request was
approved and the meeting set for June 13, 1960. Peres went earlier
to the French capital to prepare the ground. He told himself with
regret that this was not the same Paris to which he had become
accustomed in recent years: no more meetings in bedrooms, no more
friends who were prepared to help him circumvent their own
government, no more of the fraternity which began with mutual
interests and continued in some cases with genuine personal friendship.

Now Peres found that all business was conducted in an official
manner. Even friends who wanted to help made it quite clear that
they could not. This became evident to Peres in his first meeting on
June 8, with the minister for atomic energy, Pierre Guillaumat. Those
pushing for going public, explained Guillaumat, were the industrialists
connected with the project. They claimed that "it has become
impossible to maintain secrecy and that a leak might occur at any
moment because of the scale of the enterprise and the number of
Frenchmen already employed in Dimona. Their work contracts
specify that they are being sent to 'a warm climate and desert
conditions.' It's not too difficult to figure out where that is."

Afterward, Peres went to meet Foreign Minister Couve de
Murville, "the man everyone describes as the source of the coolness
toward Israel." This was the description of General Levaud, chief of
staff of the French armed Forces. "I am warning you about something
you have known for some time," said the general. "Don't talk to

Couve de Murville about practical matters. We are managing fine without him and will try to manage the same way in the future."

However, there were matters that could not be managed without Couve de Murville, and the reactor was one of them. On June 8, 1960, as Peres confided to his diary, "conditions had completely changed. I used to meet Pineau secretly in his private apartment at the Quai d'Orsay. We knew that a friend was waiting for us there. Now we were received in the official office." There Peres found Couve de Murville, sitting in the dim light of his office, impeccably dressed, very polite, tense, and attentive."

The discussion was based on the four points included in the message that Couve de Murville had sent Israel's ambassador in Paris. With regard to point number one, publicizing the Dimona reactor, Peres said that Israel did not object in principle, but felt that, prior to this, there should be a comprehensive announcement about French-Israeli scientific cooperation and that the section about nuclear cooperation should be just one of the paragraphs. Furthermore, immediately after the announcement, Israel wanted to open the Dimona center to visitors, so that "even the Soviet ambassador can visit it."

When Couve de Murville raised an eyebrow, Peres assured him that there was no cause for concern; things that should not be shown would not be. Peres further suggested that when the announcement was made, Israel would play down the French role. At this point French pride intervened, and Couve de Murville said that he was not interested in minimizing French technical achievements.

As to point number two and the question of how the reactor would be described, Peres had an answer. In view of the fact that they were talking about a twenty-four-megawatt plant, there was no difficulty in presenting it as designed for peaceful purposes only, as were similar reactors in India, Sweden, Germany, Canada, and other countries.

Point three, international inspection, Peres said, was impossible to allow. There was no mechanism for it, and that sort of inspection would mean opening the door to Russians. Peres saw Couve de Murville nodding his head in agreement.

In dealing with point four, the uranium, Peres reminded Couve de Murville that there was an Israeli agreement to consult with France.

The conversation continued for more than an hour; at the end of it, Couve de Murville said he wanted to consult his colleagues. He would give Peres his final answer on Monday, June 13, a few hours before Ben-Gurion was due to arrive in Paris.

On the whole, Peres was optimistic. It seemed to him that he had satisfied Couve de Murville on most, if not all, of the points raised. For that reason, he was surprised by the grave expression on Couve de Murville's face when they met again. Without wasting any time, he told Peres that he intended to "speak frankly and without obfuscation. Under consideration was not supervision and uranium but general intention. If it were announced to the world that France, as a responsible country, had assisted Israel in that matter, the scandal would transcend France and Israel." As he knew Peres's modus operandi, Couve de Murville quickly added that "the idea of a conspiracy on such a serious matter was out of the question."

Peres was astounded. He tried other arguments, but he seemed to have lost Couve de Murville's sympathy, as the foreign minister answered each point negatively. Ben-Gurion's visit to Paris resulted in de Gaulle's promise to reconsider French policy and in the suggestion that Guillaumat and Peres maintain their contacts.

The policy reevaluation did not lead to the hoped-for results. On August 1, Ambassador Eytan was summoned to Couve de Murville and told categorically that France would cease all assistance to Israel in building the reactor if Jerusalem continued to oppose supervision and disclosure. Couve de Murville added that, in this event, France was prepared to compensate Israel for losses resulting from a cessation of the aid.

On this point Peres decided to take an independent initiative. It was clear that France was no longer, and would never be again, what it had been for Israel, but Israel still had friends in key positions in the French administration. He now turned to them and secured a promise that, if the assistance were stopped, they would supply Israel with the necessary information to enable it to continue with its plans.

Only after he had received this promise did Peres inform Ben-Gurion. He told him that he had wanted to ask for his approval, but in the end had decided to act on his own so that, if there were a mishap, Ben-Gurion would be able to say honestly that he had not known about it. The Old Man answered laconically, "You don't argue with success."

Israel now had two alternatives, which Peres laid out for Ben-Gurion. One was to accept compensation from France and to agree that the assistance be stopped. The second was to insist that the aid continue. Peres was inclined to follow the second course. He did not disguise the fact that this would involve a bitter argument with France, but maintained that Israel would not lose anything thereby. Ben-Gurion decided, "If that's the way it is, we'll argue with them and we won't agree to international supervision."

To conduct the discussions, Peres again flew to Paris (November 8, 1960), where he met Couve de Murville and Guillaumat. He was already resigned to the fact that it would not be possible to prevent publication of the matter, so his aim was to reduce the damage as much as possible. The French demanded that the facts be published jointly. But this would mean, said Peres, that it was a joint project, and a French-Israeli joint project would inevitably arouse suspicion in the world. He suggested that Israel alone announce the existence of the project and present it as a purely Israeli matter. Questions to the Quai d'Orsay would be passed on to Israel. If anyone asked where Israel had purchased the necessary equipment, the reply would be that the source was being kept secret to avoid pressure from the Arab boycott.

Peres added that, if they accepted this approach, Israel would not emphasize the Dimona reactor, but would talk about the whole research program, including a university in Beersheba and research to develop arid zones with atomic energy, etc. It would be announced that this was a five-year plan with the aim of training engineers to develop the Negev, to introduce modern industries to Israel, and also to absorb students from Asia and Africa. The Beersheba university would have French as its first foreign language, which would explain the presence of so many French engineers in Beersheba and Dimona.

Couve de Murville, who previously had stated that he would not be a party to a new French-Israeli secret, this time accepted the proposal with considerable satisfaction. He said he very much approved of this plan and asked how and when it would be published. Peres replied that he imagined that the prime minister would make a statement in the Knesset in the coming weeks.

From there Peres proceeded to the matter of supervision of the reactor. After he had explained Israel's position at length, Couve de Murville stated that he certainly understood the reasons for Israel's objection to international supervision, but wanted to know if there was an alternative. Peres answered that there was. France, he suggested, should continue to assist Israel in building the reactor, but Israel would release it from the obligation to supply material from which the reactor could produce anything that was not for peaceful purposes. In return, France would drop the matter of international supervision. Couve de Murville gave his assent to this. It turned out later that he understood very well, or at least guessed, the reason that Peres was so forthcoming.

In a book published in 1971, Couve de Murville wrote about French-Israeli connections in the nuclear field: "Israel could look for other sources of uranium, apart from France, and that is what in fact happened."

In any case, it was clear to everyone that the disclosure of the existence of the reactor could not be delayed any longer. Reports of Israel's nuclear capability, and about its contact with France, were appearing everywhere. For example, the *Washington Post* wrote, on December 18, 1960, that Israel could become the world's fifth nuclear power. The paper told its readers that Israel had built and developed a nuclear reactor in secret and that within five years it would be capable of manufacturing an atom bomb. The French Foreign Ministry was under continuous pressure from journalists.

The day after the *Washington Post* report, the Quai d'Orsay issued an official press release strongly denying reports that France was helping Israel to carry out a nuclear program for military purposes. The spokesman added that "the plans of Israel's Atomic Energy Authority are intended for peaceful purposes only. The assistance given by France for carrying out this program include a research plant for the manufacture of heavy water and natural uranium."

On December 20, Peres gave a briefing in his office in Tel Aviv to a number of officials who were in on the secret.

"Possibly in the next few days the prime minister will make an announcement confirming that we are building another nuclear reactor of twenty-four-megawatt capacity. It could be tomorrow, the day after, or next week. The main points are:

- The Nahal Sorek reactor is a small one and the Dimona reactor is for research.

- Contrary to rumors, the Dimona reactor is part of a long-range plan for the development of the Negev.

- We must, at all costs, avoid emphasizing the importance of the partnership with a foreign power. The main initiative was our own.

- No country in the world is under international supervision. Those who suggest that Israel should be the first are also suggesting the internationalization of Jerusalem.

The world was waiting for the Israeli announcement. In order to make it less dramatic, Ben-Gurion decided that he would give an official statement, but answer a parliamentary question from two Knesset members—one from the coalition and one from the opposition. Their question was: "Is there any truth in the report that Israel is in the process of manufacturing an atom bomb?" With an expressionless face, Ben-Gurion replied: "The report is false, knowingly or unknowingly."

Shimon Peres, sitting in the plenum, apathetically scratched his chin as he leafed through, knowingly or unknowingly, a booklet of legislation.

The Last Item

Peres visited Paris again in February for the purpose of wrapping up two vital matters. One was the immediate supply of sophisticated Super-Mystere aircraft, which had been agreed upon earlier. Problems had arisen. The planes were supposed to come from the stocks of the French air force, and suddenly, France was claiming that this would disrupt the air force's training program. Peres applied directly to Air Force Commander General Johue, one of Israel's last genuine friends in the administration.

The general was not too pleased with the guided missiles that currently armed his planes, "because of their low ceiling." He was sure it was possible to develop a guided missile "with a very long range, appropriate speed, and a very high ceiling, but the government is hesitating." Peres could help the French government overcome its hesitations, suggested the general. How? He only had to hint that Israel might be interested in such missiles. He did not have to commit himself, emphasized Johue, only to express an interest.

Peres was delighted to oblige. On March 11, 1969, the first six Super-Mysteres flew in to Israel. The second purpose of Peres's visit was to conclude negotiations for the supply of the latest French combat plane, the Mirage. The negotiation reflected the change in Israel's status that had occurred in Paris. There were many ups and downs, because everyone who thought that French-Israeli ties were too strong—in particular, the Quai d'Orsay—took advantage of this matter to try to weaken them. Unexpectedly, and in a manner that caused satisfaction in Jerusalem, it was de Gaulle himself who decided in favor of the sale.

The signs of opposition to the deal, however, caused such concern in Israel that when Peres met with Couve de Murville on February 25, 1960, he asked "whether in his opinion, Israel could rely on continued French assistance." Couve de Murville was careful in his reply, reiterating de Gaulle's policy. "Israel's position is important to the entire Western world. France is, of course, part of the Western world and will play its part."

Peres was not satisfied. "Does the minister object to publicizing the fact that France is continuing to stand behind Israel, as in former days?" Again Couve de Murville was cautious. "What do you want to publicize, the matter of the Mirages?"

"No," Peres replied.

"The fact we are supplying you with weapons and planes?"

"No, just the fact that good relations are continuing. We need this, because the announcement would deter the Arabs and reassure people at home."

"I follow your argument," Couve de Murville said. "From your point of view you are right, but we are against it. It would have an undesirable effect in North Africa. The king of Morocco has just returned from a visit to the Arab countries. We have to be careful."

"But his mission failed."

"That is correct, but we still have to take Muslim reaction in North Africa into account."

"If that's the case, there are contradictory needs. What happens when there are contradictions?"

"In political life, when you come up against a contradiction, you speak with two voices."

"In that case, we'll take the tenor."

Some two months later, on May 11, 1960, "we met in the Israeli Defense Ministry with the representatives of three large French companies, who had come to conclude the first Mirage deal. The time had come for the festive signing of a $24 million agreement to buy twenty-four planes that flew twice the speed of sound."

The Mirage era had begun for the Israeli air force. Its predecessor, the Mystere, had played a central role in the defeat of Egypt in the Sinai Campaign; the faster and more effective Mirage would decide the Six-Day War.

The Mirages were the last significant item that Israel received from France. Even Peres was forced to admit, however unwillingly, that the udder of the French cow was refusing to suckle the Israeli calf.

Peres would attain other important achievements in his life, but it is doubtful that any of them would equal those of the French period. He forged the links with France at a time when it was not at all sure that the Zionist enterprise would survive. Without the French connection, it is difficult to see how a small state, with no financial or military resources, could hold out. The arms that Peres acquired from France—both in quantity and in quality—converted the Zionist idea into a political reality.

It was not just a matter of timing, though. The reactor liberated Israel from the fear that one day, when it could not continue competing with the Arab states in the arms race, the military balance of power would tilt against it, and it would face the danger of annihilation.

Egyptian President Anwar Sadat's visit to Jerusalem many years later to make peace may have been motivated by his knowledge of this reality. And some years after that, when Peres spoke of an international peace conference, the attention paid in the various Arab capitals may also have been the result of that achievement. For Peres understood from the outset that the basis of peace lies in Israel's strength, and in the Arab states' knowledge that it cannot be wiped out. The French connection that Peres initiated and fostered made the greatest contribution to the establishment of this fact.

But the time had come to look for and to cultivate new pastures.

CHAPTER THREE

OTHER DIRECTIONS

Collecting the Moral Debt

AS THE TWILIGHT of relations with France approached, Peres could congratulate himself on the fact that, several years earlier, he had initiated a step that was specifically designed to avoid a situation where all Israel's security eggs were in one basket. He did this despite the trauma of taking such a step. Every mention of Germany at that time was tantamount to playing with fire. The mortal wounds of the Holocaust were still very painful and far from being healed.

In 1952, Jerusalem and Bonn signed a reparations agreement, which provided for large-scale monetary compensation for Nazi crimes to the State of Israel and the victims of the Holocaust. When news of the agreement was published, violent street riots, which almost led to civil war, broke out in Israel. Eventually tempers cooled down, and most of the population accepted, with manifest reluctance, Ben-Gurion's stand that it would be immoral and irresponsible to absolve Germany from paying compensation.

But there is an enormous difference between accepting the payment of reparations and active cooperation. It was not easy for a young Jew, whose roots were in Poland, to come to the conclusion that it was time to inaugurate a new era with a country whose citizens had annihilated six million of his people.

"How do I feel here as an Israeli?" Peres once wrote on a visit to Munich. "Objectively, this is not a people that excites my imagination. Subjectively, my entire approach is accompanied by a feeling of reserve, an almost physical fear that a German will touch me, a feeling of guilt in case something appeals to me. We live here in an atmosphere of isolation, in which we are not just insulated, but are the insulating material. At the same time, everything is on a human level. It almost hurts to see how like us the Germans are. Is there really in this people a seed of evil that cannot be changed? Is it unavoidable that this people will create hatred and arrogance, oppression and murder? Or if they repent, can the repentance be genuine, determined, and thought through?"

If there had been an alternative, there is no doubt that Peres would have been happy to give up on Germany, but the alternative did not present itself, and therefore he concluded, "I do not see any reason to release Germany from its moral obligation toward us. Even though we may curse it in the Knesset, I never heard that it is possible to create armored divisions from curses."

This, then, was the justification. The security of the State of Israel is the highest priority of the Jewish people, the answer to the Holocaust. In order to achieve this aim, it was permissible, even necessary, to have relations with everybody—even, and maybe especially, Germany.

In 1957, Peres spelled out his thoughts to Ben-Gurion and found him ready for the idea, both morally and from a practical point of view. The conclusion of their discussion was "to approach Germany the way we started with France: to make direct contact between the Defense Ministries." On July 3, 1957, Peres met for the first time with the West German defense minister, Franz-Josef Strauss, who became a key figure in the development of relations between the two countries.

From the outset the two men understood each other. Strauss certainly won Peres's approval, because he described him in this way: "He is a mountain of a man, a hundred kilograms plus, with blue eyes full of energy, likes eating very much, and is a sparkling polemicist."

In the following months Peres and Strauss met six times, and reached agreements for the supply of further items to the IDF, including submarines, missiles, and planes. The cooperation continued and expanded.

The agreements with Germany shored up the arms supply triangle, which Peres described to the IDF General Staff: "If America gives us money and not weapons, and if France sells us weapons for cash, the Germans give us arms for nothing. This German policy is approved with some limitations, the most important of which is secrecy. If the word gets out, there is no chance of this matter continuing."

As in the case of France, the cooperation did not remain limited to arms for long. Other matters of common interest were discovered, which were given expression in a number of ways.

On one occasion, Peres brought along a guest to Strauss's home: Tom M'boya, who was, at thirty-two, one of Kenya's up-and-coming leaders. M'boya seemed both ill at ease and grateful to Peres for arranging the meeting, which took place in an informal atmosphere. As the three of them sipped Madeira, M'boya briefed Strauss on the situation in Kenya, warning that there was a danger of a complete Communist takeover, using local Communist groups which received aid from Moscow. He talked excitedly about his trip to Israel and about the promise he had received to train a group of officers.

When Strauss asked how he could help, Peres replied that, as Israel was assisting with training, Germany's aid should be in the form of equipment. Peres's diary records that Strauss instructed his aide, General Becker, to prepare, in consultation with Israeli representatives, "a list of equipment that independent Kenya needs to fight subversive forces. Tom was delighted, and Strauss was also pleased to be expanding the scope of his activities." He told Peres, "As you suggested, we went into Sudan. I hope you are not sorry about it; we certainly are not. We'll try and penetrate farther, right down the East African coast, in consultation with you."

First Steps in the United States

The significance of the German and other European deals was marginal compared to the opportunity that began to shape up at the beginning of 1963: the possibility of a genuine shift in the military assistance policy of the largest and strongest of the powers. The many years of patient work began to show results when new winds, even promising breezes, began to blow from the direction of the United States.

The change had begun to be felt in 1961 when Ben-Gurion, on an unofficial visit to President John Kennedy, requested a supply of Hawk antiaircraft missiles that Israel needed very badly. A year later, he received the answer that Kennedy had decided to accede the request, albeit at a price: Israel's acceptance of an American plan to solve the problem of the Palestinian refugees. According to the plan, the refugees themselves were to decide whether they wanted to return to Israel, or to be absorbed in their countries of residence. Ben-Gurion felt that this was too high a price—in fact, an impossible one—and he gave up on both the plan and the Hawks.

Another difference of opinion between Israel and the United States concerned the reactor in Dimona. Before his trip to the United States, Ben-Gurion made an announcement in the Knesset about the existence of the reactor, although he only gave partial information on the subject. Before he set out on his trip, a dispute broke out in Jerusalem as to whether he should give the Americans more information in his talks with them. Foreign Minister Golda Meir forcefully demanded that he do so. Peres argued that it was unnecessary, as the Americans knew very little, and Ben-Gurion concurred. Peres did not accompany Ben-Gurion on this visit, but when the prime minister returned, Teddy Kollek, who had accompanied him, assured Peres he was right.

Kennedy did not give up on the refugee question. In January 1963, he came up with a new proposal, which called for Israel to absorb 10 percent of the refugees. At the same time, he revived negotiations for the sale of Hawk missiles, and, as in 1961, the matter of the reactor became mixed up in the talks.

The refugee question was quickly disposed of, mainly because of the opposition of the Palestinians themselves and the Arab states. The linkage between the Hawks and the reactor revived the debate in Jerusalem. The Americans demanded that Israel permit them full supervision of the Dimona reactor. Peres was convinced that the two matters should not be connected.

At a discussion in the prime minister's office on January 16,

1963, he said that, if it was impossible to receive the Hawks from the United States, "let's think about getting them from Europe." This suggestion enraged Meir. "It puts the clock back several years," she declared angrily. "We seem to have an allergy to America. At a time when, after a lot of hard work, the United States takes a tiny step in our direction, we suddenly remember that in fact we can get the same thing somewhere else."

"It took them a year to check it (the radar)," Peres said.

"When did we discover that it was possible to get it in Europe? When the Americans gave it to us," Meir replied.

Ben-Gurion ruled: "We are not breaking off negotiations with America on the matter; that is clear."

It was a good thing that they did not. Peres himself flew to Washington at the beginning of April 1963 to finalize the negotiations. There, at an informal dinner party, he had the opportunity to sense the change in attitude toward the reactor. In the course of a discussion on the matter, the influential Senator Stuart Symington burst out, "Don't be fools; don't stop work at the reactor; don't listen to the administration; do what you think you should."

It turned out that even the administration had become less sensitive, as Peres was to learn "from the horse's mouth." After a meeting with presidential aide Mike Feldman, Peres was brought to Kennedy's office to meet him. British Prime Minister Harold Wilson was waiting in the adjoining room, so the president was only able to shake hands briefly with Peres.

That afternoon, when Peres was meeting with another assistant, McGeorge Bundy, Feldman phoned to say that Kennedy was sorry he had not had time to talk to Peres in the morning, and invited him to come right away. As they walked to the Oval Office, Feldman told Peres that the president had canceled a meeting with congressmen at the last minute to make time for him.

"We went in to the president's office, quite a nice room, though we have seen more beautiful rooms. President Kennedy entered. In some ways he looked better than his pictures, in some ways worse. What surprised me was the smallness of his face, smaller than in the pictures, a narrow lined forehead, dark-blond hair with a lot of gray, looks pretty tired, large gray eyes, a slightly sarcastic smile. He is quick to catch on, really telepathic, an extraordinary grasp of the subject. He keeps up-to-date, reads the papers, and knows what is happening in the world and the region. He has a remarkable memory. With all that, he behaves informally. You don't get the feeling that here sits the president of the most powerful nation on earth, a man whose very name arouses excitement. He speaks fluently, and you can at once see that he has no patience for messing around. He is brief and to the point and expects the same from you: to ask straight and clear questions and to give unambiguous answers. Our conversation began without any preliminaries. It was, in fact, his conversation; he interrogated me throughout that half hour."

Kennedy approached the subject of the reactor indirectly, starting with the question: "What missiles have been introduced into the region?"

PERES: "Egypt has four types. Recently they have introduced missiles mounted on torpedo boats."

KENNEDY: "What, they have the Komar?"

PERES: "Yes, they received it recently."

KENNEDY: "How many?"

PERES: "Four, so far."

KENNEDY: "They have a range of sixteen miles, don't they?"

PERES: "Correct. That's thirty kilometers, with a 750-kilogram warhead. In addition, they have received air-to-air missiles, and antiaircraft missiles from the Russians. The fourth type is ground-to-ground."

KENNEDY: "They didn't get those from the Russians."

PERES: "We don't have evidence that the Russians supplied them with those missiles. They have developed them with help from the Germans."

KENNEDY: "Is West Germany helping them?"

PERES: "Not the government, but German scientists and technicians. So far the missile is not too accurate. It has a range of five hundred kilometers."

KENNEDY: "How many do they have, and when will they be operational?"

PERES: "They have thirty, so far, and they will be operational in eighteen months."

At this point Kennedy began to pressure his guest slightly. "To get back to the rockets, the danger, of course, is that there is no point in missiles, unless you arm them with unconventional warheads. Don't you think the warheads are more dangerous than the missiles themselves?" His logic was clear enough: if, in fact, Israel was developing nuclear capability, why the concern over Egypt's rockets?

PERES: "Let me say that even rockets with conventional warheads are different from bombs dropped from planes. The main feature of a rocket is that it is unmanned. It causes panic and gives its possessor a sense of power. There is no effective defense against it."

KENNEDY (not yielding): "That is correct; but as you know, the atomic warheads are more dangerous than the missiles."

PERES: "The missiles are already in place, whereas the atomic warheads won't be there for some time, if at all."

Kennedy understood that his line of questioning was getting nowhere, and he became more direct. "You know that we follow with great interest any development of nuclear potential in the region. That would create a most dangerous situation. For that reason we have been in close touch with your effort in the nuclear field. What can you tell me about that?"

At this point, Peres produced a formulation which was to become the official policy of all Israeli governments on this subject. "I can tell you clearly that we will not introduce nuclear weapons into the region; certainly, we will not be the first to do so. We are not in the least interested in doing so. To the contrary, we are interested in reducing regional tensions, even in complete disarmament."

It is not clear whether Kennedy bought this answer. One may assume he related to it with more than a trace of skepticism, but he dropped the matter. "How would you suggest dealing with the matter of missiles and weapons?" he asked.

PERES: "In my opinion, diplomacy is preferable to military means. I don't see how you can persuade the Soviets not to supply arms, and Egypt is thirsty for arms. If it depended only on us, we would be prepared to give up arms altogether. You must remember that we are a democratic country, not only in principle, but with all the democratic institutions. We are under pressure not to neglect development and education. We have problems of social integration. There is a natural pressure to deal with these problems instead of stockpiling weapons. Therefore, when we talk about diplomacy being the better way, it's not just because we prefer it, but because our situation dictates this."

KENNEDY: "What do you mean?"

PERES: "I mean a declaration, accompanied by the means for keeping peace."

KENNEDY: "I'll ask you two questions. First, don't you think that, if we made such a declaration, we should also guarantee the Lebanese, the Jordanians, the Saudis, etc., and won't that create the impression in the world that we are setting ourselves up as the deciding judge? What would we think, for example, if the Russians made such a declaration? There is also the second question, but answer this one first."

PERES: "There is a difference in kind between the Israel-Egypt dispute and Egypt's quarrels with the Arab nations. The possibility of peace or war between Israel and Egypt is evenly balanced. The enormous prestige of the United States today would not be harmed if it came out openly, not against someone, but against something; that is, against any attempt to change the status quo by military force."

KENNEDY: "The second question: does this apply to Egypt also? Are you asking for a one-sided declaration in Israel's favor, or a declaration to safeguard Egypt, as well?"

PERES: "As an Israeli, I am of course speaking about Israel. We have no aggressive intentions, but I have my doubts whether you could reach an agreement with Nasser as easily as you could with us. We are talking now not about limited intervention in time of war but to prevent a war, and not behind the scenes but openly, in a way that will not only speak to Nasser but that will appear as a new reality in Arab minds, and change the history of the region."

KENNEDY: "What formulation would you suggest?"

PERES: "We can find the words; you must agree on the principle."

KENNEDY: "What would you do if there were a revolution in Jordan with the result that King Hussein is thrown out, or something happens to him?"

PERES: "There are three possibilities: (a) an Egyptian invasion, (b) a military revolt that will invite the Egyptians in, as happened in Yemen, and (c) a local revolt. In the first instance, Israel would find itself in a very difficult position, and we could not stand idly by. Ditto in the second case, and we might have to argue with the American administration (regarding the way to act). In the third instance, it would be very difficult to decide. And maybe there is a fourth possibility that we didn't take into account. We will have to decide according to developments."

KENNEDY (with a smile): "I'm sure you didn't imagine that the day would come when you would pray for the safety of Hussein and [Saudi Arabian King] Faisal. How long are you staying here?"

MIKE FELDMAN: "He came to finalize the negotiation on the Hawks, and tomorrow he has meetings at the Pentagon for that purpose."

Peres could not resist—and this was always a problem with him—the temptation to demonstrate his talent with words: "I represent a nation of doves that has come to buy Hawks."

Peres conducted the practical negotiations with the president's advisers and officials of the State Department and Pentagon. After exhaustive discussions, it was agreed that the Americans would have the right to visit the "Dimona reactor"—as distinct from the "Dimona complex."

The other outcome of the negotiation was that Israel at last received the thing it needed so much: five batteries of Hawk antiaircraft missiles. The significance of this agreement went far beyond its immediate security importance. It lay in the decisive breakthrough in the wall of American resistance against selling sophisticated military equipment to Israel. From now on, the gaps in that wall would widen, until the United States became Israel's main ally and arms supplier.

The Promise That Was Kept

On the surface, it seemed that Israel had hit a high point in matters of defense supplies. But even at times like these, Peres never abandoned his long-held view that Israel's defense posture was directly related to the degree of its dependence on others. The more he dealt with purchasing weapons, the more his basic thesis was strengthened: that there were no such things as friendly countries, only friendly people and governments—and those could change.

His conclusion was that he must continue his efforts in the direction of local production. The first big result of his labors was achieved on July 6, 1960, and he was deeply moved, as he confided to his diary:

"This afternoon there was a ceremony which concluded tremendous efforts, hopes, and difficulties over many years. At 4:30 P.M., I went with Ben-Gurion to the Israel Aircraft Industry. In a large square there were some four thousand people sitting, among them, employees of the aircraft industry, cabinet ministers, foreign diplomats, and people from all walks of life. On a whitewashed circle, small but beautiful, was the first Fouga-Magister training aircraft manufactured in Israel. On the previous evening I was still looking for a name for it, and decided that *Swallow* appealed to me. Planes should be called after birds, as submarines are called after sea creatures. It is also the first swallow. I was also taken by a tractate from the Talmud: 'A swallow may frighten an eagle.' More than 50 percent of this jet aircraft was manufactured in Israel, and that is a first-rate achievement. The Old Man was deeply moved and began his speech by saying, 'If I were a religious man and wore a hat, I would take it off to Al Schwimmer.' Al was also very moved, and read his speech in Hebrew with a strong American accent. Al was appreciative toward me, describing me as 'the pillar of the aircraft industry.'"

The ceremony was the end of a long and bumpy road, along which Peres had been forced to stand up against almost wall-to-wall opposition. The economic ministers grumbled bitterly that the plan to assemble and manufacture sophisticated weapons was wasteful and irrelevant. Others were concerned about diplomatic complications. Even the army was against it.

In a memorandum to the defense minister, written in reply to a positive recommendation from Peres, Chief of Staff Haim Laskov wrote that if this matter (assembling a jet plane in Israel) was within the sole province of the Defense Ministry, there was nothing for him to say. If, however, there was room for an opinion from someone on the General Staff, then it seemed right to him that a (third) opinion should be sought—that of the air force commander. Laskov suggested that the belief Peres had expressed in the military industries should be based primarily on its ability to provide spare parts for weapons, including bazookas, rockets, flamethrowers, up-to-date mines, etc.

Laskov and the air force commander concluded that "even if an economic solution is found, such a step is not a solution for the Bedek plant because a limited number of aircraft is no substitute for the purpose for which Bedek was planned and built; that is, the servicing of foreign airlines and El Al."

Peres refused to limit the purposes of Bedek to these fields. He wanted a plant that would manufacture everything needed in the aeronautical field—planes, in particular, but also rockets. The first missile to be manufactured by Bedek was inaugurated some three months before the flight of the Fouga-Magister. As we can see from Peres's description, it was not a fearful weapon, but he was no less proud because of this:

"At 2:00 P.M. on April 2, 1960, I flew by helicopter to a spot in the Negev, where the G-25 was being tested. The missile can be fired from an aircraft, boat, or command car to a distance of up to thirty kilometers. Three missiles were fired in that fantastic landscape of fractured mountains and plains. The first one immediately dropped to the ground, for unknown reasons. The other two missiles flew like magnificent creatures for a distance of sixteen kilometers and hit the center of the target that had been painted on the hills opposite. The hit was marvelous, and the two officers who fired the missiles—one a naval man, the other from the air force—performed with expertise and self-confidence, despite the general excitement.

"Hitting the target is the successful conclusion of four years' work, perseverance, and research. It gives the IDF not just a new weapon, but entry to the complicated world of guided missiles. Other nations have invested tens of millions of dollars just to reach the starting point. And what we could not buy, we attained through the talent and loyalty of our workers. It was a great and promising day for Israeli science, the defense effort, and the plant's management."

The name of the plant was changed from Bedek to the Israel Aircraft Industry (IAI), and from this point it rose to heights that even Peres had not dreamed of in those cold nights in Newfoundland. A daughter company was established alongside the main plant, and together they produced aircraft for various purposes, such as the Arava transport plane, with short take-off and landing ability, which was very popular in developing countries; the Westwind executive jet, which became a hit in the United States and Europe. The production of missiles was given a terrific boost, which reached a climax in the Gabriel sea-to-sea missile, mounted on patrol boats, and

Reshef and Keshet vessels. After them came sophisticated antiair-craft and air-to-air missiles.

The production line expanded to the manufacture of communications equipment of all types, radar systems, computers and testing systems, medical electronic equipment, and control systems for air, sea, and land. But the jewel in the crown was the manufacture of the Kfir combat aircraft, the first of which was transferred to the air force on April 14, 1975, as a gift from the Israel Aircraft Industry for Israel's twenty-sixth birthday.

Peres sat on the platform for distinguished guests, watching the blue sky and the maneuvering of the plane, his eyes full of tears. Beyond the plane he could see, as clearly as if it were yesterday, the night scene at Lake Kinneret with Al Schwimmer and Elhanan Yishai. And he could hear himself telling Yishai, "You know, this American boy says that he'll make a jet." And Yishai suggesting, "Come on, let's go for a dip in the Kinneret, so we remember his promise to make a jet."

The fulfillment of that night's dream was now cruising confidently in the skies: he and Al Schwimmer had made a jet, as they had promised.

The Arms Merchants

The military industry in no way lagged behind the aircraft industry. Like its more sophisticated elder sister, it also developed and diversified at a faster pace than its founders had dared to dream. In fact—and in this it equaled the aircraft industry—the military industry diverged from its basic purpose of producing arms for Israel's needs and developed foreign markets. There was opposition, and this time not only for financial reasons. Many were concerned that entry into the world arms market would involve Israel in moral problems, not to mention diplomatic complications. It would not be long before the opponents were able to say, "We told you so."

One day early in March 1958, Leo Gardiner, the pilot, noticed that one of the engines of the Constellation DC-4 that he was flying was not functioning properly. He switched it off and decided to continue the flight with three engines. A short while later, his gauges showed him that he had another problem—an oil leak. He decided to land. He was flying at the time over the small city of Bone, some four hundred kilometers east of Algiers, the capital of Algeria. Gardiner called the control tower of the French military airfield in Bone and received permission to land.

The French at the airfield welcomed Gardiner and his crew warmly. The trouble began on the following morning in the person of the airfield's French security officer. "What are you carrying?" he wanted to know.

"Arms," replied Gardiner, without hesitation.

"Where are you taking them to?"

"South America." Gardiner added in a relaxed tone, "We have an understanding with Paris about this plane."

"Fine," said the security man, "we'll check it." He phoned headquarters in Algiers, which immediately contacted Paris; no one had heard anything about the pilot, the plane, or any arrangement. Now the security officer became suspicious. He began to interrogate Gardiner, on the assumption that the arms in the plane were intended for the Algerian rebels.

This is how Peres described what happened next, in a message to Asher Ben-Natan, head of the Israel purchasing mission in Paris:

"They took the pilot and asked him, 'What have you been doing for the past eleven years?' The pilot did not realize that they suspected him of anything, and he began to tell them. 'In 1947, I smuggled American planes to Israel. In 1948, I flew arms from Czechoslovakia to Israel, and I bombed Cairo. In 1953, I flew Spitfires from Israel to Italy. In 1956, I flew arms from France to Israel.' To the Israelis it was a heroic epic; but to the French security officer, it was proof that he was dealing with a top-class smuggler.

"They asked each member of the crew what language he spoke and in which language he wanted to be interrogated. One of the boys said he had emigrated to Israel from Rumania. As soon as they heard 'Rumania,' they didn't ask him anything else, they just put him on one side, because he seemed to them suspicious. They then took the third crewman, an English pilot married to a Jewish girl, and started interrogating him. He related that he had fought in the War of Independence and the Sinai Campaign. From the security officer's point of view, it looked extremely suspicious: one of them is from Rumania, another an American, the third from England. They claim that there is an understanding about the plane, but Paris says it knows nothing about it.

"Then there was the matter of the arms themselves. They were wrapped in blankets. Asked why they were loaded like that, they answered that it saved space and crates. The security men said, 'We pack them that way for a parachute drop.' Our boys replied, 'Maybe you pack them that way for parachuting, but we didn't pack them for that purpose—anyway, we have no chutes aboard.' This led the officer to suspect that they had already dropped some of the arms to the Algerian rebels."

Despite the jocular tone of Peres's description, it was not in the least bit amusing. When the affair was published in the media, there was a public outcry in both Israel and France. Israel was suspected—even by some members of the French government—of being involved in smuggling arms to the Algerian rebels, with whom France was engaged in a tough and bitter war. And this was at the height of the friendship between the two nations, when France was going out of its way to help Israel.

What, in fact, had happened?

Peres answered when he appeared before the Newspaper Editors' Committee: "Anyone who has flown to Israel in the pilot's cabin knows that there is nothing more difficult. As you approach Israel, you are surrounded on all sides by enemy radar. It turns out that the best route to South America lies over North Africa. In view of the fact that there is a war in Algeria, we contacted a key official in the French administration—and I must say something in his favor. If there are good relations between France and Israel, it is because of this man. He has not gained materially from assisting us; he does it for idealistic reasons. (The official was Louis Mangine, the close aide of Premier Bourges-Maunoury.) Naturally, we made contact with this man and sought his advice regarding the advisability of flying over North Africa. His answer was positive. He added that the appropriate authorities would be informed. This was, of course, passed on to the flight crew. They were told that it they had problems, they could feel confident that they were flying over friendly territory, and that there was an arrangement with them (the French). And that was where the breakdown occurred. The official did not keep his promise, and he failed to inform the people he should have informed. He simply forgot."

Why, in that case, didn't Peres wind up the whole matter by informing the French government about the forgetfulness of the official?

"When we heard that he had forgotten to pass on the information, he told us, 'If you like, I'll take the responsibility, but you had better understand that it is the last responsibility I'll ever take on.' I went to Ben-Gurion, and he told me, 'We'll take the responsibility.' He instructed our representative in Paris to 'tell my friend that he is absolved of all responsibility, both because of his past service and because of the vital importance of his services in future. If you betray a friend in his hour of need, you will never make other friends.'"

Peres adds that the matter was inflated because "in this affair we were a victim of internal bickering between French government departments and of the tension between various personalities in the government."

There is no doubt that people in France who disapproved of the special relationship with Israel took advantage of the affair. Peres told Ben-Natan "to explain to our friends how ridiculous it is to claim that the weapons were ready to be dropped by parachute. The story is baseless. No arrangements of that type existed, and there were no chutes aboard the plane."

Israel's friends in Paris accepted this explanation, and there were still enough of them in key positions to wind up the matter in a satisfactory manner. First the crew was released; and, later, when the affair had died down, the plane and its equipment were returned to Israel.

Now, a new controversy started that, from Peres's personal point of view, was more serious than its predecessor. If the weapons were not intended for the Algerian rebels, for whom were they intended? Peres had said South America, but that continent was not monolithic. It contained countries with which Israel was keen to maintain relations, but also those from which Israel kept its distance because of the tyrannical nature of their regimes. One of the worst offenders from that point of view was the Dominican Republic, and that was the destination of the weapons. Nicaragua was another country with the same type of regime, and Israel also sold it arms.

Peres felt a strong obligation toward both Nicaragua and the Dominican Republic because, during the 1948 War of Independence when many countries refused to assist the Jewish state in any way, these two sent large quantities of weapons to Israel. For this reason, Peres wrote to Nicaraguan leader Colonel Somoza, on February 20, that "bearing in mind the warm and friendly relations between our two countries, we have tried, within our limitations, to give all possible help to the success of your mission."

The mission was indeed a success and Israel made a deal worth $1,218,850. While it was still being implemented, the other South American countries heard about it and raised an outcry.

"We have really screwed up with the Nicaraguan arms deal," Foreign Ministry Director General Walter Eytan wrote Peres on July 5, 1957. "All the Latin American countries abhor it (Nicaragua), both because of its foreign policy and its internal regime. It is a shame you did not consult with the Foreign Ministry before going ahead with this deal. You know as well as I do that we are very dependent on the Latin American bloc in the United Nations, consisting of twenty countries. We cannot afford to disregard their feelings. I am therefore asking you to give instructions immediately that all new deals with Nicaragua be suspended, and that all shipments not yet sent be held up."

It took Peres four months to reply to Eytan (November 13, 1957) that, "recently, several South American countries expressed an interest in buying arms from us. It is clear that we are very interested in such deals. However, in view of past experience—the Nicaraguan deal—we are most interested in coordinating with the Foreign Ministry, in order to prevent any possible political damage." In reply, Eytan sent Peres a list of countries to which it was permitted or forbidden to sell arms. Nicaragua was on the "forbidden" list, as was the Dominican Republic.

Then came the affair of the plane. It quickly became apparent— and was published—that Peres had made the deal with the Dominican Republic on his own initiative and against the explicit instructions of the Foreign Ministry. He was heavily criticized in the press. At a meeting with newspaper editors on March 13, 1958, Peres tried to explain his reasoning. The weapons sold to the Dominican Republic, he said, were taken from IDF surplus and were worth some $15 million. Selling these weapons enabled the purchase of new arms needed by the IDF. "I see the task of the Defense Ministry to change old weapons into new ones."

He went on to tell them about a discussion with Ben-Gurion,

when Foreign Minister Golda Meir was also present, concerning arms sales to the Dominican Republic, which had asked for a frigate, Uzi submachine guns, and bazookas. It was decided to turn down the deal, because the source of the weapons could be traced. Peres accepted the decision concerning the frigate and the Uzis. However, as it emerges from his own story, he decided, on his own initiative, that it would be impossible to trace the bazookas back to Israel. He therefore implemented the sale, also on his own initiative. Why did he do it? Because, in principle, he had his own definite opinion about forbidding the sale of arms. "By not selling an Uzi to a certain country, we are not implementing an embargo against that country, but against ourselves. It is absolute nonsense to embargo ourselves on an item that can be acquired elsewhere."

These explanations did not alter the fact that he had disobeyed explicit instructions. This was an opportunity to settle accounts with Peres for which many at the Foreign Ministry had been waiting, particularly Golda Meir—and, in fact, not only at the Foreign Ministry, and not only Golda Meir.

CHAPTER FOUR

I WILL NOT ABANDON YOU

Youngsters Against Veterans

THERE WAS VERY little similarity between Moshe Sharett and Golda Meir, who replaced him at the Foreign Ministry. Rough in behavior and speech, careless in dress, impulsive in deeds, and down-to-earth in thought, Meir was the diametric opposite of the eloquent, quiet, and thoughtful Sharett. But they totally agreed on one issue: opposition to the activities, and in particular to the modus operandi, of Shimon Peres. The friction with him, which had been low-key in Sharett's time, continued with far more intensity during Meir's tenure, and often required the intervention of Ben-Gurion.

The root of the conflict lay in the situation that Meir inherited when she was appointed to head the Foreign Ministry. For many years she had been isolated from day-to-day contact with foreign affairs; her experience was limited, and she had little contact with world leaders. In contrast to her own position, she saw a young man of thirty-three, plugged into a worldwide network of contacts. Achievements that were inaccessible via the accepted diplomatic channels, generally because of Arab pressure, Peres attained in back rooms by unconventional and very undiplomatic methods. It is true that he tended to enter via back doors, but they were the doors of the great—men in positions of power.

A number of people in the Defense Ministry agreed with Meir's assessment of Peres's activities, and it was to them that Peres spelled out his approach. "I know that you criticize me for spending too much time on politics," Peres told a meeting of senior Defense Ministry officials on May 13, 1957, "but defense and foreign affairs go hand in hand. The fact that the Defense Ministry did not deal with these matters in the past does not prove that it was right."

What enraged Meir more than anything was the full backing that Peres received from Ben-Gurion. The prime minister and defense minister understood that the sort of contacts that Peres maintained could be fully exploited only if they were kept secret—even from the foreign minister. Even when he felt that Peres was excessive in concealing matters from Meir, Ben-Gurion did not make a real effort to change the situation.

As most of the political and defense activity was at that time conducted in France, that was the heart of the problem. In July 1957, Meir flew to Paris for a meeting with Jean Monnet, one of the leaders of the crusade for European unity. Her purpose was to win his support for integrating Israel into NATO, or linking it to the alliance in some way. The day before the meeting, Meir learned that Peres had preceded her by four months. "She reacted extremely sharply to your talks with Monnet and the fact that she knew nothing about them," Asher Ben-Natan cabled Peres (July 10, 1957). "I explained that it had been impossible to inform her, as the meeting had been arranged at the last minute. Golda did not accept the explanation. She decided to cancel her meeting with Monnet and to return at once to Israel."

Back in Israel, Meir bitterly poured her heart out to Ben-Gurion, who wrote in his diary:

"I told Golda that I was worried and saddened by her suspicions, which are not totally without foundation, that the Defense Ministry is interfering in foreign affairs. After she told me that she is already in despair, I said that I cannot accept that she is 'beyond despair.' Golda says she has no complaints against the chief of staff, but Shimon is doing things without her knowledge, and she agreed to hold a comradely discussion on the matter."

The discussion satisfied Meir to a certain extent, but not for long. When Peres was due to leave for France on an arms-purchasing mission, she demanded that he report to the ambassador and have him participate in all the talks. When Peres demurred, the two again arrived at Ben-Gurion's office. After hearing the claims of both sides, Ben-Gurion reached a compromise: report, yes; participate, no. The practical effects of this compromise are outlined in a letter that Ben-Gurion wrote to the Israeli embassy in Paris on March 18, 1956:

"The director general of the Defense Ministry is coming to France on an arms-buying mission. He will inform you of the people he meets, but the situation demands that he meet with them alone. Some of the things between us and the French have been done, and will be done in future, in an unorthodox manner, on occasion bypassing one minister or another, often the finance minister. For this reason, members of the French government choose to talk informally, on a one-to-one basis. I am sure that you value arms acquisition above ceremony, and if the French can waive protocol, so can you."

In the case of the Dominican Republic deal, however, Peres overdid it, earning a reprimand from Ben-Gurion. "There must not be any sale of arms to a country without my knowledge and approval," he wrote Peres in an official letter on March 5, 1958. "You should only inform me when a country makes a definite offer to buy arms, and I will not make any decisions without consulting the Foreign Ministry." After the reprimand, though, Ben-Gurion felt the need to administer a complimentary pat on the back, which in effect took the sting out of the rebuke. "This order is not intended as criticism of past actions. Would that all government ministries were run with the same talent, success, and loyalty as the Defense Ministry under your administration. Nevertheless, at a serious time like the present, we must have complete coordination of our policy, and the sale of weapons is a diplomatic action, not just a financial and economic deal."

He could have added that it was also a political matter, for the confrontation between Peres and Meir was expressed not only in differences of approach on diplomacy and defense, but in a power struggle that was taking place within the Mapai ruling party. At this time, the "old guard" party leadership, in which Golda Meir was a key personality, was being challenged. The leading challengers were Moshe Dayan and Shimon Peres, who had attracted a talented and dynamic group of followers, dubbed "the youngsters" by the media.

They were indeed young, but they owed their political power—their very existence—to the Old Man. Ben-Gurion was always attracted to young people, whom he saw as the future of the nation. This affinity was strengthened by the Sinai Campaign. He attributed the military success of the campaign primarily to two people: Moshe Dayan, whom he saw as the man who successfully prepared the army for the difficult test; and Shimon Peres, who equipped the army and gave it the diplomatic-military framework in which to operate.

A group of other young people coalesced around Ben-Gurion, and their power and influence increased steadily. There were government officials such as Nehemia Argov, Teddy Kollek, Yitzhak Navon, and Haim Yisraeli, who were his close aides. On the political level were such men as Abba Eban, Giora Yoseftal, Yigael Yadin (although he was not a member of Mapai), Ehud Avriel, and Shlomo Hillel.

Ben-Gurion knew very well that the veterans would not easily accept the advancement of the youngsters. "There will be opposition in the party to this change, and we must resist it," he told Yoseftal in May 1958. His prediction was completely borne out. Even though they were relatively older, the veterans showed a fighting spirit in no way inferior to that of the youngsters. Golda Meir, Eshkol, Pinhas Sapir, Pinhas Lavon, and others did not have the slightest intention of vacating their positions to the "Young Turks" who were breathing down their necks.

The veterans found the opportunity to unveil their purpose in November 1958. A general election was due in a few months, and Ben-Gurion decided to include some of the younger men in the party leadership, including Eban, Yadin, Dayan, and Peres. The veterans rebelled and there was an uproar in the party. Ben-Gurion decided to call both sides together to bring about a reconciliation. Shragai Netzer, one of the leaders of the old guard, told Ben-Gurion that if Peres were scheduled to participate, Pinhas Lavon (by that time secretary general of the Histadrut labor federation), would not show up. "I will be sorry if Lavon doesn't come," replied Ben-Gurion emphatically, "but Shimon must not be ostracized. No one has contributed more than he at the Defense Ministry."

In his speech at the reconciliation conference on November 22, 1958, Ben-Gurion adopted the policy of the carrot and the stick: he told the veterans that he did not intend to promote the youngsters at their expense, but he aggressively defended his intention to bring them into the leadership. "Only if Mapai remains the youngest (of the parties) will it be able to fulfill its mission in the future," he declared. "Throughout history, young people have achieved great things. A youngster does not deserve a prize for being young, but he should not be punished for it. If he is qualified for leadership, his youth will be a blessing."

The veterans were not reassured by this. Lavon described the meeting as the "coronation" of Dayan and Peres. Dayan, who had just retired as IDF chief of staff, poured oil on the flames, attacking the veterans at almost every turn, angering and provoking them. The old guard was helpless in the face of his criticism. What could they do against a man who already wore the mantle of leadership, who was the hero of the Sinai Campaign? His fresh, young personality, to which his black eye patch added a touch of mystery and charisma, became a symbol of the rejuvenated Israel. It was also clearly inconceivable to confront Ben-Gurion, the unchallenged, authoritative leader. There remained, therefore, the director general, with his considerable power, the image of a young doer, ambitious and without restraint. All the rage and criticism of the old guard was directed at Shimon Peres.

Peres's opinion of the veterans was not much better than theirs of him. He dealt indirectly with their determination to hold on when he spoke about another national leader: "De Gaulle says, 'I am sixty-seven today.' Unlike the leaders of Mapai, he is convinced that sixty-seven is not the age when the fires of youth start operating, but the age to retire from public life." (It is superfluous to point out that, when Peres himself approached that age, he would change that opinion, but it is part of human nature that a man in his early thirties does not believe he will ever reach his sixties.)

Dayan confronted the old-timers head-on and in public. Peres could not do this because he was in the "padded cell" of the civil service. This started to irritate him, and on May 3, 1958, he spoke of this to Ben-Gurion, who asked him, as he wrote in his diary, "Where are you headed?" Peres replied that "he could no longer remain a government official. He was not permitted to speak out, and

the new civil service law would restrict him even more severely."
Ben-Gurion remarked, "I don't see anyone else who could run the
Defense Ministry." Peres suggested that he could "resign shortly,
run for the Knesset, be appointed deputy defense minister, and thus
continue to run the ministry, but be free to speak out like any
Knesset member."

Ben-Gurion concurred. The general election took place on
November 3, 1959. A few weeks later the new Knesset was sworn
in, and Peres took his place on the Mapai benches. Not too far away
sat his political ally, Moshe Dayan, also making his political debut.

After the session, "I had tea with Moshe Dayan. He asked me
if I felt there was anything to celebrate and, without waiting for an
answer, remarked that it was strange how little feeling of rejoicing
and significance accompanied his entrance to the Knesset and
government. I said I agreed."

When Ben-Gurion presented his government to the Knesset,
Peres was included as deputy defense minister. (Dayan was appointed agriculture minister.) On the day the ministers pledged their
loyalty (December 17, 1959), he was present in the plenum, but on
his return home that night, he wrote nothing about himself in his
diary. He was entirely overwhelmed by his impression of the man he
was coming to admire more and more.

"Moshe Dayan looked very festive in his dark suit and red tie.
He is amazingly handsome and his personality stood out in this
entirely new environment. This is not the climax of his life; rather, an
important turning point." Only two days later did he pull himself
together sufficiently to write about his own new appointment: "This
morning I saw Ben-Gurion, who congratulated me on my new
appointment, and said, 'You have to be a deputy before you become
a minister.'"

At the center of all that happened in Israel was David Ben-
Gurion. Everything was done at his command. The ideas of others
were worthless without his support, and everything important
needed his consent. Like others before him who established nations,
he saw how the bees in the beehives of officialdom buzzing around
him needed his constant attention, sapped his political power and his
physical and spiritual reserves.

On June 16, 1963, after the visit to Washington in which he
finalized the matter of the Hawk missiles, Ben-Gurion again an-

nounced his resignation from the government. Delegations of party members who begged him to reconsider came away with empty hands.

One of the people to whom he explained his reasons was Commerce and Industry Minister Dov Yosef. "The burden was heavy, too heavy to bear, particularly the burden of Defense Minister," Ben-Gurion said. "And when I saw that there were two comrades on whom I could rely, Levi Eshkol and Shimon (Peres), I felt free to break free and be responsible only to myself."

On Ben-Gurion's recommendation, Eshkol was elected prime minister and defense minister, and Peres was reappointed deputy defense minister.

To everyone's surprise, Eshkol became a popular prime minister. After the stormy years of Ben-Gurion, it seemed the public was very satisfied with a simple, smiling leader with a sense of humor; a man of relaxed compromise, rather than one dedicated to unrelenting struggle. The prime minister's status was given a further boost when he received an invitation for an official visit to the White House in Washington, where President Lyndon Johnson was now in residence. Even Peres was enthusiastic. "This is the first time that an Israeli prime minister is being officially received via the front door, with full honors. [Have we become] a normal people?" he wrote in his diary with satisfaction and pride.

Peres accompanied Eshkol on the trip (May 31, 1964), and was amazed and excited. He had already visited Washington a number of times, and meeting presidents and heads of state was not a new experience for him. For all that, this visit was somewhat different; there was a feeling that this was a historic breakthrough. On his first night in the United States, "whether because of fatigue or excitement, or jet lag and change of climate, it is rather difficult to fall asleep. Emissaries from a small nation to a great power never sleep well."

A trace of irony accompanied Peres's wonder at Blair House, the official guest residence, whether genuine or to disguise his excitement:

"The temporary residence of American presidents, and the guest house for very important persons, is located opposite the White House. Its walls are lined with silk; expensive chandeliers hang from its ceilings; it is furnished in French and Colonial style and decorated with pictures and artifacts from China, France, and America. Eshkol occupied the first floor, and I received two vast rooms of the second. They looked after us in an appropriate manner, with everything from fruit and whiskey to a box of shaving soap, the cover of which was so shiny, it looked as if it was gold-plated. There were soft carpets and luxurious towels; only the floor trembles like a wooden railway station when the steam engine goes through."

When he entered the Oval Office with Eshkol, Peres was hypnotized by the presidential telephone. "On the desk opposite Johnson's chair was a telephone with a set of buttons. This was the "hot line," from which you can call up the most destructive force that humanity has ever known. Nothing symbolizes more vividly the power, limitations, and responsibility of the American president than that isolated telephone. Apparently it is relatively new, or its location is, because the line runs under the red carpet, and to facilitate this, someone has cut a rough, improvised hole in it."

On the evening of their second day in Washington, the president gave a gala dinner in honor of his guests. Afterwards, "we went to watch a cultural entertainment program. We had not slept for thirty-six hours, and my body rebelled against my cultural spirit. I decided to find an inconspicuous place where I could catch up on my sleep, but it didn't work. Mrs. Johnson searched me out and placed me next to her. I trembled when I heard that the program was to consist of works by Bach. I haven't the patience to listen to Bach in the daytime; certainly not in the evening. On the small stage sat four well-built ladies, and opposite them four thin, weedy men (what Bach has only done to the sexes!). They began with a duet that seemed to go on forever. During the intermission, Mrs. Johnson asked me whether I did not think that Bach had composed his works principally for the organ. Taking into account my knowledge of music, I hastened to agree. (I did not see this as a departure from government policy.)

"After the concert, the guests moved to the ballroom. The orchestra played a waltz, and a critical moment in American-Israel relations arrived: the president, tall and in a good mood, grabbed Miriam Eshkol, and with a long, swift stride, propelled her to the polished dance floor. What was going to happen with Mrs. Johnson? Eshkol doesn't know how to dance! Suddenly Abe Harman (the Israeli ambassador), tired and worried, a cigarette dangling from his lips, emerged from the darkness and approached me with a threatening step. 'Shimon, you must invite Lady Byrd to dance.' Everything went black. I did not know whether the orchestra was playing a tango or a waltz, and apart from my personal hesitation, I could see the headlines in the Israeli papers: 'Young Mapai Bulldozes the Wife of the U.S. President . . .' My resistance is growing stronger by the second, but Abe also does not give up easily. He nudges my shoulder, saying, 'Well, well?' I realized that I could not hold out, and I asked the wife of the president to dance. Gradually, the dance floor filled up with the other couples, and I finally decided that it was a waltz."

Now it was the turn of the Israeli embassy to reciprocate with a cocktail party at the Mayflower Hotel. This occasion was also recorded by Peres. "A while later we were again called upon to stand in a line and shake hands. Initially it seemed to us nothing very much—a hundred guests. Then, a little later, we started becoming curious about the number of guests—there seemed to be another three hundred. (Eshkol asked whether they were going outside and then rejoining the receiving line.) After a bit our hands became swollen and our legs shook. Most of them did not know me, and after Eshkol left, they thought I was the prime minister; others thought I was the hotel manager. The line went on forever. From a distance I started to look on each guest as a real enemy—a Nasser setting out to do battle. A thousand guests, two thousand, and all of them possess hands!"

The following day the Israeli visitors were flown to Cape Kennedy in Florida for a visit, and it is no wonder that the base delighted Peres. "Here they live six years into the future—not so far that one cannot see the horizon." From there they flew to Texas, where, that evening after a brief rest, they were entertained by wealthy members of the local Jewish community in their private club. "For us it was a miserable evening. On the one hand we felt clearly that their love for Israel was deep and sincere; on the other, our conversation might as well have been between beings from different planets. We did not understand them, and they did not understand us. There was no bridge and no common language."

From a practical point of view, very little was achieved by the visit, and in fact, very little had been expected. Peres summed up the visit: "The difference between America and France, among other things, is that the Americans took us to Cape Kennedy, but told us that Israel doesn't need missiles, whereas the French give us rockets, but don't take us to their Cape Kennedy (Vernon)."

I Will Not Abandon You

Outwardly, it seemed that Ben-Gurion associated himself with the general admiration for Eshkol, but beneath the surface the old leader was again starting to become enraged about a matter that had given him no rest since it had burst forth in the spring of 1954.

At that time, the power struggle within the military junta in Egypt that had deposed King Farouk several years earlier had reached its climax. General Muhammad Neguib, the prime minister of Egypt, was ousted and his place was taken by a charismatic young colonel, Gamal Abdul Nasser. One of the first actions of the new Egyptian leader was to demand that Britain vacate the Suez Canal Zone so the canal could be nationalized. Israel was alarmed, because the British forces stationed in the zone were considered to be an effective barrier against a possible attack by the Egyptian army. The possibility that the Egyptian leader might achieve his goal caused sleepless nights for many in Jerusalem.

Several political and defense leaders came to the conclusion that Israel could not sit idly by in the light of this new development. The activist approach was espoused by Pinhas Lavon, who had become defense minister after Ben-Gurion's first resignation from the government. The IDF's intelligence branch started working out a plan to strengthen the hand of the members of the British Parliament who were opposed to withdrawing from the Canal Zone by proving that the new Egyptian regime was a threat to the Western world and to its interests in the Middle East. Accordingly, it was decided to carry out a number of sabotage operations in Egypt to create the impression of chaos and of an anti-Western atmosphere in the country.

The campaign began in July 1954, with the planting of firebombs in American libraries in Cairo and Alexandria. The fires were quickly extinguished and the damage was minimal. The following week, military intelligence set out to carry out similar actions in two cinemas and a warehouse in Cairo, and two cinemas in Alexandria. But the agent who was to plant the bomb in the Rio Cinema in Alexandria suffered a mishap. The firebomb he was carrying in a spectacle case caught fire, and he was promptly arrested by the Egyptian police.

On July 25, the Arab press carried news stories about an Israeli spy ring that was committing acts of arson throughout Egypt. It was the first that Prime Minister Moshe Sharett and Chief of Staff Moshe Dayan had heard about it. Israel, of course, issued a categorical denial, and termed the story "an Egyptian provocation." But along with the denial there was an investigation, which pointed to Pinhas Lavon as the initiator. He had not seen fit to consult with or inform anyone else. This caused shock waves in Jerusalem and in Sde Boker, where Ben-Gurion wrote in his diary: "He (Moshe Dayan) told me of an astounding order issued in his absence by Pinhas Lavon, concerning an action in Egypt that failed (and they should have known it would fail). What criminal irresponsibility!"

On December 11, 1954, the trial of the Israeli agents, who had been rounded up and dubbed "the Zionist spies," began in Cairo. In Israel an internal committee of inquiry, consisting of former Chief of Staff Ya'acov Dori and Supreme Court Justice Yitzhak Olshan, was established to discover who had given the order for the operations in Egypt. The investigation revealed strained personal relations in the senior ranks of the defense establishment, intrigues, and forged documents.

The Israeli government found itself in a dilemma. Every day, more shattering revelations on the affair came to light, but the official line was that Egypt had leveled "malicious and baseless accusations against Israel." On January 27, 1955, the trial ended in Cairo. Two of the accused were sentenced to death; six received long prison sentences; two Egyptian Jews were acquitted. Four days later the executions took place, but before that, another prisoner, Intelligence Officer Max Bennet, committed suicide in jail.

On January 13, 1955, the Dori-Olshan committee wound up its investigation without a clear verdict: "We can only say that we were not convinced beyond reasonable doubt that the head of military intelligence did not receive the order from the defense minister. At the same time, we are not sure that the defense minister did give the order attributed to him."

On February 2, Lavon resigned. The official explanation for his resignation was differences of opinion on the structure of the Defense

Ministry and the IDF. The truth was that he was forced out because of the Egyptian affair, which at that time was withheld from public knowledge. As compensation for his resignation Lavon was elected to the post of secretary general of the Histadrut Labor Federation. It seemed that the matter had been wound up, but it hadn't. The scandal would again raise its ugly head and cause a political earthquake in Israeli public opinion, lead to dramatic changes in the Israeli leadership, and affect the life of Shimon Peres.

The overwhelming feeling was that all this would not have happened had Ben-Gurion been in charge, and that his presence in the Defense Ministry was still vital for the nation. Delegations started to stream to Sde Boker and, on February 17, it was announced that Ben-Gurion was returning to the government as defense minister.

In mid-July there was a general election. Mapai remained the biggest party, but it lost five seats in the Knesset. The nationalist Herut movement (led by Menachem Begin) gained in strength. These results were interpreted as a rebuff to the moderate policy of the Sharett government. The demands for Ben-Gurion to resume the post of prime minister increased, and the Old Man acceded to them. On November 2, 1955, the Knesset voted confidence in a new government headed by Ben-Gurion. As in the past, he also held the defense portfolio.

The next five years were stormy ones, both politically and militarily. It seemed that the Lavon affair had been forgotten, and so it might well have been, had not Lavon received new information in mid-1960 from Colonel Yosef Harel, a former member of IDF military intelligence. He showed Lavon papers that indicated that former Chief of Military Intelligence Benjamin Jibli (working with others) had forged intelligence documents to clear himself of responsibility for the affair and place it on Lavon.

Lavon went to Ben-Gurion with this new material and demanded that he be fully cleared. Ben-Gurion promised to investigate the matter and charged his military secretary, Haim Ben-David, to look into it. After two months, Ben-David presented his conclusions, which showed that there had in fact been forgeries and destruction of documents. Ben-Gurion ordered Chief of Staff Laskov to appoint a commission of inquiry, headed by Supreme Court Justice Haim Cohen, with two IDF officers. This step infuriated Lavon, who demanded immediate exoneration without another inquiry, but Ben-Gurion rejected his demand.

At this point items started to appear in the press about the affair and interest in it revived. The media, almost without exception, took Lavon's side and demanded that the injustice done to him be remedied immediately, without waiting for the results of the new inquiry. Ben-Gurion continued to refuse. His stand was that, despite the evidence that Lavon had showed him, he was not qualified to resolve the guilt or innocence of anybody without an authorized inquiry. He had nothing against Lavon, he stated, nor did he support him, but the affair must be investigated in an orderly and legal manner.

Drawing encouragement from the support of the public at large, Lavon decided to launch a campaign against Ben-Gurion. He began with testimony before the Knesset Foreign Affairs and Defense Committee, which held four hearings on the matter. When his testimony was leaked to the press, it caused an uproar in the country, in the Mapai party, and above all with Ben-Gurion.

Lavon gave the committee his version of the "rotten business" in Egypt, placing all the blame on Jibli and his men, and furnished comprehensive details of forgeries and other unsavory incidents. He attacked the entire defense establishment, charging it with "economic imperialism," waste, and ineffective administration. He told of operations carried out behind his back and without his knowledge during his term as defense minister, which resulted in unnecessary casualties.

Lavon became the darling of the public—the underdog, the persecuted one—and Peres became the black sheep. Lavon had told the committee that it was beneath his dignity to argue with Dayan and Peres. The press only mentioned Peres and added—in complete contradiction of the facts, and of the words of Lavon himself—that Dayan had been loyal to Lavon, whereas Peres had not been.

The only one to come out against this presentation of facts was Ben-Gurion, who defended his deputy fiercely. In articles, letters to the press, and personal letters, he described Peres as "the one who ran the defense establishment with rare talent," and as a man "whom few have matched in working for the nation."

Ben-Gurion's stand affected Peres very deeply. "Throughout this dispute, I never asked Ben-Gurion to defend me," he told senior officials at the Defense Ministry. "I was moved by the unusual comradeship that Ben-Gurion showed for someone whose 'case' was pretty miserable. He did it without saying a word. I don't know of any other example where such a busy man has made himself available to defend the honor of his pupil, friend, or subordinate, as did Ben-Gurion. I think it was exemplary conduct."

But Ben-Gurion's defense did not help very much, as his own prestige was starting to suffer. The attack on the values most dear to him, and on people he admired and respected, brought him out of his neutral position. He waged a frontal campaign against Lavon and found himself, for the first time since the establishment of the country, in a position of clear inferiority.

Meanwhile, the Cohen Commission completed its work, concluding that documents had been forged and false testimony given in the affair of the bombings in Egypt. These findings strengthened the hands of those supporting Lavon's demand for complete exoneration, but Ben-Gurion was not prepared to accept them on the grounds that only a judicial inquiry could discover the truth.

The press determined that this claim was evidence of a lack of sincerity. Why had Ben-Gurion not said this before the commission published its verdict? Would he have demanded a judicial inquiry if the conclusions of the commission had found Lavon guilty? A feeling emerged that Ben-Gurion's struggle was not for truth and justice but to conceal the failures of the defense establishment and those who headed it. The press did not let the affair die down, and most publications demanded Lavon's exoneration as dictated by the findings of the Cohen Commission. Ben-Gurion persisted in his attitude. The leaders of Mapai found themselves in a situation that they had hoped to avoid—they had to take a stand.

Finance Minister Levi Eshkol moved into action, attempting to find a compromise to end the dispute, but he was too late. Ben-Gurion no longer saw Lavon merely as the one who had tarnished the sacred values of the defense establishment. After studying the matter thoroughly, he concluded that Lavon, and not only Jibli, was guilty in the "rotten business." This conclusion strengthened his demand for a judicial inquiry.

On October 30, the cabinet gave in to Ben-Gurion's demand, but only partly. Instead of a judicial inquiry, it was decided to set up a committee of seven ministers, chaired by Justice Minister Pinhas Rosen. On December 21, 1960, the committee presented its conclusions: "We determine that Lavon did not give the order, and that the 'rotten business' was conducted without his knowledge."

Ben-Gurion erupted like a volcano. He described the proceedings of the committee as "concealment and half-truth," and its conclusions as "a travesty of truth and justice." He again voiced his demand for a judicial commission of inquiry. "Only in this way can we arrive at the truth. Witnesses are examined and cross-examined; people are forced to confront each other; both sides have attorneys, and the attorneys investigate and interrogate." With great emotion, he asked the cabinet: "Why are you afraid of a judicial commission of inquiry?"

But the ministers, and particularly the Mapai ministers, were fed up with the affair; all they wanted was to remove it from the public agenda. They maintained that continuing to probe the matter would cause the party irreparable harm, and for this reason, the conclusions of the committee of ministers should be regarded as the end of the matter. Ben-Gurion remained adamant that the truth was more important than the party.

The cabinet met to decide the matter, and Ben-Gurion found himself in the unaccustomed position of being in a minority when the conclusions of the committee of ministers were accepted. The Mapai ministers were certain that Ben-Gurion would accept the verdict, but Peres knew him better. "The conclusions will compel Ben-Gurion to resign," he wrote in his diary. "It is clear that unless Lavon goes, Ben-Gurion will not remain." Peres was far from happy at the prospect and tried to reason with Ben-Gurion. When this did not help, he sent him a letter (December 30, 1960), which is most moving in its expressions of admiration and affection:

> *Dear Ben-Gurion,*
>   *In my opinion, you will be able to guide the ship of state to a secure shore within a few years. In four essential matters the foundations have been laid—I refrain from saying that you laid them—for a significant and serious reorientation:*
>   *(a) In defense—the nuclear deterrent.*
>   *(b) In the political regime—the chance for altering the electoral system.*
>   *(c) In the Negev—its settlement, industrialization,*

agricultural development (which received a powerful stimulus from the German loan).

(d) Foreign policy—our links with Asian and African countries.

I am concerned that all of the above will suffer, will be damaged, maybe even destroyed, if you resign from your position today. The people, who still face the danger of annihilation, have no alternative to your faith, vision, and experience.

I can well imagine what you have been through in recent months. There has never been such odious distortion, ingratitude, and treachery, but the people are not responsible. The politicians have done what they have done, and, to give them the benefit of the doubt, I don't think they always realized the results of their actions.

Your entire life has been a struggle for the Jewish fate and the great vision of their spiritual and physical regeneration. You have no right—vis-à-vis the people and their fate—to abandon the hope and the shield just when they are most needed.

A new chief of staff has just assumed command of the IDF. He needs your guidance and support more than ever before. And with regard to the army, I know that there is no service that you are not prepared to render. I have the right to say these things without exaggeration or subjectivity. It was said at the previous election, when hundreds of thousands of citizens freely chose your leadership, in complete belief and great hope.

I will not abandon a man like you.

But Ben-Gurion was beyond persuasion. On January 31, 1961, he went to the president and tendered his resignation as prime minister and defense minister, which in effect meant the resignation of the government.

Mapai panicked. Its leaders had not been prepared for the extreme step taken by Ben-Gurion, and a hysterical scramble ensued to find a compromise that would reverse this stern verdict. But Ben-Gurion was not prepared for anything less than Lavon's head, and they gave it to him in a cynical, ugly, and brutal manner. On

Saturday, February 4, 1961, the Mapai Central Committee met behind closed doors. Levi Eshkol proposed to the members that Lavon be dismissed from his post as secretary general of the Histadrut. After an emotional debate, Eshkol's proposal received a majority.

Ben-Gurion got what he wanted, but he was to pay a heavy price. The veteran leadership of Mapai would never forgive him for forcing them to bow to his dictate in such a humiliating manner. From now on he could no longer rely on the automatic support of Eshkol, Pinhas Sapir, Golda Meir, Zalman Aranne, and their comrades. At this point a process began that would, in the course of time, bring about the end of Ben-Gurion's leadership.

Lavon's ouster satisfied Ben-Gurion, and he agreed to retract his resignation and form a new government. However, a new reality became clear to him, the party, and the public. For the first time since the founding of the country, he was unable to form a government because of the opposition to his leadership by the left-wing Mapai and Ahdudt Ha'avoda parties.

He recommended to his party that a government be formed without him, and even suggested candidates for minister of defense. His first choice was Peres. "I suggest Peres as defense minister, but if this arouses the opposition of key comrades, I won't insist on it." Only as a second choice, "you can take Dayan and appoint someone else as minister of agriculture." A third possibility: "You could turn perhaps to [former Chief of Staff Yegael] Yadin."

Mapai was not yet ready to give up Ben-Gurion's leadership. There was no way of avoiding new elections, which were held on August 15, 1961. The Lavon affair cost Mapai five seats in the Knesset, but Ben-Gurion was able to form a new government. Peres was again appointed deputy defense minister. Two years later, Ben-Gurion again resigned, and Levi Eshkol replaced him as prime minister and defense minister.

Once more it seemed that the affair had been finally laid to rest, but in point of fact it was only sleeping, waiting for another opportunity to appear. At the end of 1964, Ben-Gurion, now a member of Kibbutz Sde Boker in the Negev, received new evidence that strengthened his conviction that Lavon had ordered the "rotten business" in Egypt.

Armed with these new findings, Ben-Gurion approached Prime

Minister Levi Eshkol with a request—really, a demand—to appoint a judicial inquiry commission. The very idea of dealing with the affair again made Eshkol shudder. After consulting with his colleagues, he rejected Ben-Gurion's demand, thus causing the first rift between the two men.

The action that completed the rift and made it irreversible was Eshkol's decision on May 2, 1964, to reverse the Mapai Central Committee decision ousting Lavon. This enraged Ben-Gurion and he launched an open campaign against Eshkol and the Mapai leadership. His home in Sde Boker was flooded with delegations of worried Mapai officials, asking him to abandon the Lavon affair. He sent them all away. Against this, Eshkol stepped up his resolution by deciding to recall Lavon to an active role in the party.

This angered Peres, who took a strong stand against the idea. Moshe Dayan went even further: on November 3, 1964, he submitted his resignation because of "the hostile and oppressive atmosphere that I feel in the Eshkol government."

Ben-Gurion's first success came when the attorney general, Moshe Ben Ze'ev, told the cabinet that he accepted Ben-Gurion's views on the Lavon affair. On the basis of his recommendation, Justice Minister Dov Joseph proposed that the cabinet set up a judicial commission of inquiry, and Eshkol was forced to agree. Ben-Gurion was exultant, but not for long. Under strong pressure from his party colleagues, and from Ahdudt Ha'avoda, Eshkol took only three hours to reverse his decision backing the recommendation of the justice minister. A meeting of the Mapai Central Committee was called on December 13, 1964, to decide between Ben-Gurion and Eshkol.

This was Eshkol's opportunity to show that he had learned something of Ben-Gurion's methods. A few hours before the session of the central committee was due to start, he called a cabinet meeting and submitted his resignation, thus placing before the party a clear choice: either Eshkol as prime minister, or a judicial inquiry and a government crisis. After a stormy meeting, with passionate speeches and continuous interruptions, the party central committee resolved by a large majority to approve the continuation of the Eshkol administration. In other words, for the first time since Ben-Gurion had become the leader of Mapai, the party showed preference for another man.

The final rupture occurred at the party convention in February 1965. The two camps, youngsters and veterans, prepared themselves thoroughly for the confrontation. The veterans put up an impressive performance. Moshe Sharett, stricken with cancer, his days numbered, arrived in a wheelchair and delivered a vitriolic attack on Ben-Gurion, which stunned the delegates. Eshkol and Golda Meir followed suit.

Ben-Gurion had been scheduled to reply to his opponents, but he was deeply shocked by the vehemence of the speeches against him, particularly Golda Meir's. He stood up and left the hall without uttering a single word, and his demand for a judicial commission of inquiry was voted down by 1,226 votes to 841.

Ben-Gurion returned to his hut in Sde Boker and began to think about leaving Mapai and setting up an independent political party. He told his associates that it would include nonpolitical figures who supported a change in the electoral system and Mapai members opposed to Eshkol. He believed that such a list could elect twenty to twenty-five members of the Knesset. He predicted that the Alignment of Mapai and Ahdudt Ha'avoda, which had meanwhile been formed, would win a similar number.

Assisted by his former bureau chief, Haim Yisraeli, Ben-Gurion began sounding out people he thought would join him. During this period, Hillel Cohen, the head of Sollel Boneh, the giant Histadrut construction company, phoned Yisraeli and said: "Tell Ben-Gurion to talk to [Histadrut Secretary General] Aharon Becker, and [Haifa Mayor] Abba Khoushy. If he talks to them, they will go along with him." This was important information, because they were men of power and influence within Mapai. Yisraeli hurried to tell Ben-Gurion, but the Old Man was unimpressed: "I don't care about that. I want to know whether Moshe and Shimon will join me."

Neither Moshe nor Shimon was inclined to do so. Peres did not agree with Ben-Gurion's optimistic forecast about the electoral potential of the new list. He also felt a moral reluctance to the move: "We have been educated toward unity and construction, not splits and opposition," he told a meeting of Ben-Gurion supporters, now dubbed "the Minority," at Moshav Avihayil. At a meeting of the Minority staff (June 27, 1965), Peres put forward a resolution stating that "the majority of the participants at this meeting believe that the best way to fight for our views is within the framework of the party."

After the resolution was approved, Peres was sure that a split had been averted, but two days later he found he had been entirely wrong. Following the resolution of the Minority staff, Ben-Gurion called a meeting of about twenty of his chief supporters at his Tel Aviv apartment. Peres opened the meeting with a presentation of the alternatives facing the Minority camp, clearly indicating that he preferred remaining in Mapai, and conducting the struggle within the party.

When he had finished, Ben-Gurion made it clear to all those present that there was in fact only one alternative. He had not called them together for a discussion, he stated, but to announce his intention to establish an independent list that would fight against the travesty of justice in the Lavon affair. He had even prepared a platform for the new list, which he proceeded to read to the stunned audience.

Ben-Gurion demonstrated his anger at Peres by instructing another person, Meir Barelli, to conduct the meeting. Peres, pale and insulted, did not say a word. He resumed the chairmanship of the meeting a few minutes later, but he did not mention his proposals.

That same evening (June 29, 1965), the establishment of a new list, headed by Ben-Gurion, was announced. It was called the Israel Workers' List, and became known by its Hebrew acronym, Rafi.

Peres faced a cruel dilemma, perhaps the cruelest of his political life. He did not believe in the new list, its policy, or its chances of success. He was deeply offended by Ben-Gurion's attitude toward him and the way he had presented him and his comrades with a fait accompli. He had no personal dislike for Eshkol, certainly not the deep hatred felt by Ben-Gurion, nor did he see any point in reviving the Lavon affair. In addition, he was worried about the possibly irreparable harm that would be done to his political career by leaving Mapai. But Ben-Gurion was still Ben-Gurion, his leader and mentor. Could he forsake him now, in the hour of his greatest trial? Should he sacrifice his political ambitions on the altar of Ben-Gurion's mania? Did Ben-Gurion have the right to expect it of him?

That night Peres could not fall asleep. He tossed and turned, constantly conjuring up images of the meeting in Ben-Gurion's home. He was hesitant and confused. Only when the first rays of the sun penetrated his room did he fall into a troubled sleep, and even that was not for long. At about seven o'clock he was awakened by the phone. Still groggy from his short sleep, his first reaction was to reach for the alarm clock, but the ringing continued. Without opening his eyes, Peres picked up the receiver and held it to his ear.

"Hello, are you there?"

Peres recognized Ben-Gurion's voice at once, and all traces of sleep vanished. Ben-Gurion said he wanted to come to Peres's apartment immediately to apologize for his behavior at the meeting yesterday. It had happened, he continued, because he was very tense. Peres replied that Ben-Gurion did not have to trouble himself; he would come to Ben-Gurion's flat.

Peres jumped out of bed. His wife Sonai, who had heard the phone conversation, already had the coffee on. Peres drank it quickly, refusing the sandwich she had prepared. As his driver had not arrived, he drove himself to Ben-Gurion's home in north Tel Aviv. As soon as he crossed the threshold, the Old Man hugged him warmly and again asked for his forgiveness. "You did not deserve such behavior from me." Afterward he said that he knew Peres opposed a split, but "I am in a situation where I cannot go on without Moshe (Dayan) and you." He then added emphatically, "Certainly not without you. If you tell me 'No,' I'll give up the whole idea."

Peres was deeply distressed. He felt a great sadness for this man who had established the state, led the Mapai ruling party, and now in the fullness of years had decided to set out on a new path, which, even with the best intentions, would lead nowhere. He was also sorry for himself, realizing that this path would certainly not take him where he wanted to go. Despite all this, Peres did not hesitate even for a fraction of a second. His face did not perspire and his voice did not tremble as he said confidently: "I will not abandon you."

The Orphanhood of a People

Ben-Gurion knew very well what he was doing when he told Peres that he could not establish Rafi without him. He himself was too old and tired for the hard work of establishing a new party. Dayan behaved like Dayan—a prima donna, expecting things to be served him on a silver platter. Starting a new party from scratch requires money, party workers, branches, and offices. Somebody had to do the work and it fell, as if understood, on Peres's shoulders.

Although he came with ambivalent feelings, from the moment Peres left Mapai and the government, he left behind him any doubts or hesitations and devoted all his efforts to building the new party. The first thing he realized was that the platform could not be based on the affair alone. He broadened it with issues: a new electoral system based on constituencies, in place of proportional representation; a national approach instead of a socialist one; science, industry, technology. Second, he placed himself at the head of the organized effort, and in a short time established branches, recruited thousands of party workers, and raised a considerable sum of money.

Characteristically, he adapted his calculations to the new reality, changing swiftly from moderate pessimism to arrogant optimism. He offered Gad Ya'acobi, a young Rafi candidate, number fifteen on the list for the Knesset, telling him that "it will be the tenth place before the last realistic one." In other words, he thought Rafi would win twenty-five seats, and under Israel's proportional representation, the fifteenth place would be a safe position. Ya'acobi consulted with Dayan, who was pessimistic and warned him, "the fifteenth spot will be the eighth *after* the last realistic one," envisaging seven seats for Rafi.

Peres's frenetic activity did not escape the notice of the Mapai leaders, who reacted in characteristic fashion. Despite all that had happened, they still felt uncomfortable attacking Ben-Gurion. Peres was a convenient substitute, and they attacked him in every way possible. He did not take the assault lying down, and this period deepened a hostility that eventually was moderated but never forgotten.

The election campaign was tough and brutal. Mapai fought savagely against those who had deserted it, and the former party members replied in kind. Former comrades went for each other's throats with a fury bordering on hysteria. The results proved that Dayan and Peres had both been mistaken in their forecasts. In the general election of November 1964, Rafi won only ten seats, as against forty-five for the Mapai-Ahdudt Ha'avoda Alignment.

The disappointment was acute. For the first time in many years, people such as Dayan and Peres found themselves outside the action. They were sentenced to a sterile period of opposition, and no one could say how long it would last. Tabling questions in the Knesset, attending meetings of important committees, visiting party branches were the scope of Peres's activities now—not nuclear reactors, rockets, tanks, and deals with heads of government.

Ben-Gurion, who had not achieved any of his goals, lost interest. Although he rarely made an appearance in the Knesset, the leadership of Rafi did not remain vacant. Peres had built it up from top to bottom, but his comrades did not make him leader. The leadership was bestowed, as though self-evidently—to Peres, also—on Moshe Dayan. He became the final arbiter in every matter—in fact, the first arbiter. This was the natural relationship between the two: Peres was the creator of power, Dayan the wielder.

Once they had become accustomed to the new situation, the Rafi people revived their fighting spirit. Their parliamentary campaign against the Alignment-led government was as tough as the election campaign had been. Only a common enemy could calm things down, and he soon made an appearance.

On May 16, 1967, President Nasser of Egypt demanded that United Nations Secretary General U Thant withdraw the U.N. forces stationed on the Egypt-Israel border. The deterioration in the situation reached a climax on May 21, when Nasser announced the closure of the Straits of Tiran to Israeli shipping, thus blockading Israel's southern port of Eilat on the Red Sea. For Israel the announcement was, in effect, a declaration of war. Despite this, the government did not act rashly and sought ways to defuse the crisis by diplomacy. Approaches were made to France, Britain, the United State, and the United Nations.

All of them acknowledged the justice of Israel's case and the seriousness of the step taken by Nasser, who had promised, when Israel withdrew from Sinai in 1956, to permit free shipping to Eilat. But as the days went by it became clear that, apart from trying to influence Nasser verbally, the powers and the United Nations were unable to do anything. Reassured by this state of affairs, Nasser heated the atmosphere further by moving large forces into the Sinai Peninsula and up to the Israeli border.

Israel announced a general mobilization of its forces on May 19, but the government waited, still trying to find a diplomatic solution. In Israel, the public began to show signs of impatience, and what was worse, insecurity. As the period of waiting continued, the public increasingly lost faith in Eshkol's leadership. A fear grew that the coming war might lead to the destruction of Israel. At a time like this, the public wanted the ship of state to be guided by the man who had guided it successfully through previous crises. The name of Ben-Gurion was on everyone's lips.

In its despair, the public did not realize, or want to realize, that Ben-Gurion was no longer the leader that he had been in the early years of the country. The struggles and the years had taken their toll. The activist of the 1940s and 1950s was now fearful of war and predicted grave results if it broke out. He bitterly criticized Eshkol's conduct of the crisis and blamed him for the deterioration. He suggested that the Rafi faction in the Knesset demand Eshkol's resignation. The suggestion was not adopted, because Dayan and Peres opposed such a step at the height of the crisis.

The first practical initiative for changing the leadership came from the leader of the National Religious party, Interior Minister Moshe Haim Shapiro. At a meeting with Peres, he announced that his party would support the replacement of Eshkol with Ben-Gurion. The head of the opposition, Menachem Begin, joined the initiative. He met with Eshkol and suggested that he vacate his position in favor of Ben-Gurion, and permit the latter to form a government of national unity. Eshkol refused, but the public's lack of confidence in him as a military leader at so critical a time reached hysterical proportions.

In Peres's consultations with the leaders of other parties, "it became clear to me that there is not a majority for replacing Eshkol, but what can be achieved is the appointment of Moshe Dayan as defense minister. Eshkol has already suggested to Dayan that he assume military command of the southern front. Moshe agrees. He sent Avraham Ofer to me with the suggestion that I join the government as minister without portfolio. Of course, I refused. Dayan phoned me the same day and said, 'Shimon, don't waste your time, nothing will come of it.' But I stood my ground and demanded that Dayan join the government as defense minister. I saw this as a condition for establishing a national unity government.

"I now faced one of the most difficult situations in my life: I had to go to Ben-Gurion and tell him that there was no chance of replacing Eshkol, and we had to be satisfied with getting Dayan into the government as defense minister. I knew that Ben-Gurion would react with fury. I visited him on Thursday morning and explained the situation in detail. David Ben-Gurion erupted at me like a volcano: 'I thought you were a statesman and a friend, but now I doubt whether you are either. Don't you understand that Eshkol is not capable of leading the struggle? Didn't we agree that a condition of joining the government was the replacement of the prime minister?'

"I knew that in this situation, I had to fight back without restraint: 'You always say that when one weighs ideology against security, security is the decisive thing. Does this principle obligate only us, or does it obligate you as well? Don't you see how grave the security situation has become?' He calmed down as quickly as he had erupted."

Ben-Gurion agreed to Dayan's joining the government but only on condition that Peres tell Eshkol, "We have no confidence in you as prime minister." Peres carried out this difficult task, although he knew that "I was making things very tough for a man (Eshkol) whom deep down I like, despite all that has happened recently."

Eshkol's reaction was moderate, even forgiving. "I understand that that is your position. Maybe you will change your mind one day." On June 1, 1967, Eshkol established a national unity government and gave the defense portfolio to Dayan. That evening the leaders of Rafi met at Ben-Gurion's home to celebrate. Ben-Gurion said: "I know that you all worked for this, but one of you worked very hard and very skillfully, and that is Shimon."

Four days later, on June 5, the war broke out. It lasted six days, and the victory was greater than had been envisioned. The Sinai Desert, the Golan Heights in Syria, and the West Bank of Jordan were conquered; Jerusalem was liberated. The prestige of Moshe Dayan as a national hero reached the proportions of adoration, in no way reduced by the fact that he had become the leader of the fight only four days before it started, and had therefore not exercised a decisive influence on the course of the war or the army's ability to fight it. For all that, he had played a part in the victory by restoring self-confidence to the army and the people. The public wanted a hero, and Dayan was more than ready, as well as eminently suited, to fill the role.

People like symbols with whom they can identify; they are not concerned with those who facilitate the creation of the symbols. It was the Mysteries and Mirages that Peres had bought in France that destroyed the Egyptian air force. It was the tanks that he had acquired in France, Britain, South Africa, and Italy that swept through the Sinai Desert, the Golan, and the West Bank. The great victory could not have been won without the superb quality of the Israeli soldiers and their commanders, but neither could it have been achieved without the sophisticated weapons with which Peres had supplied them. This fact received scant attention. Once again it was Peres who had created the power and Dayan who had used it. As always, the crowd carried Dayan on its shoulders, leaving Peres on the side—joining in the cheering.

The trauma of the war and the euphoria of victory put the rivalry between Mapai and Rafi in proportion. The leaders of Rafi, including Peres and Dayan, saw no point in continuing the dispute, and the atmosphere in the opposite camp was similar. The only barrier to uniting the two parties was Ben-Gurion, who was not ready to forgive or forget. He was totally opposed to Rafi's return to its parent body. His uncompromising stand again forced Peres to confront him. He reiterated the call he had made before the war for a union of the labor movements, and, to start with, the return of Rafi to Mapai. Rafi scheduled a convention in mid-December to decide for or against the union.

On December 12, 1967, Rafi held its last convention. By a majority of 52 percent against 48 percent, the convention approved the establishment of a union between Mapai, Ahdudt Ha'avoda, and Rafi, to be called the Labor party.

The war gave a tremendous boost to Israel and its position in the world community. National pride and self-confidence soared. There was unprecedented economic development. The days of austerity and economic depression were over. They were replaced by industrial and agricultural development, which led to a dramatic rise in the standard of living.

There were also, of course, problems. President Nasser did not accept his defeat. His artillery on the western side of the Suez Canal mercilessly shelled the Israeli positions that had been established on the eastern bank. In response, Israeli aircraft carried out daily bombing raids on military targets in Egypt, penetrating as far as Cairo. This war of attrition lasted for two years. Only in August 1970 did the guns fall silent, when Israel and Egypt agreed to a cease-fire sponsored by the United States.

Shortly afterward, the man who had cast a pall of fear over Israel for so many years—President Nasser—died of a heart attack and was succeeded by a new president, Anwar Sadat.

Even more difficult problems were created by ruling over a million Arabs in the West Bank and the Gaza Strip. One of the immediate results was the strengthening and increased activity of the Palestine Liberation Organization (PLO), whose members sowed death and destruction in Israel's towns and beyond.

During this period, Peres held a number of ministerial positions: transportation, absorption, communications, information, and responsibility for development in the administered territories. Although on the surface his position in the government was more senior than indicated by the positions he held, he was, in fact, dealing with marginal matters. As he usually did, he tried to invest these topics with vitality and sparkle, sometimes in an artificial and pretentious manner.

When he took over the Ministry of Posts, he found it important to change its name to the Ministry of Communications, which sounded more fashionable and sophisticated. When he became transportation minister, he proclaimed the pretentious slogan, "a car for every worker," which his rivals mocked for many years.

But together with the presumption, there was also action. Under Peres's leadership, the communications ministry built its first satellite receiving station and decided to take the phone service away from the government and transfer it to a private company (a decision that took many years to implement, for reasons outside Peres's control). As minister for immigrant absorption, he suggested that all immigrants to Israel be directed to Jerusalem, which stimulated the town's development and enlarged its population.

In his spare time, Peres tended to party affairs. The return to the parent party had not destroyed the barriers created by the split. The three sectors of the Labor party jealously guarded their separate structures. Mutual suspicion and rivalry were the norm.

Eshkol died and Golda Meir replaced him as party leader and prime minister. Like Ben-Gurion before her, Meir was not one to forgive and forget. Now, as prime minister, she had the chance to settle accounts with Peres, both for the days when he had run his own foreign policy while ignoring her and for the struggle with Rafi. She could not dismiss him, because the party unification agreement permitted each faction to choose its candidates for government positions, but she could restrict his activities and ignore him, and she did so.

Meir learned to live with Moshe Dayan, and he with her. The two of them became the symbol of Israel: Meir the proud and brave woman, a mixture of Jewish mother and angry biblical prophetess; Dayan, the war hero. The people of Israel, who had never had it so good, were confident that, with two such leaders, nothing bad could befall them.

Then another war came along and turned this situation on its head. Hostilities broke out on October 6, 1973. This time there was no period of waiting—not even a warning of what was about to happen. After careful planning, which amazingly was kept completely secret, the Egyptian and Syrian armies attacked Israel, taking the IDF by surprise.

The early days of the war were a nightmare for the citizens of Israel and their leaders. The Egyptian army managed to cross the Suez Canal and establish itself on the eastern bank. The Syrian army invaded the Golan Heights. There was a feeling of standing on the brink of collapse. After a few days, the military picture began to change gradually. Large quantities of arms arrived from the United States. The Syrians were driven back from the Golan Heights. An IDF force managed to cross the Suez Canal and conquer territory on the western side.

When a cease-fire was attained, the Israeli public was in a state of profound shock. Thousands of young men had been killed in the fighting. The thing that Israelis had thought impossible, particularly after the Six-Day War victory, had happened: the Arabs had managed to surprise Israel and to demonstrate, at least in the first days of fighting, military superiority.

Most of the fury was directed against the god who failed: Moshe Dayan. But Meir and her government did not escape the barbs of criticism and feelings of disillusionment. The government came to be called "the government of the blunder." It seemed that its days were numbered.

A general election was to have been held in November, but it was postponed to December 31, because of the war. It seemed that this time the Labor party would lose its hegemony, but then U.S. Secretary of State Henry Kissinger arrived in the region, as a mediator between Israel and the Arab states. A plan was worked out for a peace conference at Geneva, and Labor portrayed itself as the only party capable of leading the country toward the coveted peace with the Arabs, as against the militant alternative of Menachem Begin. This formula achieved its purpose. Despite the shocking blunder, a shattered, war-weary public again placed its confidence in the Labor party.

On December 1, a month before the elections, the phone rang in Peres's apartment. At the other end of the line was Haim Yisraeli, who said one word: "Ben-Gurion."

Peres wrote: "I hurried to the Tel Hashomer Hospital. His family—the children and their spouses—were waiting outside. I asked permission to enter the small room. He lay on his back, his high, pale forehead, as if carved from marble, framed by the white wings of hair. There was a strange and terrible silence about him. I thought that here, for the first time in his life, he had at last attained complete peace. A rare natural phenomenon had succumbed to the inevitable dictates of nature. The room bore witness to the orphanhood of a people."

The room undoubtedly also bore witness to the orphanhood of Shimon Peres. Ben-Gurion was much more than an admired political patron. He was Peres's spiritual mentor—his oracle in affairs of state, as in questions of morality and conscience. Peres admired in Ben-Gurion the sharp politician, visionary statesman, and man of all-embracing intellectual curiosity. All his life Peres would try to adopt these qualities, while realizing that he would never be able to achieve the same degree of greatness. But in trying, in making the effort, Peres would feel close to the man, whom he saw as the most complete personality he had ever known.

CHAPTER FIVE

ON THE WAY TO LEADERSHIP

First Encounter with Rabin

IN VOTING AS it did in the general election of 1973, the Israeli electorate had created a paradox. It returned Golda Meir's government to power, but immediately afterward, it became clear that it had not intended to do so. Although the people had preferred Labor to the Likud, there was no change in their animosity toward "the government of the blunder."

As Golda Meir labored to form a new government, attacks in the media and street demonstrations became increasingly strident. Most of the barbs continued to be aimed at Defense Minister Moshe Dayan. Wherever he appeared, he was the target of extreme expressions of deep hatred. It seemed that if he resigned, the public would be satisfied with his head, and allow Meir to form the government of her choice. But Dayan refused to go, and Meir gave him her full support.

All this time, which was undoubtedly the most difficult in Dayan's life, Peres stood by him and supported him unreservedly, although he knew that in doing so, he was not adding to his political and personal credit. On February 26, 1967, Dayan broke. "Somewhere, we have reached a point where a responsible person cannot continue to serve as defense minister," he told a meeting of the Rafi faction at Beit Elisheva in Jerusalem. He announced that he did not intend to join the new government being formed by Meir.

Peres refused to accept the decision: "Moshe has every reason to refuse to be defense minister, but the people have every reason to want him to continue as defense minister." This was not Peres at his best. He was guided by his blind admiration for Dayan that even the war had not managed to destroy. For this reason also, Peres had no doubt about his political and personal future. If Dayan went, Peres would go with him.

More surprising was the fact that Meir, too, refused to accept Dayan's departure. The more the pressure grew, inside and outside the party, the closer she became to the defense minister, whom she had so detested in the past. The prospect of a government without him threw her into a deep depression, which found its expression in a note she passed to Peres during a cabinet meeting on February 24, 1974: "Shimon, to my great sorrow, Moshe already sees himself outside. I am so upset that I cannot find the words to express it." At a meeting of the party central committee, Meir turned to Dayan and Peres with an emotional appeal: "You have no right to go—not at so difficult a time, and not from your positions." A great deal had happened since Meir and her comrades had fought fiercely against the "youngsters."

At Meir's urging, delegations of party functionaries streamed to Dayan and Peres to convince them to change their minds. To the shock and deep disappointment of the public, the efforts bore fruit, and Dayan announced his readiness to return to the government— with Peres, of course. Now the public's rage was directed not only against Dayan, but also against Meir and the entire veteran leadership of the Alignment.

On Sunday, March 3, 1974, the Alignment faction met in the Knesset to approve the composition of the new government. After some members had spoken, Meir replied. She refuted the criticism that had been voiced at the meeting and suddenly stunned her audience: "This evening I am going to tell the president that I am through with the business of forming a government, and I am returning the mandate to him. I hope you will find a way of informing him who the new candidate is."

Again delegations paraded—this time to Meir, to force her to rescind her decision. These delegations did not return with empty hands. The old lady of Israeli politics yielded and presented her new government to the Knesset, including Dayan as defense minister. The Knesset gave the government a vote of confidence, but the public did not. The demands for Dayan's resignation were no less hysterical than the demands for his appointment as defense minister on the eve of the Six-Day War had been.

Meir realized that she had the choice of dismissing Dayan or resigning herself. She took the latter course. She announced her intention to a meeting of the Alignment faction in the Knesset on Wednesday, April 10, 1974: "I have come to the personal conclusion, without regard for the parliamentary responsibility that does or does not apply to Moshe Dayan, that I have to resign. I cannot bear this burden any longer." This time the Labor party did not go down on its knees. There were no appeals and no delegations. The party and its leaders were forced to accept a reality that they had not been accustomed to during the long years of their rule—that a price must be paid for failure. The race to find an heir had begun.

In the first few days after Meir's departure, hardly anyone in the Labor party questioned the assumption that the leadership belonged to the Mapai faction.

The crucial point was the possible candidacy of Finance Minister Pinhas Sapir, who was regarded as the party's strong-man and one of Rafi's implacable opponents. When it seemed that this was about to happen, there were murmurs of discontent in Rafi, and demands were voiced that, if Sapir became prime minister, Rafi should walk out of the government and the Labor party—something Peres wanted to prevent at all costs.

In order to placate his comrades, Peres announced that he was ready to stand against Sapir—a step requiring considerable courage and, in the opinion of many, political suicide. Peres's only condition was a statement from his comrades that, if he lost, there would be no walkout or split.

When Peres announced his candidacy for the leadership of the party, he therefore thought he was standing against Sapir. But in the end, Sapir refused to assume the heavy burden. But neither he nor his associates in the Mapai leadership had the slightest intention of leaving the field clear for Peres. To foil his candidacy, the search began for another candidate.

In the situation that developed, it was almost certain that it would be Yitzhak Rabin. On paper he possessed all the necessary qualities: experience in defense matters as chief of staff, diplomatic experience as ambassador in Washington, and—most important of all—complete lack of involvement in the Yom Kippur War.

A few days before the contest, Peres met with Rabin and made the following suggestion: "If I win, you'll be number two, and vice versa." Rabin agreed. On Monday, April 22, 1974, the Labor Party Central Committee met in a grim, tense mood, to choose between Peres and Rabin. The general opinion, both among the delegates and in the media, was that Sapir's political machine would give Rabin a big majority, something in the region of 65 percent—in other words, all the delegates, except those of Rafi.

When the results were announced, there was general astonishment. Rabin won, as predicted, but with a minuscule majority. He had 298 votes, against 254 for Peres. Peres had been only forty-four votes short of victory. The significance was that dozens of Mapai delegates had defied the veteran leadership—an unprecedented occurrence. Peres was able to tell himself, "another loss like that and I'll have won."

After the delegates dispersed to their homes, it was clear to everyone that they had not only chosen a new leader, but had ended the hegemony of the veteran leaders of Mapai. From now on their strength would wane, until it completely disappeared from the political map.

From Peres's point of view, the gamble had paid off. His place as number two in the party was now unchallenged; he and Rabin showered each other with compliments. The public willingly accepted the new leadership team and even showed enthusiasm for it. On June 3, 1974, the Knesset voted its approval of the Rabin government, in which Peres was to serve as minister of defense.

At the Head of the Network

The Defense Ministry that Peres took over was very different from the one he had known during his long years of service as assistant director general, director general, and deputy defense minister. The structure had not changed, although it had become larger and more cumbersome over the years. The essential difference was the pessimism generated by the Yom Kippur War, the loss of self-confidence, the atmosphere of failure and mutual suspicion. Morale had reached an all-time low. Gossip and smear campaigns between officers regarding responsibility for the blunders of the war had become the norm. There was a general feeling of collapse and helplessness, bordering on apathy.

What should be done to stop the rot? Some felt that the need of the hour was complete reorganization of the entire establishment, including the army, but Peres came to the conclusion that, even if there were organizational flaws, they were not the root of the problem. The basic solution was the correct administration and strict supervision of the existing framework.

The differences of character and working methods between Peres and Dayan now became apparent. The previous defense minister had focused on political and military matters, the administered territories, and the operative plans of the IDF. He took little interest in the remainder. Peres did not disregard these matters, but he felt the need to exercise control over the rest of the establishment, down to the smallest detail.

At the first meeting he held with the IDF General Staff, Peres demanded to know the size of the Nahal (IDF units that serve part of the time on kibbutzim) and the proportion of women in the force. He then wanted details of the production and storing of TOW missiles and personal equipment—"uniforms, blankets, rifles, machine guns—not that they are the decisive items in a war, but do we have them?"—and so on, down to the smallest detail. He was not satisfied with the answers he received and demanded to see things with his own eyes. No less important was his determination that officers and men should know that they were subject to his supervision at all times and with no advance warning.

Among other things, he initiated a series of surprise visits to emergency stores, where the low standard of maintenance had been severely criticized after the war. "In one of these visits he astonished the commanding officers when he climbed into the tanks and checked their equipment. He asked those in charge to open equipment pouches and found that some of them lacked binoculars, signaling flags, and other vital equipment. "It is intolerable," he growled at the officers, "that a tank doesn't have binoculars, and that there is no sleeping bag for the driver."

The extent of the negligence and neglect prevalent in the army became clear to Peres at the weekly meeting with his aides at the beginning of July. It was reported that when the Syrians took the IDF position on Mount Hermon in the war, they captured a document that was described as "the most important document that ever reached a foreign intelligence service." It spelled out in detail every channel, every operating method of the air force communications system—in fact, all the information needed to permit an enemy to know the deployment of the air force at all times. How on earth had it gotten to the Mount Hermon position? It turned out that the administration branch, not knowing its importance, had distributed it in hundreds of copies. Peres was astounded. He immediately ordered the necessary steps taken to minimize the damage and the punishment of those guilty for this grave negligence.

One of the things that irritated Peres was the loss of resourcefulness and personal initiative. In the discussions with senior IDF officers about the production of a certain sophisticated piece of equipment, he demanded, "Can we do it, and should we?"

The answer came, "We can and we should. A proposal has been around for seven months."

Then Peres asked, "Why haven't you carried it out? Since when have you been so disciplined that you wait for approval? I want you to feel free in making decisions. The [military] industry should not decide what you want or what it wants of you. You decide what you want of the industry's management."

Peres did not spend all his time inspecting tanks. He made several secret trips abroad to forge new links or strengthen existing ones. One example of such relationships was with the Kurdish rebels in Iraq. Israel supplied them not only with weapons but with advisers to help them in their struggle against one of Israel's most implacable enemies. The Kurdish leader, Mustafa Barzani, was not satisfied merely with aid. He wanted to launch a joint campaign in which Israel would conquer Syria, while he conquered Iraq. When asked how Syria could be conquered, as it was defended by the Soviets, Barzani retorted: "Stop giving me excuses. You toppled de Gaulle and Nixon.

You can achieve anything!" It was impossible to convince him that the power he attributed to Israel was entirely the product of his vivid imagination.

The Kurdish connection was one of the most delicate with which Peres had to deal. Israel was interested in strengthening the Kurds as much as possible, on the principle that "my enemy's enemy is my friend." The problem was Iran. The Iranians wanted the Kurds to be powerful enough to harass the Iraqis, but no more, as Iran had five million Kurds of its own. Israel, which did not want to disrupt its relations with the shah, had to walk a very narrow tightrope.

In one way or another, the United States was almost always connected with Israel's arms deals, as the production of many items was the result of cooperation between the two, and, as a result, their export to third countries was subject to American approval. It was clear also that the United States was Israel's primary arms supplier. Israel's main role in the partnership was as a go-between. There were countries such as Iran, Ethiopia, and South Africa, that the United States wanted to assist. It was very convenient in cases such as this to give the aid via Israel, or to encourage Israel to step up its exports to these countries. In such dealings, there was no difference between the Republican administration and the Democratic one that replaced it in 1977.

Meetings with Hussein

Late at night on August 29, 1974, a Jordanian army helicopter landed on a side runway of Jerusalem's Atarot Airport. Israeli officers, who were waiting, hurried to the helicopter to help its passengers descend, and swiftly transferred them to an IDF helicopter standing nearby, its engines already warming up. The Israeli helicopter took off, and a few minutes later landed near a government guest house outside Tel Aviv. The passengers—King Hussein of Jordan; his prime minister, Ziyad Rifai; and his military adjutant— disembarked and were quickly swallowed up in the large guest house, where Rabin, Peres, and Foreign Minister Yigal Allon awaited them.

The guest house was not unfamiliar to Hussein. In fact, most of the meetings the Israeli government had had with him had been held there, and would continue to be in future. Only a few of them took place on the border between Eilat and Akaba. Very few people knew about the arrangement. In order to minimize the number of those in on the secret, the Israeli ministers' senior aides doubled as waiters, dispensing previously prepared food and drink.

The meeting was the result of the American insistence, voiced by President Nixon on his visit to Israel in mid-June, that his administration did not view the separation of forces agreements with Egypt and Syria as the end of the matter. To complete the circle, it wanted a similar accord with Jordan. Kissinger had spelled it out: Israel's option is not between negotiations with Hussein or avoiding them; the only alternatives facing Israel are negotiating with Hussein now or talking to the PLO later.

But withdrawal from Judea and Samaria was not the same, from a security, emotional—not to speak of political—point of view, as withdrawing from Sinai, or even the Golan Heights. For this reason, the Israeli ministerial team—Rabin, Peres, and Allon—were searching for solutions that did not include a pullback, and this was the main subject of the meeting with Hussein. Kissinger's position, and those of the other parties involved at the time, are particularly interesting in light of the events that were to burst forth on the West Bank some thirteen years later.

In the spirit of the times, the conversation opened with some jocular remarks about Henry Kissinger. Rabin told the king that he was about to pay a visit to Washington. Peres commented that Kissinger would also be there. The Jordanian monarch, picking up the allusion to the American secretary of state's frequent travels, remarked, "For a change."

After lengthy surveys of the situation in the world and the region, the Israeli ministers arrived at the question of an arrangement with Jordan. Rabin stated that there were three possibilities:

• Immediate negotiations for a comprehensive agreement. Rabin noted that both sides agreed that such a negotiation was too complicated to make it a realistic option at the present time.

• An agreement in principle on a comprehensive agreement and implementation in stages.

• A functional separation of forces or functional arrangements on the West Bank.

Regarding a separation of forces, which Hussein wanted, Rabin made it clear that that was not even an option because it meant a unilateral withdrawal, and Israel could not consider it.

Peres started off with a proposal he had been propounding for some time: a federative arrangement. He suggested an agreement that would include economic and security elements, joint positions, and some sort of joint administration of the West Bank. He did not mind what the creature was called—condominium, federal government, local government—the important thing was its makeup. He then went into details: the flag of the West Bank in the framework of a federation would be Jordanian, or it would resemble that of Jordan. Passports would be Jordanian. The Arab inhabitants would vote for the Jordanian parliament, the Jewish inhabitants for the Knesset. Peres allowed that the idea seemed fantastic, "but a fantasy is the only way to solve the problem."

Hussein viewed all these ideas with a degree of skepticism. It was clear, he said, that much thought had been invested in them. They should be studied, and he promised to do so, but until the study yielded results, he suggested, "We now have to talk about the present." The present was that separation of forces agreements had been signed with Syria and Egypt. For this reason, it was important that there be an agreement with Jordan based on the same principles.

Prime Minister Rifai was more outspoken than his king. He added another option to the three outlined by the Israelis: if there was no separation of forces agreement with Jordan, the Hashemite kingdom might wash its hands of the whole affair—willingly, or because of pressure from the other Arab states. Although the Israelis listened carefully, they did not budge from their opposition to a separation of forces agreement. After hearing their statements, Hussein summed up bitterly: "The irony is that, had Jordan joined in the [Yom Kippur] war, it would have attained such an agreement without any difficulty."

Later, during a general discussion, Hussein complained about the difficulty of acquiring American arms because of their high price, and Peres remarked that Israel was familiar with that problem. Thus the leaders of the two enemy states cried on each other's shoulders about the problems of buying weapons that they might even use against each other.

Hussein returned to his palace in Amman. On the horizon, the noise of the forthcoming Arab summit in Rabat, the capital of Morocco, began to be heard. The Palestinian problem was on its agenda. The Israeli government began to take stock, splitting into two camps: the Jordanian camp, led by Yigal Allon, which supported a political process with Jordan before anything else, and the Egyptian camp, led by Rabin and Peres, which believed that the next step should be a further agreement with Egypt.

A week before the Rabat conference, on October 19, there was another meeting with Hussein and Rifai, and the Jordanians again raised the subject of a separation of forces. Rabin tried to sell the Jordanians the idea that, if the Rabat conference gave Hussein a mandate to negotiate with Israel, it would still be a good thing for Jordan, if Israel started with Egypt. That way there would be an Egyptian precedent, and Jordan would be liberated from the onus of being the first. Rifai was quick to dismiss this concern for Jordan's interests. There were already precedents, he noted, and there was no need for more. Why strive for a precedent that might not occur, when there was already an existing one?

"How do you see the separation of forces?" asked Peres. Rifai gave details: the withdrawal of Israeli forces from the Jordan Valley, and the restoration of Jordanian administration. The presence of Jordanian forces in the West Bank, he said, was the most powerful weapon against the PLO. Rabin made it clear that the Israeli public would not accept a military pullback on the West Bank. It would want to know what was given in return, "and what can I tell them?" Rifai suggested that he say the same thing that had been said in the cases of Egypt and Syria. Rabin replied that this was not the same government, upon which Rifai feigned surprise and asked, "Isn't there continuity?"

In order to prevent the Rabat conference from turning toward the PLO, Hussein asked Israel to announce that, if there were a pro-PLO decision, it would consider annexing the West Bank and Gaza. However, neither the Jordanians nor the Israelis at the meeting thought that there was a chance of a development in this direction at Rabat. They concluded that after the conference they would continue investigating the possibility of finding a basis for negotiation.

The reality hit them on October 26. The decision of the Arab summit conference was unambiguous: King Hussein no longer represented the West Bank, and he was not authorized to negotiate on behalf of the Palestinians, who would be represented at the summit by PLO leader Yasser Arafat.

A further meeting, scheduled for November, was canceled at the king's request. On November 1, Rabin consulted with his senior ministers on the new situation. The discussion showed how much the unexpected decision in Rabat had thrown them into confusion. Peres's penchant for unconventional solutions reached new heights. He suggested dividing Israel and the territories into ten regions, with Judea, Samaria, and Gaza being three of them. Each region would have its own parliament.

"What do you need ten parliaments for?" interrupted Rabin. "Isn't one enough for you?"

Peres ignored the interruption, and proposed that the government consider granting autonomy to the Palestinians in the West Bank, while maintaining the IDF's control of security and the right of Jews to settle there. (Some years later, this idea was incorporated in the Camp David accords between Israel and Egypt.)

"What exactly do you mean," asked Cabinet Minister Yisrael Galili, "that there will be one state?"

"For the time being, yes." Peres explained, "If war breaks out and the PLO fights it, many Arabs will flee from the West Bank and Gaza. If they flee and there is immigration of Jews from Russia, the situation will change."

He also had an alternative suggestion: to set up administrative frameworks in Judea, Samaria, Gaza, and Jerusalem. If there were more Arabs than Jews in Judea or Samaria, Israel could give up one of the areas. All this would be carried out within borders that everyone would in time become accustomed to, provided it was done quickly.

Rabin asked Peres not to raise the proposal in the cabinet, to avoid unnecessary discussion. Peres suggested jokingly that he should bring up the idea "to confuse the enemy."

"As long as it is the enemy who is confused, that's all right," Rabin remarked drily.

The first meeting with Hussein and Rifai after the Rabat conference took place on May 28, 1975. The Jordanian prime minister did not disguise his disappointment and anger. "If you had agreed to a separation of forces, the Rabat decision could have been prevented." Later, he burst out: "Everyone keeps talking about the Palestinian problem, but nobody knows what it is. Why don't you change your policy? Negotiate with the PLO about the West Bank and Gaza, and afterward [the territories] will be returned to us."

This was to be the Jordanian line for many years hence: "We are out of the picture. Please apply to the PLO, then we'll see." If the Israelis had any doubt that this was Hussein's policy, it became abundantly clear in a further meeting with the king that took place during the period of the Rabin government on January 14, 1976.

The day before the meeting, Rabin, Peres, and Allon met to coordinate their stand. At this meeting, Peres put forward two alternative options for a territorial arrangement with Hussein:

• The town of Nablus could be controlled politically, and constituted one-third of the West Bank. Jordan could be given a corridor to it and administer the police.

• Jericho could be given up, and provided with a plan for irrigating the surrounding agricultural land situated on the eastern side of the West Bank.

If Hussein agreed to one of these proposals, suggested Peres, Israel would also agree to transfer the administration of the mosques on Temple Mount in Jerusalem to the Muslim Council, "and I don't care which flag is flown over them." Peres, Rabin, and the others present were doubtful that Hussein would agree to anything, but this could arouse his interest, and serve as a spur to further thinking. Rabin had no objection to Peres raising these ideas, and Hussein, as expected, rejected them politely but firmly. He reiterated what he had said at the previous meeting: the Palestinian problem was the most important, and "if I were you, I'd talk to the PLO."

Kissinger Shuttles Again

Hussein's self-exclusion from the negotiating process left one practical alternative: negotiations with Egypt. The hero of the hour was undoubtedly Henry Kissinger, who mediated, conciliated, smiled, shouted, and, at critical moments, applied pressure that was just short of brutal. Peres's attitude toward the United States in general, and Kissinger in particular, was, "Honor him and suspect him."

At the end of June 1974, Peres flew to the United States. His first meeting, on June 24, was with Kissinger. He found him in an angry, sullen mood. He had just returned from testifying before a Senate subcommittee on Strategic Arms Limitation Talks (SALT), and the chairman of the subcommittee, Henry Jackson, had accused him of lying about a guarantee he had given the Russians. What had particularly shocked Kissinger was that Jackson had pulled secret State Department documents out of his briefcase to prove his allegations.

With considerable feeling, he told Peres, "There is no administration in Washington right now; Jackson has more secret documents than I have." For this reason, Kissinger suggested to Peres that he avoid disclosing financial details about the arms acquisitions during the visit, because "all the numbers will be leaked."

After he had calmed down a bit, Kissinger explained that it was not a good time to visit Washington because he was about to go out of town (he was due to visit Moscow), and because the relations between the State Department and the Pentagon were very bad. He portrayed Defense Secretary James Schlesinger in a very grim light, but "you have no alternative, you have to apply to him. If he has political ambitions, you won't find him very helpful." If that were the case, said Kissinger, "you'll have to wait until I get back from Moscow, and I'll see to everything."

After hearing this, Peres anticipated an unpleasant and difficult meeting with Schlesinger, and that feeling was reinforced when he arrived at the defense secretary's office on June 26. The meeting was scheduled for 11:00 A.M., and it was agreed that at 12:30, it would continue over lunch. When Peres arrived, Schlesinger was not in his office, nor had he arrived an hour later. He finally arrived at 12:30, apologized, and invited Peres into his office, where they sat talking for three hours, and Schlesinger "completely forgot about lunch."

Right at the start, Peres discovered the reason for the bad relations between the Pentagon and the State Department. It had started with a series of TV stories by Marvin Kalb, the political reporter for CBS, suggesting that Schlesinger had been the one who had held up the airlift of arms to Israel during the critical days of the Yom Kippur War. It was generally assumed in Washington that Kissinger had inspired these articles; but Kalb had also quoted sources in the Israeli embassy that supported Kissinger's version.

Schlesinger was deeply hurt by the articles, all the more so, he told Peres, as on the day in question, he had made a special trip to his office and worked until one in the morning to facilitate the airlift "in Israel's difficult hour." He surprised his guest by saying: "Kissinger says that he supports Israel but is against its conquests. I say that I am in favor of an Israel with full military security, without relating to conquests or no conquests."

After such a declaration, there was no reason why the conversation should not proceed freely and very frankly. Schlesinger did not hesitate to voice his reservations, but Peres found him to be a good listener who was prepared to be convinced. Israel's principle requests were for:

• Lance and Pershing missiles. Peres explained that they were needed as an answer to the Scud and Frog missiles in Arab hands. Schlesinger agreed to the Lances but disapproved of the Pershings because of their potential nuclear capability.

• Cobra helicopters. Schlesinger at once pointed out that supplying these to Israel would necessitate their being given to the Arabs, which would lead to a certain escalation, both in the type of weapon and financial investment. Peres explained that the helicopters were needed for night fighting against terrorist incursions into Israeli territory. "If we can catch the gangs before they penetrate our territory, we will prevent the murder of women and children, and we won't need to cross the border to chase them."

Schlesinger replied that he had never thought of the Cobra from that point of view and immediately said, "I've changed my opinion." A similar exchange occurred regarding the next item, smart bombs and laser-guided rockets. After Peres had finished detailing the list he had brought with him, Schlesinger did a quick calculation and said: "In the United States, we spend four hundred dollars per head on defense. If we agree to all your requests, we'll be spending six hundred dollars per head. Do you really expect us to spend more per head for Israelis than we do for Americans?"

"It depends on what heads we are talking about," replied Peres. "The correct calculation is according to Arab heads—not Israeli ones. We need the weapons to use against the Arabs, not the Israelis."

Peres came away with the impression that "Schlesinger is an impressive and brilliant man. Talking to him is a real pleasure." He received the distinct impression that Kissinger's opinion of him was dictated by internal power struggles in the administration and that the secretary of state was involving Israel in his personal rivalry with the defense secretary.

From then on Peres became Schlesinger's defender in Jerusalem, possibly his only one. In one cabinet discussion, when Rabin jokingly referred to Schlesinger as "the righteous one of the era," Peres retorted, "When the day arrives that we can divide people into saints and sinners, I am not at all sure where Schlesinger will be and where Kissinger will belong."

[Peres was to discover, to his amazement, that Schlesinger, a converted Jew, was apparently a relative. In a closed meeting with military correspondents on October 1, 1975, he told them, "I have a relative in the United States called Robert Persky. Yesterday I received a letter that Persky's grandmother is the sister of Schlesinger's father."]

Even without regard to Schlesinger, Peres had strong reservations about Kissinger's modus operandi. On the eve of Yigal Allon's departure for Washington, Peres described to his top advisers what would happen to the foreign minister:

"I'll tell you how it will go: Yigal arrives in America; Kissinger comes and tells him, 'We have to work out a joint American-Israeli strategy for the next stage.' Yigal is delighted. [Egyptian Foreign Minister Ismail] Fahmy arrives; Kissinger tells him the same thing about American-Egyptian strategy. Fahmy is pleased. Each of them thinks that Kissinger is on his side. Afterward there is a leak in an Israeli newspaper harmful to Kissinger. He calls in Israel's ambassador to the United States, Simha Dinitz and says in an offended tone, 'I am your best friend.' Then we apologize and try to justify ourselves."

In a private conversation with Rabin, Peres reduced it to a single sentence: "With due respect to Kissinger, he is the most devious man I have ever met."

In October 1974, Kissinger made visits to Cairo and Jerusalem to start negotiations on an interim agreement between the two countries. It quickly became clear that there were two main points of disagreement:

- Egypt's demand for an Israeli withdrawal beyond the Mitla and Gidi passes (two strategic openings in the Sinai hills, some twenty-five miles back from the Suez Canal).

- Israel's demand that the agreement include a clause on an end to belligerency between the two countries.

For the talks with Kissinger, the Israeli ministerial team agreed in the first instance on a stand against ceding the passes. At a meeting in the prime minister's residence in Jerusalem on October 11, the American secretary of state said forcefully that Israel's stand would wipe out any chance of an agreement.

The ministerial team asked to consult, and Rabin, Peres, and Allon closeted themselves in Rabin's study, next to the lounge where the meeting with the Americans was taking place. What should they do? Peres said at once, "I'm not prepared to withdraw behind the passes."

To his surprise, Rabin said impatiently, "I am."

"I suggest that we don't give away the passes immediately," Peres said.

"I am in favor of an average pullback of fifty kilometers (including the passes)."

Peres rose from his seat. "In that case, I have no further business here; I am against giving up the passes." He started to leave the room, but Allon caught him by the arm and appealed to him to stay.

Rabin said, more calmly: "He'll ask us about the passes again."

"You don't have to answer him," Peres replied.

Rabin became conciliatory: "All right, we have agreed we won't talk about the passes to him."

This incident illustrates the confusion that prevailed in the ministerial team at that time. It was essentially the result of a lack of experience, leading to a loss of self-confidence and a tendency to pull in different directions. Each of the three members of the team had served previously in different official capacities, but this was the first time that they had carried the full responsibility, and, at least in the first few months, they found difficulty in shouldering it.

There is no doubt that Peres was the hawk of those days—the man on the Israeli team who took the toughest positions—with Rabin and Allon ultimately toeing his line. Kissinger, who was well aware of the situation, frequently attacked the defense minister. In a conversation with Ambassador Dinitz on October 6, 1974, he complained about the criticism of him in the Israeli press and suggested that Peres was behind it. Two months later Rabin phoned Peres and said, "There is a problem with Kissinger; he's got his eye on you. Let's calm him down with a personal message."

The deadlock with the United States reached a climax in the middle of March 1975, when the negotiations between Israel and Egypt arrived at their moment of truth. Kissinger carried out a number of shuttles between Cairo and Jerusalem, but they did not succeed in closing the gap between the positions of the two sides. In order to break the logjam, Kissinger demanded during his last visit to Jerusalem that Israel agree to a deep pullback in Sinai, and guarantee a similar withdrawal on the Golan Heights six months later.

At a dramatic cabinet meeting, it was decided to reject the demand, with the prime minister, defense minister, and foreign minister presenting a united front.

On Saturday evening, March 22, the official announcement on the failure of the negotiations had been made; it was also announced that Kissinger's mission in the region had ended. Prior to this, Kissinger had warned his Israeli hosts of the dire consequences of such a decision. But although they knew about this, they were not ready for what actually happened.

It began on the Boeing airliner that carried Kissinger back to Washington. In a background briefing for the journalists accompanying him he poured fire and brimstone on the ministerial team, with most of his barbs directed at Peres, whom he termed "a phony hawk, by the leave of (and in the shade of) Dayan, spreading terror over the rest of the cabinet members." Even when he scorned Rabin it was with reference to the defense minister, "a small man whose only worry is what Peres will say about him."

When Kissinger returned to Washington, he did not content himself with taunts and reproaches. At every appearance he blamed Israel for the failure of the talks. The real blow was contained in a note sent to Rabin by President Gerald Ford, at Kissinger's instigation. It stated that "in view of developments, the United States will reassess its policy in the Middle East." In case anyone did not understand the meaning of this "reassessment," it very quickly took on a concrete form.

Many items of military equipment, which had been previously agreed upon, simply failed to arrive. Economic assistance was reduced to the scale of millions of dollars, instead of the billions that had been agreed. Peres, who was due to go to Washington in April for arms procurement talks, was advised to stay at home.

As the diplomatic deadlock continued, and with it the American pressure that increasingly worried the defense establishment, Peres sought a formula to break the logjam. On Sunday, June 29, he met with Rabin and put forward a two-stage proposal:

• Israel would not transfer the Mitla and Gidi passes to Egypt, but neither would it hold on to them. American soldiers would be stationed at both ends of the passes, or, if the Egyptians objected, American troops would man the Israeli side, and Russian soldiers could be stationed on the Egyptian side. (At the time, twelve Russian observers were serving with the United Nations forces in Sinai.)

• Peres himself, or Asher Ben-Natan, would meet secretly with Kissinger to inform him about the proposal.

Rabin enthusiastically agreed to the first idea, but not the second. He preferred that Ambassador Dinitz meet with Kissinger. He phoned him at once and informed him of the suggestion, and asked him to sound out Kissinger's reaction. Dinitz tracked down Kissinger, who was vacationing in the Virgin Islands. The secretary of state replied that it could serve as the basis for discussion and agreed to a meeting. Dinitz set out without delay.

This was the breakthrough because for the first time since the start of the negotiations, Israel had agreed to give up control of the passes. Peres's suggestion seemed acceptable to the Egyptians, and the discussions were renewed. Kissinger arrived for another shuttle, and this time his efforts were crowned with success. On Tuesday, September 2, 1975, Israel and Egypt initialed the interim accord.

Signing the interim accord opened the American taps that had been closed off six months earlier. Peres was invited to Washington to discuss the details of the assistance that the United States had agreed to as part of the interim accord. On Monday, September 22, the phone rang in the room of his New York hotel, where he had made a stopover. On the line was Kissinger's secretary, John Adams, who told him that the secretary of state wanted to meet with him for "a personal conversation that would remain off the record."

The meeting took place the following day at 11:00 P.M. at Kissinger's apartment in the Waldorf Astoria Hotel. After taking off his evening jacket, Kissinger described himself as "a worried Jew." He went on to say that his strength was in his ability to assess situations correctly. He warned that there had been a significant erosion in Israel's standing in the United States. (Peres was intrigued by this concern, as he was sure that Kissinger, more than anyone, was responsible for the deterioration.)

He wanted to know what Israel would do if forced to return to the 1967 borders. Peres replied, "We'd fight." Kissinger then returned to the Jewish theme. He wondered why the Jewish people were not proud of a Jewish secretary of state, "and not just a Jew by origin, but a Jew by historical responsibility," he emphasized.

Peres replied politely that "the Jews are proud of their sons in the late hours of history when they are no longer alive." Nevertheless, he said, he had found admiration for Kissinger in wide Jewish circles and even pride in his accomplishments.

Kissinger loved these informal conversations with his shirt collar open and his feet on the coffee table. He especially enjoyed them after bringing some project to a successful conclusion, and his interlocutor was the man of whom he had gotten the better. What did he hope to achieve from this conversation? Not much—just to become closer to, and to earn the goodwill of, the man whose arm he had twisted. And that he achieved in no small way. From the moment Peres left the New York hotel, a little after three in the morning, relations between the two men grew steadily closer.

What's Gotten into Rabin?

The rows between Peres and Rabin during the negotiation of the interim accord with Egypt were the result of the tension that had been increasing since they had declared that the contest between them for the leadership of the party would not affect their working relationship.

Peres did not find it too difficult to live up to his side of the bargain. Although he was disappointed by his defeat, he did not feel beaten. He had, after all, made a good showing and won the number-two spot in the cabinet and the party. He would certainly have preferred to be the prime minister, but following years of opposition and relatively minor tasks such as transport, communications, and information, he had good reason to be satisfied that he was in the seat previously occupied by David Ben-Gurion and Moshe Dayan.

He unquestioningly accepted Rabin's authority as his superior; but Rabin, for his part, showed signs of hostility almost from the start, and missed no opportunity to belittle Peres.

It is quite possible that the conflict resulted from the contrast in character and mentality between the two. Rabin is a realistic pessimist—dry and extremely practical. Peres is the opposite. An associative thinker, he feels facts are important as general guidelines, not matters that have to be analyzed, detailed, and given emphasis. Most of the time he fluctuates between relative realism and unbelievable optimism. Rabin aimed to solve the problems on the agenda by conventional means; Peres looked ahead, searching for unconventional long-term solutions.

In a quiet discussion between the two at Rabin's apartment on May 17, 1975, Peres spoke of a plan that had been in his head for some time:

"We have to try to initiate a national revival, a sort of neo-Ben-Gurionism, to settle the area between Beersheba and Rafah (southern Gaza Strip). We have some five thousand children of moshavim, the best farmers in the world. We have to desalinate seawater and irrigate hundreds of thousands of acres there. Until we get the water, we can set up aircraft and rocket industries, exporting hundreds of millions of dollars' worth of goods. This government must get out of the coastal plain. We must build and invest only in Galilee, the Negev, and Jerusalem."

Rabin shook his head and darted a strange look at Peres. This sort of language was entirely alien to him. What Peres did not understand was that, even if he had wanted to, Rabin was incapable of thinking in terms so distant from the here and now. He should have understood this, for during all the years he served in the army, Rabin had consistently opposed all of Peres's schemes for local production, regarding them as "castles in the air," and preferred simpler solutions that his practical mind was able to grasp. In other words, he was in favor of purchase from abroad. Now, also, on the terrace of his apartment in Ramat Aviv, he must have thought to himself that Peres ought to go to bed to give his probing mind a rest.

Whatever the reason, Rabin stepped up his attacks on Peres. He found it difficult to listen without interrupting him and insulting him, even during cabinet meetings.

During the exchanges, the other cabinet ministers sat in shocked silence, their heads bowed, waiting for the storm to pass. After one such exchange, Transportation Minister Gad Ya'acobi went to see Rabin. "Listen," he told the prime minister, "you are insulting Shimon in a manner that will eventually harm the entire government, yourself included. If I were in his place, I'd have reacted long ago."

Rabin snapped, "You are not in his place, and you are not like him."

It was unavoidable that the confrontation would find its expression in army matters, also. During a discussion on the balance of power in the Middle East at the prime minister's office in February 1975, Chief of Staff Motta Gur complained to Peres, "I have the feeling that the army is being dragged into the dispute between the prime minister and the defense minister."

Certainly, the prime minister's relationship with the army started to be influenced by his relations with Peres, who often found himself in the position of mediator or conciliator. At one of the meetings, Rabin suddenly asked the head of military intelligence for an intelligence assessment of terrorist actions. The chief of staff pointed out that, as this item was not on the agenda, suitable material had not been prepared. Rabin insisted, and when Gur stood his ground, Rabin demanded that he "stop performing." Peres remarked that the chief of staff meant that if an assessment was required, it should be prepared in an orderly fashion. "So we'll take it as a disorderly situation report," shouted Rabin, sure that they were intriguing against him.

The situation reached a peak when the chief of staff refused to participate in a cabinet meeting to which he had been invited at the end of March 1976. "I did not come to the meeting because I did not want to explode," he told Peres. "I won't blame myself if I blow up one day at the things the prime minister says. A prime minister should not behave like that."

Peres's defense of the IDF sometimes pushed him into untenable positions, such as his stand in the case of Air Force Commander Benny Peled. When there was a reform of the income tax system, Peled announced publicly that he was giving up his official car because it would now be regarded as a partly taxable expense. Rabin flew into a rage. "There has never been a situation when a decision was taken and somebody demonstrates against it."

"If you think it is a demonstration, you should have called me, and I would have put a stop to it," Peres said. "I don't see it as a demonstration."

"What's the point of calling you, if you don't see it as a demonstration?" Rabin replied. "In any case, I have no intention of asking you about it. It is a concrete question and one of principle. You can think what you like."

All this time Peres tried to be patient and stay cool. The turning point in his attitude toward Rabin came in May 1975, when he learned of the prime minister's intention to name Reserves General Ariel (Arik) Sharon as his adviser. Rabin administered this bitter medicine to Peres drop by drop. He revealed something of his intentions on May 17. Almost casually, he remarked to Peres, "Arik wants to be my adviser. I told him that I do not have authority in defense matters, so he will not be able to interfere in that field. Simply as an adviser, he won't have anything to do." Rabin added that he saw some political advantage in recruiting Sharon, a Likud man, to the administration.

Peres gave his view. "The appointment will make things easier for you politically for a few months, but afterward, Arik will become disappointed and depressed." He parted from Rabin with the clear impression that it was the type of idea that is talked about but not implemented. His shock was all the greater when, a few days later, the press reported that Peres and Rabin had agreed that Sharon would be Rabin's adviser—on security matters. It was a clear violation of an understanding, not to mention a public insult to Peres, the chief of staff, and senior IDF officers. The prime minister had never previously had an adviser on security matters, for the simple reason that the defense minister and chief of staff were considered his security advisers.

At a cabinet meeting on June 1, 1975, the tourism minister asked the prime minister if the press reports were true. Rabin replied that he had decided to appoint Sharon as his general adviser.

Peres said, "The press writes that it is your intention to appoint him security adviser. I assume that is a mistake."

Rabin replied, "General adviser."

"What will his authority be as a general adviser?"

"In view of the fact that I do not require the cabinet's approval for this appointment," Rabin announced, "the matter is not on the agenda."

In fact, Rabin and Sharon had agreed that Rabin would announce Sharon's appointment as a general adviser to avert a storm, but Rabin gave Sharon a written document stating that the reserves general "will accompany the prime minister to all political and military forums that the prime minister attends."

In July, Rabin officially named Sharon as his adviser, against the strong opposition of Peres and the chief of staff. At the beginning of August, there occurred the first incident that proved how the appointment prevented the prime minister and the defense minister from carrying out their tasks properly.

In the agreement between Rabin and Peres regarding Sharon's authority, it was determined, among other things, that nothing would be done to give the impression that Sharon was superior in status to the chief of staff. On August 7, the prime minister, defense minister, and chief of staff were due to set off on an inspection tour of IDF bases. Peres discovered that Rabin intended to bring Sharon with him. He called Rabin and told him it was against the agreement. Rabin replied that Sharon's presence was in no way detrimental to the chief of staff, Mordechai Gur.

"But," Peres recalled, "you told me that Sharon would not deal with defense matters."

"He is not dealing with military matters."

"So why is he coming?"

"He's coming because I am coming," Rabin declared.

Peres warned, "You have to be careful about the prestige of the chief of staff."

"I am careful, but I'll bring whoever I want."

"If that is the case, and the person you want to bring is Arik, Arik cannot be subordinate to the chief of staff in his other post (an emergency appointment as commander of the southern front).

"I don't agree."

"I want this checked with Zadok," Peres said. "It's my right as a cabinet member." (Haim Zadok was the Justice Minister.)

"If you are appealing the matter, then let's cancel tomorrow's visit."

"Good, we'll cancel the visit."

And so an important tour by the prime minister and the defense minister was canceled because of Rabin's refusal to keep his promise. Rabin never received any appreciation for this from his adviser. Throughout the period of his appointment, Sharon made extremist statements that embarrassed the entire government, and the prime minister in particular. Finally, he submitted his resignation in December 1975. His main reason, as he told the press, was "I am not prepared to be a partner in defense blunders."

The affair harmed Rabin, particularly in the party. The appointment of a Likud man to such a senior position irritated the party functionaries, who would not forget it. Personally, Rabin was perceived as a man of questionable judgment. The general feeling was that Sharon had made a fool of Rabin and had taken advantage of him, but it was Rabin's relationship with Peres that suffered most of all. If the defense minister had harbored any illusions about Rabin's attitude toward him, this affair laid them to rest. "That process was intended to oust me," Peres told Knesset member Micha Harish. He now understood that he was in a corner and would have to use his fists to get out.

From that point on, the poor relations between the prime minister and the defense minister affected everything that the government did. However much they wanted to, the two men could not divorce affairs of state from the bitter rivalry between them. At the outset, they managed to keep it from the general public, but later on they stopped trying and became the subjects of frequent headlines in the papers.

It was not surprising, therefore, that Peres felt somewhat relieved when Rabin went abroad, as happened at the end of January 1976, when he paid a working visit to Washington. With Rabin far away from Jerusalem, Peres felt he could take a vacation from the almost daily confrontation.

On Thursday, January 29, 1976, Peres toured army bases and held meetings into the late hours of the night. When he finally got to bed, near midnight, the phone rang. It was Yosef Ciechanover, the head of the purchasing mission in the United States. As Peres listened, an expression of amazement spread over his face. After a few minutes he put the phone down, threw himself into a chair, and muttered, "What is he up to? What's gotten into him?" "He" was Prime Minister Yitzhak Rabin, and what Ciechanover had told him was published in all the media the following day in even more detail.

The reports gave the following picture: On Thursday evening, after meeting the heads of the U.S. administration, Rabin had invited Israeli journalists stationed in Washington to a background briefing in Blair House, the official guest residence. When the reporters arrived, they got the impression that the prime minister was tired and nervous. He told them about his talks with administration officials in a muddled and confused manner. When he came to the list of arms requirements that he had brought with him, he astounded the reporters with an unprecendentedly outspoken attack, the target of which was clear: "The lists of arms presented to the Americans was not a 'certificate of honor' for the State of Israel . . . they were exaggerated . . . they included items not vital for war. Thank God I corrected that . . . experience has shown us that if someone in the defense establishment thinks that he knows what he is going to think in a year's time, he is wrong."

When the reports reached Jerusalem, there was general consternation. The arms lists had been discussed in several cabinet meetings and in more intimate forums chaired by Rabin. He had never so much as hinted at any disapproval. He had the power and authority, had he so wished, to cross anything off the list that he thought advisable. He had not exercised this right even once. What, then, was he complaining about?

Peres learned the answer to this question at the first cabinet meeting after Rabin's return from the United States, on February 8.

"We have to fight for the things that are really vital," he said.

Peres countered, "The question is whether we should discuss it publicly. After all, you are as responsible for the lists as I am."

"I don't deny it," Rabin declared, "but I think we made a mistake and that we should learn from it."

Peres read out the media reports on Rabin's remarks, and when he had finished, he started to say, "We intended to ask for sophisticated surveillance equipment . . ."

"I never heard anything about it."

"Then the time has come for you to listen and learn. Maybe you would like to tell me what mistakes we made in the defense establishment?"

"I didn't say that," Rabin said.

"So, will you deny it?"

"All right, I'll deny it."

To formulate the denial, Minister without Portfolio Yisrael Galili was called in. Rabin and Peres approved the wording that Rabin read in the Knesset. He said that he had not intended to criticize the defense minister, and confirmed that he had been a full partner in preparing the arms lists.

Rabin's apology removed the matter from the agenda, but it did not result in peace between the two—only a cease-fire, which did not last long. When the dispute flared up again, it was about something far more meaningful. It became clear once more that the rivalry between the two was harming their ability to deal realistically with a matter vital to the nation: the government's attitude toward the administered territories and their inhabitants.

Ever since the West Bank had been conquered in the Six-Day War, Israeli policy had been based on the assumption that by giving maximum freedom and civil rights to the inhabitants, it would be possible to maintain the conquest with minimal problems. The main elements of this policy were freedom of movement throughout Israel proper and free movement between the West Bank and the kingdom of Jordan across the Jordan bridges.

Peres had always believed that another element should be added to this. The mayors of the towns in the West Bank had been appointed by the Jordanian authorities before the war. Peres felt that bringing the Arab inhabitants nearer to democratic values would give them a feeling of running their own affairs and soften the impact of the conquest. He proposed, and the cabinet approved, the holding of municipal elections in Judea and Samaria. They were set for April 12, 1976.

As the date drew near, it became increasingly apparent that setting up elections might have been a mistake. Information from the field indicated that many of the more moderate mayors were liable to lose out to more extremist candidates close to the PLO. It became clear also that it might be very difficult to ensure the democratic nature of the elections. PLO agents entered the picture. Riots and disorders sprouted like mushrooms after spring rain, with the clear purpose of terrorizing the population into voting for candidates acceptable to the PLO.

In Israel, voices began to be heard suggesting the postponement of the elections, if not their cancellation. Peres opposed this because reneging on their original decision would worsen Israel's situation, both in the territories themselves, and also in world opinion. At a cabinet meeting on April 4, 1976, he said that he could "not guarantee to the cabinet the results of the poll," but he added that "he was sorry to read Israeli press reports that the left and the PLO had already won when, according to the lists of candidates, there was a new, unknown element."

There is no doubt that Peres would have done well to read the Israeli press carefully, and not sorrowfully, because, when the results of the elections were announced, it became clear that the press had not erred. The results were interpreted as a victory for the extremist elements, whose representatives won key places in most of the municipal councils. Rabin behaved as if he were the leader of the opposition. In an interview in *Ha'aretz* on May 12, he contended that "the defense minister erred in his assessment and that this error prompted the Israeli government to initiate a process which did not add to its prestige." It is possible that the contention was in itself correct, but it was certainly unfair. All the information that Peres possessed concerning the probable results of the elections had also been at the disposal of the prime minister. If he had reached a different assessment, he had the authority—in fact, the obligation— to postpone or cancel the poll.

Peres, in fact, had given the cabinet ministers, including Rabin, the chance to do so. At the meeting on April 4, a week before the elections, he had spelled it out clearly. "If anyone has second thoughts about holding the elections, now is the time to voice them." None of the ministers, including the prime minister, had opened their mouths.

The *Ha'aretz* interview infuriated Peres. He took advantage of a meeting of the Labor party bureau on May 13 to demand that Rabin resign and form a new government without him if he was dissatisfied with his performance. A source described in the press as "close to Peres" said that he would no longer show restraint in the face of the prime minister's provocations. An atmosphere of crisis threatened the existence of the government. The party functionaries moved into action and succeeded in arranging a reconciliation meeting between Rabin and Peres, which ended with a statement that "the quarrel has been ended, and in future, there will be no arguments and public criticism."

It was merely another cease-fire that would last only until the next incident. It was, however, welcome, because waiting in the wings was a crisis that necessitated maximum cooperation between the prime minister and the defense minister, and the mobilization of all the resources that they could find within themselves.

Entebbe

SUNDAY, JUNE 27, 1976

Peres spent the morning at the weekly cabinet meeting. The state budget was on the agenda and the ministers took advantage of it to make long speeches about the activities of their ministries, so that they can leak them to the media afterward.

Peres's efforts to pay attention to the speeches were all in vain. From time to time he took a quiet nap, which was interrupted by a constant stream of reports that his military aide, Ilan Tehillah, passed to him. He read the notes, tore up some of them, and deposited the pieces in an ashtray, and wrote comments or instructions on others, which he returned to Tehillah.

Then he was handed a note with a laconic message: "Air France flight 139, which left Ben-Gurion Airport for Paris, has been hijacked after a stopover at Athens. Its destination is unknown."

Wide awake now, Peres tensed in his chair and passed the note to Prime Minister Yitzhak Rabin. After reading it, Rabin hastily brought the meeting to a close, asking the ministers of defense, foreign affairs, justice, and transportation to remain behind. From now on, these men would constitute the ministerial team dealing with the hijacking. After a brief discussion, it was resolved that the government held France responsible for the safety of the passengers, and that there would be no surrender to the terrorists.

Peres returned to his Tel Aviv office and summoned IDF Chief of Staff Motta Gur. The two men agreed that, if the hijackers requested permission for the plane to land at Ben-Gurion Airport, it would be granted. At the same time, Gur would mobilize a special IDF unit to take control of it as soon as it landed.

That evening, it was learned that the plane had landed at Benghazi in Libya. A little before 9:00 P.M. it was reported that the plane had taken off for an unknown destination after refueling. Some two hours later, Peres returned home. He was eating a light supper in the kitchen when his red (hot line) telephone rang. Chief of Staff Gur was on the line: he had received reports that the hijacked plane was on its way to Ben-Gurion Airport, and he had already gone there.

After phoning Rabin, and receiving his approval for allowing the plane to land and dispatching a force to take control of it, Peres showered, changed, and left for the airport.

MONDAY, JUNE 28, 1976

When Peres arrived at the airport, a few minutes past midnight, a state of alert was already in force. "There was that undefinable atmosphere of anticipation," he wrote later in his diary. "The police and soldiers were tensely polite, as if weighed down by their knowledge. Many different types were hanging around the airport lounge: a young mother with her daughter in her arms, a tired old man, a wild-haired student, a couple holding hands. Some were sleeping, others awake and bleary-eyed."

Peres went up to the third floor, where the chief of staff, Chief of Operations Yekutiel (Kuti) Adam and a number of aides had set up their headquarters. Shortly before 1:00 A.M., information was received that, after being refused permission to land at Khartoum in the Sudan, the plane had headed toward the Jordanian capital of Amman.

Those present in the room calculated that the news was inaccurate and it was more likely that the plane's destination was Israel. Consulting maps, they concluded that it would be at least two hours before the plane reached Israeli air space.

Peres decided to utilize the time to visit the special IDF unit, which was stationed outside the airport fence, awaiting developments. Accompanied by Kuti Adam, he drove out onto the main road and down a dirt road to the small hut where the force was stationed.

Entering the hut, Peres's eyes alit on the soldiers. "Here in the dimly lit hut," Peres noted later, "some of the finest boys in the country were assembled. Nothing would frighten them; no obstacle would deter them."

Peres stood to one side, listening to a briefing by one of the officers on the structure of the hijacked plane. After the briefing, at a meeting in a side room with the commanding officers, Peres asked their opinion of the plan to storm the plane on its arrival. In the ensuing discussion, most of the officers were in favor.

The meeting broke up. Peres's eyes followed the figure of the force's commander, Jonathan (Yoni) Netanyahu, who had paused in a corner of the hut, sunk in thought. He sensed a certain sadness in the young officer's expression. Within two hours, reflected Peres, this young man may find himself leading his unit in a battle against the terrorists.

He went over to Yoni and started a conversation about the coming operation. While they were talking, information was received that the plane had turned from its eastward flight and headed south. In other words, it was no longer heading toward Israel. The tension evaporated. Peres and Yoni started talking about poetry, and discovered that they shared a liking for the work of the patriotic poet, Nathan Alterman. Yoni told Peres that his favorite work was *The Town of the Dove*. After exchanging quotes from the book, the two parted, never suspecting that this was the last time they would talk to each other.

Peres returned to the airport building shortly before 4:00 A.M., only to learn that the hijacked aircraft had landed at Entebbe, in Uganda. It was now possible to attend to bodily needs. The airport director brought food—passengers' meals from one of the aircraft; someone else contributed half a bottle of brandy. Two women soldiers made coffee, and, after drinking it, everyone went his separate way.

Peres arrived home at 6:00 A.M. His wife was still asleep. He made himself a glass of tea and called Rabin. He told him about the events of the past night, pointing out that he did not see any point in waking the prime minister. Rabin thanked his colleague for allowing him a good sleep, which would undoubtedly serve him well in the coming days.

Peres skimmed through the headlines of the morning papers before setting out for his office. The idea of a rest, even a short one, did not even enter his mind. The various reports reaching the ministry indicated the hijackers thought that a party of senior IDF officers were aboard the plane. A check of the passenger list sent by Air France showed that no senior serving officer—nor any other VIP—was aboard the plane; however, about half of the approximately two hundred passengers were Israeli citizens. According to the reports from Entebbe, of which there were not many, President Idi Amin had received the hijackers as welcome guests.

That afternoon, Peres drove up to Jerusalem for a discussion about the proposed defense budget cuts. From there he returned to his office. The reports from Entebbe were still sparse, and it seemed that everyone, including the world media, was guessing in the dark. Peres arrived home after midnight and, after two days without sleep, was rewarded with six and a half hours of continuous slumber.

TUESDAY, JUNE 29, 1976

In the morning, Peres drove up to Jerusalem to participate in a meeting of the Knesset Foreign Affairs and Defense Committee. From there he looked in on the Knesset plenum, which was discussing the state budget. Only at 5:30 P.M. did the ministerial team meet to consider the demands of the hijackers for the release of forty terrorists serving prison sentences in Israel, six from Kenya, five from West Germany, and one each from France and Switzerland. There was also an ultimatum: if the terrorists were not released by 2:00 P.M. Israel time on Thursday, July 1, the hijackers would start executing the hostages.

The ministerial team already had the reactions of the countries directly concerned. Kenya had announced that it was not holding the men whose release was being demanded (terrorists arrested some months earlier at Nairobi Airport, while preparing to fire a rocket at an El Al plane). Germany had not yet made a decision. France had announced that the woman terrorist, whose release the hijackers were demanding, had already been set free. Switzerland was not inclined to accede to the hijackers' demand to release its prisoner (a Jewish woman who fell in love with an Arab on a visit to Israel and joined a terrorist group).

Rabin stated that, in the absence of other options, Israel would have to start negotiations with the hijackers. Motta Gur's rough voice broke in: "There is a military option, and it is being investigated." Peres was taken by surprise. He sent Gur a note. "What are you talking about?" Gur replied in a note that, on his way to Jerusalem, it occurred to him that he would be asked about military action, so he phoned his office and gave instructions to check the possibility of "sending a force to Kenya, which would cross Lake Victoria to Entebbe by boat, kill the hijackers, and return home."

Peres asked: "What about the passengers?"

"The passengers will remain in Entebbe," Gur replied.

"I won't authorize any plan that does not have a chance of saving the passengers. If we leave them in Entebbe after killing the terrorists, we are sacrificing them to certain death," Peres said.

"I know our clients, so I have prepared something."

Peres told Rabin, "We don't have an approved plan at this point. When we have checked it out, we will submit a plan for a military operation."

A tense discussion followed concerning the various options facing Israel. Peres informed the meeting that Malcolm Toon, the U.S. ambassador to Israel, had expressed the opinion that Israel must not surrender. It was, suggested the defense minister, a serious and unprecedented situation. No Western country was pressing Israel to give in, and Israel, which had always stated adamantly that there must be no surrender to terrorists, was going to throw in the towel.

"Nonsense," replied Rabin, almost shouting. "There are precedents. We gave in when an El Al plane was hijacked to Algeria. We surrendered several terrorists in exchange for two Israelis who were being held in Damascus. The families of the hostages have pointed out that we released terrorists for the bodies of IDF soldiers who fell in the Yom Kippur War, so shouldn't we release terrorists in exchange for live people?"

Peres commented, "We never released terrorists found guilty of murder."

Rabin at once ordered his military secretary to check if this was true. A few minutes later the aide returned with the information. Peres was wrong. The tension among the ministers increased. Rabin was nervous. He constantly interrupted his colleagues. Finally, he summed up the meeting by saying there was no military option, and therefore, Israel must negotiate with the hijackers.

Upon returning to his Tel Aviv office, Peres conducted the investigation mentioned at the meeting with Motta Gur, Kuti Adam, and Air Force Commander Benjamin Peled. Peres asked for ideas, and Gur repeated the proposal he had written in the note but in more detail: the soldiers would fly to Kenya, rent a boat, and sail it across Lake Victoria to Entebbe. On arrival at the airport, they would kill the terrorists, return to Kenya by boat, and then head home.

Peres reiterated his stand regarding the saving of the passengers. Adam suggested a more complicated plan, by which Israel would announce that it accepted the demands of the hijackers but would insist that the exchange be carried out as follows: two planes would arrive at Entebbe—one empty, one with the released terrorists. Simultaneously, the passengers would board the empty plane and the hijackers would board the plane carrying the released terrorists. The two aircraft would leave Entebbe simultaneously. As far as the hijackers were concerned, both planes would have French air crews, but in fact, the plane with the terrorists on board would have an Israeli air crew, which would, of course, fly them back to Israel.

Because it was an Air France plane, this would need French cooperation, and if only for this reason, Peres doubted its feasibility. But he agreed to dispatch Asher Ben-Natan, who headed the Israel military mission in Paris for several years, to the French capital to see if there was any point in discussing the idea. He would, of course, need the prime minister's approval for this.

Throughout the discussion, the air force commander had been sitting silently. When he finally opened his mouth, he seemed to be talking to himself: "Maybe we could send a thousand soldiers to Entebbe, take control of the town and the airport, kill the hijackers, and return with the hostages. Hercules transport aircraft could fly there and back."

It was the first time since the aircraft had been hijacked that anyone had suggested taking control of the airport. Peres smiled, caught between consternation and admiration, not sure how to react to the idea. "The plan is so imaginative," he said, "that it seems extremely practical." Gur was quick to pour cold water on the idea. "The plan cannot be carried out, and we should forget it."

On his way home that night, Peres thought over the events of the day. He half heard his bodyguard, Amos, sitting in front next to the driver, saying something. His mind registered that it was interesting, and he asked the young man to repeat it.

"I served several years in Uganda," said Amos, "and I know the way they operate. Idi Amin won't start killing white people in a hurry—he'll drag it out."

Thinking over what he had heard, Peres came to the conclusion that he would like to know more about Uganda and its president. As soon as he arrived home, he telephoned his office and gave instructions that a number of Israelis who served in Uganda be invited to the ministry the following day.

WEDNESDAY, JUNE 30, 1976

At precisely 8:30 A.M., three IDF officers who had served in Uganda arrived at Peres's office. Colonel Baruch (Burka) Bar-Lev had been the head of the IDF Mission in Uganda. He had been instrumental in getting Idi Amin selected as chief of staff, and had been at his side when he had carried out the coup d'état that had brought him to power. Lieutenant Colonel Yosef Soen headed the air force mission in Uganda; Moshe Bedichi had been Amin's personal pilot.

Peres requested, "Tell me everything you know about Amin—his character, his habits, his way of making decisions."

"Amin is very influenced by people he knows and trusts," Burka responded. "If I were with him now, I would tell him: 'Idi, you have a chance to enter history. You can carry out an operation that will win you a Nobel prize.' Something like that could capture his imagination."

"How will he act without our suggestion?"

"I don't think he will harm the passengers, but I also don't think he will start a fight with the hijackers. All this is on the assumption that he doesn't have a dream tonight, because he is a great believer in dreams. The best thing would be for someone close to him to talk to him. It is a shame that nobody like that is with him now."

Peres asked, "Is it possible to reach him by phone?"

"It wouldn't be easy, but I'm prepared to try."

Soen said, "If we mount a military operation against him, he is liable to blow a fuse and do something crazy."

"Whatever happens," said Bedichi, "I don't think the Ugandans will fight."

"Idi once told me," Burka recalled, "that before she died, his mother told him: 'Amin, if you want to succeed, never harm the Jews—they are holy people.'"

"Is he a brave man?" asked Peres.

Burka, Bedichi, and Soen agreed, "He is the biggest coward imaginable!"

Peres wrote a note to himself with the following conclusions:

(a) Amin will be interested in prolonging the affair in order to be in the international spotlight for as long as possible.

(b) Amin will not harm whites on his own initiative because he is able to kill only blacks without being afraid.

(c) Despite this, if a military action is carried out, during which Ugandans are hurt and the passengers remain at the airport, they will be slaughtered by the Ugandans.

(d) The Ugandan army is not a military problem.

(e) We should contact Amin by phone, as he can be an unwitting source of valuable information. He can also be used to reassure the hijackers and to gain time.

Immediately afterward there was another meeting. The chief of staff reiterated his suggestion with one change: the soldiers would reach Kenya in a special Boeing airliner. Apart from the question of abandoning the passengers, there was another problem which made this plan irrelevant. It would involve cooperation with the Kenyans. They had been sounded out and had refused.

An officer from one of the IDF elite units suggested that it could be done without the Kenyans. An Israeli plane could fly straight to

Lake Victoria and drop twelve soldiers and rubber dinghies by parachute. The soldiers would cross the lake, kill the hijackers, and withdraw to the middle of the lake, where another boat would be waiting to take them ashore. A Hercules transport plane, which would land in the concealed bush country, would collect them and fly them home.

This plan had two disadvantages: first, the hostages would still be left at the mercy of the Ugandans; second, at a trial exercise two days before, the dinghies had capsized and the soldiers had been unable to carry out their mission. Peres said the plan did not appeal to him.

As views and ideas were exchanged, Benny Peled continued to press for military action. Someone asked him whether he would be so determined if his own son were among the hostages. Peled responded heatedly, "I would act in exactly the same manner because that is the way I have brought up my son. I am prepared to swear by all that is dear to me that I would act the same way."

Peres's military secretary, Brigadier General Arye Braun, asked his boss, "What do you think about the possibility of seizing another area—in Kampala, the Ugandan capital, for example—and threatening Amin that if he doesn't release the hostages, something important to him will be blown up?"

"Is that a possibility?" Peres wanted to know.

"It would be a better idea to kidnap his family, or to take control of the area where his tribe lives in northern Uganda and hold them as hostages," Peled suggested.

"And then what will he do? Can he influence the hijackers?" Peres asked.

He summed up the meeting: the plan to take control of Entebbe Airport and release the passengers should be investigated.

At the same time, Burka tried to make contact with Amin and eventually succeeded. From the outset, it was resolved that his contact with Amin would be unofficial, so as not to release the French from their obligations.

Burka told Amin that he was speaking as a private citizen, although he was in touch with "someone connected with the government." Amin seemed pleased with the call. In any case, he spoke freely, informing Burka that the aircraft was booby-trapped and the airport was mined. He said he had spoken with the hijacked passengers, and they were requesting that Israel accede swiftly to the hijackers' demands. Burka told Peres that he thought Amin was lying and was saying things dictated to him by the hijackers.

Time was becoming the most vital element. There would be a military option only if the ultimatum—set for the following afternoon—was postponed. The essential aim now was to gain time.

To this end, Burka again phoned Amin. Peres's instructions were to give Amin and the hijackers the feeling that if they didn't push matters too far, they had a good chance of getting what they wanted. Amin opened the conversation by saying that "the number-one freedom fighter" had arrived forty minutes ago and told him to say that Israel must release the forty terrorists. Peres concluded from this that the terrorist commander was standing by Amin, guiding him, in the same way that he was advising Burka.

On Peres's instructions, Burka hinted to Amin that he should use his army to free the passengers, an action that would win him much support in the world. Amin pretended not to understand the hint.

That evening, the ministerial team consulted with the prime minister. Peres reported on the contacts with Amin. Reserve General Rehavam Zeevi, the prime minister's adviser on counter-terrorism, was also present. He was charged with preparing a plan for the release of the terrorists imprisoned in Israel, in the event the government decided to give in to the demands of the hijackers.

After his report, questions were raised about the possibility of cooperation with France. It turned out that not much had been done about this, and an argument developed between Rabin and Foreign Minister Yigal Allon about how to deal with this matter. Somebody said one thing; someone else another thing, until Rabin exploded: "Gentlemen, the meeting is over! You are the foreign minister. You decide the procedure. We have finished with this."

Allon said, "If I am annoying you, appoint another foreign minister."

Rabin replied, "I think that you also have to make decisions. You are being asked a simple thing. I don't know why it is necessary to make this into a half-hour argument, that's all. Do what you want!

Okay . . . if in the State of Israel today, in this forum, at this time, we have to argue, go ahead!"

Eventually Rabin calmed down and the meeting continued. At the end of it, Peres offered, in order to gain time, the following recommendations: U.S. Secretary of State Henry Kissinger should contact Egyptian President Anwar Sadat; U.N. Secretary General Kurt Waldheim should be mobilized; the possibility of calling a meeting of the U.N. Security Council should be checked; the possibility of a joint operation with France should be investigated. The prime minister added that the Pope should also be contacted and asked to lend his voice in a moral stand.

THURSDAY, JULY 1, 1976

Peres awoke at 5:30 A.M., and drank a quick cup of coffee in the kitchen. Dawn was just breaking outside. His mood was somber. The tendency in the cabinet—particularly on the part of the prime minister—was to accept the demands of the hijackers. The chief of staff was against a military operation. France did not show any signs of approving a joint operation, and in a few more hours, at 2:00 P.M., the hijackers' ultimatum would run out.

Peres drove to Jerusalem. At 7:45 A.M. another meeting of the ministerial team began. Beforehand, in the corridor, Motta Gur told Peres: "As chief of staff, I cannot offer you any military operation to save the hostages, and therefore, the bottom line is that I will recommend releasing the terrorists."

The first report was from Rehavam Zeevi. The hijackers had released forty-eight non-Israeli passengers, and they had arrived in Paris. As soon as they arrived, they were interrogated by Israeli representatives, among others. It was learned that the Israeli hostages had been separated from the others. Ugandan soldiers were helping to guard the hostages, and there was full cooperation between the hijackers and the Ugandan authorities.

Peres asked if the plan to release the hostages with French cooperation had been checked out. It turned out that it had not, because Rabin and the foreign minister had canceled the plan without consulting Peres or even informing him.

Rabin reiterated his view that there was no way of avoiding giving in to the demands of the hijackers, and an argument ensued.

Peres said, "It should be clear that negotiation and Israeli surrender will open the door to wide-scale terror in the future."

Rabin replied, "Who says that it opens the door to wide-scale terror?"

"In my opinion . . ."

"I ask you to clarify your remarks and explain why."

"If we give in," Peres said, "no country in the world will stand up to the terrorists. In all situations such as this, there are elements of time running out, of threats, of a war of nerves. So I am for checking all the alternatives—even the seemingly hopeless ones, like cooperating with the French."

"I've no objection to sounding out Michel Ponietowski (the French interior minister). If you want to receive a refusal within half an hour, go ahead."

Peres nodded his head at Asher Ben-Natan, who was present in the room. Ben-Natan left the room, en route to Paris.

Peres returned to Tel Aviv, to the room assigned to Burka. He told Burka to phone Idi Amin again and to tell him he had an important message that he wanted to bring to Kampala personally. However, the Ugandan president was in a rage. He complained that the phone conversations had been recorded. "I heard myself on the Voice of America," he said. Burka assured Amin that he had nothing to do with it and again suggested that he fly to Uganda.

Amin replied: "Tell your government to listen to the announcement of the Popular Front for the Liberation of Palestine on the radio at 1:00 P.M. Israel time. That is the only answer I can give you. If you have something serious to tell me after the announcement, call me. We have had very tough conversations so far. You had better wait for the announcement. You know that I'm not telling you any secrets because I am being recorded by the Voice of America. Ring me after the announcement. It is a very important one."

Burka asked, "Don't you want me to come?"

Amin replied, "First listen to the announcement."

Peres was somewhat reassured. It meant that nothing would be done before the announcement, and even after it, they would definitely allow more time for an answer to their demands. In other words, more valuable time had been gained.

The cabinet met. Rabin proposed that the ministerial team be empowered to open negotiations with the hijackers. Peres found himself in a tight corner, as a civilian urging military action opposed by a former chief of staff (Rabin) and the current chief of staff. He therefore said that he would vote in favor of the proposal, but he emphasized—and demanded that it be put on record—that he was only doing so as a ploy, to gain time and mislead the hijackers.

The meeting was interrupted to receive a report of the hijackers' statement on the radio. The announcement said that the ultimatum had been extended to Sunday, July 4, "and if by then the Palestinian prisoners have not been released, the hostages will be dealt with accordingly."

Peres felt a certain relief at the postponement of the ultimatum, although the announcement also stated that the hijackers were now holding "only the Israeli citizens, those with dual nationality, and the Air France crew. The other hostages will be released."

"The scene conjured up in my imagination was dreadful," noted Peres later in his diary. "Again armed Arabs and Germans were threatening innocent people, separating the passengers, not by age or sex, but by nationality—all humanity on one side; Jews on the other. That thought is particularly shocking. What is the point of the existence of the State of Israel? Is it again possible to persecute people in this way, simply because they are Jews?"

There was now more time, but there was still no operative plan. Peres continued consultations in which there was an increasing tendency to favor taking control of Entebbe Airport. Motta Gur continued to be opposed to the idea because there was not sufficient intelligence on the situation at the airport, the location of the hostages, the number of guards, etc.

Peled asked, "What is intelligence? I land, grab the first guard that I find, ask him where the hostages are being held, tell him to take me there, and he takes me. Do you think that terrorists who carry out actions have exact intelligence?"

Gur said, "The suggestions being made here are not worthy of a general staff. If we are playing at *Goldfinger*, that is another matter. If you want to play at James Bond, do not do so with me. If we don't have the intelligence for an operation, there will be no operation. The suggested plan is a beauty, with a very good chance of success, but only if we have certain intelligence information, of which the main point is to know what kind of pressure the hostages are under."

Peres asked the head of the Mossad intelligence service whether there was any chance of operational or intelligence cooperation with Kenya. The intelligence chief replied: "If we agree to kill Idi Amin, [Kenyan President Jomo] Kenyatta might cooperate." (According to Israeli intelligence, Amin had sent soldiers to murder Kenyatta. When they did not succeed in their mission, he sent other soldiers, who killed them.)

Peres requested that the head of Mossad make contact with Kenya. The intelligence chief pointed out that he needed authorization from the prime minister. Peres phoned Rabin and asked for authorization. Rabin listened impatiently, and finally snapped, as if to get rid of an irritation, "Good, let him make contact."

Peres felt that things were starting to move, and therefore the French should not suspect that Israel was planning a military operation. However, Ben-Natan was already in Paris, and was shortly to meet with the French interior minister to propose a joint rescue operation. He needed to be stopped. Peres asked to be connected with Ben-Natan. When the phone was handed to him he spoke into it, "If you meet a French girl tonight, only flirt with her. I am telling you as a friend, don't get undressed." Ben-Natan, who was used to receiving such messages, had no difficulty in understanding what was required of him.

At the end of the day, Peres assessed the situation. There was a plan that they could live with. The main obstacle to its implementation was the opposition of the chief of staff. Peres came to the conclusion that the time had come for an unorthodox step. He left his office. At this late hour the Defense Ministry and the yard outside were deserted. He made his way speedily to the office of the chief of staff.

Motta Gur was surprised to see him. The two sat down in armchairs and Peres told him he wanted to speak not as a minister but as a friend. He started by saying that he was absolutely determined not to recommend any operation of which the chief of staff disapproved. All he was asking of Motta Gur was to understand that "this time the fate of the people, the state, Judaism, and Zionism hangs in the balance. Obviously, I am not demanding a plan that will be a guaranteed success or that will not involve casualties. I am not kidding myself—it is clear to me that, if the plan fails, I will have to draw immediate personal conclusions."

Peres sipped his coffee and continued, "I respect your responsible attitude, but now is the time for daring. There are no operations without serious risks, sometimes terrible risks; but I'm convinced that if we surrender, nothing will be left of us."

Gur did not respond. After a long pause, during which he sat looking at the wall, deep in thought, he said: "We'll go ahead with the preparations."

Peres returned to his office, feeling that he had won Gur over to his side, but it made him feel his responsibility even more strongly. Wasn't it irresponsible to dispatch dozens of soldiers to so distant a target when the situation on the ground was largely unknown?

He now felt that he was the one who needed the opinion of a man he greatly admired and respected. He lifted the phone and dialed the number of Moshe Dayan's home, where he was told that Dayan and his wife were dining out in Tel Aviv with guests from the United States at the Capriccio Restaurant. Peres set out for the restaurant with his military secretary, Arye Braun. They found Dayan in the middle of the soup course.

Peres apologized to Mrs. Dayan and their guests and took Dayan to a distant table. The former defense minister listened carefully as Peres outlined the proposed operation. When he had finished, Dayan said enthusiastically: "It's a beauty of a plan." Peres left the restaurant with the feeling that "at last, there was something to work on."

FRIDAY, JULY 2, 1976

Peres awoke before the alarm rang. The toothache that had been nagging him all week had become unbearable. He phoned the dentist and made an appointment for the same day. He then swallowed two painkillers and phoned the head of the Mossad.

At last there was some encouraging news—the Kenyans were prepared to cooperate, on certain conditions. The cooperation was to be secret and Kenya's role was not to be revealed. If Uganda attacked Kenya, Israel would come to Kenya's aid. There was also a concrete demand: the supply of some aircraft. In addition, the force that came to the rescue must destroy the Ugandan MiG aircraft stationed at Entebbe Airport.

Without hesitation, Peres ordered the head of the Mossad to tell the Kenyans that Israel accepted all the conditions. Peres went to the prime minister's office in Tel Aviv and informed Rabin of Kenya's willingness to cooperate. Regarding the timing of the operation, Peres said that there was general agreement that it should be carried out as long as possible before the expiration of the ultimatum, so that the hijackers would be calm and relaxed. He was inclined toward Saturday night.

A special task force under the command of Major General Dan Shomron, the chief infantry and paratroop officer (today IDF chief of staff), was already carrying out maneuvers on a scale model of Entebbe Airport and the building in which it was thought the hostages were being held.

Rabin did not share Peres's enthusiasm. "This is an operation which, if it does not succeed, is liable to harm Israel more than anything," he says, "and it will also harm the IDF." But he was speaking less decisively than previously. Peres received the impression that Rabin was already more willing to consider a military option.

The effect of the painkillers was starting to wear off and Peres hurried to his dentist, who, apart from the treatment, was later to prove what a small world it is—or, at least, what a small place the State of Israel is. (After it was all over, the dentist told Peres that his son, a medical orderly, was a member of the task force. It goes without saying that, when he treated Peres, the dentist had no idea of what was about to happen, about his son's involvement, or about the role of the man whose teeth he was treating.)

During the day more information arrived, elicited from the released passengers who had arrived in Paris. The following picture emerged: the Israelis and those with dual nationality were being held in a main hall on the ground floor of the old terminal at Entebbe Airport. The air crew was being held in the women's rest room in the same building. The terrorists—apparently seven of them, including a German woman—were guarding the hostages. Additional guards, Ugandan soldiers, were on the roof of the terminal. Apparently the plane, parked on a side runway, was not booby-trapped, and the runway was not mined.

Motta Gur and Kuti Adam arrived at Peres's office. It was clear that Gur had experienced a complete transformation. He now spoke of the operation as certain. He asked Peres what to do if the Ugandan soldiers showed resistance. Without hesitation, Peres said that they should be shot. Gur said that this would make his planning much easier.

Gur reported on the recommended flight path of the aircraft, designed to evade the radar of the countries along the route. The head of the Mossad entered and disclosed a new problem. The Kenyans had added a condition to their permission for the Israeli planes to refuel in Nairobi—that the task force take Idi Amin hostage.

"Is it possible?" Peres asked.

The head of the Mossad replied: "The problem is that the Ugandans won't ask for him back. They will thank us for taking him."

Gur said, "This is impossible. It will greatly lengthen the operation and put it in danger."

Peres gave orders that the Kenyans be told that every effort would be made to seize Amin, but it could not be guaranteed. He then phoned Rabin and told him that he wanted to present the plan to a limited forum. Rabin told him to come right away, and they did as he said.

The chief of staff presented the plan, and, for the first time since the business started, said there is "a good chance of the operation succeeding."

Against this background, Rabin called a meeting of the ministerial team for 12:15 P.M. Views were exchanged; questions were asked—not all of them had answers. Peres sensed that most of the ministers, possibly all of them, were in favor of the operation—with the exception of the prime minister. "I'm still not sure about the operation," he said. "There are ninety-eight Israelis in that terminal. We have never dealt with numbers like that before. Although I am in favor of going ahead with all the preparations, I suggest we regard it as a secondary matter."

That evening, Peres entertained Zbigniew Brzezinski, who was slated to receive a senior position in the administration of U.S. presidential candidate Jimmy Carter. At dinner, in the middle of a discussion on the future of the occupied territories, Brzezinski turned to Peres and asked: "Why don't you try military action to rescue the hostages at Entebbe?" For a moment, Peres was stunned, but he quickly recovered and listed the problems that made a military operation impractical.

Peres arrived at his office at 6:15 A.M. He had not slept well, imagining endless problems, particularly mechanical trouble with the planes. He immediately phoned Air Force Commander Benny Peled and asked him about this.

Peled replied, "Sir, I have given instructions to tighten every screw on all the planes!"

Peres was briefed on a new feature of the plan. After the two planes landed, a Mercedes limousine, like the one used by Amin, would disembark from one of them. It would be escorted by two Land Rovers of the type used by the Ugandan president's bodyguards. The only problem with this trick was that Amin was away on a visit to the island of Mauritius, and it was not known when he was due back in Entebbe. But it was assumed that the guards at the airport—they knew of his absence—would not know he had not returned. It was another risk that would have to be taken.

At 7:40 A.M., the chief of staff arrived at Peres's office, and after him, several IDF generals. He said that last night he went on a trial navigation flight with the planes and pilots to be used in the operation, in order to experience how the planes handled at night. Now he was convinced that there would be no problems in that area.

At 9:15 A.M., the final meeting of the military team was held. The mood was good. There was that feeling of anticipation that precedes an important operation. The improvement in the atmosphere was greatly helped by the news that they would shortly receive additional information.

Peres said to Gur: "I hope you gave orders that the terrorists are to be killed."

"Those are the orders," Gur replied.

Kuti Adam reported that a successful dry run had been carried out the previous day on the scale model of the airport, and there had been no hitches. Peres asked Gur for a step-by-step account of the plan.

"Four Hercules transport aircraft will take off two hours before sunset, with one hundred and eighty soldiers aboard," Gur said. "Each plane will have a crew of five. The first plane will land at 11:00 P.M. Twenty-four Jeeps, three Land Rovers, and the Mercedes will disembark. This force will take control of the old terminal, where the hostages are being held.

"Within five to seven minutes, the other three planes will land. Armored personnel carriers will disembark from the second aircraft, carrying the force to deal with the Ugandan troops if they offer resistance. In addition, a Peugeot vehicle with a medical team and a team to evacuate the hostages will disembark.

"The other aircraft will be carrying the forces that will take control of the new terminal. The dry run carried out in Israel took fifty-five minutes. Taking into account possible armed clashes and casualties, we should allow for ninety minutes to two hours for the operation."

Dan Shomron did not attend the meeting; he was with the task force, waiting for orders to take off.

At 10:00 A.M. the military team proceeded to Rabin's office. After they again briefed the prime minister on the plan, they learned that everything now depended on the answer from Kenya. Gur said that "in the absence of an affirmative response from the Kenyans, I would not recommend going ahead."

A discussion ensued as to whether the planes could be refueled somewhere else. While they were talking, a telegram arrived from the Mossad operatives in Kenya: "In our estimation, it will be possible to land at Nairobi Airport for the purpose of refueling."

A few minutes later another telegram was brought in, also from a Mossad operative. "The prisoners are being held in what was the transit lounge of the old terminal building. I understand that it is on the ground floor, facing southeast, toward the runway. The rest of the building is apparently empty. The terrorists have asked to move the hijacked plane to the old hangar. General Amin is due to return tonight (Friday)." This meant that Amin was already back in Uganda. So now the refueling problem had been solved, and the deception with the Mercedes was feasible.

The time table was becoming overcrowded. The cabinet meeting to decide on the fate of the mission was set for noon. At 4:00

P.M., the planes were due to set off from Sharm el-Sheikh to Uganda, but they still had to get from Ben-Gurion Airport to Sharm, where they would undergo their final refueling. In order to be in a position to leave Sharm by 4:00 P.M., they would have to take off from Ben-Gurion at 11:30 A.M., and the cabinet had not yet decided. Peres authorized Gur to order the take-off from Ben-Gurion at 11:30. If the government decision was negative, they could always be recalled.

At 11:15 A.M., the ministerial team met with the prime minister. Gur started with a detailed outline of the plan. After it, Peres asked to speak. "We have to ask ourselves what we are fighting for. Sometimes it seems that we are fighting for something indefinable; but actually, it is something very specific. That something is called dignity."

Everyone looked toward Rabin. Everything depended on him. Would he stick to his line and put a stop to everything that had been done so far? Finally, Rabin looked at Peres and asked: "When do we have to order the planes to take off?" Peres sighed with relief. He sensed that, with that question, Rabin had expressed a decision in favor of the operation.

The ministerial defense committee met at 2:00 P.M. Its members heard details of the plan for the first time. To judge by the questions, there was no opposition to the operation. Rabin sent Peres a note: "Shimon, I think the planes can take off for Sharm." Peres wrote back: "They are already on their way."

At 2:30 P.M., the full cabinet met for reports, questions, objections, suggestions. Time was running out. At 3:30 P.M., Haim Yisraeli, one of Peres's aides, passed him a note: "They have to take off soon. I remind you that the planes can be recalled later, but they should take off on time." Peres did not respond. Yisraeli waited and then sent another note: "It's 3:50 P.M. Should they take off?"

By now, Peres had no doubt that the cabinet would approve the plan. He returned Yisraeli's note, on which he had written: "Let them take off." Yisraeli left the room. When he returned a few minutes later, he handed Peres another note: "Shimon, they are taking off now." Wordlessly, Peres passed the note to Rabin. Rabin read it and looked up; their eyes met. For a split second the two sworn rivals saw eye-to-eye as they never had before and never would again. More than the other ministers, the two of them sensed the crushing weight of the responsibility that they had assumed and placed on others. Both had played their distinct roles: Peres, the initiator and mover; Rabin, the one with the ultimate responsibility and the courage to decide.

Finally, with the planes already on their way, the cabinet approved decision number 819: "Regarding the release of the hijacked passengers of the Air France plane in Uganda—rescue mission. It is resolved to approve the rescue of the hostages in Uganda by the IDF, according to the plan proposed by the defense minister and the chief of staff."

At 5:40 P.M., Peres left in a hurry for his office. All his thoughts were concentrated, as he wrote later in his diary, on "the planes, which are on their way, carrying the destiny of Israel."

In order to give an impression of business as usual, Peres attended the bar mitzvah of the grandson of *Yediot Ahronot* editor Herzl Rosenblum. Everyone surrounded him and asked him what was going to happen. He replied that the hostages would soon be home. Everyone smiled.

He traveled back to his office, where his phone was linked to the operational network. Over the loudspeaker, it was possible to hear the exchanges between command headquarters in Israel and the planes, and between the planes themselves.

At 11:03 P.M., the voice of Dan Shomron was heard at last over the communications network: "The first plane has landed safely." In Peres's office, the atmosphere was tense. No one opened his mouth. All eyes looked toward the loudspeaker in the corner.

At 11:10 P.M., Dan Shomron was heard again: "Everything in order, we'll report later." Noises were heard in the background. It was not clear whether what they were hearing were shots being exchanged or the aircraft engines.

At 11:18 P.M., one word came through: "Ebb-tide." They all knew that this was the code word to say that all the planes had landed.

At 11:28 P.M., they heard, "Everything is going according to plan. We'll report in a moment. So far, everything is fine."

At 11:29 P.M., they heard, "Palestine"—the code word announcing that the action to take control of the building in which the hostages were being held had begun.

At 11:32 P.M., "Jefferson," signifying the evacuation of the hostages, came over the loudspeaker.

At 11:33 P.M., the order, "Move everything to the circuit," which meant evacuate, came through.

At 11:50 P.M., they heard a shout: "First aid to Shkedim command post," code word for Yoni Netanyahu's unit, the force that had attacked the building with the hostages. "Two Yaktrina." (Two wounded.) No one moved, but the faces showed increasing tension. Who had been wounded? Were the wounds serious?

At 11:51 P.M., "Mount Carmel" announced that the evacuation had been completed and the planes had taken off. Peres still did not betray any feelings, but inside, "his heart was jumping for joy."

At 11:56 P.M., Dan Shomron said: "There are ninety-four released passengers and twelve Air France crew members, totaling a hundred and six."

At 11:59 P.M., they heard, "Correction: there are ninety-three passengers. It appears that one of them was taken to hospital." (Later it turned out that this was an old woman named Dora Bloch.)

At midnight, the chief of staff called Peres's office, trying to keep his voice calm and matter-of-fact, but he could not disguise his satisfaction and pleasure. He quickly reported: "The operation lasted fifty-five minutes; two of our soldiers have been wounded. The plane with the rescued hostages has taken off according to plan. It will refuel in Kenya and return home. According to reports from Kenya, there are no problems."

Peres said, "I am coming over."

Peres hurried to the chief of staff's office, and the others followed him. Industry and Trade Minister Haim Bar-Lev, a former chief of staff, was also there. Everyone knew that his son, Omer, was with the task force. Bar-Lev's expression betrayed no emotion. There was no way of knowing whether his son was one of the wounded.

Also present was General Rafael Vardi, who had lost his eldest son in the Yom Kippur War. Now they learned that his only surviving son was with the task force, his fate unknown. When he heard about it, Gur was angry. "An only child should not be sent on such a mission," he growled. Vardi remained calm. "If the son serves in the paratroops, he has to remain with his comrades. That is his wish. He told his mother that he was going on leave, but she knows him and she knows where he is."

"I could hardly believe my ears," Peres wrote later in his diary. "What incredible courage!"

SUNDAY, JULY 4, 1976

At 1:00 A.M., Peres summoned Burka Bar-Lev, who arrived quickly. He explained that he was curious about Amin's reaction to the operation. He suggested that Burka phone his former friend and simply say: "Thanks for the cooperation." Burka dialed, and eventually, Idi Amin's voice boomed over the loudspeaker linked to the phone.

"President Amin speaking."

"Jambo, sir, I want to thank you for your cooperation, and thank you very much, sir," Burka said.

"You know that you did not succeed," Amin said.

"Thank you for your cooperation—what? The cooperation didn't succeed? Why?"

"Did you actually do anything?"

"I simply want to thank you for the cooperation, sir."

"Did you do anything?" Amin asked.

"I did exactly what you wanted," Burka replied.

"Ha-ha . . . what happened?"

"What happened?"

"Yes?"

"No, I don't know."

"Can you tell me?" Amin asked.

"No, I don't know. I was simply asked to thank you for your cooperation."

"Can you tell me what was the message that you wanted to give me?"

"I was asked by my friend who has good contacts with the government to thank you for the cooperation," Burka said. "I don't know what it means, but I think you know."

"I don't know because I just got back. I hurried back from Mauritius."

"What?"

"To solve this problem before the ultimatum expires tomorrow morning."

"I understand. All right, sir, but I repeat: thanks for the cooperation. Maybe I'll call you again tomorrow morning? Do you want me to call again tomorrow?"

"Yes."

"All right, thank you, sir. Good-bye."

"Okay."

Burka put down the phone and everyone present burst out laughing, releasing the tension. "Is it possible?" asked Peres. "That more than an hour after the operation, three kilometers away, the president doesn't know what has been happening at his own international airport?"

Food was brought in—chicken, stuffed peppers, salads, cakes. Only now did they realize that they had not eaten for several hours. They fell on the food. After they had eaten, Motta Gur lifted a glass of champagne and, his voice charged with emotion, said:

"We can already say that this was the IDF's most successful and impressive operation. But it is impossible to talk about the operation, even at this stage, without mentioning the drive and influence of one man. I don't know if we can award percentages to everyone who played a decisive part in deciding on this operation, but if we can, the large majority must go to the man who pushed and pressured in favor of it in all directions, upward and downward, and that is the defense minister, who deserves all the credit."

All those present looked toward Peres and applauded enthusiastically. He felt a mixture of satisfaction and surprise. The demonstration brought tears to his eyes, making him do what he finds so hard to do: show emotion.

At 1:15 A.M., an officer entered the room and passed a note to the chief of staff. Gur read it, went over to Peres, and whispered in his ear: "Yoni is one of the two wounded." An expression of pain crossed Peres's face, but he thought: "At least he is still alive!"

Conversations with Rabin and the leaders of the opposition followed. The wording of the IDF spokesman's announcement was approved.

At 3:00 A.M., "I return to my bureau to catch a brief nap before the planes return home," Peres wrote later, "but I cannot sleep. I lie on the sofa trying to imagine what the boys aboard the plane are feeling. As for the passengers, they are surely still in shock.

"At four in the morning, Motta comes in and turns on the light. I notice that his face is pale and he looks extremely upset. 'Shimon, Yoni is gone. He was hit in the back and the bullet sliced into his heart.'

"It is the first time this crazy week that I cannot hold back my tears. I remember Yoni at the airport at Lod that night. Somehow I sensed his eyes were sad, as if that wonderful boy was tired."

CHAPTER SIX

THE GREAT
UPHEAVAL

THE SUCCESS OF the Entebbe operation had a tonic effect on the Israeli public. People seemed to stand taller, and they never tired of repeating stories about the glorious rescue. Had there really been a Mercedes limousine in the plane? Had the Ugandan guards really thought that their president was inside it? Why had Idi Amin not known what was going on?

The Six-Day War had made Israel's Jewish citizens proud of their nation and army—a pride that had turned into arrogance and presumption. The disaster of the Yom Kippur War was the result of exaggerated self-confidence—of blindness and pride. After that war, the Israeli people had bowed their heads, suddenly aware, in the most ruthless manner, how vulnerable they were, and conscious of the dangers that faced them.

A perceptive observer could have seen in their eyes the difficult question: Who are we really—the invincible heroes of the Six-Day War, or the beaten incompetents of the Yom Kippur War? There is no doubt that in posing this question there was a great desire to be better, stronger, and wiser, but it was an existential question, because if the answer was that the citizens of Israel were really as they seemed to be in the Yom Kippur War, then they were in deep trouble.

Into this atmosphere came the Entebbe hostages and their rescuers, like oxygen to an invalid with respiratory problems. Once again backs were straightened and faces were wreathed in smiles. This time it was not overdone, as it was after the Six-Day War, because in the background was the memory of the Yom Kippur War, and this memory kept the rejoicing from turning into a feeling of "we are the greatest." It was quite enough for the citizens of Israel, who had been so shocked by the most recent war, to regain the feeling that their enterprise and courage had not deserted them, that they were still capable of causing surprise and amazement, of doing the impossible. Once again it was good to be an Israeli.

This pleasure was spoiled to a certain extent by the rivalry between Rabin and Peres. Anyone who thought that the success of the operation would bridge the gap between the two was swiftly disillusioned. The noise of the engines of the planes that brought the hostages and their rescuers to Israel had hardly died down when an ugly contest between the two was launched to win the larger part of the credit for the success. The media were tediously full of contradictory descriptions of the roles of the two men in the operation. Those who had played a part in planning and implementing the rescue told reporters about Peres's decisive role; Rabin's associates leaked anonymously to the press that Peres's role had been marginal, even a nuisance.

The endless quarrels, the deteriorating economic situation, the continuous strikes, and a number of scandals that disclosed corruption at the top, combined to create a general disenchantment among the public with the rule of the Labor party. A gradual desire for change developed, which focused on the personality of Professor Yigael Yadin, who had been IDF chief of staff in the early 1950s.

The mustached, charismatic scholar had abandoned public affairs in favor of archeology, where he had made an international name for himself. Over the years, he had rejected repeated pleas to enter politics. Now he announced that he was ready to establish a new party, and all the public opinion polls predicted that a party led by him would meet with considerable success.

The decline in the popularity of the government and the Labor party did not affect Peres's image. A public opinion poll published at the time showed that only 35 percent were satisfied with Rabin's performance as prime minister, and 51 percent favored Peres. Rabin's political fortunes had sunk to an all-time low, so it was natural enough that, at the first opportunity, he made a desperate gesture that brought down the government and eventually toppled the Labor party from power.

The occasion for Rabin's action was a vote of no-confidence in the government by the ministers of the National Religious party. He could, as on similar occasions in the past, have ignored the matter, but he thought that he had a unique opportunity to confound his many critics and prove that he was a leader capable of making decisive political moves.

Rabin decided to apply the law and fire the three NRP ministers, thus losing the support of the NRP Knesset members, and with it the government's parliamentary majority. On December 21, 1976, he carried out the second phase of his plan: he went to the president and submitted his government's resignation. The government now became a transition administration until the general election, which was set for May 17, 1977.

Advancing the elections also naturally brought forward the contest for the leadership of the Labor party, and in mid-January, Peres announced his candidacy. Never before had the party ousted a prime minister from his position, but there was a feeling that it was about to happen now.

The Labor party convention was held on February 23, 1977. Following speeches by Rabin and Peres, the voting began. After the polling booths closed, the two candidates sat in separate rooms with their supporters, waiting tensely for the results that slowly started coming in. There was a slight advantage to Rabin, then a slight advantage to Peres; they were neck and neck all along the track. When the final results came, Peres sat in his room, feeling as if someone had struck him on the head with an axe. His face was frozen and disconsolate: 1,445 votes had been cast for Rabin; 1,404 for Peres—a difference of forty-one. In effect, twenty-one people had stood between Peres and victory.

It was clear that the votes of the Arab and Druze delegates had swung the contest. Rabin had won 80 percent of them because of the pressure exerted (without his knowledge) by one of his supporters. Peres's campaign coordinator Aharon Harel requested and received a sworn statement from the Druze delegate concerning the pressure exerted on them by the Rabin camp. He came to Peres with the document and said, "With this we can nullify the election."

"Out of the question," was Peres's immediate response.

"Why?" demanded Harel. "We have a watertight case."

Peres smiled sadly. "Let's say we have a revote, and I win. The other side won't accept it, and there will be a split in the party. Let's swallow our bile and shut up."

From then on, Peres and Rabin directed most of their energies against the Likud and Professor Yadin's Democratic Movement for Change (DMC), which had meanwhile been established. But it gradually became evident that their display of unity had come too late. The Labor party's campaign limped along, as the Likud and the DMC increased in popularity. Every time the Labor campaign seemed to take off, something happened to return it to the ground with a hard bump. The party was especially hard hit by a number of cases of personal corruption, two of which shattered the country.

The first had already hit the headlines in the fall of 1976, when Moshe Sanbar, governor of the Bank of Israel, ended his term of office. A number of candidates were proposed for the job, but Rabin chose Asher Yadlin, the director general of Kupat Holim, the Histadrut's health fund, who was also a senior party functionary. Shortly after Rabin announced his appointment, the press discovered that Yadlin was involved in a series of scandals concerning the taking of bribes for work from Kupat Holim fund contractors. Yadlin was put on trial, found guilty, and sentenced to five years in prison. It was the first time that so senior a political figure in Israel had been found to be a criminal.

The second scandal also began at the end of 1976. News items started to appear connecting Housing Minister Avraham Ofer, one of the Labor party's front-line leaders, with cases of personal and party corruption. Ofer categorically denied the allegations published in the media, but on the morning of January 4, 1977, the citizens of Israel woke to tragic and depressing news. The reports said that a passerby had found the minister, slumped over the steering wheel of his Volvo limousine on the Tel Baruch shore, north of Tel Aviv, with a bullet in his head. A handgun was on the seat beside him, along with a note explaining the reasons for his suicide.

These events created a general feeling that the nation had lost its way. The Labor party's only hope was that, by May 1977, the public would have forgotten about these scandals. But then something else happened, and this was the straw that broke the back of Rabin and the Labor party.

The item published by reporter Dan Margalit in *Ha'aretz* on March 15, 1977, conveyed no hint of what was about to happen. It merely disclosed that Leah Rabin, the wife of the prime minister, had a bank account in Washington, D.C. Holding a foreign currency account abroad was a serious violation of Israel's currency laws. It was soon revealed that the prime minister himself was a joint signatory to the account. Rabin confirmed this, but added that only a small sum—some $2,000—was involved.

Generally, the seriousness of such offenses was measured by the amount of money involved. Where the sum was less than $5,000, the offender usually got off with a fine. Only in cases where larger sums were involved was there criminal prosecution. On the basic of Rabin's statement, Attorney General Aharon Barak advised him that he had no cause for concern, and the matter started to fade.

However, Barak, acting as he would with any citizen, demanded that Rabin produce his bank statement, which showed that the prime minister had lied. He possessed two accounts, not one, and the sum involved was not $2,000 but $23,000. Barak told Rabin that he had no alternative but to put his wife on trial. The prime minister himself would get the benefit of the doubt, based on his claim that he had not known.

On the night of April 7, 1977, the citizens of Israel were at their television sets, watching the finals of the European Basketball Cup, where Israeli champions Maccabi Tel Aviv were taking on Italy's top team, Mobilgirgi Varese. That evening Peres was invited to dinner at the home of Abba Eban. Among the other guests were the British ambassador and the Jewish philanthropist, Sir Isaac Wolfson. Eban brought a television set to the dinner table, with the sound turned down, so that they could follow the game.

Peres excused himself and left early with his wife, Sonia. When they arrived home, Sonia turned on the set; the game was still on. Peres said he was tired and went to bed. Just as he was dropping off to sleep, the light went on in the bedroom and Sonia stood in the entrance.

"Come quickly, television," she said.

"Who won?" asked Peres.

"No, no," she exclaimed excitedly. "It's Rabin."

Peres went into the living room. Rabin's face appeared on the screen, pale and depressed. In an emotional voice, he announced his resignation from the government and the leadership of the Labor party. "It is a sad ending," he said quietly.

Sonia switched off the set and looked at her husband. For several minutes he sat, his face expressionless. Then he got up and went to bed without a word.

On Rabin's recommendation, Peres was appointed acting prime minister until the elections. On April 21, the Labor party central committee met to elect its new leader. No one even bothered to count the hands raised in his favor; only eight voted against, and eighteen abstained.

After two dramatic confrontations with Rabin and a period of exhausting disputes with him, Peres had taken a further step on his path to the summit; however, the legacy he received made its achievement attainable only by a miracle.

Looking for another miracle during this period, Peres presented an absurd scenario. He spoke of "a Jewish government with the best Jewish minds." Had not Ben-Gurion himself asked Professor Albert Einstein to be the president of Israel? Peres mentioned some names. It would be a good thing if Henry Kissinger agreed to accept an important political portfolio. Another candidate was Arthur Goldberg, for whom Peres proposed a new job—minister for Jewish affairs.

But the miracle that the Labor party desperately needed didn't happen. On May 19, 1977, the Israeli public flocked to the polling booths to cause the greatest political upset that the State of Israel had ever known.

CHAPTER SEVEN

LEADER OF THE OPPOSITION

Starting Over

THE LABOR PARTY headquarters in Tel Aviv's Hayarkon Street was silent, almost abandoned. From the open window in Shimon Peres's room it was possible to hear the soft sound of the sea. Only a very few of the dozens of people who had crowded the room at the start of the evening remained. Peres sat at the head of the table, his face pale, his eyes red, watching the television screen. Anchorman Haim Yavin and his team of reporters continued relaying figures to the viewers, which bore out their startling forecast earlier in the evening: for the first time in the twenty-nine years of Israel's statehood, the Likud, headed by Menachem Begin, would be the nation's largest party.

No one spoke in the sparsely furnished room. It seemed as if those present, particularly Peres, still did not believe or could not absorb what had happened. A thought flashed through Peres's mind: *It's a good thing that Ben-Gurion isn't here to see Menachem Begin in his moment of victory.*

As the Labor defeat became increasingly clear, the oppressive silence was frequently interrupted by the horns of cars stopping in front of the party headquarters, honking ceaselessly to show their joy and derision. From time to time, a shout from the street penetrated the room: "Boo!" "You've had it!" "Thieves, at last we have caught you!"

If the jeers reached Peres, his expression did not show it; he continued to watch the small screen as if hypnotized. It was only at three in the morning that he finally placed his hands on the table and very slowly pushed himself upright, as if he needed support. "That's it," he said, turning to leave. He descended the narrow stairs with a heavy tread. The entrance to the building was deserted. The security guards who had been there earlier had left. They had gone over to Metzudat Ze'ev, the Herut party headquarters, because the man who would be the next prime minister of Israel was there.

As Peres left the building, he shivered in the chill breeze from the sea. He was about to cross the road, when suddenly a cab stopped on the other side. Two people sat in it. The driver looked at Peres and, when he recognized him, lowered the window, put out his head, and spat at the exhausted figure. Peres quickly entered his car, and drove off toward his home.

Sonia was waiting for him. She placed her hand on his arm without uttering a word. A few minutes later, his friend Asher Ben-Natan and journalist Mira Avrech arrived. The television set was switched on, and they sat down to watch. A little before 4:00 A.M., Peres turned to his wife: "I should call Begin and congratulate him, shouldn't I?" Without waiting for an answer, he got up and walked toward the telephone in the kitchen. Just that moment, Haim Yavin announced that Begin was about to speak. Peres stopped. "If he's talking now, I can't very well call him. I'll wait until he finishes."

Begin's face appeared on the screen, and a microphone was pushed toward him. He spoke of his victory, his pleasure, his gratitude. He ended by saying, "And now I am waiting for tomorrow's congratulatory cable from Shimon Peres." The shadow of a smile flickered over Peres's face as he sat down. "Good. If that's what he wants, there is no point in calling him."

The following day he rose, as usual, at 6:30 A.M., and went to his office at the Defense Ministry. For a few hours he dealt with ministry matters, but around noon, several of his close associates began to gather, wondering what they should do now.

At this point, Peres's remarkable powers of recuperation, fueled by his indefatigable optimism, became evident. All was not lost, he argued. Despite the heavy loss, it was not impossible that Labor would form the next government. His calculation was as follows: Labor Alignment (including left-wing Mapai), 32 seats; Yadin's Democratic Movement for Change, 15; National Religious party, 11; altogether, 58. Only three more seats were needed from a small faction or factions to reach the required 61.

Peres did not leave it at that but met that day with DMC representatives, who told him that the people had shown a clear preference for a Likud-led government. NRP leader Yosef Burg told him the same.

Menachem Begin had another idea. He visited Peres at his office in the Defense Ministry and suggested that Labor join his government. Peres asked him about his policy regarding Judea and Samaria, the West Bank. Begin said that he would not give up one inch of land. Peres asked: "How will you rule over a million Arabs?"

"With faith and the sword," was the reply, making it clear to Peres that they did not have a basis for partnership.

However, Peres quickly learned that Begin had found a common language with another senior Labor party figure. At the end of May 1977, Peres was sitting reading, when the phone rang. Sonia answered it, and told him, "It's for you—it's Moshe." For a split second his heart seemed to stand still, for he had heard rumors, and then he went to the phone.

"I have decided to join the government," said the rough, decisive voice.

"I am sorry to hear that."

"I decided that I can serve the nation better that way. I don't see myself sitting in the opposition for four years." There was silence. Dayan felt the need to reply to the question that had not been asked: "I didn't speak to you first so as not to create the impression that we had plotted this together, or that you were in any way responsible for my decision."

"I understand."

Peres put down the phone and returned to his chair. The words of the book danced before his eyes, and he laid it down. He recalled the period after the Yom Kippur War when the public had wanted Dayan's head. Peres had not made any calculations about "sitting in opposition, or serving the nation." Although circumstances had not obligated him, he had stood by Dayan, as he had all his life. Yet now, at the most difficult hour of his own life, Dayan had discarded him like a tool that had served his purpose and was no longer needed. He felt bitter but he could not feel hatred for Dayan, even though "the knife sticking deep in his back" was causing him great pain.

When on May 26, 1977, Samuel Lewis, the new American ambassador, wanted to know whether Dayan's move would "strengthen the cabinet on the path to peace," Peres replied: "Yes. He is a very original and flexible thinker. I hope he won't be neutralized." Peres's assessment was to be borne out in the near future, but his own partnership with Moshe Dayan was over. No other partnership in Israel's political history had been so stormy, so full of controversy, or had left so deep a mark.

The political transformation was completed when a proud, pompous Menachem Begin presented his new government to the Knesset on June 20, 1977. Two days later, Ezer Weizman came to take over the Defense Ministry. A large number of people attended the ceremony, where Peres presented his successor with three heavy files, summing up the ministry's work during his term and giving details of all the matters still on the agenda. When he shook hands with the men with whom he had worked for most of his adult life, Peres was afraid to speak, lest the tears that were choking him burst forth.

Now came the days of idleness. There was no Defense Ministry to go to, no cabinet meetings to attend. Peres's spirits fluctuated between black despair and cautious optimism. One of his close friends asked him how he felt.

"I don't know," he replied tiredly, almost apathetically. "I wake up in the morning and I don't know what for."

It did not take long for Peres to find a reason for waking up every morning. As others sank into self-pity, Peres threw all his energy into the work of rehabilitation. Within a few months, he and former Finance Minister Yehoshua Rabinovich had wiped out all the party's debts and put it back on firm financial footing. His main achievement was in restoring the party branches, which he saw as the roots from which it drew its strength. The roots had begun to decay, with local activists looking for shelter as near as possible to the new administration. Many party clubhouses were padlocked, with neither budgets nor personnel to man them.

Peres relieved the monotony of party work with activities that he enjoyed. Even if he arrived home at midnight, he read for an hour or two, and on Friday afternoons he sat in his armchair and watched the Arabic films (with subtitles) on Israel Television. He once explained that he found these movies simple and touching. If there was a gap in his timetable, he went to the beach, sat in a deck chair, and exposed his face to the sun, although he never took off his shirt. The lifeguard sometimes brought him a glass of water; people sometimes approached him for autographs.

Then and now lunch is part of his working day, and he takes advantage of it for meetings. He likes good food and can easily find his way through a sophisticated menu, a legacy from his frequent visits to Paris. But he is very careful—sometimes fanatically so—not to eat too much, believing that the public does not like fat leaders. His slim figure proves that his appetite for leadership is stronger than his appetite for good food.

Next to History

On Friday, November 18, 1977, Peres and his wife Sonia boarded a plane from Miami to Los Angeles for a fund-raising lecture tour on behalf of the United Jewish Appeal. He arrived at the Los Angeles airport tired from the long flight, and all he wanted was to get to his hotel and rest. He did not know that the next time he went to bed, it would be in his Tel Aviv apartment.

As he descended from the plane, Israel's consul general in Los Angeles approached him with a message. "President Sadat is arriving in Israel on Saturday night, and it is suggested that you return home at once." Peres was not too surprised. The media had been full of the preliminaries for such a visit. He never left the airport, and, within an hour, he was on a flight to New York. The consul general had ascertained that this flight would arrive just in time to catch an Air France connection to Israel.

But the Los Angeles plane did not make it. There had been an accident involving two planes on the runway at Kennedy, and Peres's plane spent three hours circling the airport. Sitting in the Air France plane was another distinguished passenger who wanted to return to Israel—Golda Meir. She knew that Peres was on the plane from Los Angeles, and when it was late, she asked the Air France pilot to wait. He agreed, but could only wait for one hour, and eventually set off without Peres and his wife.

When Peres's plane finally landed, there were no other planes crossing the Atlantic that day. At that point, Peres was sure he was going to miss the historic visit of President Sadat to Israel; however, members of the Israel purchasing mission in New York, who had come to meet Peres, started checking other possibilities and discovered that an El Al cargo plane, carrying industrial piping, was due to leave for Amsterdam at three in the morning. Peres and Sonia waited at the airport, dozing in armchairs in the VIP lounge. At the appointed hour they embarked, only to find that there were no seats aboard the cargo plane. They were given blankets, which they spread on the hard floor, and lay down. They arrived in Amsterdam on Saturday morning and caught an El Al plane to Israel.

Peres arrived at his home on Saturday afternoon, after a journey of thirty-six hours. Only then did he learn that he was to make a speech in the Knesset on the following day, in honor of the guest. Earlier, it had not been certain that he would speak. Several cabinet ministers objected to the idea that Peres should speak, as well as Sadat and Begin.

Faced with the task of preparing his speech, Peres called Yitzhak Navon, a political ally from the Ben-Gurion days who spoke fluent Arabic, and asked him to come and help. Peres was already writing, when Navon arrived and asked, "What exactly do you want me to do?" Peres requested that he find a "suitable passage from the Koran." Navon started searching, but meanwhile, Peres finished his speech and gave it to Navon to read. "You don't need any passage from the Koran," Navon told him. "It's an excellent speech."

It was already 6:30 P.M. Peres changed quickly and set out for Ben-Gurion Airport, which was lit up and surrounded by hundreds of security men. The runway was already packed with the thousands of invited guests. Peres was taken to his place in the center of the line waiting to shake Sadat's hand.

At 7:58 P.M. the Egyptian president stepped out of the plane, and the dream of an entire generation came true.

Peres returned home late, exhausted. But, despite his fatigue—he had not slept for two days—he found it difficult to drop off. He could not forget the sight of Anwar Sadat embracing Menachem Begin.

Lying in the dark, he felt history had touched him lightly and then turned from him to lay its hand on his great political rival. All the recent small achievements suddenly seemed worthless: the victory in the Histadrut elections, the start of rehabilitation of the party were nothing, compared with the historic visit. The Likud government would be the one to sign the first peace agreement with the largest Arab nation. Now Peres, too, began to believe that the Likud would remain invincible for many years to come.

After the first excitement of the visit had died down, it gradually became clear that completing the peace process would not be a short or easy matter, and that Peres was destined to play a part in it. His first active involvement was on February 10, 1978.

By then the negotiations between Israel and Egypt had become deadlocked. The Egyptian president wanted the Israeli leader of the opposition to know the reasons and decided to make a stopover in Vienna on his way back from a trip to the United States for this purpose. The meeting between Peres and Sadat took place at the Shlosheim Castle in Salzburg.

"I don't like formality, Shimon," Sadat said, creating a friendly atmosphere. "We'll talk as friends. I'm a country boy." He went on to complain about Prime Minister Begin's refusal to compromise on the question of the Jewish settlements in Sinai, and on the "blank wall" when it came to the Palestinian question.

On a personal note, Sadat remarked that he would rather have conducted negotiations with Golda Meir than with Begin. "She is an impressive woman, and I have the greatest respect for her." He dismissed Moshe Dayan as "a showman" and expressed disappointment at his approach. At this point he asked Peres to tell him about Ben-Gurion. When Peres had finished, the Egyptian president said thoughtfully, "I could have settled everything with him; he was a man of great decisions."

As their talk ran on, Austrian Chancellor Bruno Kreisky entered and reminded them that lunch and a press conference were scheduled. As they were leaving the room, Sadat placed his hand on Peres's shoulder in a friendly manner, apparently needing to share his personal feelings with him. "You know all Egypt is free, except for me. I feel like a prisoner serving a life sentence. Wherever I go, I am surrounded by people. Chancellor Schmidt came from West Germany to visit me, and I wanted to go for a walk with him, but every step we took, hundreds of people crowded around to encourage me and take away my privacy." He did not know then that the day was not far off when some of his people would take from him much more than his privacy.

As soon as he parted from Sadat, Peres called Begin and gave him the gist of the conversation. When he returned home, he came to Begin's office in the Knesset to give him a more detailed report. Begin received him warmly.

These were to be the last smiles between Peres and Begin in meetings of this nature. From then on, all Peres's foreign trips and meetings were to be the subject of outbursts and mutual recrimination.

Peres did not remain in Israel for long. About a month after he returned from Salzburg, he set off for Bucharest at the head of the first delegation of the Israel Labor party to be invited by the Rumanian Communist party. On March 11, 1978, he met with Rumanian President Nicolae Ceausescu. Among other things, the two men exchanged philosophical ideas about the nature of regimes. Peres started this off by remarking that Europe was becoming a socialist continent, made up of democratic socialist regimes and communist ones. "Although I am not a supporter of the communist system, I see room for pluralism and cooperation as the culture of socialism strives for peace, the abolition of poverty, disarmament, and scientific and cultural cooperation."

"There is room for pluralistic cooperation and even the dismantling of blocs," Ceausescu agreed. "However, I am not as optimistic as you are regarding the situation of the Social Democrats in Europe. They have not solved their economic problems. The system known as democracy does not permit the participation of the masses in developing and running the country."

Peres returned to Israel in mid-March, and, a couple of weeks later, was ready to set off again. This next trip was not completely random, nor was it strictly necessary. There was nothing urgent for him to do abroad, but neither was there anything urgent at home, and that was the problem. Little was happening in Israel that afforded him any satisfaction. His daily rounds consisted of endless meetings with low-level party functionaries, who came to persuade him to distribute money from the party coffers, and to seek benefits for themselves and their associates. Alternatively, they sought his intervention in local disputes. When he wasn't busy with these matters, he was forced to spend his time in verbal fencing with Rabin and his supporters, who it seemed would never let him rest.

He spent most of his time in the Knesset in his capacity as head of the opposition, and that was also very difficult. Almost every time he spoke in the plenum, he became involved in verbal duels with Begin, in most cases emerging defeated, sometimes even humiliated. Begin had always been a superb public speaker; now he also had authority, and the combination was invincible. Time after time, Begin mounted the Knesset podium, and dispatched verbal slingshots at Peres, mocking him both with his words and with the tones of a first-class actor. The Knesset public galleries rewarded him with bursts of laughter. The Labor members tried to keep straight faces, but it was not easy, and sometimes laughter could also be heard from the Labor benches. Everyone could see how much Begin enjoyed these occasions, with Peres sitting only a few meters away, stumbling after Begin's rhetorical barbs.

Going abroad became a blessed escape. Begin and Rabin were not around to irritate him; he did not meet party functionaries always asking for something. There he was received with respect, and he looked forward to these respites, as a losing boxer looks forward to the bell that signals the end of the round.

At the beginning of April, he flew to the United States for a lecture tour on behalf of the United Jewish Appeal; however, as was usual with such trips, his activities were not confined to raising money. In Washington, meetings had been arranged with Vice President Walter Mondale, Secretary of State Cyrus Vance, and National Security Adviser Zbigniew Brzezinski. The talks centered on the deadlock between Israel and Egypt that was holding up the continuation of the negotiations. He was interested to note the differences in the attitudes of his American interlocutors to these matters.

Mondale and Vance tended to see both sides of the coin, and showed understanding of Israel's difficulties in Judea and Samaria. They put forward ideas with the aim of finding a middle path between Egyptian demands and Israeli positions. Brzezinski was far more outspoken, putting all his eggs in the Palestinian basket and blaming Israel for the deadlock in the negotiations. The essential problem, he said, was Israel's refusal to agree in principle to withdrawal from the West Bank. This refusal prevented Sadat from formulating a declaration of principles on the West Bank that would justify his independent initiative to the Arab world.

Peres's visit to the United States would have been routine, even tedious, if not for a phone call he received in his hotel room. "Shim, could you come to dinner?" Peres immediately recognized the warm, hoarse voice of Harry Belafonte. The famous black singer added that it would be an intimate dinner party, "so that we can talk as we want."

The two had met previously only two months earlier in Canada, when Belafonte had told Peres that he was part Jewish. His grandfather had been a German-Jewish adventurer who had roamed the world, generously distributing his blood and seed. "I am the only vestige of his visit to Jamaica," Belafonte said.

In Belafonte's apartment on Manhattan's West End Avenue, Peres entered an environment that bore witness to its owner's main interest: Africa. "Apart from large, bright paintings on the struggle for liberation, the shelves were full of attractive African statuettes. The furniture contained an Asian element, with wood and metal chairs in consummate good taste. A model of a donkey and three pioneers, which Belafonte had brought back from a visit to Israel, stood out in this decor. The only American features were the bar and the waiter in evening dress, with gleaming white gloves."

Looking around him, Peres discovered that all the other guests were black: the American ambassador to the United Nations, Andrew Young, and his wife, Belafonte's sister and her husband. Including his host, Belafonte, and his Jewish wife, Julie, a former ballerina, Peres noted that, "All six belonged to the new black aristocracy of New York—fashionably dressed, weight-conscious, widely traveled, and extremely articulate."

Young told of his visit to Israel with his wife, where they "saw the great man there on the kibbutz." (Ben-Gurion at Sde Boker.) That man, he said with a smile, had asked him if his wife was a

Yemenite, whether he had found her in Israel, and what right he had to steal her from Israel.

Belafonte suggested that Peres and Young go off for a private chat. The two of them went into a corner with their drinks, and Peres told Young that whenever he heard black music or listened to the speeches of black leaders, he found a strong biblical content in them. "The songs, 'We Shall Overcome,' and 'Let My People Go,' and the speeches of Martin Luther King, Jr., and others deeply affect me, and remind me of the words of the prophet Amos: 'Are ye not as children of the Ethiopians unto me, O children of Israel?'"

Young appeared confused, and it was not clear whether he accepted this musical analysis. In any case, it did not prevent a political discussion. Young raised the question of rule over the West Bank Arabs, and Peres explained, "To us it is a Jewish question, not just a Palestinian one. We don't want to rule a million Palestinians; we are not interested in being overlords."

At this point, Peres was both pleased and surprised to hear that Young did not consider the PLO a suitable partner for solving the problem of the West Bank. He said clearly that he did not support the PLO because of its extremist stand.

"There are moderates among them," he said, "but they are not the ones who decide policy. It's difficult to understand Jordan and Saudi Arabia. Why don't they support the Sadat initiative? I'm going to take part in a cabinet discussion in Washington on that subject. Do you think I should suggest that the United States should pressure Saudi Arabia and Jordan?" Peres definitely did think so.

At dinner other subjects were raised. Someone asked why Israel was supplying arms to Somoza. Peres replied, "At the outbreak of our War of Independence in 1948, the family of Nicaraguan dictator Anastasio Somoza helped Israel acquire arms for its defense; we can't forget that."

The question of Israel quickly became marginal as the African continent occupied center stage. The discussion heated up, with the guests all very well informed of African developments. Peres thought that Africa had the same meaning for American blacks that Israel did for the Jews. He was surprised when Young spoke with a certain warmth of the way the South treated blacks, as opposed to the northern United States. "Northern liberalism is only an intellectual performance," he stated. "In practice, the southerners were more tolerant and understanding of the blacks than the northerners."

The meal lasted over five hours, and afterward, Young offered Peres a lift back to his hotel. On the way, they talked about President Carter. Young mentioned that it was not true that he was an intimate friend of the president. "Carter is a wise man, quick on the uptake and able to absorb an amazing amount of information, but he is not the Messiah." Young added that he did not think he himself had achieved much by being appointed U.N. ambassador. "When all's said and done, I am the representative of twenty-five million blacks, who discovered that their electoral clout is worth more than anything they can get by demonstrations and riots."

In June 1978, Begin and his cabinet were very nervous. The negotiations with Egypt were deadlocked over Sadat's demand that an agreement between Egypt and Israel include a declaration of principles concerning the West Bank. Begin categorically rejected this and demanded that the two matters be treated separately. Sadat announced a suspension of negotiations and refused to meet Begin or his representatives.

At the same time, there was a continuous deterioration in the functioning of the government and the prime minister. Secrets were leaked from cabinet discussions while the meetings were still in progress; inflation soared to new heights. Persistent rumors circulated about the state of the prime minister's health, which necessitated his taking drugs that led to extreme fluctuations in his mood and judgment. A change of government was openly discussed.

Peres received a phone call from Austrian Chancellor Bruno Kreisky, who was worried about the crisis and convinced that something ought to be done about it. He felt sure that a meeting between Peres and Sadat would help matters. Was Peres prepared for him to sound out the Egyptian president? Peres gave his approval, making it clear that such a meeting required the prime minister's approval. On June 30, 1978, Peres received the news that Sadat was ready for a four-way meeting in Vienna, with the participation of Kreisky and former West German Chancellor, Willy Brandt. Peres at once called Begin's office and made an appointment to see him Saturday afternoon.

When he arrived at the prime minister's residence in Jerusalem, he found Begin in a hurry to attend a reception for Vice President Walter Mondale, who was paying an official visit to Israel. He did not have much time to talk. Peres told Begin about the Kreisky initiative. Begin gave his assent and suggested that Peres talk with Foreign Minister Moshe Dayan, in order to coordinate the stand to be presented to Sadat. Peres arranged to meet with Dayan in the Knesset on Tuesday.

Meanwhile, the news of the proposed meeting between Peres and Sadat had been leaked to the media, and there was good reason to believe that Sadat had leaked it in order to embarrass Begin. That same morning, Dayan appeared before the Knesset Foreign Affairs and Defense Committee to report on political developments. He began by severely criticizing Peres's intention to meet with Sadat. He knew that the prime minister had given his approval, but he disagreed with Begin. In his view, the meeting would devalue the conference of Egyptian and Israeli foreign ministers, which was due to take place in London at the end of July.

Peres now found himself in a situation to which he was not accustomed; he faced a direct confrontation with Moshe Dayan. He had made strenuous efforts to avoid this ever since Dayan had deserted the Labor party, but now he had no choice. Peres retorted very angrily that Israel was a free country, and he was going to meet with whomever he chose.

Two days later, on Thursday, July 6, there was another switch. Peres met again with Begin and found him hesitant and distraught. The prime minister told him that there was something in Dayan's criticism of his forthcoming meeting with Sadat. In fact, he remarked, to Peres's amazement, he had not given his consent to the meeting, because he had not thought such consent necessary. In view of the media criticism, said Begin, he intended to announce publicly that he had "not welcomed" the meeting, without discussing the question of consent. The shocked Peres said that, if the prime minister had so much as hinted at disagreement on Saturday, he would have canceled the meeting at once. But now that he had given his assent, on the basis of the prime minister's former approval, cancellation of the meeting would be seen as a very extreme step against Sadat. Begin relented and said he would not mention the matter publicly.

From the prime minister's office, Peres flew north for a tour of Druze villages in Galilee. While he was having lunch at the guest house of Kibbutz Gesher Haziv, he received a call from Begin, asking him whether, after all, he would not reconsider, as he, Begin, had to say something about it publicly. Peres realized that Begin was under heavy pressure from Dayan. Peres replied that he did not think he should cancel the trip; however, at the Labor Party Political Committee meeting that night, he would consult with his colleagues and inform Begin afterward of his decision.

The members of the political committee with whom Peres discussed the matter were also in a state of confusion, but all of them, including Golda Meir, were in favor of holding the meeting with Sadat. Yigal Allon phoned Begin, explained the committee's decision, and asked him to refrain from public declarations against the meeting because of the resultant damage to Israel's status in Europe. Begin agreed.

After the committee meeting, Peres went just before midnight to Dayan's house, where the foreign minister told him that he had already heard from Begin about the political committee's decision to cancel Peres's trip. Peres expressed his astonishment at the misunderstanding. Dayan gestured impatiently with his hand, saying: "What is Begin, and who is Begin? Did we have to waste half a day on this affair?" When he returned home, Peres called Allon, who was equally amazed at what Begin had told Dayan. He promised to call the prime minister in the morning to clarify the matter.

After three hours' sleep, Peres set off for Ben-Gurion Airport, from where he flew directly to Vienna. In the plane, he told Micha Harish, his political aide who was accompanying him, that they had not arranged for a car in Vienna and would have to make arrangements to rent one. When the plane landed, however, Peres was welcomed like a head of state; a convoy of motorcycles, dozens of bodyguards, and two helicopters accompanied him wherever he went.

On Sunday, July 9, 1978, at 11:30 A.M., Sadat, Kreisky, Brandt, and Peres met in the Austrian chancellor's office. The four sat down in soft leather armchairs under a large Viennese chandelier in the hall where the famous Congress of Vienna had once taken place. As the four exchanged small talk, reporters and photographers buzzed around them like bees. When the media men left, the talks began. When the time came for discussion of Middle East affairs, Kreisky suggested that he and Brandt withdraw, leaving Sadat and Peres alone, but their curiosity must have gotten the better of them, and the two European leaders remained for that part of the discussion.

Sadat said that he had received a letter from President Carter asking him to meet Dayan. He had refused, he said, because he did not trust Dayan. Neither did he see any point in a meeting with Begin because he was a figure of the old generation, and it was difficult to make progress with him. Even though Peres did not in his heart of hearts disagree with these assessments, he felt he had to defend the two in such a forum. He reminded Sadat that Dayan was the architect of the "Open Bridges" policy that permitted free travel between the West Bank and Jordan and that Begin had made wide-ranging concessions regarding Sinai and in his autonomy program for the West Bank.

At 2:00 P.M., the four of them emerged for a news conference and lunch. At 5:00 P.M., Peres and Sadat met at the Imperial Hotel, where the Egyptian president was staying, to continue their discussion. Sadat started by praising Peres. "I trust you completely. You have proved that you conduct yourself as a responsible man and a statesman. I am sure that with you, Shimon, I could reach an agreement about everything. When you said at the news conference that government and opposition are a parliamentary matter, but that you are one people, I almost burst out and shouted, 'Bravo, Shimon, bravo, that is the way to talk!'"

Sadat then spoke at length about his doubts before his journey to Jerusalem, and of his difficulties since with Begin and Dayan. In view of the fact that there was no solution in sight, he was considering resigning from the presidency in September (1978). He constantly thought of retirement. He spoke nostalgically about his predecessor, President Nasser, whom he described as a man who found it difficult to make decisions.

Peres wanted to know how Sadat arrived at decisions. Sadat replied that he had to think on his own, "a habit from prison, from the cell in which the British shut me up." Even when his wife was around, he found it difficult to think, although he was very much a family man. His wife, he told Peres, had a Christian mother who had lived with them until she died. When he traveled abroad, he would bring her a crucifix. He never concealed it. People of all religions could live in peace, he emphasized.

Toward the end of their discussion, Peres showed Sadat the

draft of a declaration that he had prepared for the International, which Brandt and Kreisky had already approved. Sadat clapped his hands, summoning his personal aide, who brought him his reading glasses. Peres noticed that he was having difficulty with the first clause, which called for the renewal of the negotiations that had been broken off in January. It spoke of "renewing contacts." Peres suggested instead, "renewing the Sadat initiative," and Sadat approved the clause.

(It is interesting to compare the Vienna document with the Camp David Accords. Regarding the borders that would be determined in the framework of a peace agreement, Sadat agreed in Vienna to "secure borders according to U.N. Security Council Resolutions 242 and 338." At Camp David, he secured from Begin agreement to "complete withdrawal to the international border." With regard to the Palestinians, the Vienna document says that, "in order to find a solution to their problem, the parties must recognize the Palestinians' right to participate in the determination of their future by negotiations with their elected representatives." At Camp David, Begin signed an agreement that included explicit recognition of "the legitimate rights of the Palestinians.")

Peres flew to London, where meetings had been arranged with Prime Minister James Callaghan and Foreign Minister David Owen; however, Peres was not the only foreign guest meeting these personalities. King Hussein was also on a visit to London. The idea of a meeting between Peres and Hussein was raised by Callaghan. He had received a message about it from former King Constantine of Greece, who was living in exile in London. According to the message, Hussein was interested in renewing the dialogue that had begun when Peres was defense minister. Peres asked Callaghan to check with Hussein about whether they could discuss shared rule in the West Bank or territorial compromise. Otherwise, he said, there was no point in a meeting. A few hours later, Callaghan called to say, "Hussein says that he is prepared to talk about shared administration for a transition period."

Peres called Labor Party Secretary Haim Bar-Lev and told him to report to Begin on these developments and to ask him what he thought of Peres's meeting Hussein, emphasizing that the matter must be kept completely secret. Bar-Lev did as he had been requested, and returned Peres's call: "Begin is against it." The prime minister would explain his reasons when Peres returned to Israel.

Peres informed Callaghan regretfully that, under the circumstances, he could not meet with Hussein.

He did, however, have a meeting with another Arab king. From London, Peres flew to Paris, and then disappeared for forty-eight hours. Curious journalists were informed that he was taking a quiet vacation in a secret hideaway. In fact, Peres spent those days, July 17 and 18, 1978, at the palace of Morocco's King Hassan in Rabat. The two of them had long conversations about the crisis in the negotiations between Israel and Egypt, Sadat's status in the Arab world, relations between the great powers, and many other subjects—nothing to justify the hysteria that burst forth as soon as Peres returned to Israel on Tuesday, July 18.

As soon as he arrived at the airport, Peres called Begin at home to arrange a meeting so that he could report. It was set for the following day at the prime minister's office in the Knesset. Before the meeting Begin spoke in the plenum, opening a political debate. When he reached the subject of Judea and Samaria, Begin became frenzied. He seized a piece of paper, tore it in two, and cried, "Behold: this is territorial compromise!" He then went on to say that during the Vienna meeting, Peres had not asked Sadat whether he agreed to territorial compromise. Peres interjected that Begin had not yet heard his report, that in point of fact he had put the question to Sadat, who had replied (that it was a subject for discussion). Begin ignored Peres's remarks, and continued to criticize his conduct.

When he finished his speech, Begin descended from the podium, strode toward Peres, smiled as if nothing had happened, and asked, "Shall we have lunch together?" They went into the Knesset members' dining room, which was crowded with people, and sat down at a central table.

After they had given their orders, Peres asked Begin if he could speak on the assumption that "nothing will get out." With an expansive gesture, Begin replied, "Certainly. I won't tell anyone—not even my wife." Peres started reporting on his talks with Sadat and King Hassan. From time to time Begin rose to shake hands with acquaintances. Each time he sat down, he apologized, "Please understand, I have to do this. When you were in power, you also did it."

Peres asked the prime minister why he had vetoed his meeting with King Hussein. Begin replied that Hussein had refused to meet representatives of the government. "How can he refuse to meet with us and meet with you? Ben-Gurion would not have permitted it either."

That evening Begin sat in the Knesset members' dining room with a group of Knesset members from his party. He was in a buoyant mood, shouting and joking to the loud laughter of his admirers. There is general agreement about what was said at this boisterous gathering, but disagreement about one outburst. A witness said afterward: "Begin started talking about Peres's trip. To the surprise of those present, he disclosed that Peres had visited Morocco, adding, 'With me he won't see as much as an earlobe of Morocco-Shmorocco again, just as I did not let him see Hussein.'" Then, according to the witness, he spat out the word, "*khoi!*" (Russian for penis).

At the time, the rumors were multiplying about the medication Begin was receiving and its effect on his behavior. In view of these rumors, Peres, when he heard about the incident, did not want to make anything of it. But Knesset Member Yossi Sarid told the prime minister's associates what he thought of Begin's behavior.

After midnight, the Knesset was still full of members, waiting for the end of the political debate. Peres was in the members' dining room when suddenly Begin strode up to him. In a tone of great excitement, Begin demanded to know whether he had heard him use the word *khoi*. Peres replied that he had not heard it himself, but others said they had heard it. Begin claimed forcefully that he had said no such thing. Peres then asked him why he had spoken in public about his visit to Morocco and the cancellation of his meeting with Hussein, after promising that it would remain confidential. Begin was embarrassed. He did not deny it; he simply said, tiredly, "I am sorry." Peres looked at him in consternation. What was happening to this man? He was surprised to discover that he felt pity rather than hatred for his great rival—pity for the man and great concern that he was guiding the affairs of the nation.

The deadlock in the negotiations continued, and in an attempt to break it, U.S. Secretary of State Cyrus Vance planned a mediation mission to Cairo and Jerusalem in August 1978.

Vance's mediation did not produce the hoped-for results, and the negotiations between Israel and Egypt continued to limp along. At this point, President Carter decided to throw the whole weight of his prestige into the balance by inviting the leaders of Israel and Egypt to a conference at Camp David, at the beginning of September 1978.

The discussions at Camp David were difficult, with many ups and downs, but on September 19, 1978, the three leaders appeared before a specially invited audience and the television cameras and signed the Camp David Accords, which were to be the basis for a peace treaty between Israel and Egypt, to be signed within three months.

The Israeli public initially reacted with emotion and unrestrained jubilation, but within a few days this cooled down somewhat as it became clear that a heavy price had been paid. Especially painful was the need to dismantle the Jewish settlements in Sinai. Many saw this concession as a betrayal of Zionist principles and treachery toward the settlers, who had built their homes, with the help and encouragement of the government.

Before the Knesset debate on the Camp David Accords, the Labor Party Central Committee met to discuss the party's position. The atmosphere was tense. Yigal Allon led the group opposed to dismantling the settlements. He proposed that the central committee demand separating the vote on this from the vote on the accords themselves. Peres saw this and similar suggestions as futile parliamentary maneuvers. He agreed with Allon and those like him that Begin had paid too heavy a price, and he strongly criticized him for it; but he insisted that the Camp David Accords were a single package, and the party had to decide for or against them.

"The choice is not between a good agreement and a bad agreement," he pointed out. "The choice is between the chance for peace and returning to the state of war." It was a fateful hour, he said, "and the party must not stutter; it must say yes, seriously and unambiguously." After a stormy discussion, Peres's stand was adopted by a large majority. The Labor Party voted in the Knesset in favor of the Camp David Accords.

The time frame resolved at Camp David for signing the peace treaty was not adhered to. Four extra months were needed to overcome the obstacles that appeared during the negotiations; however, by March 1978, all the parties were able to welcome the completion of the process. The signing of the peace treaty was scheduled for March 27, 1979, in Washington.

Peres arrived in the U.S. capital in a parliamentary delegation that accompanied the prime minister to the signing ceremony. The military aircraft that took them made a stopover in New York to pick up the prime minister, who had gone on ahead. It was then that Yehiel Kadishai, the head of the prime minister's office, told Peres that Sadat wanted to meet him in Washington for a private talk.

Peres found Sadat slimmer than ever, suntanned and in an exceptionally good mood. After exchanging compliments, Sadat made some comments about his contacts with Begin. Yesterday they had met privately, he told Peres, and Begin had asked him why he had refused to come to Jerusalem to sign the treaty and why he hadn't invited the prime minister to Cairo. He had, after all, promised Carter that he would. Sadat said that he had been ready to come, but on that same morning, Begin had appeared on television and announced, "Sadat will come to Jerusalem, to the undivided capital of Israel, to the eternal capital of Israel." What was he up to? asked Sadat. "Doesn't he have any understanding of psychology? Couldn't he simply have said, 'Sadat is coming to Jerusalem, period'?"

With regard to Begin coming to Cairo, Sadat explained to Peres that he had told Begin he had created a bad image of himself in Arab eyes. Begin had asked him why this was, and Sadat had replied, "Too many speeches." Afterward, Begin had complained to Sadat about his meetings with Peres. The Egyptian president said he had replied, "Every time that Shimon and I are in the same place at the same time, we will meet!"

But Begin was not the only one about whom Sadat had complaints. "Arafat, that big liar, that boaster! Let him go crazy if he wants to. You don't have to pay him any attention. Even if there is a Palestinian state, he won't be its leader."

He displayed much greater tolerance for Knesset Member Geula Cohen, one of the fiercest opponents of the peace treaty. "I like her—she has feminine charm, and beautiful eyes." With a wink, he added, "She described someone as a dictator, a Nazi general. She was surely talking about me." And he burst out laughing.

Dayan continued to cause him uneasiness. "Did you see Dayan on American television this morning? He is a strange man. Why is he so pessimistic? Will he try to return to the Labor party? Will you accept him back? That man can spoil lots of things!" At the end of the meeting, Sadat escorted Peres to the door, parting from him with a warm handshake and an invitation to visit Cairo.

On the day of the signing, Peres lunched with Henry Kissinger. "Sadat is a great admirer of yours," the former secretary of state told him, then went on to criticize Begin's autonomy plan for the inhabitants of Judea and Samaria. "What do you need it for? It means a return to the 1967 borders, sooner or later."

Kissinger thought that Begin had conducted the negotiations with Egypt in an amateurish manner, without sufficient planning. "Why did he put forward his own proposals? Sadat had to reject them, if only for the reason that they were Israeli proposals. Begin should have told Sadat: 'You did a brave thing in coming to Jerusalem. Well done. Now, what do you suggest?'"

Begin's strategy with the United States also seemed strange and misguided to Kissinger. He said that Begin had neglected to say one good word about the Republicans. He told Peres about a visit paid to him by Howard Baker, the Senate Republican minority leader, and a very powerful man. Baker had complained, "I spoke in favor of Israel three times in the past two weeks. The Israelis are always coming to me in the Senate. Now I see that the president gets all the praise and no one else. I'll remember that when the Israelis come to me next time."

Kissinger summed up with a sigh. "Every time Begin appears on television, he decreases the number of supporters of Israel."

Leadership Under Siege

The historic political achievement did not disperse the heavy clouds that increasingly darkened the skies over the Likud government. Inflation continued to soar; quarrels between the Likud ministers increased in frequency and sharpness; the image and authority of the prime minister suffered unbelievable erosion, and rumors about his inability to function spread. The Labor party was no longer talked about by its members or its opponents as doomed to be the opposition for many years. Its ratings in public opinion polls improved continuously, and the way seemed open for a return to power after only one term in opposition.

Peres's meetings with world leaders strengthened his prestige as a statesman. His appearances in the Knesset, with their strong challenge to the government, afforded him an unassailable position as leader of the opposition. The party had finished paying its debts and now had a firm economic basis. During 1978, officeholders had been elected to their positions without any personal or factional tension. Peres started to believe that after several years of hard work and effort, he had at last won the right to some rest and relaxation, and that the only contest ahead was for the national leadership.

It was a grave error on his part. Paradoxically, it was his very success and the improved standing of the party that brought him trouble. Now there was something worth fighting for—the big prize was not just the leadership of the opposition but the premiership itself. The "slave" had done his job and had rehabilitated the party; now there were those who wanted to see him go.

The actual challenge to his leadership came in a very unorthodox way. It had been known for several months that Yitzhak Rabin was writing his memoirs, and it was also known that Peres was not likely to enjoy reading them; but the reality was worse than the darkest predictions.

On August 8, Israel Television broadcast extracts from Rabin's book on its regular 9:00 P.M. news. They fell on Peres like stones from a siege catapult. The former prime minister accused the former defense minister of every sin imaginable, and attributed to him every negative character trait known to man. He charged that Peres had intrigued against him throughout his premiership, that he had leaked state secrets, that he was untrustworthy, unfit to be defense minister, and certainly was not fit to be prime minister. Rabin said he would never serve in a government headed by Peres. The most remarkable thing of all was that not one of the charges was backed by any proof, or even an attempt at proof.

The Labor party was stunned by the publication. There was a feeling that a "Pandora's box" had been opened, just when the Likud government was starting to go downhill.

On July 12, 1979, the party executive committee met to discuss the book in an atmosphere of great tension. One after the other, former ministers of the Rabin government spoke, all of them criticizing the book as expressing a subjective opinion and not the objective truth. They asked Rabin numerous questions to which he did not have the answers. If Peres was so worthless, why had he made him his replacement after the scandal over his wife's foreign bank account? Why had he agreed to run for the Knesset on a list headed by Peres? Typical of the general feeling was the remark of former Justice Minister Haim Zadok: "This book harms Yitzhak Rabin's credibility and his judgment. The author was unbalanced by his personal animosity."

The general feeling was that the meeting should be wound up with a resolution condemning Rabin and his book, but Peres decided to refrain from this. "I have no resolution to present," he said. "The conclusion is, in fact, the things that were said here and the confidence in me on the part of all the members."

Peres's friends and supporters were downcast. His moderation seemed to them soft-headed. "He cannot make decisions," they said. "He hesitates and compromises too much." Were they right? Certainly, when Peres had predicted that the book would boomerang on its author, he was right, but only partly so. He was right as regards the party. Even when he was prime minister, Rabin had not understood the political system and the feelings of those who ran it. They could support one candidate or another, but they would never excuse a public assault on the party and its leader. Dirty laundry must be washed behind closed doors.

Peres was wrong, though, about public opinion in general, and his mistake was extremely damaging. Because of his weak response, Rabin's version of events was accepted by many, and the accusations against Peres took root. Rabin took on the image of a victim; Peres, of an intriguer and saboteur.

Meanwhile, Yigal Allon, the former foreign minister, was energetically pursuing his "noncandidacy" for the party leadership. The drop in Peres's popularity gave him a serious advantage. A strange thing happened: although Allon had been in politics for thirty years, he became the symbol of freshness, idealism, and integrity.

During this period Peres was extremely depressed. One Friday night he saw an astrologer on television predicting that Yigal Allon would be Israel's next prime minister. Normally, Peres would not have attributed any importance to such a thing, but these were not normal times. When it was suggested he should see an astrologer, he agreed. Ilan Pecker, a well-known Israeli astrologer, came from Jerusalem to Peres's Tel Aviv office late one night, and in secret. The two remained closeted for an hour and a half, and Peres emerged slightly encouraged, but not for long.

Allon went ahead and announced his official bid for the leadership, but less than two weeks later, on Thursday, February 2, 1980, he suffered a fatal heart attack.

With the death of Yigal Allon, Ahdudt Ha'avoda, and its Kibbutz Hameuhad movement, were left without a leader. Although many of the younger members felt that the imperative of the hour was to unite under Peres, the movement's leaders had other ideas. They were concerned that, without a leader, and without a contest, they would lose their strength in the party and be dominated by the former Mapai and Rafi factions.

Many of the kibbutz members were not too happy with Rabin as their flag-bearer because he was essentially an alien element, but he was available and more than ready to carry their standard. And then something else happened. A public opinion poll taken in January, when Allon was still alive, had shown the following scale of popularity: Peres, 18 percent; Allon, 8 percent; Rabin, 5 percent. But immediately after Allon's death, there was a dramatic increase in Rabin's popularity. Although Peres's position remained stable, Rabin soared to 18 percent in March, 22 percent in April, and 27 percent in June, and continued to rise.

There were two explanations offered for this phenomenon. First, the popularity that Allon had accumulated, and which reached a peak with his death, was transferred to Rabin. Second, Rabin added to it with his periodic television appearances, where he looked perplexed, spoke hesitantly, and came across as decent and credible, compared to the polished, professional performance of Shimon Peres, who projected the image of a smooth politician. As opposed to Peres, who constantly attacked the government, Rabin seemed moderate, objective, responsible, and honest. Whatever the reason, Peres had to face the hard fact that Rabin was back, and he was very popular—more popular than Shimon Peres.

The party was appalled at the prospect of yet another confrontation between the two of them. Conciliation attempts got under way, but Peres took the position that, before any dialogue, Rabin must publicly repudiate the things he had written in his book. Rabin did backtrack, to a certain extent. He announced that he no longer ruled out the possibility of serving under Peres, or vice versa, but when he was asked about his book, he replied that he did not retract a single word.

As in the case of Allon, Peres sought ways of heading off a contest. He was armed with the central committee decision, declaring that he was the party's candidate for prime minister, but the validity of this decision was due to expire as soon as the convention was held in December 1980. (It had been postponed, due to Allon's death.) The only thing that could put off the convention was the fall of the government and early elections.

Peres tried for this in a series of meetings with leaders of the National Religious Party (NRP). The prospect became more likely when Yigael Yadin's Democratic Movement for Change (DMC) split, and the government lost six of its Knesset votes as a result. In one of the meetings, NRP leader Yosef Burg made an interesting suggestion. Noting that there was no certainty that the government could survive, and bearing in mind that the Labor party did not want to join Begin's coalition, he asked whether Labor would consider joining a government headed by himself.

There were other meetings at which the NRP asked Peres to help secure the postponement of the election of the chief rabbis to enable the party to ensure the reappointment of its own candidates. Overcoming strong opposition in his own party, Peres delivered the votes; but the NRP did not help him bring down the government.

Nevertheless, Peres persisted. Moshe Dayan and Ezer Weizman resigned, and a number of Knesset members crossed the floor. It was clear that the government's survival hung by a thread.

In April 1980, Peres was due to go to the United States for a lecture tour. On previous visits he had met with senior administration officials, and some weeks before this trip, President Carter's special ambassador, Saul Linowitz, broached the possibility of a meeting with the president. It was an unusual idea, for it was very rare for a U.S. president to meet with the leader of the Israeli opposition. This time the president decided to do the unconventional thing, and he announced his intention to meet with Peres.

The meeting was scheduled for Thursday, April 24, 1980. Such meetings are normally attended by the Israeli ambassador, but the day before the meeting, Ambassador Ephraim Evron received instructions from the Foreign Ministry in Jerusalem that he should not accompany Peres. Instead, Counselor Ya'acov Nehushtan, the number-two man in the embassy and a Likud man, should go along. The purpose of this move was twofold: first, to detract from the importance of the meeting; second, to receive a report of the conversation from a person acceptable to the government. Peres's first reaction was to dispense with an escort altogether. Evron passed on the message to Jerusalem, and was told that if Peres wished it so, he could go to the president on his own. At 5:00 A.M., Evron was awakened by a phone call. Foreign Minister Shamir told him that it had been decided he could accompany Peres.

When they arrived at the White House, they discovered that there had been no need to disturb Evron's sleep. The president asked that the discussion be a private one, and Evron waited outside with Vice President Mondale. Very little was said about the progress of relations with Egypt. Most of the talk was devoted to Jordan, with Carter expressing an interest in Peres's views on the possibility of Jordan's joining the peace process. The president proved to be well informed on internal developments in Israel, and assumed that the Labor party would return to power. "Will you form a coalition with Yosef Burg, Ezer Weizman, and Moshe Dayan?" he asked. Peres replied that he did not think it possible or desirable to form any coalitions before the election.

The president only spoke of the forthcoming elections in the United States obliquely, but his intention was clear. He did not decide the composition of the Israeli government, he said, and he "assumed" that Israel did not want to interfere in the electoral process in the United States. In case he did not understand, the vice president, whom Peres saw later, was far more outspoken.

"You know the record of this administration on Israel," he said. "You know that we are sensitive to Israel's security needs, and that we are opposed to a Palestinian state and to the PLO." In view of this, he said, the White House was disappointed with the vote in New York. (He was referring to the New York primary, where Senator Edward Kennedy had defeated Carter.) Although there were some places where the Jews had voted for Carter, the New York vote had been a clear demonstration against him. Mondale expressed confidence that Carter would be elected for another term as president, and if this was the case, what was the point of the Jews voting against him? The vice president hastened to add that he was not asking Israel to do anything specific; he simply wanted to make the president's feelings clear. "He is human, after all; don't forget that."

In July 1980, it became clear that the confrontation between

Rabin and Peres was not only affecting the Labor party, it also had an influence on political decisions of national and international importance.

The Knesset was considering a private member's bill proposed by Knesset member Geula Cohen, of the right-wing Tehiya faction, which would declare that the united city of Jerusalem was the capital of Israel. From a legal point of view, there was nothing new in her draft law. Israeli sovereignty had been extended to all of Jerusalem shortly after it was unified in the Six-Day War of 1967. The significance of the proposed measure was political. In view of the fact that President Sadat had raised the question of Jerusalem's future, the proposers of the law intended to confirm this established fact.

As the law was about to be presented for final approval, the Israeli government found itself under considerable pressure. The United States warned that the passage of the law would disrupt the peace process. Other nations announced that if the law were passed, they would move their embassies from Jerusalem to Tel Aviv. World opinion was united against the law—friends as well as enemies. Begin announced his support for the measure, but, as it was such a fundamental issue, he said he would only vote for it if it was clear that a wide consensus existed. In other words, he was passing the ball to Labor's court.

It was a difficult dilemma. On the one hand, there was no doubt about the dire international consequences of passing the law. On the other hand, how was it possible to vote against united Jerusalem as the capital of Israel?

In point of fact, the bill could have been voted down if the Labor leadership had been strong and united, but Peres was not a strong leader at that time. His leadership was being eroded every hour of the day by Rabin and his supporters. He could not permit himself— or thought that he could not—an unpopular move such as voting against the proposed law. Consequently, the Labor party voted in favor of the bill, and the Knesset passed it by a large majority. The reactions were even more serious than the most pessimistic forecasts. Of the eleven foreign embassies that had been in Jerusalem, only one remained; the others all moved to Tel Aviv.

On October 10, Rabin took his long-anticipated step. He wrote to Peres, "I wish to inform you that I intend to put forward my

candidacy, at the third convention of the Labor party, for party
chairman and candidate for the premiership of the government to be
formed after the elections for the tenth Knesset." The letter was a
long one, replete with acceptable party expressions. Peres fired off
a one-sentence reply: "I hereby acknowledge receipt of your letter."
That evening, Knesset member Adi Amora'i called Peres and told
him in French: "*La guerre comme la guerre.*" (It means war.)

And it was war. The contest bore no resemblance whatsoever
to the previous one with Allon—not in style, nor in aim. As the
convention neared, the tension increased. It reached a peak on
Saturday, November 22, when Peres's close aide, Yossi Beilin,
learned that Yitzhak Rabin was due to give a news conference that
evening about some libel action. He told Peres, who asked for more
details. Toward evening, Beilin received a fuller picture.

That day the French journal, *L'Express,* had published a story
linking Rabin with Betzalel Mizrahi, a Tel Aviv building contractor,
whose name had been mentioned in connection with the underworld.
The story claimed that Mizrahi had given Rabin a loan to pay the fine
levied on Leah Rabin in 1977 for holding an illegal bank account in the
United States. It further alleged that Peres had a photocopy of the
check that Mizrahi had given Rabin.

Peres and his aides were in shock. The item in the French
magazine appeared only three days before the Labor party branches
were due to elect their delegates to the convention. The obvious
conclusion was that Peres and his people had leaked the story to
discredit Rabin in advance of the elections. There was something
curious about the publication of the item just then, and in a French
publication, at that. The rumor had been current in Israel for several
months. Several hundred people knew about it, and several papers
had considered publishing it, but had eventually decided not to do so
for lack of proof. The question of who had leaked it was therefore
irrelevant. There was nothing to leak. The story had been going
around Israel, and nobody was interested in it.

But Rabin, using the right tactics, from his point of view, made
it very relevant indeed, as he tried to squeeze maximum political
value out of the affair. His first action was to call a news conference
for eight o'clock Saturday evening.

Rabin categorically denied the story in *L'Express,* characterizing
it as a gross libel. He was asked who he thought had given the story

to the French journal. Rabin did not name names, but used expressions such as, "it's not difficult to guess," and "certainly not someone interested in my welfare."

That night Peres issued a statement condemning the publication in *L'Express* and denying that he had any check in his possession. In response to this, Rabin demanded that Peres sign an affidavit to enable him to prove he had paid the fine out of his own pocket. Meeting with the editors of daily newspapers, Rabin displayed a photocopy of a check for 250,000 Israeli pounds made out to the Tel Aviv District Court and signed by his wife, Leah. His appearance before the editors was emotional. "I am simply ashamed that I have to go into all these details," he said. But the shame did not prevent him, even in this forum, from telling half truths that bordered on outright lies.

How had he in fact paid the fine? Rabin was asked. He replied that he had received two loans. One, from a relative, was for 70,000 Israeli pounds, and he had paid it back the same year. The second loan was more curious. It was from an American friend named Norman Bernstein—an interest-free loan for $10,000, which he had not yet paid back. He displayed his bank statement from the Ramat Aviv branch of Bank Hapoalim, which showed an overdraft. The impression was of a man in financial difficulties because of having to pay the fine.

A few days later, the truth emerged. The account that Rabin had shown the editors was not his only account in that branch. He also had a foreign currency account with $73,000 in it. Why had Rabin showed the editors only part of the picture? Why hadn't he repaid Norman Bernstein the $10,000 out of the $73,000? Why had he received an interest-free $10,000 loan from Bernstein in the first place? There were reporters who wanted to ask these questions, but their editors vetoed it. The matter of the second (dollar) account was also not published. There was general feeling that the story in *L'Express* had been injurious to Rabin, and that further revelations could be construed as persecution. The questions remained unanswered.

The matter had died down by the time of the party branch elections, which showed the highest turnout of voters the party had ever known. When the results came in, it was clear that Peres had scored a victory, although there were differences of opinion as to how large it was, as not all the delegates elected to the convention were clearly identified with one camp or another.

On election night at the convention it became clear that the victory was greater than expected. Peres had broken the 70 percent barrier: 71.12 percent to 28.88—the biggest majority in the history of the Labor party.

Peres ascended the platform to a thunderous standing ovation. After a few introductory remarks, he announced his intention to shake hands with Rabin, who was sitting nearby, and advanced with his hand outstretched. The television cameras zoomed in on Rabin's face. He looked like a wounded beast who knows that the hunters have closed in on him. He grimaced and looked sideways, seeking a way of escape, but there wasn't one. He rose, stuck out his hand, and sat down quickly, his face pale and depressed. The gesture set the delegates alight. They cheered, clapped, and stamped their feet. For a moment they were in love with themselves, their party, and their leaders.

That evening, Peres's friends came to his home on the eighth floor of an apartment block in Ramat Aviv. When Gad Ya'acobi arrived, he went up to Peres with a broad smile on his face. "I haven't come to congratulate you," he told him, "but to congratulate Sonia." Peres looked surprised. "I saw a notice in the entrance that she had been elected to the neighborhood committee."

Mira Avrech, the newspaper columnist, took from the bar a bottle of Napoleon Armagnac, which Peres particularly liked. She had brought it to him as a present from one of her trips abroad. They had decided to open it on victory night. She went up to Peres with the bottle: "Now we can open it." Peres took the bottle and returned it to its place. "Not yet," he said. "This is not the victory."

Now the struggle with Menachem Begin began; however, as it got under way, the word "struggle" seemed exaggerated. In one corner stood Shimon Peres, victorious and self-confident, at the head of a party that all the polls indicated would win an overwhelming victory. In the other corner stood Menachem Begin, ill, depressed, alienated, at the head of a disintegrating government riddled with leaks and internal squabbles. The party he led was in despair, its members accepting the inevitability of an electoral rout.

Begin's appearance during those days aroused pity. When he came to the Knesset, he seemed to sit gazing into space, his face disconsolate, as if he hadn't the slightest interest in what was going on around him. He appeared to be waiting for the political demise that would put him out of his misery. After futile efforts to save his government, Begin came to the conclusion that there was no way of avoiding early elections. On February 19, the Knesset approved, by a large majority, advancing the elections from November to June 30, 1981.

It had been the resignation of Finance Minister Yigael Hurvitz that caused the government to fall. His resignation also initiated one of the strangest and most dramatic political developments that had ever occurred in an Israeli election campaign—the Likud rose from the dead, and with it Menachem Begin.

The reason for the dramatic transformation was the replacement of Hurvitz as finance minister by Yoram Aridor, a man in his early forties—a trained jurist with a minimal background in economics. But what he lacked in economic experience, Aridor made up for in insolence and daring. As soon as he received the appointment, long before he had time to assimilate the complex background information, he turned the economic policy of his predecessor on its head.

No more the tight fist. No more, "I haven't got the money." No more demands for belt-tightening. All that was over; the days of candy had arrived.

The government embarked on a policy of unprecdented price reductions, as customs and purchase taxes were slashed. On cars, color television sets, and air conditioners, Aridor cut prices by 30 percent, and even 40 percent. An orgy of buying ensued. In the stores, the shelves groaned under the weight of the goods.

It was without any doubt a most irresponsible and shameless squandering of the nation's resources for electoral purposes, but it worked even better than Aridor had predicted. The public was delighted—more, it was grateful. Gradually, three and a half years of soaring inflation and unsuccessful economic policy were forgotten.

The Labor party was taken by surprise and was unprepared to deal with this challenge. In fact, it was caught in a trap. Its reaction focused on the drastic effects of this policy after the elections. However, after the years of constant price rises, the public did not want to hear criticism of the new policy. The public also got the message that if Labor won the election, the party would be over.

With the polls going more and more the Likud's way, Peres had to fulfill an obligation that he had undertaken in the days when his path to power had seemed smooth and assured. In the middle of March, he was scheduled to go to Geneva to open the United Jewish Appeal campaign. A few days before his departure, he received a phone call from his friend, Jean Friedman, in Paris. A messenger had come from King Hassan of Morocco, said Friedman, and asked Peres to pop over for a visit during his European trip.

Peres left for Geneva, as planned, on March 16. After fulfilling his obligation to the fund-raisers, he returned to his hotel, where a phone call from London was waiting for him. On the line was Lord Sieff, one of the owners of the Marks and Spencer chain store and a leader of the British Jewish community. He told Peres that King Hussein's brother was in London and had suggested that they dine together. Peres was sure that Sieff meant Crown Prince Hassan of Jordan, and he accepted at once.

The meeting took place the following day in Sieff's house. Four people sat down to dinner: Peres, Sieff, Al Schwimmer, and the brother of King Hussein. Peres could not take his eyes off the king's brother. He seemed about thirty-five to forty, portly, with a neatly trimmed mustache. The more Peres looked, the more he felt a nagging doubt. He had met King Hussein several times, and the man opposite bore a distinct resemblance to him. He had never met Crown Prince Hassan, but he had seen plenty of pictures of him, and this man, introduced as Hussein's brother, did not resemble Hassan! Peres felt that something very strange was going on.

The riddle was solved later in the conversation. It was not Crown Prince Hassan, but Muhammad, Hussein's other brother, who was not well known outside Jordan. So Peres found himself in the shoes of King Saul, who searched for the kingdom and found the asses instead.

The next day Peres was off to Morocco, where he was told by King Hassan that, if he was elected prime minister, Hassan would invite him publicly and officially to Morocco, inaugurating a new era in relations between the two countries. Peres hastened to ask whether this was "a royal undertaking." The king answered affirmatively. When it actually happened—several years later than either of them had anticipated—the king would keep his promise.

Defeat

Peres returned to a very different reception from the former subjects of King Hassan of Morocco, and it illustrated the transformation that had occurred in public opinion in Israel. On April 6, Peres came to deliver greetings to a crowd of former immigrants from Morocco, who were celebrating their traditional Maimona Festival in Jerusalem's Sacher Park. Prime Minister Menachem Begin also attended the festival. When Begin appeared on the platform, he was received with enthusiasm bordering on ecstasy. When it was Peres's turn to speak, he was met with a shower of tomatoes, and he had to leave the platform without delivering his greeting.

The following day, the Histadrut Labor Federation held its elections. A few months earlier, no one had had any doubt that the country's workers and wage earners would punish the Likud for the inflation and continuously rocketing prices. Everyone expected an overwhelming victory for Labor. Labor did in fact gain ground, and increased the decisive majority it had always had in the Histadrut, but despite this, it could not be considered a great victory. Before the election, Likud leaders had said they would be satisfied to win 20 percent of the votes. In fact, they scored 26 percent.

On the night the results were announced, Begin underwent a transformation that he himself described as a "resurrection." All at once it dawned on him that all was not yet lost, and this affected him the way spinach affects Popeye the sailor. His political muscles started to bulge, his chest expanded, despair gave way to euphoria, and he mounted a charge against his enemies with fire and wrath.

It was a medical and political miracle: his lethargy, depression, and apathy vanished, as if he had never suffered a heart attack and a stroke. The more he worked—and particularly, the more speeches he made—the more his vitality increased.

The immediate outcome of this revitalization was the missile crisis in Lebanon, which resulted from the order Begin gave the IDF to shoot down two Syrian helicopters that were on their way to attack Christian forces. This action departed from the unwritten status quo that had existed for years between Israel and Syria with regard to

Lebanon. Damascus reacted with its own departure from the status quo: the stationing of ground-to-air missile batteries near Beirut. Begin strongly demanded the immediate removal of the missiles. If the Syrians did not remove them voluntarily, he warned, the Israeli air force would destroy them.

The situation rapidly deteriorated to the brink of war. This development did not escape the notice of President Reagan, who dispatched Special Ambassador Philip Habib to mediate between the two sides. The crisis dominated the headlines and became the main issue of the election campaign. Peres strongly criticized the decision to shoot down the Syrian helicopter. Begin responded that Israel was committed to the security of the Christians in Lebanon. Peres and Rabin both pointed out that this commitment had been expressed over the years only by giving assistance to the Christians. Extending the obligation to active military intervention meant that Israel would find itself forced to react according to Christian moves, even when they were contrary to Israeli interests.

In the Knesset debate on the affair, Peres refuted Begin's claim that there was a national consensus regarding the crisis. He sharply criticized Begin's boastful declarations, which he said aggravated the problem. "It is out of the question to put the fate of the nation in the hands of a person whose mood fluctuates so violently from unrestrained and complete euphoria to the deepest depression."

However, much of the public liked the euphoric declarations, and Begin started to dole them out in large portions. He used his rhetorical talent to lash out at anyone in his path. The pro-Palestinian statements of West German Chancellor Helmut Schmidt and French President Valery Giscard D'Estaing brought a sharp oratorical retort from Begin. "Those who speak like Schmidt and Giscard are consumed with greed. They only see two things: how to sell arms dearly, and how to buy oil cheaply!"

Next in line was Netherlands Foreign Minister Van der Klauuw. When he met Begin in Jerusalem, he told him that he had met with Yasser Arafat. "You shook a hand dripping with Jewish blood," Begin reproved him. From Europe, Begin moved to Saudi Arabia. When Philip Habib told him that there was a possibility that the Saudis might help find a solution to the Lebanese missile crisis, Begin saw fit to give his views of them in public: "A rich family, and a weak medieval regime that would not be able to pump oil without Western aid."

The public stood up and cheered. Here was a proud Jew, who did not bow down before the leaders of the world and who was not afraid to talk back to them! The Labor party's criticism of his irresponsibility and the damage he was causing to the nation was regarded as mean-spirited and defeatist.

Of course, Begin did not content himself with targets overseas. His choicest rhetorical pearls were reserved for Shimon Peres. With considerable oratorical skill, he mocked Peres's statements and ridiculed his policies. He particularly focused on his credibility, reading with great pleasure extracts from Rabin's book. The campaign veered away from political matters, toward personal attacks. This exchange between Peres and Begin at a meeting of the Knesset Foreign Affairs and Defense Committee was typical:

"You have converted the Likud's election headquarters into a government, and you are conducting the Lebanese crisis from there," Peres said.

"We are?" Begin replied. "What about that [election] advertisement showing me with an open mouth, talking about runaway inflation? Who else is running wild?"

"Didn't you blame me for a helicopter accident in 1977?"

"Do you deny you told me that they deceived Ben-Gurion with the Altalena?"

"I do deny it. And afterward, you were reading from a book in the Knesset plenum. Was that statesmanlike?" Peres asked.

"That was the answer."

"Read Ezer Weizman, Moshe Dayan, and Shmuel Katz—what do they say about you?"

"You read them," Begin said.

"Are you talking about style and content? Your cabinet ministers said that Teddy Kollek and I were bordering on treason. Can't you restrain them?"

"Shimon, I'm not your defense counsel. You've got a mouth. Defend yourself."

"Do I need your defense? It is Israeli society that needs defending!"

And so it went on.

Three weeks before the election, Begin dropped his real bomb, four days after his meeting with Sadat. At 4:00 P.M. on Monday, June 8, 1981, during the festival of Shavuot, the Israel Radio news announcer told his astounded listeners about the bombing and destruction of Iraq's atomic reactor by Israel air force planes.

It was certainly an impressive military operation, but naturally, questions arose about the timing. Had it really been necessary to do the job before the elections? Begin had prepared his answer. He said that Israeli Intelligence had information that the reactor was going "critical" in July. Bombing the reactor after this would cause radioactive radiation that would severely harm the citizens of Baghdad. Obviously, there was no alternative to carrying out the operation in June.

Reacting to this, Peres raised doubts about the credibility of the information. The reactor had been supplied to Iraq by France. After Francois Mitterrand, a friend of Israel, had been elected president, claimed Peres, diplomatic means could have been found to prevent its being used for military purposes. In any case, it was certain that Mitterrand's France would not have given Iraq the material in the coming months to manufacture an atomic bomb. So Peres's criticism fell short of an outright condemnation of the action. In fact, his words implied that, if diplomatic means had failed, he too would have supported the destruction of the reactor.

Then Begin took an unconventional step. He sent the chairman of the Knesset Foreign Affairs and Defense Committee a letter he had received from Peres the previous month (May 10, 1981)—the day of the French presidential elections. Peres had written it in his own hand, so that even his secretary would not see the contents. It was headed, "Personal and Top Secret." Begin asked the committee chairman to circulate Peres's letter among the members of the committee, in order to prove that his statement about only disapproving of the timing—and not of the action itself—was untrue. As Begin had anticipated, the contents of Peres's letter were leaked to the media, and so the whole affair came out into the open.

Some six months before the bombing, Begin had told Peres about the plan. Peres had asked whether the possible Iraqi reaction had been taken into account. Begin did not reply. On the night of May 9, Peres was informed that the action might take place the next day. Realizing that this was the day of the French presidential election, Peres sent Begin a message warning against carrying out the operation that day for fear of offending the French. He added assessments that could be construed as opposition to the operation, as such. He even emphasized (using code words) that there could be negative results in view of Israel's own vulnerability in that field.

In fact, Peres did not retract these opinions, even after the bombing of the reactor. His first reaction did not spell out his views, so as not to cause Israel political and security damage. Begin took advantage of this to create the impression that there was a gap between what Peres had written in the letter and what he had said after the bombing. From an electoral point of view, Begin achieved his aim, but as it violated the confidentiality of personal and secret documents, it was an atrocious thing to do. Begin had grossly betrayed the trust that Peres had placed in him, and had not hesitated to publish the letter for electoral purposes, despite the fact that it contained information on nuclear matters related to Israel and had been marked "Personal and Top Secret."

Electoral considerations also dictated the Israeli government's announcement, taking responsibility for bombing the reactor. In the past, Israel had always denied involvement in actions of this type, in order to make it easier for friendly nations to avoid condemnation. As long as there was only suspicion, however well-founded, these nations could satisfy the Arab states by general expressions of disapproval. But once Israel accepted responsibility, they would have to take action, and that is just what happened. The Reagan administration immediately announced it was suspending the supply of F-16 combat aircraft, despite its contractual obligations.

Even if Israel's vital interests had been harmed, Begin profited in electoral terms. The public, drunk with success, did not want to see or hear how matters really stood. Now Peres understood, and the party with him, that the campaign had become a "catch as catch can" wrestling match, with no holds barred.

Furthermore, it was too late to do anything about it. At this point, mid-June 1981, the Likud had made stupendous progress, not only catching up with Labor but even overtaking it in the polls. The process had begun with Finance Minister Aridor and continued with the resurrection of Menachem Begin. Not that Yitzhak Rabin's notable contribution to the situation should be ignored. The Likud was making effective use of his book, quoting extensively from it in its election propaganda. From the Likud's point of view, it was an asset that any party would dream about. The number-two man in the rival party writes that the number-one man is an indefatigable

intriguer, unfit for public office. Who are we, the Likud, to argue with
him? And how dare you, the public, doubt his word?

Rabin himself did not lift a finger to neutralize the sting of the
arrows that the Likud fired at Peres. He participated in the election
campaign; but in his appearances he spoke of the party, without ever
mentioning the name of its leader. Party functionaries appealed to
him to demand that the Likud stop using his book. They asked him to
say something to the effect that, despite what he had written, he
preferred Peres to Begin. Rabin gave evasive replies and did nothing.

Six days after the bombing, Eliezer Zurrabin, head of the PR
agency working for Labor, and his researcher, Mina Tzemach, came
to Peres's office at party headquarters with a bitter message. A poll
taken after the bombing of the reactor indicated that the Likud was
ahead by the astounding margin of twenty seats. It also showed that,
if Rabin replaced Peres at the head of the Labor list, the gap would
be closed. The conclusion was obvious, and Peres understood it well
enough. He at once announced that he was prepared to resign, but
first he wanted the matter thoroughly checked.

There followed one of the toughest days of Peres's life—maybe
the toughest. The goal for which he had worked all his adult life, and
which, just a few months ago had seemed well within his grasp, now
appeared to be lost forever. The next day he intended to resign from
the Labor leadership, and he had no doubt that this meant retiring
from public life altogether.

He continued to function as if nothing had happened. In the
evening he appeared at an election rally, returning home very late.
Sonia, his wife, was awake. He told her about the talk with Zurrabin
and Tzemach and asked her what she thought. As always, she
assured him that she would support whatever he decided, but, "I
think you ought to decide to go." The following morning Zurrabin
phoned. The situation had changed again. A later poll indicated that
the Likud was only six seats ahead and that the gap was closing.
Peres no longer had to resign. What had happened?

The very factor that had initially worked against Labor now
started to plague the Likud: overconfidence. Buoyed up by a wave of
popularity, the strength of which surprised even him, Menachem
Begin lost all restraint and sailed into the rhetorical stratosphere. For
some time the results had been positive, from his point of view; but
then he went too far.

It happened on Sunday, June 14. Begin arrived at an election rally in Netanya. The scene had become familiar to him: a huge, enthusiastic crowd, thunderously shouting, "Begin! Begin!" and "Begin, king of Israel!" Every word he uttered drew roars of approval and admiration. His face was pale with emotion and dripping with sweat as he wagged his finger and yelled threats at Syrian President Hafez Assad: "Beware, Assad, Yanosh and Raful are ready for you!" (Officer in charge of the Northern Command Avigdor Ben-Gal and Chief of Staff Rafael Eitan.) There was a roar of delight from the crowd, and Begin continued: "Special Ambassador Philip Habib is coming to Israel on Wednesday, and I'm going to ask him, 'Well, are you going to get the missiles out of Lebanon or not? Because, if you don't get them out, we'll get them out!'" The crowd went wild.

When this was shown on television the following night, it caused general shock and revulsion. The same evening, Peres appeared in Petah Tikva, and he also received his customary welcome: a barrage of tomatoes and shouts of "Begin! Begin!" from Likud supporters. But this time, he was not the only target. Labor supporters were beaten up; cars were set alight; shop windows carrying Labor posters were smashed.

"Violence," cried Labor. "That is the true face of the Likud and its leader!" Entertainers, artists, writers, university professors, and other public figures rallied to Labor under the slogan, "Anything but the Likud!" An ugly ethnic conflict surfaced: Oriental, Sephardi Jews on the Likud side; European, Ashkenazi Jews for Labor.

These were Peres's greatest hours. He did not flinch from the waves of violence that greeted his every appearance, and gradually he started winning admiration for his guts and his nerves of steel. He displayed a quality of leadership that breathed the spirit of life into the Labor campaigners, who held their heads high and went forth into the fray as if it were their last battle.

The polls now indicated a neck-and-neck race; and therefore, the last event of the campaign—the television confrontation between Peres and Begin—assumed a decisive importance. Peres forced the debate on his unwilling aides and assistants, who remembered only too well the debacle of 1977. With Begin at the height of his rhetorical powers, they were sure he would crush Peres. Peres insisted that he could not back down. Deep down, he was convinced he could beat Begin.

At the same time a new development occurred, featuring once again Zurrabin and his poll researcher, Mina Tzemach. This time, they showed Peres a poll indicating that, if Rabin were the candidate for defense minister, Labor could gain as many as six or seven Knesset seats.

Party functionaries started pressuring Peres to announce that Rabin was his candidate for defense minister. The public was waiting for the announcement of the great reconciliation, and it was impossible to backtrack by then. So Peres made the announcement and Rabin retracted his statement that Peres was not fit to be prime minister.

Peres spent election day, June 30, touring different neighborhoods in Tel Aviv. In the evening, he returned to his office. About eight o'clock, he was shown the results of a last poll conducted by Mina Tzemach, which showed the Likud winning by seven seats.

Peres went home to shower and change his clothes. Back in his office, he received a phone call from Rabin. "Did you hear about the last poll?" he asked. "I just wanted to say that I see myself as a full partner with full responsibility for the defeat." Peres felt his throat constrict with emotion. "I appreciate your attitude," he replied.

Two hours later, the picture seemed to have changed. Peres felt as if a stone had rolled off his heart, as he heard the television anchorman announce that, according to the TV exit poll, it was neck and neck, with a possible lead of one seat to Labor. An hour later, Hanoch Smith, the television pollster, announced that Labor was now four seats ahead, 51 to 47.

Peres left his office and walked to the Labor party election headquarters at the nearby Deborah Hotel, where he was received by hundreds of ecstatic reporters with loud cheers. On his way to the table where the leaders were sitting, people were shaking his hand and slapping him on the back. Rabin stood up and approached him. To riotous applause, the two rivals embraced each other.

Everyone joined in the ensuing sing-song, until it became apparent that their joy had been premature. At 1:00 A.M., Hanoch Smith admitted he had been mistaken. Labor was not leading. He returned to his original prediction: 47:47. Everyone understood the significance. Labor had greatly increased its strength—from thirty-two to forty-seven Knesset seats, but it was not enough to be able to form a government because the religious parties, which held the balance, had already announced that they preferred to continue in a coalition led by Menachem Begin.

The singing and the cheering died down. The headquarters quickly became deserted. Peres too returned to his home, frustrated and depressed. Once again he had been mocked by fate. Again the big prize had been dashed from him, when it was within reach—even in his hand. He would not be the man to lead the government of Israel—at least, not this time.

CHAPTER EIGHT

OPPOSITION IN
TIME OF WAR

IT WAS DIFFICULT for Peres to wake up on the morning after the election and remember that in the months and days ahead he would again have the obligation of sitting in opposition. Possibly it was even more difficult than it had been four years earlier. Although the election result in 1977 had been upset, it had not been completely unexpected. The writing had been on the wall for anyone prepared to read it. This time it had been unexpected. Labor had started the campaign with an enormous lead. Peres had every reason to feel the deep disappointment of a thirsty man who has reached the spring for the umpteenth time, but has not been allowed to drink from it.

Apart from his bruised personal feelings, he faced the real prospect of losing the leadership of the Labor party. Party activists do not choose a party framework only on the basis of ideology. They also expect—and sometimes this is the main reason—that the party will compensate them for their efforts with appointments to various positions at home and abroad, and by other means within the power of a government. If Peres could not hand out these rewards, sooner or later they were likely to look for someone who could.

This consideration, allied with the desire to be part of the decision-making process, led Peres seriously to consider joining a national unity government, headed by Menachem Begin.

Not that it was easy for him even to think about it. He no longer had any respect for Begin, and he knew that the feeling was mutual. Accepting Begin's leadership was tantamount to admitting defeat, to bowing his head before the decisive victory of the Labor party's number-one political enemy. For Peres, even considering the idea was bordering on treachery to the memory of his guide and mentor, David Ben-Gurion, who had never disguised his dislike and contempt for "the Knesset member who sits beside Dr. Bader," as Ben-Gurion used to call Begin in the days when he refused even to mention his name. Ben-Gurion, however, was dead and buried, and the new reality belonged to Begin. It was possible to retire into a corner and mourn, and Peres sometimes did. Late at night, after a drink or two, he permitted himself to sink into the comfort of self-pity, but these occasions were the exception. Essentially Peres was a pragmatist: the situation was bad, unpleasant, unjust, but that was the situation. Decisions had to be made on the basis of what was—not on what might or should have been.

The first time Peres publicly expressed his thoughts about joining the Likud-led government was a few weeks after it had been formed. At a meeting in Haifa with leaders of Mapam, Labor's left-wing partner in the Alignment, Peres warned that Ariel Sharon, as defense minister, was starting to plan the next war, and only Labor's joining the government could prevent it. Was the warning a prophecy or an excuse? Apparently, it was a mixture of both. It was not too difficult to gauge the intentions of the new defense minister.

Anyone who knew Sharon was convinced that the man would not be content until he had conducted his own war in order to allay the heavy burden of frustration that he carried. He had always been under the authority of others—mostly people to whom he felt superior. He saw himself as a military genius, although many others felt that this was questionable. Despite his military achievements— and these were considerable—he had never achieved the position he wanted most—that of IDF chief of staff. He had seen men younger than he—and in his opinion, less talented—receive the appointment, while he remained behind. Despite his undoubted ability, no defense minister had been prepared to give him the top army post. In general, his superiors in the defense establishment had agreed with David

Ben-Gurion's assessment that Sharon was a congenital liar and therefore not to be counted on.

Throughout his military career, Sharon had not managed to persuade those in authority that he had overcome the grave defects in his character. Finally, he retired from the IDF and went into politics, for which he showed great aptitude. In this new field of endeavor, his defects were converted from liabilities into assets. Boldness bordering on irresponsibility, difficulty in telling the truth, obsessive ambition—all the qualities that had blocked his path in the IDF were now revealed as extremely effective in the far more tolerant atmosphere of politics. They sometimes even won the admiration of his fellow politicians.

Peres's statement to the Mapam leaders had also been an excuse. He wanted very much to be in the government. But he also knew that the bitter pill he was offering his party was not easy to swallow. There would have to be very good—even sensational— reasons for the party to justify to itself and its voters a step of this sort. And what could be a better reason than saving the nation from Ariel Sharon?

Peres's remarks in Haifa made headlines and caused an immediate row in the Labor party. A few days later the Knesset faction met to discuss the matter. Some supported him, others opposed him, and some, like Yitzhak Rabin, were ambivalent. The man who swung the balance was Ya'acov Hazan, the veteran leader of left-wing Mapam, Labor's junior partner in the Alignment. His face red with emotion, his clenched fists raised to heaven, he shouted: "National unity will mean the end of unity in the Labor movement!"

It was the end of Peres's flirtation with the idea of a national unity government. Peres did not possess the political or moral strength to split the Labor movement for the sake of a partnership with Begin. So it meant a return to the gray reality of opposition, although this time it was a much more significant opposition than the one he had headed in the former Knesset. The cooperation of the three Knesset members from Shulamit Aloni's Citizens Rights Movement (CRM), with his own forty-seven members gave Peres the leadership of the largest bloc in the Knesset. The sense of power that this situation afforded to the party members mitigated their disappointment to some extent that the government was still in the hands of the rival party. There was a feeling that ousting the Likud from power was only a question of time—and not so much time, at that.

There is no doubt that this feeling contributed to the process of reconciliation between Rabin and Peres—a process that had begun on election night. Rabin appeared to accept the fact that he could not put the clock back and that a safe number-two spot was preferable to the risks of another confrontation with the leadership. Accordingly, there was no reason for him not to act as an exemplary, disciplined party member in order to neutralize the criticism of him for writing the anti-Peres book that had served the Likud so well in the election campaign. He behaved as a man determined to forget the past, and to play the game according to accepted rules, while at the same time keeping his finger on the political pulse. If the situation changed one day, he would play by different rules in order to get back the leadership of the Labor party and the premiership, which he still thought—and thinks to this day—were taken from him unjustly.

Another reason for Labor's cautious optimism was Menachem Begin's personality. Everyone who came into contact with him could see that he was deteriorating. His fluctuations between euphoric optimism and dark pessimism became increasingly frequent and extreme. Often, during meetings, he sat with his head on his chest, dozing or meditating. His close aides were constantly having to deny the persistent rumors about the prime minister's depressed state of mind. But in the corridors and committee rooms, the facts were well known and the general feeling was that things could not continue this way.

It was against this background that Peres was invited to the prime minister's office on April 30, where Begin informed him that a few hours earlier the air force had bombed three terrorist bases in Lebanon. If the bombing did not stop terrorist activities against the northern settlements, he declared, "another six camps were lined up." Peres assumed from this that Begin was no longer enthusiastic about Sharon's plans to cross the Lebanese border, but had decided to limit himself to retaliation raids by the air force.

The following weeks were crammed with incidents, mainly the firing of Katyusha rockets that made life in the northern settlements unbearable. The feeling in political and military circles was that the question was no longer *if* Sharon would go to war in Lebanon, but when, how far, and on what pretext? The answers to all these questions were not long in coming.

On the evening of June 3, 1982, Israel's ambassador in London, Shlomo Argov, was attending a banquet at the Dorchester Hotel. After the meal, which was attended by several other ambassadors, the guests went upstairs for drinks. Argov felt tired, and decided to return home. He had left the hotel and was walking to his car, when suddenly a man emerged from the darkness and strode quickly toward him. Before either he or his bodyguards could see what was happening, the man fired several shots at the ambassador. Argov fell, gravely wounded, and was taken to the hospital. The ambassador's desperate struggle for his life was successful, but it was bitter success, for Argov remains totally paralyzed.

Sharon now had the pretext for action. Some hours after the attempt on Argov's life, air force planes bombed terrorist command posts in and around Beirut. The terrorists replied with a Katyusha barrage on Kiryat Shmona.

On Saturday night, June 5, 1982, Peres called together the top political and defense experts of the Labor party to discuss the tension on the northern border, and reported that the government intended to carry out only a limited action to clear the terrorists from south Lebanon. In other words, the IDF would advance forty kilometers from the border, and no more. Why forty kilometers? Because that was the maximum range of the artillery at the disposal of the terrorists.

This, then, was supposed to be the answer to the question of how far, only it wasn't. On the following day—Sunday, June 6, 1982, in the early morning—large forces crossed the border into Lebanon. At 8:00 A.M., Peres was at home, drinking his morning coffee and listening to the radio, which reported that the inhabitants of Kiryat Shmona had spent another night in the shelters, when the phone rang. The prime minister's office asked him to come to Begin's office at 10:45 A.M. with Yitzhak Rabin, Haim Bar-Lev, and Mapam leader Victor Shemtov.

When he arrived at the prime minister's office, Peres found the corridors swarming with excited army personnel. Defense Minister Ariel Sharon arrived, wearing a sort of military jacket, striding along purposefully, surrounded by aides and military men carrying maps— the very embodiment of the "great leader." His bearing and behavior were those of a man fulfilling a lifelong dream. The war was his. He had not been allowed to be commander of the army—now he would show the world how to wage war!

Peres, Rabin, Bar-Lev, and Shemtov sat down in the prime minister's private office, detached from, and uninvolved in, the frenetic activity going on around them. Peres could not avoid nostalgic memories. He looked at Sharon, who now headed the defense establishment, whose creation Peres had dominated. Sharon had sent forth an army armed with weapons mostly produced by the factories that Peres had developed. Even the political logic of cooperation with the Lebanese Christians, on which Begin and Sharon were basing the campaign, had started with Peres.

He remembered how, on May 4, 1960, a young British colonel called Slade Baker had arrived at his office in the Defense Ministry and had been introduced to him as a staff member of the London *Times*. Baker had told him that on May 12, there would be general elections in Lebanon, supervised by the army in case of disruptions. The problem was that many of the Lebanese army officers were pro-Nasser, and there was concern that they would spread propaganda in his favor and cause other problems.

At that time, President Nasser of Egypt was regarded as Israel's most dangerous enemy, and the Lebanese Christians were also worried by him. Baker said he wanted to deliver a message to Peres from General Shehab, the commander in chief of the Lebanese army, whom he had met in London. Shehab's request was for the IDF to create tension on the Lebanese border about a week before the elections, to give him a pretext for dispatching Lebanese army units to the Israeli border. He would make sure that the pro-Nasser elements were the ones sent.

Israel had complied fully and effectively, and the cooperation had continued quietly, until it was given a boost by a common enemy in the form of the PLO. In the middle of September 1970, King Hussein had turned his army's Bedouin units on the Palestinian refugee camps in the vicinity of Amman to counter the PLO's arrogant behavior in Jordan, which increasingly threatened the king's regime. In a few days of what came to be called "Black September" by the Palestinians, Hussein's soldiers carried out a savage massacre in the camps, resulting in hundreds of casualties and a mass flight of survivors, mostly to Lebanon.

As a result, the delicate communal balance of Lebanon between Christians, Muslims, Druze, and other groups was altered. The Palestinians, many of them PLO members, represented an accession of strength for the Muslims, which threatened the position of the Christians. PLO forces in Lebanon were, of course, also strengthened, and this was a threat to Israel.

The resulting common interest led to increased cooperation and eventually direct meetings between the two sides, starting at a low level, later reaching the highest levels when leaders of the Christian community came to visit Israel.

One of the important meetings took place in Peres's office at the Defense Ministry in Tel Aviv on April 1, 1976. Peres's guests were Joseph Abu-Halil, the political secretary of the Christian Phalangists and editor of their journal *Al-Amal,* and the Phalangist military commanders of the Beirut and coastal regions. At this meeting, Abu-Halil declared that they were striving for a different Lebanon, and "we see Israel as our ally."

Three months later, on July 29, Peres met Danny Chamoun, another Christian leader, and in his conversation with him, laid out his Lebanese doctrine: Israel would continue to give assistance to the Lebanese Christians, he said, "without conditions and without political directives." In return, Peres asked the Christians to establish a military force that would control southern Lebanon as far as the Israeli border and expel the PLO forces from there.

"We are prepared to assist with the organization, training, and arming of this force," he stated, "as long as the Christians provide the manpower—particularly, the officers." On this principle, the Christian South Lebanon Army was established, under the command of Major Sa'ad Hadad. For several years this cooperation had the desired effect. Hadad's small but well-equipped forces managed to stop many planned terrorist incursions from Lebanon. But then the PLO increased its strength to a point where Hadad's force could not prevent its activities.

Now, Peres's thoughts were interrupted by the voice of Begin. For the first time, Peres was hearing officially, and of course very solemnly, that the IDF's tanks were crossing the border. Somebody asked how long the battle would last. Begin started to answer, but Sharon got in first: "We'll finish it in twenty-one hours." Begin, who was very scrupulous about giving accurate information, interjected: "The fighting will continue for twenty-four hours at the most."

On the following day, there was a Knesset debate on the motions of no-confidence that the extreme left-wing factions proposed because of the incursion into Lebanon. On the basis of the information they had received from the prime minister, the Labor members—with the exception of Knesset member Yossi Sarid— voted against the no-confidence resolution, and it was rejected by a large majority. Peres's speech was cautious, so as not to disrupt the national consensus about the war.

The following day Sharon briefed the Knesset Foreign Affairs and Defense Committee on the progress of the fighting in what at that stage was called the "Peace for Galilee Campaign." In this briefing he continued to aver that it would be a short campaign with limited objectives. To more specific questions concerning reports that the limited campaign was being expanded, Sharon replied with notable evasiveness.

In the discussion that Labor members of the committee held after the briefing, Yossi Sarid warned that the defense minister was pushing the army beyond the limits set by the government and beyond the forty kilometers that Begin had talked about in the Knesset. "The affair has the smell of the 'Cedars of Lebanon plan,'" he warned. He did not have to give details. Those in political circles knew that a plan had been worked out in the Defense Ministry to invade Lebanon, advance to Beirut, take control of the city, and make the Christians the rulers of Lebanon. In return for this, the Christians would sign a peace treaty with Israel. When Sharon had been asked about the plan, in the meeting at the prime minister's office, he had strongly denied that it was being implemented, and Begin had confirmed his assurance. Sarid suggested that they send Peres and Rabin to Begin to tell him that Labor's support stopped short of a campaign that was taking on the character of a prolonged and arduous war.

Peres called the prime minister from his Knesset office, and Begin agreed to receive him at once. When Peres arrived a few minutes later, accompanied by Rabin, Begin took time out from the cabinet meeting to see them. Peres told Begin about his colleagues' reservations, and Begin promised to inform the cabinet on the matter. Peres suggested that, in order to calm the suspicions, Begin announce in the Knesset plenum that there was no intention of reaching Beirut, or the Beirut-Damascus road. Begin agreed, and said he would do so on the following day.

Peres returned to his colleagues, who had been waiting in his Knesset office, and he and Rabin reported with satisfaction what they had just heard from the prime minister. Rabin commented, "It was a good thing that we went. It's now in the protocol that we said we should not advance to Beirut and the Beirut-Damascus road and Begin promised that there was no such intention."

The following day, Begin repeated his assurance in the Knesset, and quoted Peres to the effect that there was no point in fighting the Syrians, that they should be persuaded to remain in their positions in Lebanon's Bekaa Valley, and that the battle would be against the terrorists.

As Begin was giving this assurance in the Knesset, the IDF was continuing to advance to Beirut and toward the Syrian forces, without—as it afterward became clear—Begin's knowledge. A few days later, it was impossible to conceal the fact that the IDF was advancing toward Beirut and toward the region where the Syrian forces were stationed, but the public was in no mood to hear criticism. The atmosphere in the street was of drunken exultation. Once again the IDF was marching as a conquering army; again, positions were being captured; Israel had once more proved its power to the world. Public figures such as Yossi Sarid, who pointed out that the Knesset and the people had been deceived about the aims of the war, were met with a solid wall of hatred. Journalists who wrote in a similar vein found themselves and their families threatened with violence. Even those who were not infected with the general euphoria said that criticism must not be voiced in time of war, that accounts should be settled when the guns stopped firing.

Peres, one of the soberest people imaginable, found himself in a dilemma that did not leave him throughout the war. His experienced mind absorbed facts that told him the government was leading the nation on an adventure from which no good could come. But he was no Yossi Sarid, a courageous and unruly backbencher who bore no responsibility to anyone or anything. Peres was the leader of one of the two large parties, and as such, he had to act responsibly and ask himself, if I'm wrong, can I lead my party in a political struggle against the government in the midst of a war, which—against all logic and experience—might, in the end, prove to have been justified and effective? There are no easy answers to such dilemmas, and Peres felt he must adopt a policy of wait-and-see.

On Thursday, June 10, when it had become clear that Sharon lad led the nation into a war with the Syrians and into a long stay in the suffocating mud of Lebanon, Peres and his colleagues were again invited to the prime minister's office. For the first time since the war had started, Begin's face showed signs of tension and worry. On his table was a cable from President Reagan, who reported on a message he had received from Soviet leader Leonid Brezhnev, warning against an escalation of the situation. "The United States is concerned about a more serious confrontation between Israel and Syria, and calls for a cease-fire as of tomorrow at 6:00 A.M.," said the cable. In diplomatic but unambiguous language Begin was informed that an Israeli refusal would harm relations with the United States. Begin told his worried listeners that the IDF would expel the Syrians and the terrorists beyond the forty-kilometer line. He promised that there was no intention of conquering Beirut or remaining on the Beirut-Damascus road.

"There is no intention of anything beyond forty kilometers," Begin repeated his worthless pledge. He agreed that the press release issued after the meeting would include this declaration, together with a promise that the IDF would not enter Beirut. In fact, Peres received information the next day that Sharon had ordered the IDF to fabricate an excuse to break the cease-fire so that the army could continue its advance to Beirut. When Mordechai Gur demanded that Labor send another delegation to Begin, Peres dismissed the idea with a tired gesture. "He's making fun of us," he said, meaning Sharon, not Begin, who obviously was also being deceived by Sharon.

Even now, the Labor leadership did not dare to come out with public criticism of the progress of the war. Two days later, when it had become clear to everyone that Sharon had initiated a long war that would leave hundreds dead or wounded, the Alignment Knesset faction met to draw conclusions from the fighting. Paragraph twenty-one of the recorded decisions of that meeting read: "Publication of the stands that the Alignment conveyed to the appropriate authorities at the various stages of the war should be delayed until a suitable occasion."

Peres argued with his friends that, "by preserving loyalty to the government, I am keeping open a line of communication to Begin." He wasn't just talking. The importance of that line of communication increased, as the reports Begin received from Sharon became increasingly infrequent. For example, when Peres called Begin on June 21 and told him that the IDF had started bombing Beirut, it was the first that Begin had heard about it.

That same week there were numerous media reports about the bombing of Beirut, about the destruction that the IDF was causing wherever it reached, and about the hatred it was arousing among the Lebanese, who had formerly been allies. The pages of the newspapers were full of black-bordered death notices for the soldiers who had fallen in battle.

In this atmosphere, the Knesset Foreign Affairs and Defense Committee set out on a tour of Lebanon, where committee members met with IDF soldiers. They were impressed by the high morale that many of them still possessed, in contrary to the impression conveyed in the media.

That evening the committee members were flown back to Sde Dov Airfield, near Tel Aviv. On the way, Peres passed a message to the Alignment members sitting near him: "I want urgently to talk to you. Please come to my office in Hayarkon Street, immediately after we land." They were all tired from the long and exhausting trip that had taken them from southern Lebanon to the environs of Beirut. Shlomo Hillel and Victor Shemtov pointed out that it was already late, and they still had to get home to Jerusalem, but Peres insisted.

Peres opened the meeting impatiently with the following statements: "Friends, this war is going to end in a big victory." Raising his voice, he told Sarid and Shemtov, "This is going to be a great success for the Likud, and I demand that both of you refrain from criticism. You are entitled to harm your own political futures, but you have no right to cause damage to the party." There was a short silence, following which most of the members nodded their heads in agreement. Sarid and Shemtov had been rebuked. The following day, the papers reported that, "The members of the Foreign Affairs and Defense Committee received the impression that media reports about the damage to Beirut and its environs have been greatly exaggerated."

On July 4, Peres and his colleagues were again invited to see

Begin, who had with him Sharon, Shamir, and David Kimche, the director general of the Foreign Ministry, a former Mossad agent, and one of the originators of the concept of the "Christian connection." It was at this stage that Peres began to feel nagging doubts. "I am against the use of water and electricity cutoffs in the siege of Beirut," he said, but Rabin contradicted him: "Closing off their water is an extremely effective measure."

Peres was not surprised, for, as the war continued, the friendship between Sharon and Rabin had been renewed. Sharon had effectively made Rabin into his adviser, and the two of them were frequently seen at the various war fronts. It is doubtful that Sharon needed Rabin's advice, but the fact that one of the two leaders of the Labor party completely supported the siege of Beirut greatly helped Sharon to continue the war until he achieved the targets he had set for it.

However, it became increasingly evident to everyone that those targets were not attainable. The United States was concerned that other aims had intruded, possibly unplanned, because of the war. Peres learned about this assessment when he visited Washington on August 10, 1982, after the United States had also become embroiled in Lebanon in a big way. The return home in coffins of dozens of U.S. marines (after their base was blown up by a car bomb) was undoubtedly a major factor in the replacement of Secretary of State Alexander Haig by George Shultz.

In all Peres's high-level meetings at the State Department, it was not even hinted to him that a special team, consisting of Charles Hill, Dennis Ross, and Wat Cluverius, was sitting in the same building, preparing a new peace plan for the Middle East. Nicholas Veliotes, who sat beside Shultz during his talks with Peres, would be secretly sent in two weeks' time to Jordan, to elicit the reaction of the king to what would later come to be known as the "Reagan plan."

Peres would hear about the initiative from another special envoy, Saul Linowitz, only two hours before President Reagan told the American people about it on television. The reason for the conduct of his hosts was later explained to Peres as being the result of a desire that he not be accused of complicity, and that the Reagan plan, incorporating as it did Labor's idea of territorial compromise on the West Bank, should not be portrayed as being the result of a plot between the administration and the Labor party.

The Labor party did, in fact, welcome the initiative, but it got a very different reception from Begin. When U.S. Ambassador Samuel Lewis brought it to him, the prime minister told him, "This is the saddest of all our meetings. It is a serious diversion from the Camp David Accords."

Begin had many better reasons for being sad—and all of them came from Lebanon, not Washington. IDF soldiers became cannon fodder for anyone bearing arms in Lebanon. The dream that had created the Cedars of Lebanon plan had become more like a nightmare. The most dramatic expression of this disastrous and hopeless state of affairs came in an event that shook the citizens of Israel and the entire world.

On Thursday evening, September 18, 1982, when Israelis were emerging from their synagogues after prayers for Rosh Hashana, the Jewish New Year, several dozen militiamen of the Christian Phalangist forces advanced into the Palestinian refugee camps of Sabra and Shatilla, near Beirut. Two days later they withdrew, leaving behind them the bodies of hundreds of slaughtered men, women, and children.

The protests of the killing of women and children under the noses of the IDF soldiers who were supposed to be protecting them went beyond the borders of Israel. The United States and the Jewish organizations there did not hold back their condemnations. Egypt quickly summoned Ambassador Sa'ad Mortada home from Tel Aviv, and a crisis developed that threatened the fragile peace between Israel and the largest Arab nation. The Israeli public made its opinion clear in a gigantic protest demonstration, when hundreds of thousands of people gathered in central Tel Aviv to demand that the government appoint a commission of inquiry.

The press kept up the pressure, and eventually, the government was forced to appoint an official commission of inquiry headed by the president of the Supreme Court, Justice Yitzhak Kahan. After hearing dozens of witnesses and reading thousands of documents, including the minutes of the relevant cabinet meetings, the committee decided that several IDF officers would be disciplined. The main conclusion, however, related to Defense Minister Ariel Sharon. The commission resolved unambiguously that although his responsibility was indirect, Sharon was personally responsible because he had known what was going to happen and had done nothing to prevent it. The commission recommended that Sharon, the architect of the war, be dismissed as defense minister, and expressed doubts about his fitness to be a member of the government. After a long struggle, Sharon agreed to resign from the Defense Ministry, following the ruling of Attorney General Yitzhak Zamir that the recommendation of the commission did not prevent him remaining in the cabinet as minister without portfolio.

Only now did the Israeli public start to recover from the Lebanese euphoria. Instead of fighting a war of advance and conquer, the IDF now found itself up to its neck in the Lebanese swamp, with its soldiers a target for all the warring factions in Lebanon, including the Christians, who gradually also became enemies of the occupation army. Every day the papers were full of death notices of youngsters who had fallen victim to the bullets of rival factions, without reason or purpose, except for the fact that the government could not find a way to withdraw. At the same time, the economy continued to deteriorate. The cost of the continuing war necessitated the spending of vast sums, which fueled an annual inflation rate of several hundred percent.

While the army remained in Lebanon, Begin withdrew into himself. People who met him found him uninterested, distant, apathetic. His state of mind worsened when his wife, Aliza, his lifelong companion and the person closest to him, died. The people around Begin observed that he had apparently lost all interest in what was going on. The government seemed to have lost its way, and kept going only by inertia.

On Sunday, August 28, 1982, at the end of the weekly cabinet meeting, Begin rose from his place at the head of the table, and without having warned anyone of his intention, forced out the words: "I can't go on." Walking slowly, his back bent, he left the cabinet room.

Two weeks later he submitted his resignation to the president and retired from public life to complete isolation in a small Jerusalem apartment, from which he emerged only rarely. He has never disclosed what broke him. However, the political campaign that his son, Binyamin Ze'ev, declared against Sharon reinforces the assumption that Begin resigned because the man in whom he had put his full trust had deceived him and led the nation under his rule to a disaster.

The Herut Central Committee met to elect a replacement for Begin. The choice was Foreign Minister Yitzhak Shamir, a short, soft-spoken man of sixty-eight, who had been commander of the Lehi underground during the British mandate period. Shortly after being sworn in, Shamir initiated a meeting with Peres in the home of a former Lehi member in Jerusalem. He suggested that Peres immediately join a government of national unity, citing the economic crisis and the Syrian threat.

Peres brought Shamir's proposal to the Labor leadership, expressing his own opinion that there was no point in Labor climbing aboard the Likud "wagon," which, slowly but surely, was reaching the end of its road. And, in fact, on January 25, 1984, the Shamir government fell, just four months after it had been established. The general election was called for July 23, 1984.

On the face of things, it seemed that this time, nothing in the world could prevent a clear victory for the Labor Alignment. It would be difficult to imagine a worse starting point for the Likud. Its popular, charismatic leader was hiding in his apartment. His successor was a dull personality, with none of his predecessor's rhetorical talent. Inflation had soared to spectacular heights, and the IDF was still trapped in the Lebanese swamp.

Despite all this, many Labor activists were worried. There was a feeling—and it crossed factional lines—that if anyone could spoil this (from the party point of view) rosy picture, it was in fact their leader, Shimon Peres. From all sectors of the party the opinion was voiced that Peres was a congenital loser, that his image was that of an undistinguished politician—a politician, and not a leader.

Even those who thought that he was the best of all the available leaders to head the nation—and there were many who thought this—felt that, though it was a shame, possibly even unfair, the man was incapable of leading himself and his party to victory.

More and more party members began to say aloud that a new leadership was needed. In normal circumstances, they may have turned to the popular Rabin. But to his misfortune, there was another man who had wrapped himself in an even more statesmanlike mantle: Yitzhak Navon, the fifth president of Israel, who had resigned the presidency a year earlier than scheduled in order to return to the political arena. A group of Knesset members, led by Uzi Baram, head of the Jerusalem Labor party branch, suggested to Peres that Navon should head the party list for the elections.

Peres felt insulted and betrayed. Since 1977, he had led the party through its most difficult years in opposition, and now, just when it seemed they were on the brink of a new era, there were those trying to replace him with somebody else. He had no intention of permitting this.

Peres met with Navon, his friend from the days of Rafi and Ben-Gurion. At the meeting, which took place in Jerusalem's Shemesh Restaurant, Navon rejected the proposal that he be given the number-two spot under Peres. When Peres realized that he could not achieve an understanding with his friend, he turned his attention to his rival. Peres learned that Ahdudt Ha'avoda leaders Yitzhak Ben-Aharon and Yisrael Galili, who afforded Rabin his political base in the party, had persuaded Navon to stand against Peres for the party leadership and promised him their support.

Now it was Rabin's turn to feel betrayed. He rejected proposals by his supporters that he enter the contest against Peres and Navon, to take advantage of the split in the Rafi votes between the two of them. He made a careful calculation that the worst possible strategy was to give Navon the leadership of the Labor party, as Navon would receive the support of Rabin's camp, leaving Rabin without a base in the party. On the other hand, if Peres remained party leader, Rabin would retain his camp intact. In other words, if Navon became leader, he was likely to lose all his political power; allied with Peres, he could maintain his number-two position. It was a simple case of a bird in the hand being worth two in the bush.

Uniting against the threat of Navon, Peres and Rabin agreed that Rabin would receive the Defense Ministry, in return for backing Peres, if and when Labor formed the next government. This ministry would ensure Rabin's number-two position in the government and the party. Informed of the agreement by Peres, the former president had to decide whether to be satisfied with the "bird," which Peres was at this point prepared to promise him, or to take the risk of losing both birds for something that now seemed unattainable anyway.

Navon lost no time in calling a news conference, at which he announced that he supported the continuation of Peres's leadership of the Labor party and would not stand against him.

On April 2, 1984, Peres was again elected party chairman and party candidate for prime minister.

The Labor party was now free to wage a tough and brutal election campaign. The Likud was fighting for its life, and it did so with fury and anger. As the Likud campaigners had no achievements in which they could take pride, they directed their barbs at a single target: Shimon Peres, and his personality. This time they did not content themselves with reading extracts from Rabin's book; they unleashed a campaign of vilification that had no limits whatever.

They tried to portray him as a man who had exploited the nation. They started a rumor that he was a partner in Tadiran, the big electronics company, and hinted that he used his official positions to benefit the firm. Many accepted as a fact the rumor that his mother was of Arab extraction and that he had sent his two children abroad to avoid military service in the Lebanon war. (In fact, his son served as a pilot, and his son-in-law was a paratroop lieutenant colonel in the thick of the fighting.) The libels were specifically angled to blacken his name among the Oriental Jews. One rumor told how he enjoyed humiliating the Moroccan maids who cleaned his apartment.

The climax of the campaign—the live television debate between the prime minister and the leader of the opposition—arrived soon enough. Peres prepared for the contest with simulations. Yossi Sarid, who had played the part of Begin on previous occasions, was now called in to play Shamir.

Sometimes Peres and Sarid forgot that they were engaged in a simulation, and they shouted angrily at each other. The advisers awarded points to both men. In the first rounds, Sarid lashed out without mercy and on one occasion, Peres burst out: "I can't go on like this; Shamir will never say things like that." But by the time of the final rehearsals, Peres felt more than ready for the real contest.

Peres arrived at the television studios with Sarid. When he met Shamir, he shook hands and inquired politely about the prime minister's throat, which had become hoarse giving campaign speeches. Peres's advisers were pleased that Shamir had received the right to reply first to the questions of the moderator, Dan Pattir. Peres hit the Likud mercilessly on Lebanon, and on the grave economic crisis to which they had brought the nation. Shamir hesitated, stammered, and mumbled his answers. Everything indicated a decisive victory for Peres.

When the time came for summing up, Shamir proclaimed his philosophy in a monotonous, colorless voice. But then something happened. At the end of his speech, when it seemed he had nothing to add and was already withdrawing into himself, Shamir issued a call for the establishment of a national unity government. It was unconventional, unexpected, and—as it turned out later—effective. Here was a political leader not asking for victory. He was, for the sake of the people, in order to solve the nation's difficult problems, ready and willing to share power and achievement with the rival party. Likud activists who had been watching the contest from an adjoining room burst out in applause and cries of joy. Asked about it by reporters who were waiting by the studio entrance for his reaction, Peres responded, "The Alignment does not intend to join a national unity government, but to set up an alternate government."

At Labor party headquarters there was the feeling that Peres had soundly beaten Shamir and that there was no longer any doubt that the Likud would be defeated in the elections. The party completely ignored the positive effect that Shamir's call for national unity had had on public opinion.

CHAPTER NINE

MARRIAGE
WITHOUT LOVE

THE MORNING OF the election was sunny and hopeful. Peres left his apartment in Ramat Aviv for the local polling booth at the neighborhood's Arazim School. In the corridor, he shook hands with early voters and flashed smiles at the cameras. From experience he knew to wait for the photographers, and to hold his ballot over the ballot box. From there he proceeded to his office to Hayarkon Street to receive reports from the field.

The Labor party offices in Tel Aviv were decorated with giant posters, with the party symbol, "Alef-Mem-Taf," and with colorful flags. At noon he went to lunch at the nearby Dan Hotel, accompanied by a security man. A party activist remarked with a smile that soon he would have "several bodyguards," as is usual with a prime minister.

In the evening, as the voting drew to its close, party veterans began streaming toward Peres's office. There were friends there from his days in the Defense Ministry—Al Schwimmer and Michael Piron—and the French millionaire, Jean Friedman. Additional reporters joined the media team who had stuck to Peres during the past days. When the polling booths closed, they crowded around the television in Peres's office. Only the sound of the air conditioner could be heard. As the face of the popular TV anchorman, Haim Yavin, appeared on the screen, everyone in the room, seemed to hold his breath, but Yavin had appeared only to announce that there had been a technical hitch with regard to the TV exit poll, and the results were not yet available. There was a certain amount of nervous laughter, and feeble attempts at jokes at the expense of Israel Television. Everyone became quiet again when Yavin reappeared to announce the results of the exit poll: Labor, forty-six seats, Likud, forty-three.

No one moved; no one opened his mouth. Peres and the others continued to gape at the screen, unbelieving. After Lebanon, after the shocking inflation, after the atmosphere of social collapse—only a three-mandate difference?

The sandwiches and drinks that the party workers had prepared in the Palace Hotel sat untouched. The party workers started to disperse and go home. Peres continued to sit in his chair, his grim face showing his shock and disappointment.

Peres told reporters who questioned him that he would try to form a government, but he understood very well how difficult the task would be. As always, the religious parties held the balance; without them, it would not be possible to form a coalition. But the small left-wing factions opposed a coalition with the religious parties, and their six votes were also needed to form a government.

Peres continued to gaze at the television. He made an impatient gesture when Yitzhak Shamir's face appeared on the screen, grinning from ear to ear. To the cheers of his supporters at Likud election headquarters, he announced that he had the sixty-one seats needed to form a government. He was relying on the support of the religious parties, which had been the norm since they had formed their alliance with Menachem Begin in 1977.

The final results became known the following morning. Labor had won forty-four seats to the Likud's forty-one—almost a tie. The leaders of both parties started making calculations, and reached the conclusion that neither of them could form a government with more than a minuscule majority in the Knesset—one or two seats, at the most.

After both the large parties had tried, without success, to form a narrow coalition, more and more voices were heard favoring the formation of an administration based on a partnership. The big

question was: Who would be the prime minister of such a government?

Peres and Shamir began meeting privately to find a way out of
the deadlock. The first meeting, which dealt with the premiership,
got nowhere. At the second meeting, at the beginning of September,
Peres and Shamir decided to set aside the matter of the premiership
and tackle the other problems first—the most important of which
were policy differences, such as peace negotiations and settlement
policy in the West Bank.

Peres opened the third discussion by saying, "Each side has its
own ideology, and neither side expects the other to accept its policy,
but there are times when the people decide to bypass political
matters to save the economy. We are looking for a bridge, with the
two large parties standing in the middle, and the issue of the economy
standing at the head." Shamir accepted this in principle, and the two
leaders agreed to set up teams to formulate political and economic
guidelines.

At the fourth meeting, the question of the premiership was again
raised. It was at this meeting that Peres first suggested the idea of
rotations: one of them would be prime minister for two years, the
other foreign minister, after which they would swap positions.

After Shamir had accepted the idea, they began to deal with the
question of who would be prime minister first. Another question:
What about the second most important post—defense?

Shamir suggested the following: Labor would get the post of
prime minister for the first two years, during which Likud would have
defense and foreign affairs; at the end of the two years, there would
be a rotation of all three. At the meeting of the Labor party
executive, where the proposal was discussed, Rabin, who was
Labor's candidate for defense, bent toward Peres and whispered in
his bass voice, "Shimon, you know this is very important to me." The
reminder was enough. Peres knew that he must not endanger the
delicate web of relations he had labored so hard to build with Rabin.
The idea of rotating the Defense Ministry fell as quickly as it had been
raised. The negotiations were about to break down, and Peres began
to contemplate the unattractive possibility of a new appeal to the
voters.

Help came from an unexpected quarter. Businessman Azriel
Einav, an old acquaintance, called Peres and invited him to his home

in the luxurious suburb of Savyon for a secret meeting with Ariel Sharon. Einav told him that Sharon was interested in hearing firsthand about the deadlock in the coalition negotiations—possibly he could help. Peres was doubtful both about Sharon's motives and his ability to help; but, after further pleas from Einav, he came to the conclusion that even if the discussion did not help, it could not do much harm.

Peres came to the meeting on his own. Sharon brought Rafi Eitan, who was later to become famous as the controller of the spy, Jonathan Pollard. In a series of secret meetings that began in the presence of Einav and Eitan, and continued with Peres and Sharon meeting privately, Sharon agreed to give his blessing to a scheme whereby Peres would be prime minister for the first two years, then Shamir would take over; but Rabin would be defense minister for the entire four-year period.

What about ideological and political differences? Peres had given that subject a lot of thought, and he proposed the idea of an inner cabinet, consisting of five ministers from Labor and five from the Likud. Important issues would be discussed in this forum, which, because of its balanced structure, would not be able to decide on anything really objectionable to one of the large parties. Sharon wanted to convey these suggestions to his party; in return, he wanted a senior ministry and a seat in the inner cabinet.

There remained ideological and political differences. The extra twenty-one days that the president had given Peres passed without agreement. The teams working on it had difficulty in arriving at a formulation that could reconcile the program of the Alignment, accepting territorial compromise in the West Bank and Gaza, with the Camp David autonomy scheme, which was the limit of the Likud's concessions. Peres rejected the stand of his party colleagues, who showed a tendency to argue every dot and comma. He reiterated time and again, "We don't have any time. These are the results of the election, and we have to live with them." In fact, he believed in his ability to lead the Likud to far-reaching political moves that no coalition agreement could prevent.

In the end a compromise formula was found, a call to Jordan to negotiate without prior conditions. The deadlock over settlement necessitated a concession by Labor, which, during its years in opposition, had sharply criticized the "provocative settlement policy" of the Likud. Peres proposed that Labor agree to the establishment of another six settlements. Shamir, worried and fearful of Sharon, was not satisfied. The compromise was to approve the twenty-eight settlements already decided on by the Likud, but the actual establishment of each new settlement would be decided by the inner cabinet.

At last, the agreement was complete. It resolved that Peres would be prime minister for the first two years, during which Shamir would be foreign minister. At the end of two years, they would switch roles. Rabin would be defense minister for the entire four years. Sharon received the Ministry of Industry and Trade.

There were quite a few Labor party members—those associated with the dovish camp—who said out loud that Peres had sold out the party's principles in order to fulfill his dream of becoming prime minister. Peres took the opportunity to reply to his critics when the central committee met to approve the agreement. After surveying the election results, he clarified the alternative: "Let's say we go to elections, and we get the same results—what then?"

"We'll change the head of the list," someone interjected.

"We can change everything," Peres said. "If there are members who think that I did not do my job properly for the past seven years, they have the right to say so."

Peres went on to outline the important tasks facing the government at this difficult hour for the country: "We must overcome the split in the nation that we have reached and bring to an end our involvement in Lebanon."

After three hours of discussion, it was evident that the majority of central committee members supported Peres. The vote in favor of establishing a national unity government was 70 percent.

On September 13, 1984, Peres presented his government to a festive Knesset—and an excited family in the visitors' gallery. The emotion was evident on his face. He had waited so long for this occasion, but his heart was torn: "This government was born on divided ground, constructed on unknown precedents, and completed with the delicate work of straightening things out."

First on the government's list of urgent priorities, he emphasized, was the need to stabilize the economy, renew growth, and bring down inflation, while avoiding unemployment and guaranteeing a living wage for the workers. He then promised to bring the IDF home from Lebanon while safeguarding the security of the Galilee settlements. He went on to appeal to King Hussein to come to the negotiating table to talk about a real peace.

In an interview he gave to *Ha'aretz,* only a few minutes after being sworn in as prime minister, Peres said: "I felt a certain relief, after an effort that was almost beyond human capacity, and continued five weeks, day and night. We went through so many crises, and often there was the feeling that everything was about to crumble . . . I know that my seven years in opposition have been portrayed as my struggle to reach the top. I had the feeling that my task, during the party's most difficult hours, in days of disillusionment and loss of belief, was to stand firm and not to be pushed into demagogy, on the one hand, or despair, on the other. I knew that there was no alternative to stubborn endeavor, which was not always understood and often aroused criticism. It wasn't easy or simple, but I knew what I was working for, and therefore, there was no question of whom I was working for. It was that feeling that made me immune to much of the unjust accusations and envy that was voiced."

Asked how he felt, sitting in Ben-Gurion's chair, he replied: "I don't feel I'm sitting on his chair—on his path, yes. To this day, I still believe in his path, which is to see Israel as a whole, rather than its parts. I learned from Ben-Gurion not to be afraid of criticism, and that only with an iron will can impossible difficulties be overcome. I learned uncompromising realism and unlimited faith."

On the following morning, a Friday, Peres arrived at the prime minister's office with his aides. Photographers recorded the change of guard for posterity. A quarter of an hour with Shamir followed. This was all the outgoing prime minister needed to bring his successor up-to-date.

From his new office, which already had a giant portrait of Ben-Gurion on the wall, Peres drove to the presidential residence in his official car, driven by Burba, his veteran driver, and surrounded by an enlarged contingent of security men. After presenting his twenty-four-member cabinet to President Chaim Herzog, he returned to his office, not allowing himself a pause for thought, reflection, or consideration of the greatness of the moment. He rolled up his sleeves and started to deal with the problems of the nation in the order he had laid out: economy, Lebanon, peace.

CHAPTER TEN

THE STRUGGLE AGAINST INFLATION

It would be difficult to imagine a worse economic situation than the one Peres inherited. There were no precedents in any of the textbooks, where yesterday's records swiftly gave way to the new records of today. Inflation fluctuated between 12 and 14 percent per month, and was still rising. In fact, it had reached a rate that was impossible to calculate accurately. The trade deficit was $2.5 billion. The foreign currency reserves had plunged well below the "red line" of $2 billion. There was nothing on the horizon to halt the deterioration. On the contrary, the outgoing government had left a deficit budget that necessitated the injection of $1.3 billion a year, and this threatened to bring the nation to the threshold of bankruptcy.

Something of this situation had even begun to permeate the public's consciousness. After the people had purchased their new cars, their color television sets, and their videocassette recorders, they began to realize that their private celebration would end in the destruction of the very fabric of the society in which they were living.

Peres was aware of all this, and of something more. He realized that his ability, or inability, to put the economy back on the rails would make him or break him. Anything else that he might achieve, however great, would be worthless if the economy was bankrupt. To some extent, fate was mocking him. This was not the "baby" to which Peres had looked forward. More than anything else, he had wanted to be prime minister in order to implement his ideas and utilize his capacity for getting things done. New political initiatives, sophisticated industries, the greening of the desert—these were the things he believed in. Instead, he was now forced to go in the opposite direction: to curb initiatives, to hold up new industries, to cut back on growth.

Peres started to carry out this task with determination, and without wasting a single day. As his secretaries were still trying to work out how the phones operated and porters were carting in the crates of books that Peres took with him wherever he went, he met in his new office with two key economic ministers: Finance Minister Yitzhak Moda'i from the Likud, and his Labor colleague, Gad Ya'acobi, minister of economics.

Peres knew that Moda'i would be a problem. He was highly intelligent, but nevertheless given to inexplicable and unpredictable outbursts. More than anything else, he was sensitive to the fact that the public expected Peres—in other words, Labor—to pull the economic wagon out of the mud in which the Likud had mired it.

Peres's only navigating equipment was a secret economic plan prepared by an economic council that Peres had established about two months before the elections. The principles of the plan were a notable cut in government spending, erosion of wages, a price freeze, and the creation of a new currency.

Peres presented the plan in the form of "ideas," taking care to point out that Moda'i himself had mentioned several of the proposals before. Ya'acobi, who had coordinated with Peres in advance, proposed an immediate cut in the budget, if only to create a new atmosphere and restore public confidence in the government. But Peres was going too fast for Moda'i. He expressed determined opposition to any immediate step, and he suggested that a cabinet discussion on a complete and properly worked-out plan be brought forward. As an alternative, he pulled out of his briefcase his own plan for the dollarization of the economy—replacing the Israeli shekel with the U.S. dollar.

Peres categorically rejected dollarization, and he was not prepared to consider a cabinet discussion. He knew that a discussion of a comprehensive program would be accompanied by endless pressures from all sides, which could torpedo the process before it was started. He cited, as an example, the fact that a similar program for budget cuts, proposed by the Likud government in October, had failed because of Prime Minister Shamir's inability to stand up to the pressure of his cabinet colleagues.

When his persuasion had no effect, Peres told Moda'i that if he persisted in his refusal, he would bring the proposal to cut the budget to the cabinet and put it to the vote. The threat had its effect, probably because of Moda'i reluctance to be defeated in the cabinet on the first economic proposal brought before it. It was resolved to bring to the first cabinet meeting, due to take place in two days' time, a proposal to cut the national budget by a billion dollars.

Some of the Likud ministers—David Levy and Ariel Sharon being the most vociferous—protested with words such as "tragedy," "social crisis," and "the economy is on the verge of destruction." But eventually, the proposal was approved by a large majority. It was a tough decision, involving a sharp cut in subsidies. It meant a rise in prices, a lowering of the standard of living, and dismissals on a scale that could not be foreseen. Despite all this, the public welcomed the step, perceiving in it the government's willingness to take painful steps to heal the economy.

This fact did not deceive Peres about the speed with which he would be able to advance. He had no illusions about his political ability to maneuver successive, painful measures, taking into account Israel's delicate social fabric. The public was starting to understand the threatening significance of concepts such as the "deficit in the balance of trade," and "dwindling foreign currency reserves."

On the personal level, however, half the population—the Oriental Jews—were very aware of the fact that when the Labor Alignment was in power, they never had a cent in their pockets. It was only after the Likud came to power that they were able to permit themselves the consumer goods that previously had been the exclusive possessions of Jews of European origin. The Oriental Jews were not particularly interested in the fact that the price of the candies they had been given had been the destruction of the national economy. As long as the economy had been more or less healthy, it had been the European Jews who had benefited. Now it was the turn of the Oriental Jews to receive their slice of the national cake. If the result was an economic crisis, let the rich Europeans pay the price of remedying it.

Was this stand justified? Was it a correct picture of the situation? These questions were irrelevant. That was the perception that prevailed, and few had received more painful lessons than Peres on the pointlessness of arguing about the facts.

In order to neutralize the blow to the poorer sectors of the population, Peres needed something to balance his budget-cutting, and that could only come from the direction of Washington. Peres had in his pocket an invitation to come to the U.S. capital for a working visit, brought to him by Ambassador Samuel Lewis only three days after he became prime minister. The invitation had come just as American involvement in Israel's economy had reached a peak. The civilian and military economic cooperation had reached levels during the 1980s for which there was no precedent in U.S. relations with another nation.

After he had forced the budget cut through the cabinet, Peres decided to take advantage of the invitation, receptive as he was to the voices from Washington, whether directly from the administration or indirectly from the media. The message was unambiguous: the United States expressed a willingness to help Israel overcome its economic problems, but only after Israel had shown a willingness to help itself. The budget cut was one example, and it was welcomed. Peres gave the Americans another example, just before he set out for his visit to their country. He called a meeting of the Ministerial Economic Committee and forced through, with a one-vote margin, import limitations and foreign currency controls.

As soon as he arrived in the United States, Peres realized that neither the administration nor the media thought the measures he had taken had been drastic enough. In an article in *Foreign Affairs,* summing up Peres's period as prime minister, Samuel Lewis (who by then was no longer the American ambassador to Israel) wrote of Peres's three days in Washington:

"He gave a brilliant analysis of the dilemmas facing Israel and the plans of his government. He impressed President Reagan, Secretary of State Schultz, and their senior advisers, congressional leaders, and influential newspaper columnists by the seriousness with which Israel was tackling its problems. By the end of his visit, personal contact with the senior American leadership had been revived, the support for Israel of the American public had been restored, and the vital relations between the two countries had been raised to a level of closeness and trust."

In addition to all this, Peres achieved the main aim of his visit: American agreement to grant Israel emergency aid, in the event that the economic steps that Peres intended to take put dangerous pressure on the nation's foreign currency reserves. Peres described this as a "financial safety net" for Israel's economic recovery program.

In due course this "safety net" would be translated into $1.5 billion, and the question that remained was when, and under what conditions, the money should be transferred to Israel. At Reagan's suggestion, a joint U.S.-Israeli economic committee was established to investigate Israel's economic position, its economic plans, and the aid needed to carry them out. Alan Wallis, a senior U.S. Treasury official, served as chairman of the committee, which began meeting in December 1984. Professor Stanley Fisher of the Massachusetts Institute of Technology, who had spent several years in Israel, knew the economy, and knew Hebrew, was co-opted to the American team. Reagan also promised Peres to consider favorably requests to increase American military purchases from Israel.

Four days after his return to Israel, President Reagan gave Peres the opportunity of proving that the money he had agreed in principle to give Israel was not only a favor. In a letter to the prime minister, President Reagan explained the importance of the broadcasts to the Soviet Union of the Voice of America radio station. He expressed the hope that Israel would view favorably the American request to build on its soil giant transmitters for broadcasting Western propaganda to Soviet citizens.

Peres knew that U.S. allies in Europe had refused a similar request, and for this reason, the president had personally written him a long letter. Determined to achieve as much goodwill as possible from the matter, he wrote in reply: "As you surely know, the matter is likely to cause damage and to increase the pressure on Soviet Jews. We hesitated a great deal concerning your request, but after your personal appeal we decided to check the matter again." It was understood that reconsidering the question would result in a positive answer. Only a thoughtless person—or a shameless one—could refuse a president about to give him a billion and a half dollars.

Two days after Peres's message reached Washington, he received a letter from Secretary of State Schultz, thanking him for agreeing to the president's request. Immediately after it arrived, another letter signed by the secretary of state, this time expressing admiration for Peres's determination to tackle the economic problems: "If this progress continues, the success of the plan is assured, and we will be ready with our support."

But it turned out that the compliments were not the only reason—not even the main reason—for this letter. In fact, the mention of the financial aid that Israel needed so much was a reminder to Jerusalem not to be deaf to another administration request, this one concerning planned arms deals with Jordan and Saudi Arabia: "The administration asks that Israel refrain from raising difficulties on this matter." In other words, the administration would greatly appreciate—and, in fact, anticipated—that Israel would not oppose the deal too determinedly, and, in particular, would not encourage its supporters in Congress to vote against it.

This sort of request always creates a difficult dilemma. Israel has always opposed arms supplies to the Arab nations. The pro-Israel lobby in the United States was always mobilized to foil such deals. If Israel refrained from opposing the deal with Jordan and Saudi Arabia in the present instance, it would undermine its ability to mobilize the lobby to oppose deals of this type in future. On the other hand, there was real concern about losing the goodwill of the administration at a time when Israel needed it so much.

Peres called a special meeting with Shamir and Rabin. They did not hesitate for long. The three of them understood that Israel was in the position of a beggar who could not afford to bite the hand that was feeding it. They decided on "passive opposition" to the deal, assuming that AIPAC, the pro-Israel lobby in Washington, would, in any case, do what had to be done in Congress; however, Tom Dine, the head of AIPAC, reported a few days later that the administration had decided to postpone its decision on the deal.

With the American safety net in position, Israel could now perform its own acrobatics without fearing that, in the event of a fall, it would fracture its elbow. In fact it was forced to act, both because of its promise to the United States, and because an economy in such dire strats cannot be healed by outside financial assistance alone.

At the end of October 1984, Finance Ministry Director General

Emmanuel Sharon presented Peres with the plan he had worked out with his team. It contained many of the elements of Labor's plan, with some additional features that ran counter to the promises that Peres had brought from Wasington. The proposed start of implementation of the plan was January 1, 1985, instead of April 1, which was the beginning of the financial year.

While the discussions of the Treasury plan were in full swing, Moshe Sanbar, the former governor of the Bank of Israel, asked to meet Peres. He surprised the prime minister with a proposal that could bring down inflation without causing too many disruptions. Speaking in the name of another former governor, Arnon Gafni, and the present governor, Moshe Mandelbaum, Sanbar suggested that Peres reach an agreement with the Histadrut on a "package deal" involving a freeze on wages and prices. According to Sanbar, Histadrut Secretary General Yisrael Kessar had already agreed to the deal in principle.

Peres quickly saw the advantages of the proposal. The most important was that its implementation, unlike that of the Treasury's plan, did not involve large-scale unemployment, the social and political consequences of which concerned Peres greatly. It should also be added that the package deal involved a general agreement, which was much more Peres's style, rather than confrontation.

Accordingly, Peres put the Treasury plan aside for the time being, infuriating Moda'i, and instead established a committee of six ministers to work out a package deal. A parallel economic and social council, consisting of representatives of government, Histadrut, and employers, was also established.

The first stage was a disappointment. It quickly became apparent that Kesar's agreement to the package, which Sanbar had reported, was only partial. He did agree in principle, but he had a number of reservations, which naturally related to the wage freeze. Tough and exhausting negotiations ensued, in which Peres found himself in perpetual confrontations with the Histadrut secretary general, one of the senior figures in the Labor party. In these discussions, which often became heated, Peres had to take insults from Kessar, who sometimes, in the presence of Likud members, gave vent to scornful references to Peres as "His Highness."

Peres absorbed the insults without responding. Accepting insults while continuing to push for his target was Peres's specialty—

almost his way of life. Finally, the secretary general was restrained by members of his own party, who demanded that he show respect for the party leader.

Peres devoted all his time to this process. Night and day, without sleep, he pursued the tough negotiations, during which he also had to deal with Moda'i, so that he would not be affronted. Never before had an Israeli prime minister intervened in economic matters in such an intensive and dominant manner. In the end, in January 1985, Peres's endeavors were rewarded with success when the three main elements in the economy—the government, the Histadrut, and the employers—signed a package deal for an eight-month period. Its principal features were comprehensive supervision of wages and prices, cancellation of most of the subsidies, and a 10 percent cut in the state budget.

Peres's success in bringing the government, the Histadrut, and the employers to agreement was reckoned by everyone to be a remarkable achievement. It was also a big step in the right direction from an economic point of view, but insufficient, as it turned out, for such a sick economy. This was the opinion of many economists in Israel; it was also the opinion of many economists in Washington— and not only economists. A gigantic advertisement in the *New York Times* proclaimed: "Mr. President, enough! Stop the endless, immoral donations paying every Israeli citizen more than $1,000 a year." It was signed by "American taxpayers, the unemployed, and the homeless."

On December 8, 1984, Ambassador Lewis brought a forceful message from Secretary Shultz. "The United States will not transfer the emergency assistance until there are signs that you have achieved your purpose, and until you clarify the plan for healing the economy." Officials in the U.S. State Department kept up a continuous barrage of criticism about Israel's economic policy, the package deal, and the steps taken by the government to control prices. At one of the meetings with the American team, which had come to Israel to check on what was being done, Peres lost some of his patience: "What do you suggest? Let's hear your remedy." The Americans, who had strict instructions not to become involved in the "Israeli cauldron," replied, "There are many good Israeli economists, who know the system and who are perfectly capable of finding the best solutions. It is not our job to propose economic plans to you."

At the beginning of February, a second package deal was signed, which, as anticipated, caused disappointment in Washington, where it had been assumed that the economic plan would be implemented when the first package deal ended. Ambassador Lewis met with Peres and left no doubt about the intentions of the administration. "Additional economic measures are necessary," he said, "and we cannot yet recommend further assistance. The United States is concerned about the creeping devaluation of the dollar, and the Israeli shekel is inflated in relation to the European currencies." The ambassador recommended that the government show its ability to act by implementing a significant cut in the state budget.

Peres was under pressure from the Histadrut on one side and the United States on the other. The exhausting discussions with the Histadrut and the employers, the arguments with Kessar and Moda'i, the constant dealing with prices and budgets, the fact that the end was not in sight—all this challenged his legendary patience. He began to show clear signs of irritation and physical and mental fatigue. At a meeting with Lewis, he burst out angrily at the Undersecretary of the U.S. Treasury, Alan Wallis, who had told the presidents of economic organizations that day that Israel had already wasted $1.2 billion of American civilian aid. "That is an unjust and insulting comment," complained Peres. "The entire sum was used for debt repayment. Not a cent was used for maintaining an easy standard of living or current expenses. I was personally insulted by Wallis's remarks."

One may assume that Lewis reported on Peres's plight to his superiors in Washington, for two days later a special letter arrived from Shultz. The letter was replete with expressions of admiration for the efforts Peres was making to heal the economy, but the most important part came at the end: "There still have not been sufficient steps to justify receiving the emergency aid."

This letter is particularly interesting because this time, Shultz did not content himself with saying that not enough had been done. He also wrote what he thought should be done: reform of the economy, including granting the central bank independence; a deep cut (again) in the state budget; and a reduction in the standard of services that the government provided the public.

Peres wrote back: "I am confident that the combination of our determination at home, and the friendly support of the administration under the leadership of the president, will preserve the stability of our economy." These were not simply expressions of courtesy. By now Peres, and the entire government, understood that Shultz's increasing involvement in the Israeli economy was the result of a genuine desire to contribute to its recovery. Even if Peres differed with the secretary over the means, he knew that they agreed over the ends. And when one of his associates asked Peres what right Shultz had to tell Israel what to do, he replied angrily, "He has earned the right."

In order to translate his recommendations into concrete action, Schultz invited Moda'i, in that same letter, to come to Washington for talks with the American team. Moda'i went to the meeting, and immediately after his return, economists Stanley Fisher and Herbert Stein were sent to Jerusalem for talks with Treasury and Bank of Israel officials.

In the middle of March, a paper was produced that was described as "Stein's ten points." They were the basis of an economic plan to stabilize the economy. In fact, the ten points had been worked out by Peres's economic adviser, Amnon Neubach, and Treasury Director General Sharon. Both of them were convinced that the package deals had done what they could, but in fact had not led anywhere. They agreed with the Americans that only a tough and brave economic plan could put the economy back on track. As they were well aware of Peres's political problems, they understood that the only way to get the cabinet to endorse the plan was for the Americans to make it crystal clear that the promised assistance would be granted only if the government approved an economic plan based on the principles agreed on in Washington and Jerusalem. In other words, the Israeli government did not possess the political courage to decide on the painful and difficult economic steps that it knew were unavoidable. It needed an external factor to force it to do what it wanted, so that it could say afterward, "We were raped!"

This work was accomplished by Treasury Director General Sharon, with the approval of Moda'i. He went to Washington and told Fisher and Stein that if the administration made its assistance conditional on Israel's adoption of "Stein's ten points," the government would not be displeased, even though it might voice some formal expressions of protest.

Sharon returned to Israel, and a few days later it was announced that the U.S. administration was making its assistance conditional on an agreement to implement the "ten points of Stein and Fisher." (In fact, of Sharon and Neubach.)

At the end of May 1985, a professional team was set up, headed by Director General Sharon, and it began a series of intensive and secret meetings to work out the detailed program, based on a major cut in subsidies and devaluation of the Israeli shekel. Some of the Treasury officials involved in the discussions were not happy. They came to the prime minister with their objections to such far-reaching measures and suggested that a budget cut and an adjustment of the exchange rate would be sufficient.

Peres listened, but did not make a decision. The calendar on his desk indicated the approach of May 13, 1985, the day of the Histadrut elections. Before that date passed, no economic program, including measures that were liable to lose Labor a considerable number of votes, would be announced.

On the day after the Histadrut poll, which resulted in a smashing victory for the Labor Alignment, Peres returned in the early evening from one of his weekly trips around the country. Despite his fatigue, he called a meeting in his home with Moda'i, Director General Sharon, Neubach, and Professors Michael Bruno and Eitan Berglass.

In telling them that the situation was not good, he was not revealing any secrets. By then, the second package deal was showing sure signs of crumbling. Despite supervision, prices were rising, and under-the-table wage increments were being granted. The budget cuts remained on paper only, and almost every day there were strikes in some part of the country. Everyone wanted more money: the cabinet ministers wanted it for their ministries, the workers wanted wage increases, the manufacturers wanted to raise prices.

Peres opened the meeting by saying, "From this moment on we are going to sit here, day and night, twenty-four hours a day, until we have finalized all the details of the economic plan." It was agreed to keep the meetings entirely secret so as not to further harm the stability of the economy, which, in any case, was none too stable, and to avoid rumors of a devaluation, which was scheduled to be part of the program. They believed that, the greater the surprise, the easier it would be for the public to accept the new measures. And, in fact, the meetings in Peres's home lasted into the morning hours almost every night. Peres did not sidestep a single detail or economic statistic, and made numerous mathematical calculations, putting special emphasis on the budget-cutting possibilities in each ministry.

The discussions on the economic program became more frequent and longer in the last ten days of June 1985, as the date for the expiration of the second package deal, July 5, approached.

In the prime minister's office, finishing touches were being added to the plan. Peres proposed to meet with some of the economic ministers on Friday afternoon to report on the main features of the program and, at the same time, to call a special cabinet meeting for Saturday evening, June 29. The following morning, Peres was scheduled to address the public on radio and television.

Almost at the last moment, the Treasury announced that it did not have all the documentation needed for Saturday evening. Gad Ya'acobi, who had only been told about the plan on Friday, was asked on Sunday morning to present to the cabinet the five-year plan worked out by the Economics and Planning Ministry, in order to gain time.

Only on Sunday afternoon was everything ready. Ya'acobi's lecture on his five-year plan was interrupted; Peres informed the ministers of the economic plan and outlined its main elements. After he had finished, he warned forcefully that failure to accept what he called the "emergency plan for stabilizing the economy" would mean the breakup of the national unity government. And he said further, "Anyone not prepared to support the plan after it has been accepted will have to resign."

Professors Bruno and Berglass, who had been invited to the cabinet meeting, explained to the ministers that the program was designed both to bring down inflation and to reduce the balance of payments deficit. They presented the document that outlined the main points.

The plan would be implemented for one year. At the outset, the government would declare an economic state of emergency for three months. At the heart of the program was a reduction in the state budget deficit of $300 to $400 million, below what had been planned for fiscal year 1985. To this end, there would be a budget cut of $750 million for the next two years. Other steps included a devaluation of 20 percent; cutting subsidies of goods and services; freezing of prices, wages, the exchange rate, interest rates, and other monetary steps; together with steps to distribute the tax burden more justly.

The toughest part was the need to use emergency regulations because the plan was complex and had to be implemented comprehensively. These regulations would be used, according to the plan, to fire employees in the public sector. Never before had the emergency regulations (which dated back to the time of the British mandate) been used to implement a government program. Those who had worked out the plan were well aware of this, and they did not like these methods any more than the plan's opponents; however, they believed that there really was a situation of grave emergency, requiring economic measures that could not be implemented without emergency regulations.

The economic plan split the government right through party lines. The battle against the program was waged by the "social lobby," in which Deputy Prime Minister David Levy competed with Industry Minister Sharon and Welfare Minister Moshe Katzav in voicing criticism of the effects on the weakest sectors of the population. Using their aides, these ministers leaked their speeches, while the meeting was still in progress, to journalists who were waiting in the parking lot outside the prime minister's office.

Minister Without Portfolio Moshe Arens presented a plan similiar to the dollarization plan once suggested by former Finance Minister Yoram Aridor. Science Minister Gideon Patt also suggested an alternative scheme. Some of the Labor ministers joined the criticism of the effect of the program on the poor, but by the end of the discussion, they had accepted Peres's discipline. The main problem was Yitzhak Rabin, who objected strongly to the cuts in the defense budget, but he also gave way in the end, so as not to destroy the plan.

At 2:00 A.M., the ministers stopped speaking in generalities, and the bargaining began over the budget cuts for the various ministries. Treasury officials attending the meeting bit their nails nervously, fearing that this was going to be the downfall of the entire plan. As the discussion continued into the morning, the ministers wanted more than anything else to get to bed, and the process of giving in began. At 6:00 A.M., it was Ariel Sharon's task to deliver the swan song of the opponents. Smashing his fist on the table, he shouted, "In another month we'll sit here with an economy in ruins. I will not be a partner to this." Before too long, he would very much want to forget this statement and to cause it to be forgotten.

At 6:50 A.M., Uri Savir, Peres's media adviser, passed him a note informing him that Israel Television was ready to begin the special broadcast on the meeting in ten minutes' time. Peres told him that he would not leave the room until "the last cent" of the cuts had been resolved.

At 9:00 A.M., twenty-five hours after he had opened it, the prime minister brought the cabinet meeting to an end. The plan was approved over the votes of the Likud ministers, with the exception of Vice Premier Yitzhak Shamir, who did not open his mouth throughout the proceedings, Finance Minister Moda'i, and Transportation Minister Haim Corfu. The only Labor minister who did not vote for the plan was Yitzhak Rabin, who abstained.

The program was unprecedented in its scale: deep cuts in government spending, a freeze on wages and prices, new tax regulations, significant dismissals in the public sector, renewed subsidy cuts that the package deals had not managed to achieve, and devaluation of the Israeli shekel by 18.8 percent. The most painful measure of all, from the point of view of the wage earners, was the cancellation of the linkage that existed in all wage agreements between wages and the cost-of-living index, and the related decision not to compensate workers for the subsidy cuts—something that had been automatic in the past. In effect, all wages had been cut 25 percent.

Economists and most of the press gave the plan their full backing, but the workers reacted with fury to what they called the "economic decrees." Within hours of the announcement of the government's decision, news reached Peres's office of demonstrations, strikes, electricity stoppages, and the disruption of other public services. No less speedy were the ministers opposed to the plan, who hastened to criticize it sharply and publicly, the most active of whom were Sharon and Levy. The result was that, although Moda'i was a senior if not equal partner, and although Likud leader Shamir had voted for it, the plan came to be identified with Peres alone. Furthermore, as the strikes and protests grew, Moda'i's claim to be the originator of the plan lessened and finally disappeared altogether, and he too began to express criticism of the program, as if he were in the opposition, and not the finance minister whose ministry was charged with implementing it.

The campaign against Peres became uncompromising—even violent. The Histadrut ordered television employees to prevent his appearing on the screen, and the head of the Electricity Workers Committee announced work sanctions, under the motto, "The people are enslaved and starving." The Histadrut secretary general opened every speech with the words, "I have come here under a military regime." Peres faced Kessar and the Histadrut Central Committee alone, as most of the other ministers stood aside and waited for the result of the confrontation.

These were difficult months for Peres. He was pressured from all sides to modify the severity of the economic measures. During this period, maybe more than ever before, he demonstrated his typical patience and coolness, as he was convinced of the justice of his cause. Gradually the storm died down, particularly as the plan began to show its first positive effects.

The economy started to slide into a depression, and the ranks of the unemployed increased, although on a far smaller scale than the Likud pessimists had anticipated. On the other hand, for the first time in many years, there was a clear rise in productivity. Imports, particularly of consumer goods, dropped dramatically as exports started to increase. The public started to feel that there was a reward for their wage erosion, that the economy was on the road to stability, which was concretely expressed in the introduction of the new shekel, worth a thousand former shekels.

Not only in Israel was satisfaction expressed. Washington saw the introduction of the plan as the fulfillment of the condition it had laid down for granting the emergency aid, and $1.5 billion was transferred to Israel at the end of 1985 and during 1986. The combination of American aid with falling imports and increasing exports led to a dramatic increase in Israel's foreign currency reserves, which at last reached a reasonable level.

Another increase—and in a manner hitherto unheard of—was in the popularity of the man seen by the public as mainly responsible for the economic turnaround. Public opinion polls taken at the time showed that more than 70 percent of those asked were completely satisfied with Peres as prime minister. Even Ben-Gurion never reached such levels of approval.

The finance minister might have been expected to be pleased with the success of the economic recovery plan, but in fact the opposite occurred. As the signs of the success of the program became increasingly clear, the impulsive Moda'i went from panic to hysteria, which developed slowly but surely until it reached its peak in April 1986.

While the prime minister was visiting Washington, Moda'i gave two newspaper interviews, charging that the Labor party was milking the national purse in favor of Histadrut industries and kibbutz factories connected with the party. This charge in itself was very serious, but Moda'i did not content himself with it—he also dealt personally with the prime minister. He complained about Peres's regular trips abroad, scornfully dubbing him "the flying prime minister." One of his interviewers provoked him by asking him what he thought of "the claim of Shimon Peres's friends that the success of the economic program is that of the prime minister and not of the finance minister."

"Peres had nothing to do with the planning or the implementation . . . because Peres understands nothing of economic matters, and he is an appeaser by nature," replied Moda'i.

When Peres returned on Saturday evening from his short trip to the United States, he was already in a bad mood because the peace process had become bogged down in one of the complications concerning an international conference. On Sunday morning, before the weekly cabinet meeting, Peres called in Moda'i and asked him about the interviews. He had the two papers on his desk, and, pointing to them, he said: "Yitzhak, look at the terrible things you said." Moda'i squirmed and said, "I was not quoted accurately."

Peres informed Yitzhak Shamir that he intended to fire Moda'i as finance minister, and he asked him to suggest another candidate for the post. Shamir protested that the coalition agreement prevented the prime minister from dismissing a minister from the opposing party without the agreement of the leader of that party. Peres replied that the agreement referred to dismissals from the government as a whole, not from one of the ministries.

The Likud ministers met, and Moda'i demanded that they resign en masse when Peres delivered his letter of dismissal. The ministers listened, and then decided to continue trying to prevent the dismissal of their colleague. None of them seemed eager to accept Moda'i's pleas that they follow him out of the government.

On Sunday, April 27, 1986, the Modai affair came to an end, one week after it had started. After Peres had rejected Shamir's proposal to appoint Ariel Sharon finance minister—he did not want to replace one problem with a bigger one—the Likud ministers decided after a long meeting, replete with shouting and tension, that the ministers of finance and justice—both of them from the Liberal party—would exchange portfolios. Peres and the Labor ministers, who had to wait a long time for the decision of their colleagues, voted in favor. The cabinet took three minutes to approve the arrangement, which again disappointed some Labor activists, who had been looking forward to celebrating the death of the unity government, and of the rotation agreement.

Moshe Nissim, the son of a former Sephardi chief rabbi, a rival of Moda'i's in the Liberal party, and a man with no knowledge of economics, became finance minister the next day. In character and temperament, he was the exact opposite of Moda'i. Patient, very restrained, balanced in word and deed, Nissim achieved his purpose without rows and without emotion. Gradually he and Peres developed an excellent working relationship. In a short time, the moderate but determined Nissim overtook Moda'i in popularity and became an important electoral asset for the Likud.

With the Moda'i affair behind him, with the monthly inflation rate down to 1 or 2 percent and with the foreign currency reserves stable, Peres confided to a few of his close colleagues his thoughts about the campaign he had waged. "No Western democracy undertook such a burden on its citizens and took such a gamble: to be or not to be." Peres had every reason to pat himself on the back, but in no way could he see the task as accomplished. Stopping the inflationary spiral was not in itself enough to create a healthy economy. To achieve this, it must be brought to a process of growth, particularly in the field of exports. This had not yet been achieved, and until it was, the economy was walking a tightrope, likely to fall once again into the abyss of consumption and inflation. To prevent this, care must be taken to prevent the loosening of belts. This fact would compel

Peres, in the second period of the national unity government, to make one of the most difficult and painful decisions of his life, when he had to decide whether to continue with the production of the Lavi combat aircraft.

CHAPTER ELEVEN

THE LION THAT DIDN'T ROAR

THE SEED THAT originated the Lavi (Hebrew for "lion") project had been sown in 1974, when the Israel Aircraft Industry (IAI) presented the defense minister a document outlining the production of a combat aircraft for the 1990s. In the next few years, the proposal spent far more time in desk drawers than on the discussion table.

It was not until 1980 that the defense minister at that time, former Air Force Commander Ezer Weizman, proposed to the government that Israel manufacture the Lavi combat aircraft. His reason was Israel's inability to afford the escalating prices of the advanced and sophisticated aircraft being manufactured in the United States. The government approved his suggestion.

Weizman's proposal related to a relatively small plane with one F-404 General Electric engine. Meanwhile, Weizman resigned from the government and, pending the appointment of a new minister, Prime Minister Begin took over the Defense Ministry. In two meetings in May 1981, he heard from Air Force Commander David Ivri that the manufacture of "Weizman's plane" did not fulfill the operational needs of the Israeli air force, and therefore, its manufacture would not obviate the necessity to purchase F-16 combat aircraft from the United States. Ivri recommended that if Israel was going to manufacture a plane, it should have a far larger engine. Begin, an admirer of military men and with a marked dislike of dealing with technical details, resolved that, "the air force commander is the expert. If he says he needs a plane with a larger engine, we must do as he says."

A larger engine naturally led to a larger and heavier plane. It also led to a larger project team and greater expense. This, however, did not worry the government, because talks with the United States elicited the agreement that all the money needed for the project would come within the framework of military aid, and the Lavi would be a specific item in the budget. In exchange, Israel undertook to purchase the engine and most of the body in the United States. The Israel Aircraft Industry (IAI) dealt mainly with the electronics and aeronautics of the project.

As the various stages of production passed, it became clear that the basic estimates of the cost of the project had become irrelevant. At the outset, a cost of some fifteen million dollars per plane had been estimated. It now emerged that tens of millions of dollars per plane were involved; exactly how much became the subject for a debate that was never resolved. It also turned out that the IAI's hopes for exporting the plane, which would have a decisive effect on the cost, were baseless, as the interest shown by other countries in buying the Lavi was minimal.

That was the situation when Peres became prime minister. The sum of $1.5 billion had already been spent on the project, all of it received from the United States. However, as the cost estimates increased continuously, it became evident that sooner or later—apparently sooner—Israel itself would have to participate in financing the project in a very big way. This fact was mentioned at a meeting that Peres called in his office at the end of May 1985. The actual reason for the meeting was a proposal by Amnon Neubach, Peres's economic adviser, for an additional $500 million budget cut. Neubach suggested that the cancellation of the Lavi project, now in an advanced stage of planning, be considered as a significant demonstration of the seriousness of the government's intention to cut its spending.

Peres understood that there was no way of avoiding serious and difficult decisions, and he called a meeting with Finance Minister Moda'i, Economics Minister Gad Ya'acobi, Deputy Finance Minister

Adi Amora'i, and a group of six senior economists. Peres opened the meeting with a serious, almost angry statement about the need to bring down inflation.

Professor Haim Ben-Shahar, who had once been Labor's candidate for finance minister declared that, "The Lavi project is a burden on the budget. It is increasing all the time, and you know it." Peres did not like the remark, and he snapped impatiently, "Why does it disturb you?"

Ben-Shahar said: "It constitutes an enormous burden on consumption in the economy, in manpower, in expenditure, and in the deficit."

Peres replied: "I can tell you that the Lavi is currently earning two hundred fifty million dollars and I can definitely call it an export." (He was referring to the American assistance.)

Ben-Shahar said: "I see the Lavi as an expenditure of several hundred thousand dollars a year."

"What do you want of the Lavi? Is Zim [the national shipping company] any better? Is El Al [the national airline] better?"

Dan Halperin (Israel's economic counselor at the Washington embassy) said: "When it reaches the production stage, it will be a real problem, and you are minimizing it."

Peres interrupted angrily: "I supported a project to which there was powerful opposition. They said the soldiers don't have uniforms and food. What do we need it for? I am telling you that Israel has already earned a huge sum on that project. So I am saying, wait a minute, a nation without reserves that does not invest in the future . . . what will we do with the three thousand engineers working on the Lavi project?"

When Ben-Shahar asked where Israel would find the money needed to complete the Lavi project, Peres replied with impatience, "When we get to the problem, we'll look for it; we'll break our heads. Maybe we can find a partner. You cannot always see the solutions in advance."

It was an answer typical of the man who saw advanced technology as a vital component of Israel's security and survival. In that matter he was not a compromiser, particularly when the Israel Aircraft Industry was the subject. He was the man who had established IAI, and the Lavi project was now the jewel in its crown.

He would not be the one—so he thought at the time—to lend his hand to harming it in any way, or to clipping its wings.

The claim that there was no budget was not new to him. He had heard it when he had established the IAI, the military industry, and the atomic reactor, and when he had bought advanced weapons systems from France. If he had listened to these claims, Israel would now be lagging behind in both production and know-how. He accordingly answered Ben-Shahar as he had answered his earlier accusers. He had always regarded those who maintained that there was no money for large-scale projects as people of little faith and no vision. If the passing of the years had changed his opinion on other matters, on this it remained the same. It was difficult for him to grasp that, even if he had been right in many other cases, he could be wrong in this specific instance.

The Israelis were not the only ones doing their sums. They were making calculations in Washington, also, and the Americans started getting worried. The project was increasingly becoming a bottomless barrel. They were seriously concerned, and not without reason, that, despite the fact that specific sums had been allocated, Americans would be the ones who would have to pay the balance in the end, for the simple reason that Israel had no chance of being able to do so. They also came to the conclusion that it would be cheaper for them, in the long run, to continue giving Israel the money originally promised for the plane, on the condition that the billion-dollar-swallowing project was stopped.

The upshot of this reassessment was that a Pentagon mission arrived in Israel at the beginning of January 1987, after Peres had already moved to his position as foreign minister under the rotation agreement. The U.S. delegation was headed by the assistant to the defense secretary, Dov Zackheim, a religious, Hebrew-speaking Jew. Zackheim presented a number of alternatives to the continuation of the Lavi project, worked out by the U.S. Defense Department, the main object of which was to prevent unemployment, if it were canceled, among the thousands of engineers and technicians who were working on it. The main proposal was that, instead, delicate parts for the F-16 combat plane should be manufactured in Israel.

The Israeli Defense Ministry disputed the high estimates that Zackheim presented concerning the cost of each Lavi plane, and challenged his pessimistic assessments of the prospect of finding markets for it. The atmosphere was tense. The Israeli experts contended that another 2 billion dollars was needed for the project. Zackheim maintained that it would be far more, and he warned that Congress would not approve of increasing aid by converting Israeli shekels, the method used in the past to facilitate the maintenance of the scale of the project.

Zackheim spoke favorably of the future American plane, the ATF, which would go into operation in the mid-1990s. When asked to compare it to the Sovet MiG-29, Zackheim described the latter as "the poor man's F-15."

Peres promised Zackheim that the government would consider all the alternatives seriously. But the cabinet meeting on the subject, which was held on May 20, was less serious and more inclined to the visionary: discussing the technological gap of the twenty-first century and first-line combat aircraft made in Israel. Rabin arrogantly dismissed Zackheim's alternatives as worthless—not worthy of discussion. Minister Without Portfolio Moshe Arens, an aeronautical engineer by profession who had been defense minister when the Lavi project had soared to its present expenditure, declared: "The plane has not cost us a single cent." The less enthusiastic voices of Finance Minister Nissim and Tourism Minister Avraham Sharir were drowned out by the chorus of praise.

For this reason, the remarks of Dan Shomron, the new IDF chief of staff, had the effect of a very cold shower. Using slides and diagrams, he and his assistants proved that not only would the Lavi not contribute to the IDF's power, it would in fact fatally harm it. The senior officers explained that, because of the huge outlay on the Lavi, the IDF would not be able to purchase the sophisticated weaponry it needed so urgently.

The IAI people did not give up. They presented the other side of the coin: thousands of engineers and technicians fired; a billion dollars in severance pay for the employees and in compensation for canceled contracts; a brain drain to the United States; and other claims that sounded convincing.

At the next cabinet meeting, ten days later, the defense minister was far less self-assured. Rabin announced that continuing the project would necessitate a special additional budget because he could not agree that such a massive project should be funded out of the current defense budget. The doubts now began to be felt by other ministers, most of them on the Labor side. Judging from statistics they had received from the Treasury, they realized the need to allocate to the Lavi huge resources from the state budget, and none of them was prepared to give up any of his ministry's budget in favor of the Lavi, however much it was touted as a "national project."

Washington increased its pressure and demanded a decision. U.S. Ambassador Thomas Pickering passed on letters from every level of the administration, but the cabinet continued to hesitate. The IAI continued working on the project, and public criticism increased. Peres was not in the spotlight at this point. Prime Minister Shamir, Defense Minister Rabin, and Finance Minister Nissim were at center stage. When he was asked, Peres would speak of his concern about a brain drain, of the need for faith, and of the necessity of tightening the belt to fund a project so important for the development of Israeli technology.

Between the two cabinet meetings, Rabin flew to the United States to learn firsthand what the Americans were really prepared to offer in exchange for canceling the project. When he returned, he reported to the cabinet that he had received promises from Defense Secretary Caspar Weinberger and Secretary of State George Shultz to provide extensive compensation for the cancellation of the Lavi.

At the fifth cabinet meeting on the Lavi, Rabin made the big jump: he threw all his political prestige and weight behind the chief of staff, calling on the government to give up the Lavi and accept the American compensation, which would come largely in the form of increased orders from Israeli industry. From then on, he became the leader of the plane's opponents.

For the first time since the government had been formed, Peres found himself opposed to his party colleagues—and concerning a subject of prestige and principle that had become the main concern of the Israeli public. His stand in favor of continuing production of the Lavi put him in the same camp with Yitzhak Shamir and most of the Likud ministers, except Finance Minister Moshe Nissim. Nissim refused even to consider the allocation of a special budget for the Lavi, out of concern for the stability of the economy and the balancing of the state budget. Almost all the press lined up behind Rabin and Nissim. Peres found himself in a most difficult political position. The Labor ministers swung, one after another, to the side of those opposed, until Peres was left with only one Labor party minister on his side—Health Minister Shoshana Arbeli-Almoslino.

During the five weeks between the fifth and sixth cabinet meetings on the Lavi, demonstrations were held, and heavy political pressure was applied. The employees of the IAI, the largest industry in the nation, proclaimed that they and their families would not vote in the next election for a party whose ministers had caused the grounding of the Lavi.

Shamir hesitated and dithered between the pressure of Moshe Arens, who threatened to resign from the government if the Lavi were canceled, and Moshe Nissim, who indicated that he would resign if he were forced to print money to keep the project going. Proposals presented by the IAI to increase efficiency and thus bring down the cost of the project were found to be impractical.

Peres called Al Schwimmer back from New York. He wanted to hear the opinion of the man who, together with him, had established the IAI and run it for many years. He spent long hours in his home with Schwimmer, until he was finally convinced that the Lavi was too expensive and would be obsolete by the time it went into operation. However, dropping it just like that was unthinkable, because Peres was genuinely concerned about the future of IAI. He therefore worked out with Schwimmer a proposal involving the cancellation of the Lavi and the allocation of $100 million for the IDF alternatives, and for developing the technology of the next-generation aircraft. The proposal also promised that an effort would be made to increase the scope of production of parts for the F-16 at IAI.

On Sunday morning, Peres invited Rabin for a meeting with Schwimmer to inform him of their proposal. The defense minister listened silently to their explanations and then said he wanted to hear what the IDF general staff thought about it.

The army gave its unenthusiastic approval to the plan. The following morning, Peres visited the prime minister's office. Shamir, who had just returned from Rumania, listened quietly to the explanations, asked a number of questions, and said finally: "Talk to Misha Arens; I want to hear what he thinks." Peres understood that Shamir would not risk a confrontation with his most important Likud ally on a subject so important to that ally. Schwimmer returned from a meeting with Arens without achieving anything. He had not managed to budge him from his position, and from then on the Lavi became a straight party issue, with the Likud (except for Nissim and Sharir) in favor, and Labor (except for Arbeli-Almoslino) against.

Peres tried to persuade the Iraqi-born Arbeli-Almoslino, the wife of one of the Histadrut leaders, to support his proposal. He promised her that there would not be large-scale dismissals from the IAI, but the effort proved futile.

Before the decision, Peres asked U.S. Ambassador Thomas Pickering to "nail down" all the American assurances of compensation in writing, in the hope that this would persuade the doubters to back his proposal. Political adviser Nimrod Novick spent many hours with the ambassador, and together they worked out an agreement that guaranteed Israel's participation in the next generation of American planes.

On Saturday afternoon, on the eve of the decisive cabinet debate, Pickering received approval from Washington and set out for the homes of Shamir, Rabin, and Peres with a document that gave full details of what the Americans would provide in exchange for cancellation of the Lavi. There was also a promise to reduce the cost of weapons systems that Israel bought from the United States, a benefit hitherto limited only to NATO countries.

At the same time, Shamir was talking on the phone to Tourism Minister Avraham Sharir, an opponent of the Lavi, who was in New York. Shamir was explaining to him that the Lavi had become a party matter, and therefore, he had to vote with his party colleagues for the Lavi. The tourism minister gave in and said in a radio interview that the prime minister had enforced party discipline on him. This left Nissim as the only Likud minister maintaining his opposition to the Lavi. Because of Nissim's great popularity, and his success as finance minister, Shamir rejected calls to fire him and appoint another finance minister who would support the Lavi.

On Sunday morning, about an hour before the fateful cabinet meeting, Shamir called a meeting of the "prime ministers' club" (Shamir, Peres, and Rabin) to discuss another matter. Peres had the impression that Shamir was inclined to agree to his proposal for yet another delay so that such a fateful matter would not be decided by one vote, but in the cabinet room a surprise awaited him.

Shamir opened the meeting by saying, "I hoped that the decision on this matter would not be decided by a small majority, but there is no alternative. The cabinet has before it two proposals: that of the

ministers of defense and finance, and that of the foreign minister."
Peres understood that Shamir had decided to take advantage of his
small lead and was going to announce the vote in another minute.

The only way to ground the Lavi now was to twist the arm of
Health Minister Arbeli-Almoslino. And the only person who could do
that was the man who had backed the project all along and who even
now felt torn on the subject. But Peres decided that he had to put
aside his personal feelings and act as a party leader. He asked for a
recess so that the Labor party ministers could consult. They went
into an adjoining room, and Peres turned to Arbeli-Almoslino without
any superfluous introduction. "Shoshana," he said, "you can see that
the Lavi has become a political party plane. Shamir has twisted
Sharir's arm. I appointed you to the government, and you are sitting
here as a representative of the party, not as a private person." The
atmosphere was very tense, and all the other ministers tried to avoid
looking at the health minister, whose distress showed on her face.

"If it's a party matter, why didn't you summon the party bodies
yesterday?" she demanded. "You can't pressure me like this at the
last moment. I stood up to strong pressure from the media. Why
can't I vote for the Lavi, when the Likud finance minister is voting
against it?"

Peres answered that "Herut enforced party discipline on its own
members, and not on Nissim, who is a liberal."

Gad Ya'acobi came to the health minister's defense: "We cannot
force Shoshana to vote for Shimon's plan. Let her abstain—that is
sufficient."

Arbeli-Almoslino refused and said in a tearful voice, "I don't run
away from decisions, but this is against my conscience."

Peres decided that there was no avoiding a vote, and he asked
the ministers in favor of party discipline to raise their hands. The
result was clear: the health minister was ordered by her colleagues
to vote with them.

She was agitated and annoyed. "I won't raise my hand for your
proposal," she told Peres on the way back to the cabinet room,
where the other ministers were waiting.

Shamir did not know what had happened in the adjoining room.
Rabin and Nissim had announced that they were waiving their
proposal, and Shamir accordingly asked the ministers to vote for or
against Peres's proposal. Twelve hands went up for the proposal, and

Shamir anticipated twelve against, which would mean the proposal was rejected. To his amazement he counted only eleven hands. One remained on the table—that of Arbeli-Almoslino.

Peres's proposal was adopted, and at once a storm blew up. Arens announced his intention to resign from the government. Peres passed a note to Arbeli-Almoslino:

"I know that I hurt you. I understand how deeply you feel hurt. I did not do it for personal reasons, and I greatly respect your views. If what happened on Friday (the change in Sharir's intention to vote against) had not happened, I would never have turned to you. I really believe that we have saved IAI."

Arbeli-Armoslino refused to be comforted and went out to cry in the corridor. Ministers went out to console her. Outside, the voices of thousands of angry IAI workers, who had surrounded the area of the government offices, could be heard. In the coming days, Peres was foremost among those who were abused in fiery demonstrations, which followed him wherever he went. Six months later, a public opinion poll indicated that a large majority of the public backed the decision to ground the Lavi.

CHAPTER TWELVE

GETTING OUT OF THE SWAMP AND THE TWA AFFAIR

THERE WAS NO doubt that the IDF had to be pulled out of Lebanon, but how to do it remained a burning question. Even though the Likud continued to maintain that the war had been justified, its leaders made this claim halfheartedly. They hoped that Peres and the Labor party would do the job for them, so that they would not have to admit what the decisive majority of the public already knew: that the war had spilled—and was still spilling—a great deal of precious blood, completely out of proportion to the hoped-for achievements of the campaign, and certainly wildly out of proportion to what had actually been achieved.

The policy that Peres and Rabin inherited from Shamir and his defense minister, Moshe Arens, was that the IDF would withdraw only after local security arrangements had been made. Peres brought with him to the prime minister's office a "hundred-day program," which a team of experts had prepared for him just before the elections. The team had recommended a speedy withdrawal from

Lebanon in stages, without wasting time and blood trying to reach pointless agreements with the various communities and gangs who roamed southern Lebanon and were incapable of agreeing to a cease-fire even among themselves.

The most that could be expected was an agreement with Syria that, in return for an Israeli withdrawal, the Syrians would restrain the terrorists stationed in the areas under their control. Peres, the new prime minister, wanted a quick pullback, but he could not achieve this without the agreement of Yitzhak Rabin, the new defense minister. This fact forced Peres to put aside the hundred-day program because Rabin's position, which to a certain extent matched that of the Likud, was that "a bad agreement was better than a withdrawal without an agreement."

The IDF general staff continuously demanded that the government withdraw the IDF from the Lebanese swamp. "Parents Against Silence," a pressure group of parents of soldiers who had served in Lebanon, returned to demonstrate outside the prime minister's office to demand a speedy pullback.

The Likud—particularly Ariel Sharon and Moshe Arens (with Shamir lining up behind their extremist stand)—threatened that withdrawing the army from Lebanon without an agreement would bring the Katyusha rockets back to Kiryat Shmona. As the deadlock continued, Israel Television continued to screen nightly pictures of military funerals of men who had fallen victim to one or another of the Lebanese gangs.

On November 6, Assistant U.S. Secretary of State Richard Murphy arrived in the Middle East on a mediation mission between Israel and Syria, and the Nekura talks between representatives of the IDF and the Lebanese Army began. The most notable result of these negotiations was the waste of valuable time.

The main obstacle to an agreement was Israel's demand that UNIFIL (United Nations) forces be stationed in any area from which the IDF withdrew. In mid-December, Murphy reported to Rabin that the Syrians were against this. Syria did not want U.N. forces stationed anywhere north of the River Litani, which ran from east to west across Lebanon, some forty kilometers north of the border with Israel. Israel's contention that if the IDF withdrew without a U.N. force replacing it, there would be bloody battles between the various Lebanese factions in the area, did not worry the Syrians in the least.

Damascus was dedicated to depriving Israel of any political gains as a result of the war.

Egypt, which during this period was speaking with two voices, also came into the picture. Publicly, Cairo demanded that Israel withdraw immediately from Lebanon, but in a conversation with Secretary of State Shultz, Egyptian Foreign Minister Ismat Abdel Maguid expressed deep concern about the violent clashes that would occur between the Lebanese communities if Israel's withdrawal were not properly coordinated.

Gradually, Rabin began to understand the pointlessness of trying to find a settlement, and he ordered the IDF to prepare a detailed plan for unilateral withdrawal in stages. Peres was not overly pleased with this. He had promised to bring the IDF home that same winter, and he reminded Rabin of that fact. Rabin, however, convinced Peres that this timetable did not allow enough time between the various stages, and Peres promised his full support for the IDF plan.

On January 13, 1985, the defense minister and the heads of the defense establishment presented to the cabinet their plan for a withdrawal in stages to the international border. In the first stage, the IDF would withdraw in five weeks to the Litani-Nabatiya line. In the second stage, it would withdraw on the eastern front also to the area of Hasbaya. In the last stage, only very limited IDF forces would remain in a "security zone" along the border to give support to the South Lebanon Army (SLA), which was loyal to Israel.

Arens was extremely displeased, and described the plan as "a gamble with the security of the northern settlements."

"They gamble at Las Vegas," retorted Weizman.

"At Las Vegas you can make calculations," replied Arens.

Weizman refused to give way. "Maybe you can," he responded, "because you are an engineer. I know the IDF officers, and I know they are not gamblers."

Shamir also was not quick to back down. "Why do we have to announce that we are withdrawing from Lebanon?" he demanded. "They already believe we are going to get out. The plan of the defense establishment is a surrender."

That evening, after discussing the plan (which was approved by the IDF) for ten hours, a vote was taken. Sixteen ministers, all the Labor members, plus David Levy and Gideon Patt of the Likud, and the three religious ministers, voted in favor. Shamir and the other Likud ministers remained in the minority.

Leaving the cabinet meeting, a delighted Peres was able to say, "This will be the last winter in Lebanon. I am particularly pleased, because many people said the national unity government could not make decisions. This was one of the most serious discussions in which I have ever taken part." The first stage of the pullback began immediately.

The withdrawal from Lebanon improved Israel's international image and helped better relations with Egypt. More important, it was welcomed by the Israeli public, including those who lived in the north. The public understood that there was no point in eroding the IDF's strength and lowering the morale of the troops in a vain effort to keep order among the warring Lebanese communities. The SLA, backed by limited IDF forces, successfully blocked infiltration attempts by the PLO and extremist Shi'ite organizations. Katyusha rockets did occasionally fall on northern Galilee, but they did not cause casualties or damage. IDF soldiers who helped block the infiltration attempts did suffer casualties, but these were incomparably fewer than the IDF had known between the start of the war in June 1982, and the withdrawal to the narrow security zone.

And so, the war that should never have started came to an end, but it had brought into being forces that hitherto had been dormant— at least upon the international scene, where every group and faction tries to prove itself by violent actions. Israel adapted to the experience with difficulty, as did the United States. The result was an affair that disrupted relations between the two governments and caused problems for both of them.

On June 14, 1985, a short while after the IDF pullback from Lebanon, a TWA plane was hijacked by two Shi'ite terrorists from Lebanon. Flight 748 had been on its way from Athens to Rome with 135 American citizens on board. The hijackers demanded, in return for the lives of the hostages, that Israel set free hundreds of Shi'ite prisoners who had been captured during the fighting in Lebanon and were being held in a special detention camp at Atlit, near Haifa.

As U.S. forces in the region made plans for a rescue operation, the hijackers removed thirteen of the hostages to an unknown location. The rescue operation was canceled out of concern for the lives of the thirteen. In the United States, the relatives of the hostages put pressure on President Reagan to ask Israel to release the Shi'ite prisoners, while others took the position that one must not give in to terrorist blackmail. Television teams from the American networks descended on the Atlit camp and incessantly nagged Peres and Rabin about the possibility of a deal.

Peres was very keen to prove that Israel was prepared to help its great friend in its hour of need, but how could this be achieved? Simple logic dictated a surrender to the hijackers' demands, but President Reagan had taken a stand in principle against giving in to terrorists, and the media in his country watched every word and action to see whether he would stand firm. If Israel gave in to the hijackers' demands, it would be assumed that it had done so at the behest of the United States. No one would believe that Reagan, even if he swore on all that was dear to him, had not requested or pressured Israel to do it. In other words, Israel, in its desire to help, would be responsible for portraying Reagan in a negative light. Such an outcome would certainly not earn the gratitude of the American president.

On the other hand, if Israel did nothing, its inaction would be interpreted, particularly by American public opinion, as sitting on the fence. After weighing the situation from all aspects, Peres worked out a formula that he thought would make clear Israel's willingness to help, without obligating Washington. He announced publicly that Israel was prepared to accede to the hijackers' demands, but only if Washington requested it. It quickly became apparent that he had misjudged. The declaration of good intentions grated on the ears of the nervous administration officials dealing with the crisis.

Ambassador Meir Rosenne reported that he had received an angry phone call from Shultz's office. "What's going on? What are you guys up to? Secretary Shultz and National Security Adviser Robert McFarlane are confused and angry at your government's stand. You know our position. Why do you say that you will release them if we ask? You know that we refuse to surrender to terrorists and we won't ask you to surrender. The announcements from Jerusalem are a nuisance, and I want you to tell your government that."

On Friday, June 12, Peres decided to sound out George Shultz. He phoned the secretary and said, "George, I am offering assistance with friendship and discretion. We are with you in our concern for the safety of the hostages."

But Schultz did not help Peres solve the problem of the president's position. "I greatly appreciate your call," Shultz told him. "I would be grateful if you would publish a statement that all the stories of our pressuring you to release the prisoners are baseless."

Three days later, Peres decided to send a long message to Reagan. He reiterated his admiration for the president's firm stand against international terror, but emphasized Israel's genuine concern for the fate of the hostages and its prayers for their safety. "We are concerned about the passengers as if they were Israeli citizens; we stand united with you." And, in case that was not enough, Peres added a sentence, the meaning of which was unambiguous. "As you know, Israel has exchanged terrorist prisoners for hijacked civilians on more than one occasion." And, in case even that was not enough, he ended the letter, "We are entirely ready to coordinate our efforts with you, and to maintain continuous contacts at the highest level, according to your wishes."

There was no official reply, but unofficially, Peres received an answer. Three days later, he received a call from a senior administration official who was also a personal friend. After emphasizing the need for discretion, the official explained that Reagan could not permit himself to appeal to Israel, but the president was very interested to know whether Israel would release the prisoners if the passengers were released. Peres understood that the question indicated that a settlement was being worked out, and he made it clear that Israel would do what was expected of it.

On June 26, twelve days after the hijacking, the French foreign minister, who was mediating in the matter, called Peres and told him that the negotiations with the hijackers were progressing promisingly. According to the settlement that was shaping up, the Americans had contacted the French and asked them to arrange for the hostages to be received upon their release at the French embassy in Beirut. The foreign minister said he was speaking for President Mitterrand, who wanted to know what would happen to the Shi'ite prisoners in Israel if the French received the hostages. Peres promised him a speedy answer.

As soon as he had put the receiver down, he lifted it again, called Rabin to report on the developments, and suggested that a meeting of the inner cabinet be called in another hour, at 7:30 P.M. Afterward, he called Shamir, reported on his conversation with the French foreign minister, and emphasized that Shultz was "counting on us to be ready to release them."

"Did the Americans apply to us?" asked Shamir.

"No, but we can't play around anymore," said Peres. "If we don't deny it, it will be assumed that we agree. If we don't say no, the matter is wound up."

At the subsequent meeting of the inner cabinet, Peres, Shamir, and Rabin presented a united front in favor of releasing the Shi'ite prisoners held in Israel, and the decision was accepted without opposition.

The exchange deal was implemented so that it looked on the surface as if there was no connection between the release of the hostages and the release of the Shi'ite prisoners. On June 29, two weeks after the hijacking, the hostages were released and returned to their homes. The Israeli government announced that it was freeing three hundred Shi'ite prisoners who were due to be freed shortly anyway.

Two days later, on July 1, at 7:00 P.M. in Israel, a few hours after the government had approved the big economic plan, Peres called Shultz, and the two conducted a conversation consisting of veiled hints. Israel presented the matter as if it had intended to release the Shi'ites in the near future. Shultz knew that Peres had acted to please the United States, as he had indirectly asked him to do. Peres knew that Shultz knew that he knew—and the conversation went as follows:

"I congratulate you on the way you handled the matter of the hostages," Peres said. "Tomorrow or the next day, we are going to release three hundred prisoners from Atlit."

"It's a good decision," Shultz said. "I think I understand what you are doing."

"We will go on releasing them, according to our previous plan."

"I understand and approve."

"Please pass my congratulations to the president on the way he dealt with the matter and on his refusal to give in to blackmail and terror."

"I'll tell him," Shultz replied. "I have a private meeting with him shortly."

The release of the hostages, however, did not release the United States from involvement in Lebanese terrorism. The Americans continued to be concerned over the fate of seven of their citizens, among them the CIA station chief in Beirut, who had been kidnapped in Lebanon by the extremist Shi'ite Hizbullah (Party of God) organization.

Ambassador Thomas Pickering asked Peres that same summer to ensure that Israel would refrain from any action in Lebanon not vital for its defense, in order not to interfere with the efforts for the release of the seven. Pickering did not understand what Peres was talking about, when the prime minister blurted out, "You will hear very soon that the first one has been released." That sentence belongs to another affair, which came to be called "Irangate."

CHAPTER THIRTEEN

INTELLIGENCE AFFAIRS

Irangate

ON MAY 29, 1985, Howard Teicher, a member of the U.S. National Security Council, was on the line to the prime minister's office in Jerusalem, asking to talk to Peres's political adviser, Dr. Nimrod Novick, whom he knew well from the days the two of them had studied together in Philadelphia. Speaking in the name of National Security Adviser Robert McFarlane, he asked that Peres receive Michael Ledeen, who was due in Israel in a few days' time. Ledeen advised the National Security Council adviser on terrorism, the Middle East, and in particular, Iran. Teicher hinted that Ledeen was "deniable," which meant that his employer would not acknowledge him if his identity and actions were exposed.

Novick passed the request on to Peres, who decided to see him. At the end of the week, when Ledeen called, he was at once granted a private interview with the prime minister. Peres knew the strange young man slightly from the time he had been an adviser to Secretary of State Haig and had been responsible for contacts with the Socialist

International, in which Peres had been very involved. Ledeen did not bring an official letter from McFarlane, but spoke confidently about the situation in Iran, and the mutual interest of Israel and the United States in exchanging information as to what was going on there. Peres agreed there was room for cooperation on such an important matter and promised to consult quickly with the relevant people.

That evening, June 3, Peres remembered Shlomo Gazit, a former head of IDF military intelligence and now the president of Ben-Gurion University in Beersheba. He called Gazit and asked him to come to Jerusalem. A few hours later, Gazit appeared at the prime minister's official residence in Jerusalem and heard about the talk with Ledeen. Peres explained that the man worked for McFarlane on an unofficial basis and had suggested that Israel cooperate with the United States on the Iranian issue. According to him, the Americans were not as informed as they would like to be of what was going on inside the Iranian regime, and were convinced that Israel had plenty of information. Peres said that Ledeen was going to call him that same evening, and the prime minister wanted to arrange a meeting between him and Gazit.

As they were still talking, the phone rang. Peres lifted the receiver and said, "I have a man called Gazit with me; he is my operative in this matter." Gazit took the phone and made an appointment to see Ledeen that same evening, after a dinner with an American donor to his university.

The meeting took place at the Sheraton Hotel in Jerusalem, and the two went for a stroll along King George Street until they reached the walls of the Old City. Gazit had met Ledeen once before, when he was studying at Harvard in 1980. Ledeen presented himself as an author-journalist, collecting material for a novel about the rescue of American hostages held in Iran, and as a "free-lancer" employed by McFarlane without an office or official status. According to him, contacting Peres had been his initiative, and not McFarlane's. He expressed concern about the elimination of opponents of Ayatolla Khomeini in Iran, and the prospect that the fundamentalist regime would survive the death of the aged leader. It was therefore considered important to bring down the regime before Khomeini's death.

The United States did not know anyone who could lead an Iranian underground movement, nor did it know any of the Iranian

exiles who possessed sufficient authority with the potential of
organizing a revolution. Ledeen ended by saying that the Americans
had reason to believe that Israel could point them in the right
direction. He explained his approach by pointing out that the rules of
the game in the United States did not permit a direct, open operation,
and therefore, there was need for outside partners.

Gazit wanted to know about the relations in this matter between
the United States and Iraq, which had been involved in a bloody war
with Iran for several years. Ledeen's evasive reply aroused the
suspicions of the veteran intelligence officer. A doubtful opinion he
later received concerning Ledeen reinforced his view that the matter
should be handled with extreme caution. In the report he sent Peres
several days later, Gazit recommended that contact be maintained,
but that the man be checked most thoroughly.

A whole month passed after the secret meeting between
Ledeen and Peres before Secretary Shultz received a report from
U.S. Ambassador Samuel Lewis concerning Ledeen's mysterious
mission "on behalf of the White House." Rabin, who had been briefed
by Peres about the meeting, had refused to give Lewis any details
beyond the fact that the matter was "hot," and to promise that he
would report to Shultz at their forthcoming meeting in Washington.
But Rabin did not keep his promise.

Shultz foresaw the disaster when he wrote to McFarlane, "I am
astounded at the way you are dealing with the matter, and concerned
that there are likely to be serious mistakes and confusion in the
future." He would not forgive Peres for several months for the
affront of his having cooperated with administration elements that had
bypassed Shultz and the embassy. As anticipated, McFarlane disassociated himself from Ledeen, claimed that the initiative had been
Israel's, and said that Ledeen had operated independently.

An important development at this time concerning the Iranian
connection was the entry into the picture of businessman Ya'acov
Nimrodi, who had been Israel's military attaché in Iran in the shah's
time. He came to Peres and laid claim to ramified connections with
opponents of the Iranian regime. He told him about an arms deal that
Iran wanted to put through, using Israel, with the mediation of Saudi
millionaire Adnan Khashoggi. Nimrodi also mentioned an Iranian
mediator—Manucher Ghorbanifar—and related his efforts to raise
money via strange connections with the Irish Republican Army

(IRA). Nimrodi complained to Peres that the defense establishment was holding back from the deal. Peres also referred Nimrodi to Gazit.

On June 19, Gazit met with Peres and recommended that no American arms or equipment should be sent to Iran without the agreement of the U.S. administration. He also suggested finding out what McFarlane thought. Peres summoned Foreign Ministry Director General David Kimche, formerly a senior Mossad operative, who was about to go to the United States on a working visit. He asked him to see McFarlane and ascertain his opinion on the matter. Foreign Minister Shamir was not brought into the picture, and he approved Kimche's mission. Rabin had been in the know for some time.

While Kimche was meeting McFarlane, Ledeen met, at Kimche's recommendation, with Al Schwimmer, from whom he heard that Schwimmer had met recently with Ghorbanifar through the mediation of his friend, Adnan Khashoggi. Schwimmer spoke with amazement about Ghorbanifar's knowledge concerning power struggles in the Iranian regime and suggested that Ledeen meet him. Kimche returned to Israel and reported to Peres and Gazit that he had received a "green light" from McFarlane. He also emphasized that McFarlane told him that he had spoken to President Reagan, who had approved making contact with the Iranians.

Despite this, Gazit was still unhappy, and he told Peres that something was not entirely "kosher." He pointed out to Peres that the president had approved the operation after waking up from his operation for the removal of a cancerous growth on his nose, and it was quite possible he had not understood what he was approving. Gazit was also suspicious about a clarification that Kimche had brought from McFarlane, indicating that the president had told McFarlane that, if the affair blew up, "we'll deny it from beginning to end." It did not seem to Gazit to be the president's style.

Gazit also drew Peres's attention to Nimrodi's modus operandi, in which he frequently spoke to Khashoggi and Ghorbanifar about arms deals on open international phone lines. Gazit warned that the CIA was likely to listen in and learn about Israel's involvement behind its back in a plot with an American setup.

Peres accepted Gazit's suggestion, first of all, to check the contacts of Khashoggi and Ghorbanifar with the Iranian regime. At this point the seven American hostages kidnapped by the Hizbullah entered the picture. The idea was raised to make use of them in two ways: to tempt the Americans, who were hesitant to make any contact with the Iranians, and as a test of Khashoggi's and Ghorbanifar's contacts, by proposing an arms deal with Iran in exchange for the release of the hostages.

On the basis of Peres's guidelines, Gazit spoke to Ghorbanifar and told him that Israel was interested in the political situation in Iran, and not in arms deals; but at this point, the matter was taken out of Gazit's hands. Nimrodi and Schwimmer started setting up arms deals. Only one of the hostages was released—Reverend Benjamin Weir—and it was impossible to say for sure whether there was any connection between his release and the 408 TOW missiles supplied by Israel to Iran.

In October 1985, Gazit told Peres that he was withdrawing from the Iranian business. At the end of the month, Peres visited the United States and had two long conversations with Shultz on political, economic, and military matters. Shultz would remember, when the time of accounting came, that Peres did not say a single word about the Iranian operation.

Matters became increasingly complicated when the Iranians held up a plane with eighteen Hawk missiles from Israel, which they claimed were of an obsolete type. They said they had been swindled. No more hostages were released. McFarlane was succeeded as National Security Adviser by John Poindexter. In Jerusalem, Peres's adviser on counterterror, Amiram Nir, persuaded the prime minister to drop the Kimche-Nimrodi-Schwimmer trio and give him the sole responsibility for continuing the operation. He was helped by the argument that he had forged special relations with several members of the U.S. National Security Council.

The balance swung more and more from the political toward straightforward arms deals, involving millions of dollars deposited in secret Swiss bank accounts. In May 1986, the affair degenerated into a dangerous adventure. An Israeli Boeing touched down at Teheran Airport, with McFarlane (who had been brought back into operation for the purpose), National Security Council official Oliver North, and Amiram Nir on board. The plane returned four days later, after the Iranians had tried to extort vast quantities of arms in exchange for the hostages.

At the end of July, when Vice President George Bush visited Jerusalem, Nir made contact with his aides, and asked to speak to him. Bush asked North for his opinion, and the latter told him that Prime Minister Peres thought it important that the vice president meet with Nir. Peres later maintained that North had never approached him on the matter and that his whole story was untrue. At any rate, Nir met Bush in his suite at the King David Hotel and spent twenty-five minutes briefing him on the operation.

When the affair was revealed in November 1986, North claimed that Nir had suggested to him that the profits from the arms deals be transferred to a secret account to assist the Nicaraguan Contras, bypassing the U.S. Congress. Nir denied this. So did Vice President Bush, who, when his name was dragged into the matter because of this meeting, was forced to release the minutes of his talk with Nir. He even sent Peres a copy of the minutes in January 1987 to support his version that support for the Contras was not discussed at the meeting. At the same time, when Peres met with Shultz in Washington, he again took care to avoid the Iranian connection. Shultz kept quiet, as if he knew nothing about it, although by then he had already heard most of the details.

When the affair blew up, the Israeli government received a nasty shock. Peres was particularly concerned about reports that it had been Nir who had suggested transferring funds to the Contras. By then, Shamir was already prime minister.

The Shamir-Peres-Rabin trio at once summoned Nir and sharply interrogated him, particularly over his suspected contribution to the connection with the Contras. Nir excitedly swore that he had never discussed the matter, and claimed that North's testimony on this point was entirely untrue. Once he was convinced that Nir was telling the truth, Peres appeared before the media and explained that Israel had felt obligated to help its friend (the United States), in return for its assistance in securing the release of the Ethiopian Jews. Apart from its desire to develop relations with moderate elements in Iran, he said, the Israeli government had wanted to help secure the release of the American hostages. The government promised the investigating committees of the U.S. Congress full cooperation. Everyone connected with the affair was interrogated by a special team headed by Cabinet Secretary Eliyakim Rubinstein, and the material was forwarded to the congressional committees after the approval of the inner cabinet.

The Irangate affair left a stain on Peres's success as prime

minister in the political, military, and economic sphere. The hostages
were not released; Iran remained as hostile as ever to the United
States and to Israel; the names of Israelis were again connected to
shady arms deals and to money that has not been located to this day.
The affair caused a crisis in relations with the United States, and with
the moderate Arab nations opposed to Khomeini's regime. Israel was
portrayed in the United States as an impulsive youth who dragged his
big brother into a dangerous and unnecessary adventure.

No less serious was the deterioration of Shultz's opinion of
Peres because of the affair, to the point where the deep trust that had
formerly existed between the two was seriously eroded. Peres felt
this very keenly in May 1987 at his first meeting with the secretary
of state after the affair had been uncovered. Shultz kept his distance
and took care not to depart from the cold, official tone of a diplomatic
meeting. Soon after Peres returned to Israel, he told Ambassador
Thomas Pickering, "In my worst nightmares, I never imagined that
this would happen with the administration." Trying to explain his
behavior in the affair, he said, "Dave Kimche went specially to
Washington. McFarlane told him, 'George knows.' Now George says
he didn't know. It turns out that they lied to us about his involvement."

At the first opportunity, Peres placed the subject of Iran on the
table with Shultz in an attempt to "clear away the crumbs" disturbing
their relationship. Toward the end of the year, at Shultz's breakfast
table, when Charles Hill had been called to the phone, Peres asked
his adviser, Nimrod Novick, to leave him alone with his host. It was
the first time that Peres told Shultz openly and honestly about the
developments resulting from Kimche's mission. He even offered to
show him Kimche's written report that vindicated Peres's claim that
he thought Shultz was in the know. The secretary answered
immediately, "That's not necessary. I believe you."

The easygoing secretary of state did not ask, and Peres did not
volunteer, the obvious question: if Peres believed McFarlane that
"George knows," why did he avoid talking about it with the secretary
of state on all those occasions when he met him, from the start of the
affair to its disclosure? The question that was not asked, like the
answer that was not given, would henceforth cast its shadow over
the relationship between the two men.

Pollard and the "Other Matter"

One of the most remarkable things about the Iran affair was that it developed at a time when the Israeli leadership already knew about another affair that was not exactly healthy for relations with the United States.

This affair began, from Peres's point of view, on November 19, 1985, when his bearded military secretary, Azriel Nevo, came to the prime minister's office and told him about an employee of the American navy, Jonathan Pollard, who had been arrested outside the gates of the Israeli embassy in Washington.

At the time, Peres was totally immersed in preparing for an international peace conference. Just one month earlier, he had emerged from one of the friendliest meetings he had ever had with President Reagan, and, according to his guidelines, American emissaries were now working overtime in Jerusalem and Amman with the objective of calling an international conference within a few months, possibly even that same year.

Peres's first reaction to the information Nevo brought him was to see it as an unimportant incident. He lifted the receiver and asked for the defense minister. A short conversation with Rabin made it clear that the matter was serious and that Israel had been caught red-handed. The reports streaming in from the Washington embassy only served to worsen the picture. It turned out that the American Department of Justice had been listening continuously to stories about the deeds of Jonathan Pollard and about the sensitive material he had been passing to Israel. The American Jewish community began to show signs of anxiety.

Embassy Counselor Eliyakim Rubinstein, who was standing in for Ambassador Meir Rosenne, sent a shocked cable that he had been summoned to a meeting with Deputy Secretary of State Michael Armacost. Also waiting for him there were the State Department's legal adviser, Abraham Sofaer, and Assistant State Prosecutor Mark Richards. They informed Rubinstein officially that Pollard had confessed to selling intelligence material to representatives of the Israeli government. The U.S. administration was requesting that Israel

assist it in its efforts to discover the facts and to expose the Israelis
who had been in contact with Pollard. They also insisted that Israel
conduct its own inquiry and pass the results to the United States.
The first man the Americans wanted to interrogate was a marginal
figure, the Israeli embassy security officer who had escorted Pollard
out of the embassy when he had arrived asking for asylum.

It was clear that Pollard, a Jew and an intelligence agent, had
sold information to Israel, and the questions started streaming in
from all quarters. Was the political echelon in Israel involved? Did it
know, instruct, or approve?

It turned out that Pollard had initiated contact with Israel in May
1984, when Shamir had been prime minister and Moshe Arens
defense minister. An additional fact that speedily emerged was that
the key figure was Rafi Eitan, head of Lekem, the Scientific Liaison
Bureau of the Defense Ministry, who had also been the prime
minister's adviser on counterterror until Peres had replaced him with
Amiram Nir.

Eitan was summoned by Peres and admitted that he had not
received approval and had not reported to any of his superiors about
contacts with Pollard. He took full responsibility for the operation and
said something to the effect that Pollard had presented himself as a
semiofficial emissary of American Intelligence. Peres permitted
himself a sigh of relief. If Pollard really worked for the Americans, as
Rafi Eitan said—and Peres very much wanted to believe—he could
now announce publicly that the Israeli government was opposed to
spying in the United States and that this was against its policy; and he
did so.

From then on the matter was dealt with by "the prime ministers'
forum." Its members were Prime Minister Peres and former Pre-
miers Yitzhak Shamir and Yitzhak Rabin. Rabin missed the first
meeting, on November 22, because he was abroad. It was reported
that Pollard had mentioned as his two contacts at the Israeli embassy
in Washington Aviem Sella, an Israeli air force officer, and Yosef
Yagur, a Foreign Ministry official. The chief handler, Rafi Eitan, again
reassured those at the meeting. He repeated his story that Pollard
had presented himself as an official representative of American
Intelligence, and had even produced documentation showing that his
position permitted him to take out classified material without being
checked. Eitan described Sella's role as marginal and slight. On this

basis, it was resolved that the Foreign Ministry would inform Secretary Shultz that Israel was prepared to cooperate with the United States in investigating the affair.

At 3:30 A.M. on December 1, Peres was awakened by a phone call from George Shultz. Peres started by apologizing: "Pollard was an exceptional case. I did not know about it, and my political colleagues did not know anything. It was an unauthorized initiative, without official permission." He informed Shultz of Eitan's dismissal and promised that the Lekem intelligence unit would be disbanded.

Peres repeated to Shultz the assurance about cooperating with the investigation, and promised to return all the documents that Pollard had stolen.

At a meeting of the prime ministers' forum on December 1, it was decided to establish a special team to coordinate the cooperation with the Americans. At Shamir's suggestion, Peres summoned Hanan Bar-On, the deputy director general of the Foreign Ministry, who had wide experience of Washington, where he had served for many years, home from abroad. It was decided that the legal matters would be handled by private attorneys who were not obligated by the rules of diplomacy or identified with the government.

Two well-known attorneys were suggested, but they were not available, so Peres recommended his friend, Ram Caspi. He asked Shin Bet chief Avraham Shalom, who had been appointed to head the coordinating team, to meet Caspi that same evening and bring him into the picture. Within two days, Caspi and Bar-On were attending a meeting in Jerusalem with the prime ministers' forum and the heads of the intelligence services. An American investigation team was due to fly to Israel, and it was decided that the Israeli team should preempt them and fly to Washington that night to decide the terms of the cooperation. Caspi suggested that a cabinet minister be attached to the team—preferably, someone on good terms with Shultz. Peres decided on Moshe Arens.

When the Israeli team arrived in Washington, Arens went straight to Shultz's home. From there he went with the rest of the team to a meeting at the State Department. Legal adviser Abraham Sofaer chaired the meeting, which was attended by Joseph DiGenova, the U.S. Attorney for the District of Columbia, who was prosecuting Pollard and a couple of dozen aides and advisers.

The Israeli team immediately announced that its government

stood by the principles of Israel's independence and security, and therefore reserved the right to object to any question that might hinder the investigation by Israel's intelligence services. This led to dozens of objections, and the argument on wording lasted for three days. For example, the first paragraph of the American draft contained the statement that Pollard's operation had been espionage against the United States. At Caspi's insistence, the American jurists agreed to write "espionage in the United States," instead of "against the United States." Other paragraphs included these points:

1. It was accepted by the State Department that the operation had been contrary to the policy of the Israeli government.

2. Because of this, Israel decided to take the unusual step of full cooperation with the U.S. government in the investigation of the breaking of U.S. laws.

3. In order to carry out this aim, the U.S. government would send a mission for the purpose of applying the principles of the cooperation. This agreement was achieved as a result of the historic partnership between the two governments, and safeguarding the principles of that partnership would help to convince the U.S. administration of the Israeli government's bona fides in this affair.

That was the declarative section. Afterward, the conditions of cooperation with the mission of American jurists that was coming to Israel were detailed:

1. The U.S. government confirms that the agreement to cooperate was given voluntarily by the Israeli government, in accordance with its independent rights.

2. The U.S. government will endeavor to interview those people who are in Israel in order to elicit information from them relating to this exceptional spying affair, and to obtain the documents in their possession.

3. The interviews in Israel will take place according to the individual rights of the interviewees, and according to their personal agreement.

4. The U.S. government declares that it agrees to grant

immunity from legal proceedings in the United States to the people connected with the matter, and agrees to weigh any other requests by them, such as free entry and exit from the United States.

5. The interviews conducted by American representatives in Israel will not be used as evidence in any legal process.

6. The interviews with Israeli citizens in Israel will be limited to the matter of Pollard only, and the Israeli government will not permit its citizens to answer questions concerning the gathering of intelligence.

7. The U.S. government undertakes to guard the secrecy of all the information resulting from the visit, and will not publish any public declaration by any government on the fact of the visit, its aims, and the people interviewed.

8. The Israeli government agrees that all the original documents in it possession that are the property of the United States will be returned to the U.S. government by the accepted channels.

9. The Israeli government agrees to afford full cooperation to the U.S. government, while reserving for itself the right to take any steps necessary for safeguarding its security interests.

10. At the end of the visit, both governments will continue to discuss the above matter.

Arens, Bar-On, and Caspi returned to Israel, and the document was immediately brought before the prime ministers' forum for discussion. On December 9, after the three ministers had approved it, the document was signed simultaneously at the U.S. embassy in Tel Aviv and at the Israeli embassy in Washington. The American mission was delayed for four more days to permit the Israeli team to question all the possible candidates for interrogation: Rafi Eitan, Aviem Sella, Yosef Yagur, and Irit Erb, who was also an embassy employee.

In this interrogation also, Eitan reiterated that Pollard had offered his services, as if with the knowledge of the American authorities. Sella said that his role was confined to being the original contact between Pollard and Eitan. He related that after he had given a fund-raising speech an unknown person had approached him and asked him to meet with a Jew who wanted to transfer important material to Israel.

At the meeting, Pollard had presented plastic certificates authorizing him to take out classified material, and he had suggested giving Israel information. After that first time, Sella said, he had talked to him once more in Paris, together with Yagur and Eitan. Sella told the team that he had never received documents or paid out money. Finally, to the surprise of the team, he proved that he had operated with the permission of the chief of staff and the air force commander. Disclosing this to the Americans would immediately raise the suspicion that the defense minister had been involved in the affair.

The next surprise came when the American team submitted its list of interviewees. It included Eitan, Yagur, Erb, and somebody else, but Sella was not on the list. According to the conditions agreed to between the two governments, the Israeli team was not obliged to volunteer interviewees, but it was decided that it would be bad if Sella's involvement were discovered by the Americans from their interviews of the others. Caspi reported to Sofaer and Pickering that "there is another man who put Yagur in touch with Pollard, but his role was marginal. He did not spy and did not pay out money." Caspi even asked Pickering, "What would you do if a man approached you in a Paris street and offered you information important to the United States?" As expected, Pickering replied, "I would transfer the matter to my superiors." Caspi smiled. "That's just what our man did. Let's call him 'Mr. X.'"

When the American team asked Yagur how he got to Pollard, he replied: "Mr. X made the contact between us, and told me that Pollard wanted to pass information in a semiofficial manner, that there were certain people in the administration that wanted to pass on to us information on Soviet weaponry in the Middle East and on the weapons systems of Arab nations."

So Sella's existence was not concealed—only his identity. The basic assumption of the team was that Pollard would not disclose him and his real position. The version that Eitan and Yagur believed—that Pollard was operating with the permission and authority of the U.S. authorities—had collapsed during the interrogation conducted by the Israeli team. The team's members came to the conclusion that it was not possible to sell the Americans a version whereby an employee of the U.S. Navy, acting officially, could receive payment from Israel for the most sensitive information. This was also reported to Peres, Rabin, and Shamir, but the decision to play down Sella's role was not reported to the political echelon.

After five days of intensive interviews, conducted at a country club near Tel Aviv, away from prying eyes, the American team completed its work. Only then were the documents stolen by Pollard transferred to it. The team left for home satisfied. On December 27, Shultz sent Peres a warm letter of thanks. "The cooperation reflects the close relations between us, and I thank you for the vital role that you personally played in implementing the cooperation that we requested."

Everything seemed to have calmed down. But the following summer, the decision of Industry and Trade Minister Ariel Sharon to to appoint Rafi Eitan to the post of chairman of the board of Israel Chemicals, the largest industrial complex in the country, infuriated the Americans. Pickering was dispatched to Shamir to make it clear that this appointment was not consistent with Israel's announcement that those guilty in the Pollard affair would be punished. Shamir replied that he could not oppose Sharon, and Peres replied that he was unable to do anything, because the signature of two ministers on the letter of appointment was sufficient, and both Sharon and Finance Minister Moda'i were members of the Likud.

In a conversation with Sofaer, who had come to Jerusalem on another matter, Peres said half-jokingly to Sharon's former judge (Abraham Sofaer had been the judge in Sharon's libel case against *Time*), "Maybe you should speak to him; you've got influence over him." The Americans protested the appointment, but Sharon refused to rescind it.

At the same time, the Americans discovered Sella's real role in the Pollard affair. Caspi and Bar-On went to Washington to deal with the matter of immunity for the Israelis against being put on trial in the United States, against the background of Sella's appointment to command the Tel Nof Air Base, the air force's largest. Rabin decided that backing down from appointing Sella to the post he was slated for would contradict the Israeli position that his role had been marginal in the affair, as the Americans would think, if he did not sin, why should he be punished? In addition, there was no sign that the matter concerned the Americans in the least.

The Israelis involved in the affair very quickly learned the reason. In a conversation with one of the American prosecutors, Caspi heard that Sella and the other Israelis were insignificant. Caspi went pale when he heard that the Israelis involved in the Pollard affair were hostages for the American prosecutors to ensure cooperation in an entirely different matter that the Americans regarded as far more serious. Their anger over Eitan's appointment was also because of what the Americans believed was his involvement in "the other matter."

Sella's attorney, Haim Zadok, who also participated in the discussions with the Americans, heard, together with Caspi, that the Americans wouldn't bat an eyelid if Sella was appointed to command the air base, or even if he were appointed air force commander, provided they received assistance in what they called the "other matter"—the Americans' firm belief that there was "another Pollard," far more important than the Pollard who had been caught. District of Columbia Attorney DiGenova demanded that the Israelis give him the name of the "additional Pollard." Caspi shrugged his shoulders and replied, "I don't know what you are talking about." The prosecutor did not give up. He offered the Israeli representatives a written carte blanche of immunity if they wrote on it the name of the man. He explained that the fact that a spy was walking free in the corridors of the administration kept him awake at night. The shocked Israeli representatives repeated that they knew nothing.

Caspi and Bar-On returned to Israel and reported to Peres. Pickering added that there were inconsistencies between the testimony of Eitan and Yagur, and that of Pollard. Sella's evidence could remove the doubts. There were also leaks that reported the prosecution claim that the Israeli team had not given the American delegation all the documents it had received from Pollard. DiGenova announced that, in view of these doubts, he saw himself freed from all the assurances he had given concerning immunity and not serving subpoenas to the Israelis.

In the winter of 1987, Pollard was sentenced to life imprisonment, and his wife, who had assisted him in the operation, received five years. U.S. Defense Secretary Caspar Weinberger contributed to the severity of the sentence, giving a tough assessment to the court and saying that he would not hesitate to hang Pollard.

The Israeli public, the media, American Jews, and other friends of Israel in the United States pressured the government to appoint a committee of inquiry. Yitzhak Shamir, who was by then prime minister, and the other two members of the forum, Peres and Rabin, resisted the pressure.

Meanwhile, the subcommittee of the Knesset's Foreign Affairs and Defense Committee dealing with covert matters started summoning the people involved in the affair for questioning. Shamir, who was one of those questioned, continued to express strong opposition to an inquiry on the Pollard affair. Only on March 11 did the inner cabinet decide to set up an investigating team, but one without any real authority. A former president of the Supreme Court, Justice Moshe Landau, refused to head the team, which detracted still more from its standing. In the end, the elderly attorney Dr. Yehoshua Rottenstreich and former IDF Chief of Staff Zvi Tzur headed the investigating team.

The decision to set up the team and a cabinet committee to assist the Knesset subcommittee, which was headed by Abba Eban, the chairman of the Foreign Affairs and Defense Committee, calmed matters down for a few weeks. But then a foul "war of leaks" started from the Eban subcommittee. It quickly became apparent to some of the subcommittee members that their colleagues were determined to take advantage of the opportunity to settle party political accounts, and they turned all their efforts to defending their patrons. Peres had reason to believe that subcommittee members Simha Dinitz and Micha Harish, who were close to him, would neutralize the efforts of the Likud members—Ehud Olmert, Eliahu Ben-Elissar, and David Magen. Neither Peres nor Rabin had much faith in Abba Eban, who certainly had no reason to be grateful to either of them.

On May 25, the investigation team presented its report to the inner cabinet. The conclusions were very mild and were gladly accepted by the prime ministers' forum. It was found that the three of them had dealt with the matter on a more or less equal basis, and most of the blame was put on the team of Avraham Shalom, Hanan Bar-On, and Ram Caspi, who were criticized for not conducting their interrogations properly and thus causing unnecessary complications with the Americans. Finally, the current investigating team suggested that the entire cabinet accept parliamentary responsibility for the shortcomings in the way the affair was handled.

Just as the investigation team's report was presented, things were heating up in the Eban subcommittee, which was closeted in a police rest home near Netanya. The Likud members wanted to put most of the blame for the shortcomings in dealing with the matter on Peres, since Pollard was arrested and presented as an official emissary of U.S. Intelligence. When it was learned that the Rotten-streich team had already presented its report, the race for the newspaper headlines began. The members of the Eban subcommit-tee decided to compromise on a moderate conclusion, accompanied by a dissenting comment of the minority, which condemned the incomplete version that Peres had presented to the subcommittee. The subcommittee also placed most of the responsibility on Peres for the mistakes made since Pollard was discovered, explaining that the prime minister was the "first among equals."

Peres, as opposed to Rabin, who showed self-restraint, could not overcome his chagrin. He rejected the form of the statement that Eban and Dinitz prepared for him, in which the main element was to accept ministerial responsibility. Late at night he emerged from a meeting of the inner cabinet and fired off sparks at the microphones. He continued to do so at a meeting of the Labor party central committee, where he directed his remarks mainly at Abba Eban, and drew penetrating criticism as a result. In one of his conversations with Pickering at this time, he complained: "They are criticizing me for cooperating with the United States on the Pollard affair."

Pickering consoled him by saying, "That is what saved you."

Security Versus the Law

One day in November 1985, Reuven Hazak, the deputy head of the Shin Bet, Israel's security service, asked for an urgent meeting with the prime minister. Peres knew Hazak only from a few meetings with the senior officers of the Shin Bet, and he knew that the head of the service, Avraham (Avrum) Shalom, saw Hazak as his successor when the time came. Hazak asked for the meeting to be a private one, and said that his superior, Shalom, had given permission. Peres agreed. He could not have known that this meeting would initiate an affair that would focus on one of the toughest dilemmas of the country, which since its establishment had been in a state of war: the needs of security, as opposed to the rule of law.

The good-looking man who came to see Peres in Jerusalem had a shocking story to tell. He said that Shalom was responsible for the death of the two terrorists who had been captured alive in 1984 after they had hijacked a bus on Route 300 near Ashkelon. The affair had raised a storm at the time because, in defiance of the ban of the military censor, a photograph had been published in the press of the two terrorists being led away alive from the scene of the incident. The picture contradicted the official version of events, according to which the two had been killed in the storming of the bus and the freeing of its passengers. The picture proved that the two had been killed—were, in fact, executed—a short while after the operation.

No less serious—and possibly even more—was Hazak's account that the head of the Shin Bet ordered his operatives to mislead two inquiry committees that were established after publication of the picture to determine who was responsible for killing the terrorists. One of the committees had been appointed by the defense minister, and had been headed by Reserves General Meir Zorea; the second, appointed by the attorney general, had been headed by State Attorney Yona Blatman. On the recommendation of both committees, Brigadier General Yitzhak Mordechai, the IDF's chief infantry and paratroop officer, had been put on trial. This happened about two months before Peres's meeting with Hazak. After the sentencing was repeatedly postponed for several months, Mordechai was acquitted of charges of killing the two terrorists. The political echelon in Israel and the general public were left without an answer as to who had, in fact, killed the two.

Now Peres received the reply from Hazak, who admitted that he had participated in the falsification of evidence before the two committees of inquiry. He suggested that Peres fire Shalom at once, in order to clean up the service. Peres wanted to know, "Why did you only come to me now?" Hazak explained that his conscience had been troubling him for many months, and he had spoken to Shalom about the necessity of "cleaning house." He had waited until the end of the disciplinary hearings of the five Shin Bet agents that had resulted from the Blatman inquiry. (All of the agents had been cleared in the hearings.)

Peres at once summoned Shalom, whom he knew from his service in the Defense Ministry. Shalom was regarded as a totally honest man, a harsh disciplinarian who was utterly devoted to the security of the nation. He arrived late at night at Peres's house. In an excited state, he tried to remind Peres that in a previous meeting, he had started to tell him about the affair, but Peres said that he did not remember such a conversation.

Shalom was due to retire at the end of 1986, and he claimed, "Reuven was in a hurry, and he [allied himself] with Peleg Radai and Rafi Malka, with the purpose of advancing my retirement." The prime minister accepted his claim that this had been an attempt at a "putsch," despite the fact that the three of them had not coordinated their approaches to Shalom, and despite the fact that it was clear—or should have been—that Rafi Malka, at any rate, had nothing to gain from the resignation of his boss, with whom he was on excellent terms.

Peres talked to Shamir, who supported Peres's theory of a putsch. The two agreed that Hazak and his colleagues should be dismissed from the Shin Bet, and that everything should be done to hush up the matter and to prevent the opening of ugly wounds that could cause the Shin Bet great damage. Peres summoned Hazak and told him that he did not accept his explanation of his long silence, when he himself had been an active participant in the shameful affair. He demanded his resignation from the Shin Bet, and those of his colleagues, Malka and Radai. The three had no choice but to resign.

The rumor about the resignations of three senior Shin Bet employees, including the man considered most likely to succeed the present head of the service, spread quickly, and reached the ears of the attorney general, Professor Yitzhak Zamir. When he realized that the matter was connected with the bus incident, he invited the three dismissed operatives to a meeting.

The three Shin Bet men made written statements, and Zamir again turned to the prime minister, this time demanding to be permitted to investigate suspicions of serious criminal offenses in the Shin Bet. Zamir explained that there was a suspicion that pressure was being exerted on Shin Bet employees to give false testimony to official inquiry boards to conceal the deeds of their chief. Zamir spoke heatedly about the resulting injustice to Brigadier General Yitzhak Mordechai. According to the law, he said, he was obligated to investigate the suspicions.

Peres again spoke to Shalom, who categorically opposed the investigation of himself and his men. He reminded Peres that withholding the truth from the courts was not a new practice in the case of secret operations of the Shin Bet. Shalom claimed that this was the norm, because the nature of the work of the Shin Bet did not always allow the truth to be told, even to the courts.

Peres tried to persuade Zamir to find some other way of satisfying the requirements of the law. He spoke of his great confidence in the head of the Shin Bet and of how sensitive the affair was from a security point of view. Zamir was not convinced and continued to insist on an inquiry.

A short while before he heard about the affair, Zamir had asked to be relieved of his position of attorney general, after serving seven years, and the process of selecting a successor had begun. Peres assumed that, just before his retirement, Zamir would not be worried about a clash with the political echelon. He therefore asked Justice Minister Moshe Nissim to speed up the process of appointing a new attorney general. At the same time, he decided to bring his attorney friend, Ram Caspi, into the picture. He knew that Caspi and Shalom had become friendly during their joint work on the Pollard affair. "Rami, Zamir is making trouble for Shalom," he remarked in enlisting his assistance. When Caspi asked to know what he was talking about, Peres simply said, "It's about the hijacked Bus No. 300. Talk to him, see what can be done."

Caspi invited Shalom to his home and heard his version of events. Shalom claimed that when Shamir had been prime minister, he had told him the following day about the killing of the terrorists, and had declared that he, as the head of the Shin Bet, was responsible. Shalom said that Shamir had also met with Yossi Ginossar, a senior Shin Bet operative, and spoken to him about his role in the Zorea Committee appointed by the defense minister.

Shalom admitted that he had sent Ginossar to the committee in order to disrupt its work and to report back to him about what was happening there. His reports had made it easier to coordinate the testimony of the Shin Bet operatives appearing before the committee, in order to mislead it. Afterward, Ginossar had signed the committee's report, which threw suspicion on Brigadier General Mordechai, knowing that the information in it was false. Shalom tried to justify the action by saying that he and his colleagues had vowed that if Mordechai was put on trial for killing the terrorists, they would reveal themselves and admit to the deed. Mordechai was tried for a lesser offense and acquitted. All that time, the Shin Bet operatives had remained silent.

On April 6, Peres received a memorandum from Caspi, in which he recommended that a ministerial team consisting of Peres, Shamir, Rabin, and Justice Minister Nissim suspend all action in the matter until Zamir's successor was appointed. The new attorney general, suggested Caspi, could deal with the matter without being bound by his predecessor's stand, and with a serious consideration for state security.

Caspi also suggested that the police minister order the police inspector general to delay action on the complaint that Zamir was threatening to lodge. Zamir had warned he would file the complaint if the prime minister insisted on hushing up the matter and refusing to take steps to ensure that such things could not happen again. In addition, Caspi warned Peres that an inquiry would expose Shin Bet operations to the attorneys hired by the accused, who would seek to prove that their clients' actions had not deviated from accepted norms in the service.

The prime minister's forum, which had been established earlier to deal with the Pollard affair, met several times. One of the possibilities suggested to the forum by Zamir was that Shalom resign. Peres rejected this possibility forcefully, saying, "I am not a judge, and I won't be a judge." On April 13, the forum decided to appoint Meir Gabbai, the deputy director general of the Justice Ministry, as acting attorney general, and to put the affair in his hands. Nissim was about to tell his deputy director general of this decision when he heard that Gabbai had been taken to the hospital with a heart attack.

On the following day, Peres fired Yitzhak Moda'i from his position as finance minister, after his outbursts against the prime minister. The Likud resolved that Moda'i and Nissim would swap ministries, which meant that Peres had to tell Moda'i, now justice minister, about the affair. Moda'i, who was full of bitterness toward the prime minister, demanded time to study all the facts before giving his opinion about relieving the attorney general of his post.

A month later, on May 16, Zamir informed Peres that Rafi Malka, one of the the Shin Bet operatives who had been fired after demanding Shalom's resignation, had filed an application to the high court of justice against the prime minister and the head of the Shin

Bet, appealing his dismissal. The hearing was set for June 5, behind closed doors, and publication of details of the affair was forbidden.

Previously, however, the Shin Bet affair had been leaked to Israel Television, which broadcast an unclear report—many details had been cut out by military censorship—about an inquiry against a "senior personality." Further details of the affair began to be published in the press, and the first signs of a looming public scandal became manifest.

Before the high court hearing, Prime Minister Peres called an urgent meeting with Shamir, Rabin, Zamir, and Caspi in his office. The conversation quickly became heated. Zamir announced that he was not prepared to defend the head of the Shin Bet before the high court. He pointed out that a serious criminal offense was involved, and suggested that Shalom be represented by a private attorney. He demanded that the head of the Shin Bet be suspended, along with the two legal advisers of the service who had cooperated with him. Peres briefly lost his cool and shouted repeatedly, "I am not ready to decide who will be dismissed." He charged Zamir with causing great harm to the Shin Bet and to state security, but the attorney general was insistent: "It is my duty to present the high court with the full and true picture." Peres asked Zamir and Caspi to retire to an adjoining room to coordinate an answer to the high court. In the ensuing conversation, Zamir undertook the defense of the prime minister in the legal discussion, and Caspi agreed to defend the Shin Bet employees. Caspi insisted on requesting an interim injunction from the court, giving them forty-five days to answer Malka's application. It would eventually dawn on Zamir that the time could be used to get rid of him and appoint a new attorney general, who would obey the instructions of the political echelon.

It became clear to Zamir that Peres did not plan to take any steps against the head of the Shin Bet. On May 18, the eve of Independence Day, Zamir drove to the home of Police Inspector General David Kraus in Ramat Gan and submitted a formal complaint against Avraham Shalom, Yossi Ginossar, and the two legal advisers of the Shin Bet. It said that they were suspected of committing serious criminal offenses. Shalom was suspected of giving the order to kill the two terrorists, and all of them were suspected of disrupting the legal process. Kraus put the complaint in his safe, and went abroad for a previously planned vacation.

It was now clear to Peres that the only way to stop the situation from snowballing was to dismiss Zamir. He did not meet with any opposition from the Likud to the dismissal and the hushing up of the affair. Two ministers on his side, Moshe Shahal of Labor, and Amnon Rubinstein of Shinui, however, objected to concealing the truth, and they said so publicly. On Friday afternoon, less than a week before the high court hearing, Peres invited the two to his home to meet with Shalom and possibly moderate their stand. Rabin, Caspi, and Azriel Nevo also came.

Shalom gave a lengthy account of Shin Bet operations, which had not always been within the letter of the law. He described actions that, had they reached the courts, would have placed many good operatives of the security services—and even members of the political hierarchy—behind bars. He then described the Bus 300 affair, concluding emotionally: "I swear to you on everything dear to me that everything was with Shamir's permission and authorization."

Rubinstein, a professor of jurisprudence, warned about a possible clash between Shalom and Zamir in the high court and suggested that the Shin Bet chief and his colleagues resign. Rabin supported the proposal and told Shalom: "You are likely to end up in jail." The formidable man, who had killed many terrorists and had commanded courageous operations, burst into bitter tears. All those present were embarrassed. Only Peres calmed him: "Avrum, I won't abandon you."

As opposed to all the previous occasions, when he had refused to consider such a possibility, Peres now asked Rubinstein to check with Zamir as to whether he would be prepared to stop all legal proceedings if Shalom and his colleagues resigned. Rubinstein called Zamir and arranged a meeting immediately. Before leaving, he asked Shalom whether he could tell Zamir that he, Ginossar, and the two legal advisers were prepared to resign. Shalom replied that he could not speak for the others, but gave the impression that he was ready to.

After a short while, Rubinstein returned to the prime minister's house with this message: "Zamir did not give a negative reply. He is not asking for blood; he just wants to see these men out of the Shin Bet. He wants to meet with his team. I've arranged to see him again on Sunday afternoon." Caspi again suggested that they should solve the problem by dismissing Zamir.

Shahal and Rubinstein persuaded Peres not to do this, saying that "only Zamir will have the public backing to resolve the problem." Rubinstein later said that he thought he had convinced Peres.

On Saturday night, Moda'i called Peres and told him he had two candidates to succeed Zamir as attorney general—Judge Yosef Harish and another judge of the Tel Aviv District Court. Moda'i added that the matter should be settled quickly, because he was about to go ahead. On Sunday morning, a few minutes before the weekly cabinet meeting, Peres called Rubinstein and told him about the two candidates. He said he would announce that one of them was replacing Zamir, and mentioned that Moda'i favored Harish.

Rubinstein was shocked. "But Shimon," he said, "we decided differently. How can you do this?" Peres replied impatiently, "There is no time. A decision must be made. Tell me which of the two is the better candidate." Rubinstein refused to give an opinion.

At the cabinet meeting, it was proposed that Zamir should wind up his duties and be replaced that same day. The cabinet approved the appointment of Judge Yosef Harish, a pleasant, indecisive man without strong convictions. Harish's first step in the affair did not live up to Peres's hopes for him. He gave an advisory opinion that it was not possible to order the police not to investigate Zamir's complaint. Peres understood that getting rid of Zamir had not solved the problem. The legal process had already been set in motion.

Then Caspi came up with a new idea: to investigate the possibility of presidential pardons for those involved, and in this way to free them from any investigation. He used the precedent of President Gerald Ford's pardon of Richard Nixon. Peres agreed that Caspi should go to President Herzog and sound him out as to whether he would cooperate. Caspi took along Ya'acov Ne'eman, another attorney, who had been Herzog's partner in a law firm before the latter had been elected president.

This new undertaking began to accelerate with impressive speed. At 7:00 P.M., Avraham Shalom came to the presidential residence and confessed to President Herzog about his deeds. He also told the president, himself a former head of Military Intelligence, that all his actions had been with the permission and approval of the political hierarchy. At 7:45 P.M. Shalom came out, and Caspi and Ne'eman entered. After a brief conversation, Herzog agreed to grant a pardon on condition that he was asked to do so by the justice minister, the attorney general, and the inner cabinet.

At 8:00 P.M., Peres called a meeting of the prime ministers' forum, with Moda'i and Attorney General Harish. Caspi reported on his meeting with the president, which only Peres had known about previously. Harish asked for a recess so that he could check whether the president had the legal authority to grant a pardon before a trial. He needed only a few minutes before he was able to give the politicians the answer: the president did have the authority. Meanwhile, journalists were gathering outside, and Peres felt he must finish the matter that night.

Caspi and Moda'i drove to the presidential residence, and the president repeated his willingness to grant pardons to Shalom, Ginossar, and the two legal advisers of the Shin Bet. At the same time, Peres instructed the cabinet secretary to call a meeting of the inner cabinet for the following morning at 6:00 A.M. All the candidates for pardons were summoned to Shin Bet headquarters. Caspi drove there with Shalom to persuade them to submit requests for pardons, and after two hours of emotional discussions, they agreed.

In the early hours of the morning, Ne'eman opened up his Jerusalem office, where he was joined by Moda'i and Harish, in order to formulate and type the requests for pardons. Caspi arrived from Shin Bet headquarters and found drafts already prepared. He insisted that the requests should include the statement that everything had been done "with permission and approval." Otherwise, he said, "the document will be a terrible disgrace. They did everything for the security of the state." The attorney and the justice minister added the phrase, "with permission and approval," which was to raise a political storm that would lead to the Shin Bet Report, about the involvement of the political hierarchy in the affair.

The Shin Bet employees also requested that the term "exceptional actions" be used, instead of "criminal offenses," but Caspi explained to them that the president could only grant pardons for criminal offenses. Harish, the linguistic purist, who by now had completely fulfilled all the hopes placed in him, suggested, "It is said of me that I carried out criminal offenses," and thus it was written. A few hours later, when the pardons became public knowledge, and the criticism started to pour in from all sides, Harish said in a radio interview that he had played no part in formulating the requests for pardons.

Meanwhile, the cabinet agreed to appeal to the president, with the exception of Ezer Weizman, who went to the president to explain his reservations. At 9:00 A.M. after consulting with his legal adviser, the president signed the pardons for the Shin Bet men. Harish came to congratulate him on "the great thing you did for the people of Israel."

In the ensuing public storm, the media and the legal establishment competed with each other in criticizing the prime minister, the inner cabinet, the president, and the new attorney general. The main legal point made by the critics, which was, in fact, supported by all the senior jurists in the country, was that the president's authority to grant pardons was limited by law to cases where the offenders had been found guilty, and did not apply to cases where the accused had not even been put on trial.

Public opinion was divided between those who felt that the affair should be laid to rest because it was harming the Shin Bet's ability to function, and those who criticized the use of the pardon system to protect from justice people who were suspected of committing grave criminal offenses. In fact, as always, it was the classic division between left and right: the right-wingers in favor of the pardons and of winding up the affair; the left-wingers talking about the rule of law, which must not be disregarded even by those working for the nation's security, even when their achievements in this field are generally regarded as considerable.

This atmosphere appeared to Yitzhak Moda'i (who had neither forgotten nor forgiven his dismissal from the Finance Ministry) suitable for another attack. When he was asked about the prime minister's handling of the Shin Bet situation, he replied, "Mistakes were made in dealing with the affair." That wasn't so bad, but he added, "I did not find it necessary to consult with Peres over the appointment of Harish." Even that was not so outrageous. What fanned the flames was his reason for not consulting Peres: "Because he is as ignorant about the law as he is about economics."

Somebody made sure that Peres heard about the remarks that same night. The following day was Sunday, when the weekly cabinet meeting always took place. Peres arrived at his office around 8:00 A.M., and the first thing he did was to call Shamir and ask to meet with

him privately. Shamir arrived a little before 9:00 A.M., the time the
cabinet meeting was due to begin. The two of them closed themselves in Peres's office, and Peres, with a grave expression and
without preliminaries, told Shamir he intended to dismiss Moda'i a
second time—this time from the Justice Ministry.

Moda'i was in a difficult position. If he did not resign, and the
government fell because of him, he would arouse the wrath of
Shamir, who all this time was walking on tiptoe in order not to give
Peres a pretext to torpedo the rotation agreement that would restore
him to the premiership. Moda'i, accordingly, did the only thing he
could do. He called a news conference to announce his resignation
from the government. At the special cabinet meeting, he gave Peres
his letter of resignation. (Later, he returned to the cabinet as
minister without portfolio.) The entire affair lasted less than one day,
and was not sufficient to distract attention from the other affair, which
was the occasion—at least, in a formal sense—for his dismissal.

The government was forced to bow to public pressure and to
appoint a commission of inquiry into the moral and judicial aspects of
the matter. The commission, headed by a former president of the
Supreme Court, Moshe Landau, ruled that it was forbidden to lie in
the name of security—the question that had hovered all the time over
the Shin Bet affair. "The affair called 'Bus Number 300' was very
different from the custom of giving false testimony in minitrials, and
in matters far more grave," the commission said. "Here, in addition
to deliberately false testimony, there was an attempt to disrupt the
work of an inquiry committee by means of appointing a man to the
committee for that specific purpose."

The Landau Commission also ruled, "The heads of the Shin Bet
failed by not understanding that no security operation—however
vital—can put its operatives above the law."

The government of Israel, the heads of which had also failed to
understand this, adopted the commission's report in full.

CHAPTER FOURTEEN

THE RISE AND FALL OF THE INTERNATIONAL CONFERENCE

The Murphy Rendezvous

IN ITS SEVEN years of power, the Likud managed to cause grave damage to the nation's economy, and to embroil the country in a long, unnecessary, and costly war in Lebanon. Both failures were the result of bad judgment, possibly stemming from a lack of experience with power. In the case of Lebanon, personal megalomania was also involved. This was not the case on the international front, where the Likud government deliberately took steps to block any possibility of a political settlement based on territorial compromise. In this the Likud was faithful to its ideology, which holds that territory— especially the West Bank—must not be surrendered, even for the sake of full peace.

There were, in fact, no other territories, or at least they were not relevant. The Egyptians had already received the whole of the Sinai Peninsula. The Syrians were ready to have the Golan Heights back, but not for peace, or anything resembling it. There remained, therefore, King Hussein of Jordan, who expressed a willingness to sign a peace treaty with Israel, but this involved big territorial concessions in the West Bank.

In order to prevent such concessions in the future, the Likud government carried out a policy of creating facts in the form of settlements. Their presence would forestall the possibility that areas of the West Bank, in part or as a whole, could ever be returned to Arab hands. This policy was not the invention of the Likud. It had been started by Labor Alignment governments, almost immediately after the areas were conquered in June 1967. The implementation, however, had been very slow and emphasis placed on areas outside the Arab centers of population, which kept open the option of giving up certain territories.

All this changed during the Likud administration, which set as a main task for itself the increase of settlement to the greatest possible extent, particularly in or next to Arab population centers. The success was not complete. Members of Gush Emunim, fired by religious belief and extremist ideological fanaticism, served as the spearhead of the settlement drive. But, on the whole, the Jewish public showed little enthusiasm for settling in the territories. In all the years since 1967, only a few thousand settled, many of whom live there but work inside the "green line"—the borders of the State of Israel.

One of the main reasons that Labor joined the national unity government was to halt the settlement, and it was in fact part of the coalition agreement that new settlements would not be built without the agreement of the two large parties—the practical effect of which was to freeze the status quo. This was not an end in itself, just a means of preparing the ground for the real target, the renewal of the peace process with Jordan and the Palestinians, which had ground to a halt when the Likud was in power.

Peres advanced toward this target every day, in one way or another, even while he devoted most of his time to healing the economy, the withdrawal from Lebanon, and the different scandals that surfaced during this period. A significant change in his political thinking had occurred since the days when he and Rabin had permitted the establishment of settlements in the West Bank by Gush Emunim. In those days he had been regarded as one of the leading hawks in the government—perhaps *the* leading one.

His years in opposition, the peace treaty with Egypt, the Lebanon war, the endless terrorism, and the extremism of the Likud had all brought him gradually to the conclusion that the only solution to the continuing conflict was by political means, which meant giving up territory—making even painful concessions. The hawk of the early 1970s was transformed in the mid-1980s into the leader of the camp proposing "territory for peace."

Peace with whom? In this, Peres did not go all the way to the left. He still believed, and continues to believe, that the PLO is not a partner for peace, and that the establishment of a Palestinian state would be dangerous to Israel and to the whole region. In his view there has always been only one option, which in Israeli political jargon is called "the Jordanian option," and it has become completely identified with Peres.

When Peres became prime minister at the head of the unity government, Hussein understood that there was a chance for a dialogue that had not existed before, although he had a problem that Peres could not solve for him. However much he wanted, Hussein knew that the inter-Arab situation did not permit him to enter negotiations without Palestinian representatives acceptable to the PLO. Syria, which remained a permanent threat on his border, demanded it; Saudi Arabia, which funded a significant part of his national budget, insisted on it; most of the inhabitants of the West Bank wanted it.

The best solution would be to use the PLO itself. Of course, it had never been absolutely clear if Hussein wanted the PLO as a negotiating partner or whether his declarations on the subject had been lip service. After all, it had been Hussein who had once slaughtered PLO members and expelled them from his kingdom, believing that they were a threat to his regime. In the Arab world, where confrontation and intrigue are rife, it is difficult to assess the credibility of open declarations. At any rate, it seemed that the Jordanian monarch had come to the conclusion that he could not make peace with Israel without the blessing of the Palestinians, and the Palestinians saw the PLO as their leadership for this purpose.

Also blocking this scenario for movement toward peace was Israel's absolute refusal to talk to an organization which was dedicated to its destruction, and continued to pursue a savage and bloody terrorist struggle against it. Israel's refusal was absolute, however, only in relative terms. When Moshe Dayan had been foreign minister in the government of Menachem Begin, he had worked out a formula which postulated that if the PLO rescinded its charter calling for Israel's destruction and recognized Israel's existence, it would no longer be a terrorist organization, a fact that would make it a suitable negotiating partner. This stand was also adopted by the United States. The only logical process, therefore, was to try to get the PLO to adopt a position that would make it, in American eyes—and subsequently, in Israeli eyes—fit to take part in the peace process.

Hussein made this attempt in 1985, when he held talks in Amman with PLO leader Yasser Arafat. The talks resulted in an agreement that would solve the problem of the West Bank by means of a confederation between Jordan and a Palestinian entity to be established on the West Bank. They further agreed that the negotiations with Israel would be conducted within the framework of an international conference, to which all the "relevant Arab states" would be invited.

Hussein was not greatly rewarded for his efforts. The United States expressed complete opposition to an international peace conference because such a process would necessitate Soviet participation. Peres was not prepared to accept the participation of the PLO in the negotiations, whether in an international conference, or in any other forum. He received support for his stand from an unexpected quarter.

On the eve of a trip to the United States on February 26, 1985, President Hosni Mubarak of Egypt made statements in an interview with Judy Miller in the *New York Times* that went beyond anything he had said previously: the Jordanian-Palestinian delegation to talks with Israel did not have to include people directly identified with the PLO. Regarding the international conference, he said that the great powers attending it would not play an active role; they would only provide the framework for the direct negotiations and would give their blessing to the solution that was agreed upon. In order to advance in this direction, Mubarak urged the Reagan administration to invite Israel and a Jordanian-Palestinian delegation to the United States to hold preparatory talks for direct negotiations.

Mubarak's initiative was coolly received by the PLO and most of the Arab nations, but he did not give up his idea, as Peres was to find out in a strange and unconventional way. On March 21, the Saudi Arabian millionaire, Adnan Khashoggi, phoned Foreign Ministry Director General David Kimche, who was in Geneva. He told him that Mubarak was in Washington and was asking for Peres's approval of his idea for a meeting between the Americans and a Jordanian-Palestinian delegation to prepare for direct negotiations between the delegation and Israel. Kimche immediately called Jerusalem, but received a negative answer from Peres. Khashoggi called Kimche again, saying that it would be a tragedy if Mubarak returned from the United States empty-handed. "He is looking for any way he can to get the feeling that his idea has not collapsed," Khashoggi explained.

In order to help Peres help him, Mubarak now came up with a new idea: a one-time meeting between the United States, Egypt, and Jordan, without Palestinians identified with the PLO, followed by direct negotiations. Kimche promised an answer that same day, before Mubarak's meeting with President Reagan, which was due to be held in a few hours' time. This time, Peres told Kimche to say yes, on condition that the Palestinians in the Jordanian delegation were Jordanian members of Parliament from the West Bank and that the Israeli approval was kept secret. Khashoggi thanked Kimche emotionally, asked him to call Mubarak personally in Washington to tell him, and also to report to U.S. National Security Adviser Robert McFarlane.

Kimche called Mubarak's hotel, and an Egyptian security man informed him that Mubarak was in a meeting. A quarter of an hour later, the phone rang in Kimche's Swiss hotel room. The Egyptian president was on the line. He thanked Kimche for his efforts, expressed satisfaction at Israel's stand, and conveyed greetings to Peres. Kimche told Mubarak that it was a personal gesture toward him, and emphasized that only direct talks were envisioned. As requested, Kimche reported to McFarlane, who voiced reservations about the three-way meeting, lest it harm the principle of direct negotiations.

Khashoggi later tried to institutionalize this channel between Peres and Mubarak, and passed Peres a message that Mubarak wanted to talk to him. The phone call was scheduled twice, but Mubarak did not call. Peres decided that the channel was not to his liking, and the contact with Khashoggi was terminated.

The reports of Mubarak's visit to the United States related that he discussed with Secretary Shultz the idea of a secret meeting in Washington with the foreign ministers of Egypt and Jordan, but Mubarak told Shultz he did not believe that Hussein was prepared for the condition that the Palestinians should be members of Parliament, for fear of the Syrians and the PLO. For this reason, Mubarak made a strong effort to soften the American stand on the PLO, by appealing to President Reagan's anti-Soviet sentiments during their meeting. He quoted Arafat's deputy, Abu-Iyad, as saying in closed meetings that the PLO supported the Soviet Union in order to gain the support of Moscow, but as soon as it had achieved relations with the United States, it would cut its ties with the Russians. Reagan listened, but said he was not prepared to change U.S. policy toward the PLO. However, he gave his blessing to the meeting between the U.S. secretary of state and the foreign ministers of Egypt and Jordan, on condition that Israel welcomed it and that it would be followed by a meeting with the Israelis.

At this point it emerged that Mubarak was not able to carry out his proposal. He admitted that he could not promise that after the three-way meeting, Jordan would agree to direct negotiations. With this, the whole process appeared to have reached a dead-end.

Peres did not accept that. When he had received all the reports, he called in Defense Minister Yitzhak Rabin for consultations, in which Cabinet Secretary Yossi Beilin and the head of Military Intelligence, General Ehud Barak, also participated. He put forward an alternative to Mubarak's plan that won Rabin's approval. It had three stages:

1. A meeting between Jordan, Egypt, and the United States.
2. A meeting between Israel, Egypt, and the United States (secret or open) to improve relations between Israel and Egypt, and to discuss the matters in dispute between the two states.
3. A four-way meeting: Israel, Egypt, the United States,

and a Jordanian-Palestinian delegation (including Palestinians not directly identified with the PLO).

Peres conveyed the plan to Shultz and suggested that he send an emissary to the region to advance it. He ended the message to Shultz with the sentence, "I derive benefit from the combination of you and President Reagan. It is the enjoyable part of my job." The enjoyment was apparently mutual. Shultz saw the plan as having potential promising enough to send his personal assistant, Richard Murphy, to the region for what was officially described as a "fact-finding mission," with the result that the plan for the meetings came to be called the "Murphy rendezvous."

It was Murphy's task, wrote Shultz, to try to advance the three-stage Peres plan; and according to the instructions of the secretary and the president, he would hold informal meetings in Amman with a group of Jordanians and "acceptable" Palestinians. Aware of Peres's sensitivity to the issue, Shultz added that the United States did not agree to any American meeting with declared members of the PLO.

The more the contacts between Israel and Jordan developed, the more the signs of nervousness increased in the PLO, the leaders of which feared that eventually they would be left out of the process. To prevent this, they decided to demonstrate their existence in the manner to which they were accustomed.

At the end of September 1985, the bodies of three Israeli vacationers were found brutally murdered on a yacht in Larnaka Harbor in Cyprus. Counterterror adviser Amiram Nir went at once to Larnaka, from where he reported to Peres that the murderers were members of Force 17 of the Fatah, the largest movement in the PLO, under the command of Abu-Tayib, who was stationed in Amman. Several members of Force 17 imprisoned in Israel identified the three Larnaka terrorists as fellow members of their force. According to Peres's information, it was the climax of a wave of terrorist acts planned and carried out by this Palestinian force with the authorization of Arafat.

To Peres it was clear that Israel could not ignore the murders. The question was where and how the IDF would respond. The answer, worked out by Peres, Defense Minister Rabin, and his men, came on October 1 in Tunis. Under cover of darkness, and using

sophisticated electronic countermeasures against surveillance, Israeli air force planes flew over Arab radar stations en route, bombed
PLO military headquarters, and returned safely to base.

At the end of November 1985, Murphy met with Peres after a
visit to Amman. He reported that the king had reiterated that he
could not move without the PLO. His prime minister, Zaid al-Rifai,
tried to sweeten the pill by saying that it was possible to nominate to
attend the Murphy rendezvous "better Palestinians than you might
imagine."

The truth was that Hussein was far from enthusiastic about the
idea of a meeting under U.S. auspices. He was not at all sure that
with American sponsorship, and Egyptian participation, he would get
a fair deal. From his point of view, the international conference was
far more desirable, and he said so, while emphasizing that he did not
mean an active conference but "a framework, an umbrella, a
necessary cover." He suggested that the conference be held in
Geneva. He did not care whether the invitations to the great powers
were sent by the U.N. secretary general or by President Reagan,
and "anyone who wanted to should turn up."

Hussein's words at this time fell on deaf ears. Murphy expressed the view of the U.S. administration when he said that
experience had proved that it was impossible to limit a conference to
ceremonial functions only. He was not at all in favor of Soviet
involvement.

Peres was not any more receptive, judging by what he told
Murphy about the conference. "If we are talking about an international conference," he said, "it is a complete waste of time. It is
inviting Israel to a forum where it will be attacked—not engaged in
dialogue. We have had bad experiences of United Nations involvement. The Soviet Union will not agree to participate in an empty
framework."

It would have been better for Peres had he found some other
forum to give his opinion of an international conference, because
Shamir also attended the meeting with Murphy, and subsequently,
when Peres became the chief proponent of an international conference, Shamir would remind him of his remarks.

Secretary Shultz was also entirely forthright when he told Peres
at a meeting in Jerusalem on May 10, 1985, that when Hussein came

to Washington at the end of the month, "we'll make it clear to him that there is no point in a conference."

What happened was the exact opposite, for during that visit of Hussein's, the first breakthrough occurred regarding the international conference.

"We are still opposed to this," wrote Shultz to Peres the day after his meeting with Hussein. But this time, after "decisive rejection," there was also a "but." Shultz wrote, "We understand the king's wish for international support in opening direct talks."

Who's Afraid of an International Conference?

The process of the Murphy rendezvous is dead; long live the international conference. Peres was not the man to speculate on what might have been or to mourn procedures that are no longer used. His pragmatism was expressed by always looking forward. There was only one thing that was completely alien to his belief and personality: a freeze, a standstill. He saw such a situation as more dangerous than any possible move—even an international conference to which he had originally been opposed. Now there was a new situation, which meant either an international conference or a freeze. Peres had no hesitation, particularly as the conference under consideration was a forum that was not coercive or active.

To kick off the new idea, Peres revived an old tradition. On his way to visit the United States, he made a short stopover in London to meet an old acquaintance, King Hussein, who was accompanied by his prime minister, Zaid al-Rifai. The two had not met for several years, and after a courteous exchange of inquiries about their families, the two leaders settled down to business.

During this discussion, Peres for the first time adopted the idea of the international conference, after becoming convinced that this was the only way acceptable to the king. He also managed to convince himself that this was not as dramatic a change in his thinking as it seemed. After all, he was still categorically opposed to a conference where the sponsoring great powers could play an active role in the negotiations. The international conference that Hussein proposed—and to which Peres agreed—was to come into session at the start of the discussions, and then to allow the countries involved in the dispute to hold direct talks, without further interference.

When he returned to Jerusalem, Peres at once reported to Foreign Minister Shamir on his meeting with the king. The foreign minister listened, and encouraged him to continue. On October 3, 1985, U.S. Ambassador Pickering told Peres that King Hussein had already appealed to the Soviet Union to renew its ties with Israel to facilitate its participation in the conference. He had also tried to enlist Arafat's agreement to representatives for preparatory talks for the conference, and to recognize Resolution 242 and stop terrorist actions; however, his efforts had not succeeded either in Moscow or with the PLO command.

In this atmosphere, Peres set out for Washington in mid-October, exactly a year after his first visit as prime minister. This time he came crowned with the laurels of savior of the Israeli economy (which was showing signs of recovery), as the leader who had brought the IDF out of Lebanon, and as the man who had persuaded the administration of his serious intention to bring Jordan into the circle of peace. Under Peres's leadership, Israel no longer said no to all peace initiatives; it was not only ready to stretch out its hand, but when matters reached a deadlock, its prime minister was the one to come up with fresh ideas for breaking out of it. Even if nothing came of his contacts and initiatives, Peres's strategy was to do everything he could to create continuous momentum because he both believed in it and wanted it, and also so that nobody could lay the responsibility for failure upon his government. He planned his moves in a way that always placed the ball in the other side's court. If someone must destroy a move or an initiative, let it be Jordan or the PLO.

On October 17, 1985, President Reagan received Peres warmly at the White House. Reagan's main concern was an arms deal with Jordan. He gave two reasons for his concern. One was, "the price that the king has paid for advancing toward peace is genuine." The second reason was, "if they don't buy arms from us, they will get them somewhere else." He meant the Soviet Union, "and without the conditions we impose on them."

"With a little effort, possibly the start of direct talks, we can advance toward what you want and we are concerned about," Peres said.

"Hussein contends he needs the weapons because of the Syrian threat—not because of you," Reagan said.

"Let him make peace with us and then be strengthened against the Syrian threat. If you encourage the process, perhaps we can start negotiations before the arms supplies reach Jordan."

"The arms will reach Jordan later, in any case," Reagan said. "The delivery date is in another three years. I very much hope that in that period there will be negotiations resulting in this."

"In Israel, there is a consensus against the supply of arms to countries that are in a state of war with us. It is not a personal matter. Direct negotiations will change the entire atmosphere in the region."

The following morning at his breakfast table, Secretary Shultz proposed a deal. The United States would agree to supply Jordan the arms it was requesting, but delivery would be dependent on holding direct talks with Israel. The president would give his personal assurance that the arms would be sent only after the start of direct negotiations, possibly accompanied by a declaration of nonbelligerency by Hussein. Peres agreed to check the matter without promising what his position would be.

On Shultz's instructions, Richard Murphy quickly packed his bags and, before setting out for the Middle East, held another conversation with Peres and his party. The main aim of his mission this time was to secure a declaration from Hussein that would change the mood in Congress and the Israeli position on the arms deal.

A week later Murphy returned to New York to report to Shultz, and also to Peres, who was back for the official opening of the U.N. General Assembly. He had news. The king had made it clear that there was no substitute for PLO participation in the peace talks. He also rejected Shultz's proposal that the arms deal be conditional on the start of negotiations. In other words, even if the king had wanted the American arms with all his heart, he was not prepared to pay the political price demanded by the seller.

Up to this point, the plan of an international conference as a framework for opening direct negotiations was an idea that had been kicked around at meetings. The first time Peres presented it as an official plan, which Israel supported, was in his speech before the U.N. General Assembly in October 1985. If he did so to test the reactions to the plan at home, he succeeded.

The Likud ministers did not wait for him to return to Israel to voice, loudly and angrily, their very negative opinions. The loudest complaints, not surprisingly, were heard from Ariel Sharon.

A combination of insolence, unbridled ambition, and an arrogant lust for headlines had made Sharon the bad boy of Israeli politics. His coarse, overbearing personality, which won him the title of "bulldozer," and his rough language had confounded many good people in his party and outside it. Unfortunately for Peres, he had become one of Sharon's favorite targets, and from time to time was favored with his crude comments. Sometimes Sharon was not satisfied with arrows, and he used shells.

One of these times was after a cabinet discussion during which Peres had expressed his determined opposition to the establishment of more settlements on the West Bank. Sharon knew full well that the reason was economic as well as political, but this fact did not prevent him—in principle, he never let the facts interfere with his actions—from telling a party meeting on August 21, 1985, that "what Peres and the Labor ministers are doing is to implement in full the policy of the White Paper." This was no light accusation, for the "White Paper" was the collection of decrees that the British mandate had issued against Jewish immigration to the land of Israel.

When, in response, Peres declared that it was "impossible to continue, with these attacks from Sharon," the stout minister looked left and right, and saw that no one was applauding—not even his Likud colleagues. Without any hesitation, he immediately expressed his unqualified regret to Peres, who accepted it. At the same time, Peres announced in the cabinet, and insisted it be entered in the minutes, that "any minister who expresses himself in an unacceptable manner will be responsible for the existence of the government." This threat to dissolve the government achieved its purpose, until Peres's speech at the United Nations about the international conference.

In a public speech, Sharon charged that "the prime minister has been having secret talks with Jordan and the Palestinians for the past seven months and has already agreed to bring Syria into the negotiations. The international conference has already been approved." And further, he declared, "Their (Peres and the Labor ministers) derision and cynicism has cost us much blood over the years, and what is now happening will cost us much more blood." Without stuttering or blushing, the architect of the Lebanon war went on to announce, "Today we are in a very grave situation in which a man with incomparable cynicism, and in utter disregard of orderly government procedure, is leading the government on a crooked path."

On the day after his appearance, his remarks were published prominently in the media. That same evening, Peres called together the Labor ministers, who were agreed that attacks on the prime minister's honor could no longer be excused. With the support of his ministers, Peres summoned Shamir the following morning and, as detailed in a letter he afterward distributed to all the cabinet ministers, "I told him that according to my understanding he should have demanded the sacking of Sharon, who had violated the elementary rules of the existence and management of the government."

It is possible that Shamir would have kissed both of Peres's hands if he had liberated him from the minister, who had more than once made his life miserable; however, the leader of the Likud had no alternative but to give his party rival his full support. He said he "opposed dismissing Sharon from the government, and doing so would be a violation of the coalition agreement." (The agreement said that a minister of one of the large parties could not be fired from the government without the agreement of the leader of his party.)

Peres replied that "Sharon's behavior is against the law (of collective responsibility), and the coalition agreement cannot become a refuge for someone who violates the Knesset regulations."

Peres distributed this letter to the ministers, who arrived at a special cabinet meeting called to discuss the crisis. It also contained the following: "There are moments in the life of a people, when one must get up and say, enough anarchy, and put an end to negligence and incitement." Peres summed up by allaying the fears that the Likud expressed, and the public felt, during the crisis: "The national unity government has achieved much in the fourteen months of its existence. For my part I am making, and will make, efforts so that it can continue to exist for a further three years."

Peres opened the cabinet meeting by stating, "According to the basic law (government), I announce my intention of dismissing Minister Sharon from his post." The Likud ministers and their allies in the coalition began to urge Sharon to apologize and settle the matter. All Sharon was prepared to say was, "I support government policy." More quietly, he added, "As laid down in the government guidelines, of course." Peres was not satisfied. "That is a conditional apology; it does not contain an expression of confidence in the prime minister."

Sharon exploded. "This is a deliberate attempt to humiliate, to make me bow, to bring me to my knees. I have never gone down on my knees. No one has ever made me bow down." As it turned out, Sharon, who always found it difficult to tell the truth, did not depart from his custom with regard to these words either.

At the end of the discussion, Peres announced that he was prepared to wait twenty-four hours for a suitable apology. When he returned to his office, he was overwhelmed by a stream of delegations, colleagues, and party activists, who urged him to take advantage of the opportunity to fire Sharon and, thereby, prevent the rotation agreement from being implemented. It was justified politically, they told him. He would be able to go to the elections with his achievements in the economy and Lebanon and win a majority that would enable him to set up a government without the Likud. Many told him it was a national obligation. With the Likud, it would be impossible to achieve a peace agreement on the Jordanian front. There were even phone calls from Likud members, who hinted that Sharon's dismissal would not necessarily cause the breakup of the government.

At home, Peres heard another story. Sonia, his wife, who very rarely interfered in his actions, told him: "You mustn't do it. People will again say that you are an intriguer and lack credibility."

This was Peres's own feeling, and for that reason he did not take action when the twenty-four hours he had allowed for a letter of apology had passed. At a special meeting of the Labor Party Central Committee, where he attacked Sharon and repudiated his accusations, he said: "I intend to show stamina. I am not going to act hastily, and I am not standing with a stopwatch in my hand."

A number of formulas were worked out by both sides and rejected, until, eventually, a redeeming one for Sharon's apology was found. It said, inter alia, "Blood is the result of terror, and, if anyone thought I meant that the blood was the result of derision and cynicism, I did not intend that." On the other things he said, Sharon expressed complete regret. The affair came to an end. There were those who sighed in relief; there were others who were disappointed at what they saw as a lost opportunity to dismantle the partnership with the Likud—or at least to get rid of Sharon. Sharon himself, who had been forced to his knees, waited for the next opportunity.

During all the furor, Peres's political statement to the Knesset, which he made a few days after his return from New York, passed almost unnoticed. In it he repeated his United Nations speech, almost word for word. The statement, as is customary, was put to the vote and passed by a large majority—including the Likud members.

The Americans Shuttle

Peres managed to introduce the international conference into the Israeli political scene, but everywhere else at the end of November 1985, less than a year from rotation, the conference seemed to have reached a dead-end. Richard Murphy, who had been sent to Jerusalem to report to Peres on the Reagan-Gorbachev summit in Geneva, had nothing new to report. He estimated that more time would have to pass, possibly several months, before any progress could be achieved.

Peres was extremely displeased. He told Murphy: "I am not worried about a few days, but we can't wait several months. Opposition to the plan is building up everywhere. We raised the hopes of the public since the United Nations speech; we have moved in the right direction. I don't want to lose that."

"Do you still prefer to begin the process with the unity government?" United States Ambassador Thomas Pickering asked when he met with Peres.

"Certainly," Peres said. "Once it begins, I won't be concerned about a crisis because I can present the public with a clear choice."

"Is there a final date for that?" Murphy asked.

"I am a patient man, but every day wasted is a shame," Peres said. "If the king continues to wait for Arafat, it will be like the empty chair awaiting the Messiah."

Later, when the Likud claimed that Peres had not received a mandate to advance the idea of an international conference as an open forum, Peres would point to this speech, which had been approved without any disagreement by the foreign minister.

Peres's pressure led to a new American mission to the region in December, this time in the person of Ambassador Wat Cluverius. Cluverius was well-known in Israel from his service in the U.S. embassy in Tel Aviv, and later, as consul-general in Jerusalem.

Schultz had charged Cluverius with trying to bridge the gap between Israel and Jordan concerning the modalities of the conference. In his talks at the royal palace in Amman, Cluverius learned, and explained to the Israeli team (Peres, Rabin, Shamir, and several aides), that although the Jordanians agreed that one should not talk in advance about the results of the negotiations, it was important for them to know in advance the parameters of the envisioned Israeli withdrawal in the West Bank that the United States supported. Why was this so important? Because American support for a sufficient withdrawal would enable Jordan to waive the necessity of referral back to the full conference. On the other hand, if Jordan had to stand alone against Israel and the United Sates, the option of referral to the conference would be imperative.

In other words, King Hussein had withdrawn considerably from his previous stand that the conference would be only technical. It was late at night. The participants in the meeting were relaxing around the dinner table in Peres's residence with food and drink, in a slightly melancholy atmosphere. Peres was disappointed—it seemed as if they had returned to square one, if not farther back. He delivered a monologue quietly, in a tired voice.

"All of us are getting old . . . the king has to start somewhere. If I were a Jordanian, I would realize that if nothing happens, they can forget about the West Bank. Settlement will start up again and that settles it. All the Palestinian pressure will then focus on Jordan."

In the following months there were more journeys by Murphy and Cluverius, and more formulas and suggestions, all of which came to nothing.

Peres had hoped so much that before he handed over the premiership to Shamir, he could initiate a process that even a Likud-led government would not be able to stop. And possibly he had hoped, deep down, that if such a process started, there would not be rotation, and he could go to early elections on a proposal that the Israeli public could not refuse. As the days passed, his nervousness increased. In a conversation with Ambassador Pickering, he said impatiently: "You should tell the king that Peres might be the last idiot making an effort to squeeze something out of nothing."

This was precisely what Peres tried to achieve with a series of programs that his creative mind produced. He proposed the "Marshall Plan of the Middle East." The seven major economic powers would invest in economic projects in the moderate Arab states and the administered territories. The size of the investment would be in direct proportion to the willingness of the recipients to make concessions for peace.

In one of his meetings with Hussein, he spoke about another project: a canal between the Red Sea and the Dead Sea, passing through both Israeli and Jordanian territory. It would solve the problem of the drop in the level of the Dead Sea, about which both states were concerned. It would also make Israel and Jordan each other's hostages, with a joint interest in preserving good neighborly relations.

He also had a plan for Mubarak. Knowing the Egyptian president's admiration for Israel's achievements in agriculture, he proposed the establishment of a "Council for the Greening of the Middle East," with a program to push back the desert by means of solar energy, settling the wastes, and irrigation.

It was difficult not to respond positively to the plan and to the goodwill that doubtlessly accompanied it, and Peres received many compliments for it—but nothing more. The same problems that made the Arab states reluctant to make peace with Israel—or even to negotiate with it—stood in the way of any sort of cooperation with the Jewish state.

Wat Cluverius continued to journey back and forth over the Allenby Bridge with alterations and additions to the proposal for the parameters of the conference, when Zafer al-Masri, the mayor of Nablus, was assassinated. It was clear to all that the PLO had a hand in the murder of the first Palestinian who had agreed, in full coordination with Jordan, to take over the running of the largest town in the West Bank from the IDF officer who had been in charge for several years. Despite this, Al-Masri's funeral was turned into a PLO victory march. The pictures of Arafat and the Palestinian flags carried by the multitude escorting the coffin of Al-Masri (a protégé of Hussein's) influenced the king more than the thousands of words that he had heard from the Americans and Peres to the effect that, in the absence of a settlement, the PLO would take control of the West Bank.

How to avoid this development was the subject of a series of meetings held by the king—one with Peres on the border between Akaba and Eilat, the others with Shultz on a visit to the United States. In these meetings, the king presented eleven points designed to weaken PLO influence in the West Bank and to strengthen that of Jordan:

1. Appointing pro-Jordanian mayors in four or five West Bank towns.

2. Granting municipal tax concessions in the towns by means of widening the municipal boundaries. Detailed requests, accompanied by maps, would be submitted to the Israeli authorities by eight municipalities. Six other municipalities, and twenty-four village councils, would follow.

3. Easing credit terms to West Bank inhabitants by re-opening banks in the West Bank towns.

4. Reexamining the level of taxes imposed on the inhabitants of the territories.

5. Canceling crossing fees on the Jordan bridges.

6. Extending public health services.

7. The ceasing of Israeli expropriation of land, and granting the inhabitants permission to use land already expropriated for farming or pasture.

8. Taking steps against the West Bank papers supported by the PLO.

9. Taking steps against PLO supporters in the West Bank universities.

10. Freezing new Jewish settlement, and not extending the existing settlements.

11. Approving requests for family reunions.

Hussein received only part of what he requested. A branch of the Arab Bank was reopened in Nablus. Military censors exercised stricter supervision over the PLO press. The appointment of three mayors was approved from a list submitted by Jordan. Defense Minister Rabin, who was responsible for the territories, did not seem inclined to grant Jordan's requests in the important fields of making land available for the inhabitants' use, significantly increasing approval of family reunion requests, altering municipal boundaries, or making tax concessions.

Hussein was not the only Arab king with whom Peres held meetings at this time. Another king who put in an appearance—or rather, a reappearance—was King Hassan of Morocco. Up to this point, relations with him had been similar to those with Hussein: officially no contact, no relations. Unofficially, the king of Morocco regularly received Israeli guests, including senior leaders such as Peres and Rabin, for talks on regional matters. When asked, the king denied the existence of these meetings, which were always held on condition of absolute secrecy.

On Tuesday, July 22, 1986, Peres arrived in Morocco for a three-day visit, the first open meeting between an Israeli prime minister and the king of that country.

On the face of it, nothing practical—certainly not in the immediate future—came out of this visit. More ice melted. Another Arab state had received the Israeli prime minister in view of the whole world, particularly the Arab world. Another Arab leader prepared to be an honest broker in the peace process, and one could never know where or when he would carry out an action or say a word that would be the last straw breaking the back of the camel of enmity.

Peres was again forced to take a partial break in his political moves, when Ariel Sharon broke the silence in which he had wrapped himself since the previous government crisis had ended with his apology.

On Saturday, September 6, 1986, terrorists entered a synagogue in Istanbul, Turkey, and murdered Jewish worshipers while they were at prayer. On Sunday, September 7, Peres listened, as he was accustomed, to the 7:00 A.M. news magazine on Israel Radio. He paused with the coffee cup halfway to his lips, when he heard Sharon's reaction to the murderous event: "The terrible program carried out against Jews praying in a synagogue in Istanbul is the terrible single answer of the Palestinians and their supporters to the peace maneuvers, and Israeli concessions—from concessions to the PLO, King Hussein, King Hassan." To put it simply: Peres's moderate policy was the cause for the murders in Istanbul.

That same morning, Peres called together his Labor colleagues and enlisted their support for any action he wished to take. Unlike the previous occasion, Yitzhak Rabin also supported punishing Sharon.

Once again Peres faced the old dilemma. There was no doubt that Sharon's remarks were serious and totally unfounded. It was an opportunity—almost definitely the last. Should he break up the government a month before rotation? Would anyone believe that his motives were clean of party considerations—or even more, of narrow personal interests?

Peres opened a meeting of the inner cabinet with a grim face by stating that Sharon had placed indirect responsibility on the government for the murders in Istanbul, and he had therefore decided not to fire Sharon, but to refrain from calling a meeting of the inner cabinet or the full cabinet until Sharon publicly apologized for his remarks.

Sharon found himself isolated in his own party. His Likud colleagues disassociated themselves from his remarks. Shamir supporters even hinted that he had done it deliberately to prevent Shamir from becoming prime minister. Sharon started to see himself outside the government, with all that it meant for his political ambitions.

He wrote a letter of apology, beginning: "I retract my remarks on Saturday night, as they were interpreted." Peres was not satisfied. He demanded that the phrase, "as they were interpreted," be removed. Sharon refused. Again, Shamir's associates warned Sharon about the lonely life outside the government, and the man who had declared that he would not be forced to his knees removed the phrase. He also added: "There is no connection between government decisions and what happened in Istanbul. There is no connection between our general and honest desire for peace and the murder of Jews," and several other expressions of apology, regret, and retraction dictated by Peres.

And so, the last obstacle to the implementation of rotation was removed.

At the same time, all the obstacles on the path to arbitration of the dispute with Egypt over Taba were also removed. On September 11, 1986, Peres flew to Egypt for an official visit. From Cairo Airport an Egyptian army helicopter took him to the luxurious Ras a-Tin Palace in Alexandria. The Israeli flag was raised over the palace as the helicopter landed opposite a presidential guard of honor. Egypt's prime minister, Ali Lutfi, escorted the prime minister as he inspected the honor guard. They were followed by Ezer Weizman, Abba Eban, and Likud Knesset member Dan Meridor, who had been invited to represent Shamir. The strains of "Hatikva," Israel's national anthem, sounded on Arab soil for the first time since Menachem Begin had visited Egypt five years before. Egyptian warships were at anchor in the calm bay. Only the security men in every corner, with their two-way radio sets, were nervous. Hundreds of reporters and photographers, from the United States to China, surrounded the palace in which the two leaders sat in armchairs, showering compliments on each other.

Mubarak congratulated Peres on the improvement of the quality of life in the administered territories and on concluding the Taba matter. Peres replied in kind. "It would be better if you, Mr. President, were leading the political process in the region." Mubarak was in a buoyant mood, although he did not disguise his concern about the difficult economic situation in his country. He said that he had inherited an infrastructure in ruins and a state that was disintegrating, and he had no illusions about the intentions of the Arab world to extend him assistance.

Gossip about Arab leaders was a permanent part of the agenda in regional summits, and this meeting was no different from the others. The star of the lighter part of these discussions was Libyan leader Mu'ammar Qaddafi, about whom the Arab leaders competed in telling stories. Mubarak told Peres how Qaddafi had changed his clothes three times a day at the Islamic summit, proposed unification with China, and even asked to buy an atomic bomb from Peking. He was annoyed with former U.S. President Jimmy Carter for preventing him from acting against Qaddafi. Peres told Mubarak a story that drew loud laughter from the Egyptian president. It seems that Arafat had wanted to hold a formal conference in North Yemen. The local regime made it conditional on his depositing thirty million dollars in cash in the local banks. He did so, but when he later changed his mind about holding the conference, he was told he could only have the money back in local currency.

In the practical part of the discussion, Mubarak showed interest in Israel's talks with the United States regarding the reduction of interest on old loans. He was very interested in a similar arrangement, he told Peres, but he was keen that Israel should set a

precedent and clear the way for him. If it were possible, he would be
most grateful if Peres, on his visit to the United States in three days'
time, would put in a good word with the pro-Israel lobby. Peres was
in excellent spirits. He believed that he would return home the
following morning with a formula that would move the Middle East
peace process a large step forward.

However, despite the friendship and mutual regard between the
two leaders, they were unable to bridge the gaps and issued instead
a short, anemic statement about the need to work for peace.

At noon on Friday, Peres returned to Jerusalem, and on Sunday
morning he flew off again in the Israeli air force Boeing. His
destination was the United States, where he would be conducting his
farewell visit as prime minister with the American administration.
They were also aware of the fact, and they went out of their way to
sweeten the bitter pill.

Reagan was particularly friendly. "Call me Ron, so that I can call
you Shimon," he urged him at the start of their conversation. Peres
smiled and remarked: "No problem. Ron is a genuine Israeli name."
He explained to the president that the Hebrew meaning of the name
was "joy." Immediately afterward, they started to compete in
exchanging compliments.

"The past two years have been a real success for Israel,"
Reagan said. "Summit meetings with Arab leaders, economic
achievements, and a dynamic peace policy. All this is the result of you
and your leadership. I congratulate you, and it is important to me that
we continue our cooperation in the future."

Peres responded in kind. "Under your leadership, special
relations have developed between our two nations. We have stabi-
lized the Israeli economy, and removed obstacles on the road to
peace."

All the compliments in the world, however, could not make
Peres forget rotation. At one of the official banquets, relaxed with
good food and wine, he turned to Vice President Bush and remarked,
"It's better to be a vice president than a prime minister—especially
when there is rotation." Bush laughed and tried to console him.
"Whatever happens, Shimon, we'll continue to work together."

The many compliments could also not disguise the fact that
there was disagreement in the political field. Peres had thought that
the idea of an international conference was the cornerstone of

American Middle East policy, but he discovered that this was not quite the case.

American second thoughts about the idea were even more concretely expressed in Reagan's reply to Peres's suggestion that he discuss the idea of the conference at his meeting with Soviet leader Gorbachev in Reykjavíc. The president wrote, "The United States is of course ready to consider the forum of some international conference, but my reservations—like yours—are very strong. We must ensure that the suggested framework will encourage direct talks leading to progress, and not to a deadlock."

The hint was clear. In the president's opinion, Soviet participation would lead to a deadlock. Was this, in reality, the Soviet intention? Peres was given the opportunity to examine it for himself during the same visit to the United States.

On Monday, September 22, 1986, in the office of the president of the U.N. General Assembly, who was currently the Soviet delegate, Peres met with Soviet Foreign Minister Eduard Shevardnadze.

Peres spoke at length about the Middle East dispute, international terror, the difficult economic situation in the Third World. He ended with a survey of the latest steps connected with an international conference, and stressed the need for the renewal of diplomatic ties between Israel and the Soviet Union.

Shevardnadze replied that he would keep his remarks short because of the pressure of time. He regretted this, because the problems that Peres had raised merited serious thought and deep discussion. He looked at note cards that had been prepared in advance, put them aside, and told his guests, "The Soviet Union played a decisive role in the establishment of Israel. We remember this with pride. We were guided then by historical justice because we believe that the Jewish people, with their rich history, are entitled to their own state. The same principles of objectivity and justice are before us when we demand justice for the Palestinian people. We believe that the approach of you and your people to the Palestinians has not changed since the diplomatic relations between our two nations were severed. Therefore, it is not possible to say anything positive about renewing ties between us."

In fact, he told Peres, while asking him not to be offended, "Your policy is openly anti-Soviet. Take, for example, your joining the dangerous Strategic Defense Initiative (Star Wars). We cannot be indifferent to that because we are convinced that it is a new step in the arms race. It also gives Israel a new military potential . . . we feel insulted—even if the damage is not so great—by the three radio stations to be established on Israeli soil for the Voice of America and the Voice of Europe, which broadcast propaganda to the Soviet public. We are following this development, and we have to draw conclusions. We and you must strive for normalization of relations between the Soviet Union and Israel. Don't let us do anything that will damage this process. We know that the Jewish people feel close to the Jews of the Soviet Union, and therefore, you should feel increased pressure for normalization between us. I am sorry, Mr. Prime Minister, that you are creating tension artificially." With a half smile, he added, "You are a very experienced man. I know your biography well."

"That's dangerous," Peres said.

After the laughter had died down, Shevardnadze turned to the international conference and made it clear that in his country's view, the conference had to be "active"—in other words, the Soviets felt they should have the right to intervene in the negotiations.

Peres made it clear that, under certain conditions to be determined in advance, he did not oppose a role for the international conference. "Also, on the Palestinian issue—I do not disregard their rights, and I agree that their participation is required in finding a solution. Many things have changed over the years. I regret that, while you cannot make an omelet without breaking eggs, you cannot get eggs out of an omelet."

Shevardnadze replied, "Maybe Reagan's new technologies make it possible."

"Only in outer space," Peres answered.

Again the two of them burst out laughing. Shevardnadze became serious. He leaned forward and said, "I want to make sure I have understood. You say that you are not indifferent to the future of the Palestinians. Can you tell me how you would define these people, their rights? Do the Palestinians have the right to a separate state? To self-determination?"

Peres replied, "We recognize the existence of the Palestinian people. There is no longer any argument about that. If there were only one people, and one land, there would not be a problem. But we are talking about two people on one land. In this situation there are two alternatives: to divide the land, or to divide the government in a federation and union—like the Soviet Union."

Shevardnadze said, "But the peoples of the Soviet Union voluntarily defined themselves in this manner. Lenin recognized self-determination."

"I am familiar with Lenin's writings, and also with Stalin's writings on the rights of minorities. I agree that everything has to be carried out on the basis of agreement."

"Very good. Think about our approach, and if there is anything in your ideas that resembles ours, possibly we could correspond through our Washington embassy or some other channel. We are talking in an excellent atmosphere. Please put an end to the campaign I referred to, which gives an incorrect picture of the Jewish situation in the Soviet Union. I can assure you personally that this angers Gorbachev. He is furious about the distortions and untruths."

The conversation ended, and in contradiction of what had been agreed in advance, Shevardnadze escorted Peres to where the Israeli party was waiting outside. Although his aides had tried to get rid of the photographers, the Soviet foreign minister smiled at the photographers as he shook hands warmly with the Israeli prime minister.

The London Agreement

At the prime minister's office in Jerusalem, secretaries and security men were busy packing. There were large cartons everywhere, creating an atmosphere of farewell. On October 20, Peres took his papers, personal effects, and assistants, and went over to the foreign minister's office, determined to carry out what he had said on the plane taking him on his last visit to the United States: "I will continue with my initiatives, even if I have to feed Shamir snakes and scorpions—not only frogs—and he will swallow everything."

He paid this promissory note in full. Released from the tasks and obligations of the premiership, he could devote even more energy to peace initiatives. As soon as he entered the Foreign Ministry, Peres began a series of trips and meetings with the intention of getting the wagon of the international conference out of the mud in which it had become mired because of the prime minister's attitude. If he thought Shamir would agree to this, he quickly discovered his mistake.

Peres's activity managed to bring Shamir out of his lethargy. He chose the most marginal platform imaginable. At a political discussion of the middle generation of the Liberal party (the junior partner to Shamir's Herut in the Likud), he launched an uncompromising attack on Peres and his party.

Normally restrained in his style of speech, Shamir described the international conference as "a trap for Israel—suicide—an insane and monstrous idea." Shamir could only explain the attempt to advance this idea by saying, "Labor leader Shimon Peres conceived the idea on a night of calamity when he was suffering from pessimism and despair." But all was not lost: "Thank God the Israeli government is not only in Labor's hands today. The Likud is there, and it will save the people."

If Peres had thought that this was a one-time outburst from Shamir, he was disabused of this the following day. An interview with the prime minister was published in *Ha'aretz* in which Shamir said, "The situation in the national unity government today, whereby the vice premier and foreign minister is working against the opinion of the prime minister, cannot continue. We have to recognize that there is one government and one prime minister in Israel. There is a subject in dispute that cannot be resolved, and therefore, the devil's dance around the international conference must be stopped."

Had Peres been able to look at the matter objectively, he would not have found Shamir's outburst so difficult to understand. In fact, he would have had to admit—and deep down he possibly did—that Shamir had a point. The fact was that although Peres brought the idea of the conference to the inner cabinet to make it binding government policy, he never brought it to a vote because he knew that it would not win the necessary majority. Accordingly, Shamir was right when he stated that the foreign minister was advancing a process about which the government had not decided and which at least half the government did not support.

Bringing the proposal to the Knesset, even if the Likud and Shamir did not vote against it, was no substitute for an inner cabinet decision. This was even more the case in a government where the inner cabinet had been created specifically to prevent one of the large parties from implementing a policy that the other found unacceptable. There is also no doubt that a situation in which the foreign minister was working against the opinion of the prime minister was extremely disorderly, to put it mildly. An extremely unhealthy phenomenon had been created: a government with two voices and, in effect, concerning the matter at the head of the political agenda, two governments.

In order to keep the confrontation from escalating, and maybe out of a realization that his case was not cast-iron, Peres refrained from reacting directly to the prime minister's remarks; however, his "associates" rejected Shamir's criticism, saying the prime minister was putting party considerations above national interests. This might or might not have been a correct interpretation of the motives, but it was an irrelevant reaction. A fair assessment would have recognized that the bare facts were on Shamir's side. He was prime minister, and there had been no government decision in favor of an international conference.

The problem was in limiting the matter to the bare facts of the case. This was not a budgetary matter, or even a serious security matter. It was a matter at the existential core of the nation: peace or war. Peres could, and maybe should, ask himself whether he had the right to abandon the idea just when it seemed that there was a marvelous opportunity to advance it.

Peres did ask himself the question, and gave himself a determined answer: he was going ahead. No other course was acceptable. He could not conceive of permitting a political freeze to continue until the end of the term of office of the national unity government, particularly as Shamir had contented himself with saying no without any attempt whatsoever, despite Peres's urging, to suggest an alternative that could form the basis for continuing the political process. Peres believed with all his heart that the nation could not permit itself the luxury of political stagnation.

Peres continued—even stepped up—the pace. The day after Shamir's *Ha'aretz* interview, Peres again received Pickering at his home, and the ambassador reported on talks that Cluverius had held with Hussein in London. The main point was that the king was showing flexibility, and there was a chance for progress.

Less than twenty-four hours later—it was a Saturday—Peres himself was sitting opposite King Hussein in London. Before leaving Israel, he had reported to Shamir about the meeting, and even told him of his intention to warn Hussein about a Likud victory in the elections. Shamir smiled and remarked, "As long as you tell me, it's all right."

Yossi Beilin, now Foreign Ministry director general, accompanied Peres on the flight. The two did not betray any excitement. They found it difficult to see much value in the meetings with the king over the past two years, and in fact, Peres had no reason to believe that this meeting would be different from previous ones. He intended to concentrate on pushing his idea for a Red Sea–Dead Sea canal, the Iraqi pipeline to Akaba, and matters concerning the quality of life in the administered territories.

For this reason, Peres was very surprised when, after talking about the conference, Hussein remarked that the time had come to do something practical. "Let's try to work out a draft on the points we agree on." Peres jumped at the opportunity, and the small group (Hussein was accompanied by Premier Al-Rifai) worked for eight hours, until they had summed up all the points in one document.

Yossi Beilin, who felt the importance of the moment, wrote in the margin: London, April 11, 1987. The document read as follows:

SECTION A: Agreement for calling a peace conference and face-to-face negotiations between Israel and its neighbors.

It is resolved to accept the document presented by the U.S. ambassador to the prime minister of Israel on April 22, 1986 (London document) including the role of the U. N. Secretary General and the role of the conference, as follows:

1. Definition of the role of the U.N. Secretary General in inviting the participants to the conference:

The Secretary General will send invitations to the five permanent members of the Security Council and the parties involved in the Arab-Israel dispute, in order to conduct negotiations for a peace treaty based on Security Council Resolutions 242 and 338, with the purpose of bringing a comprehensive peace to the region, security to the states there, and to relate to the legitimate rights of the Palestinian people.

2. Definition of the role of the conference as inviting the parties to enter peace negotiations in bilateral, geographic committees:

The participants in the conference agree that the purpose of the negotiations is a peaceful solution of the Arab-Israeli dispute, basing themselves on Security Council Resolutions 242 and 338, and a peaceful solution of the Palestinian problem in all its aspects. The conference will invite the parties to form bilateral geographical committees to conduct negotiations on bilateral issues.

SECTION B: The Israeli position concerning the conduct of direct negotiations, identity of the participants, and other relevant subjects.

1. Procedures

a. The conference will be called to initiate, immediately on its being convened, peace negotiations between Israel and each of its neighbors. The conference will not be a forum for negotiation.

b. The negotiations will be direct, face-to-face, and will be conducted in bilateral geographic committees.

c. A third party will not intervene in the direct bilateral negotiations without the agreement of both parties.

d. The discussions in one bilateral committee will be conducted independently from the discussions in the other bilateral committee.

e. The conference will not impose a solution and will not cancel an agreement reached between the parties.

f. The Palestinian problem will be discussed in a bilateral negotiating committee between the Jordanian-Palestinian delegation and the Israeli delegation.

g. Any alteration in the negotiation procedures or in the composition of the participants which is not with the agreement of Israel will result in the cessation of its participation.

2. Participants

a. All participants in the conference must accept, as the basis of their participation, Security Council Resolutions 242 and 338, and disassociate themselves from violence and terror.

b. The Israeli delegation will not participate in a conference, or negotiations, in which members of the PLO participate.

c. The participation of the Soviet Union and China in the conference obligates them to demonstrate greater balance in their policy; in particular, by establishing diplomatic relations with Israel. The participation of the Soviet Union is also dependent on a change in policy toward Soviet Jews; in particular, to recognize their right to immigrate to Israel.

SECTION C: Memorandum of agreement with the United States.

It is resolved to empower the U.S. Secretary of State to formulate a memorandum of agreement, committing the U.S. government in the following areas:

1. The support of the United States for the procedures of the conference as stated in section B above.

2. Violation of the procedures of the conference by any third party will result in the U.S. delegation leaving the conference together with the Israeli delegation, and publicly announcing that the United States sees that third party as responsible for the cessation of negotiations.

3. The continuation of U.S. commitment, as detailed in the memorandum of agreement of 1975, and including the U.S. conditions for talks with the PLO.

4. Prevention of a Security Council decision on the subject of the negotiations, as long as negotiations between Israel and at least one of its neighbors continue.

5. Willingness of the United States to consult with Israel continuously before raising with a third party any procedural or technical proposal.

SECTION D: The next stage—application of sections A, B, and C.

It is resolved to invite the U.S. Secretary of State to Israel, at the soonest possible opportunity, to complete bilateral consultations between the United States and Israel, in the following areas:

1. Formulation of the memorandum of agreement between the governments of Israel and the United States in connection with the above peace conference.

2. Coordination of investigation of the willingness of other parties to participate in the proposed conference.

To protect King Hussein, who was concerned that the contacts be kept secret, it was agreed the document be presented as an American paper, and that its third section, detailing the limits on the power of the conference plenum, would not be made public until after the opening of the conference.

Peres returned home with a feeling of optimism. He had never before possessed—nor had any Israeli before him—such a detailed and significant political document, agreed on with the king of Jordan. He hastened to report to Rabin and Shamir. The prime minister listened and kept silent. Peres did not believe that Shamir would prove a stumbling block to such an agreement. At the same time, intensive contacts with Ambassador Pickering, who was in on the secret, got under way, concerning an American memorandum of agreement that would give Israel extensive guarantees that the United States would not permit the conference to become a forum, which would impose solutions that it did not want.

The ambassador suggested sending a special emissary to report to Shultz and get his permission to present the London agreement as an American invention. The morning after the summit with Hussein, Yossi Beilin flew secretly to Helsinki, where Shultz was preparing for a visit to Moscow. Beilin presented him the agreement with Hussein, and Shultz did not disguise his excitement. "Tell Shimon I'm coming right away. On May 1, I'll be there."

In the political air, electric tension could be felt—a feeling that at last there had been a breakthrough to the conference and direct talks between Israel and a Jordanian-Palestinian delegation. Even Shultz threw off his doubts and joined in the atmosphere of enthusiasm with all his heart. Like Peres, he assumed that Shamir, in the face of such an important and fair agreement, would give up his previous positions to take the opportunity that presented itself. He and Peres were entirely wrong.

Shamir did not wait for Shultz to set off. Without wasting any time, he sent Moshe Arens to Washington, under the guise of a lecture tour for Israel Bonds. Arens met with Shultz, as instructed by Shamir, and told him flatly that, if he came to the region to advance the London agreement, the Likud would accuse the president of the United States of interference in the internal affairs of Israel. Shultz took his advice and stayed home.

In one of the many conversations he had with Pickering, Peres poured out his bitterness. "I don't believe that Shamir will change. He relates to the whole matter as if it were something personal between him and me. We were wrong when we thought he would show flexibility."

The main reason for Peres's impatience during those days was without doubt the dispute with the Likud and Shamir, but there was another reason. A few weeks earlier, Peres had been in Rome for a meeting of the Socialist International. One night he was sitting with his aides in his hotel suite, when one of them remarked that there was a man in Rome who could stop people from smoking by manual contact. Peres's attitude to smoking—he finished two packs a day—had changed over the years. Until a short while ago, he had been saying that he enjoyed smoking, and he had no intention of stopping. Meanwhile, he had not grown any younger, and—no less important—smoking had become a very unacceptable habit. A smoker was regarded as someone who could not give it up because of his weak character. Peres told his aides, "Let's try it. It may not help, but it won't do any harm." They immediately started searching for the man, who was brought to the hotel late at night. He touched Peres's face and chest a few times, and told him that from then on he would not smoke. He did not smoke another cigarette, but for a few weeks he showed the signs of nervousness that everyone who has stopped smoking knows well.

The tension between the two large political blocs increased daily, as the chances of softening the Likud's stand decreased. Peres announced publicly that he would work to bring forward the elections if the Likud foiled his peace efforts. The Likud took advantage of that statement to claim that Peres was frustrated in the Foreign Ministry, and was looking for an excuse to break up the government.

On May 6, 1987, Peres brought an official proposal to the inner cabinet to approve the political document based on the London agreement. After a long night of heated arguments, the five Likud ministers stood as one against the five Labor ministers. A tied vote would mean that the proposal was defeated. Peres did not want to fail on a vote calling for the approval of the London document, and Shamir did not want to fail on a proposal, which had been raised among the Likud ministers, to instruct the foreign minister to cease his peace efforts. The meeting ended without a proposal, without a vote, and without a decision.

This great political struggle ended, then, with Shamir prevailing. The small, mustached prime minister managed to let the air out of the tires of the political chariot, which remained by the roadside like an unwanted vehicle. Peres was portrayed—in Amman, in Washington, in Moscow, and the whole world—as a man with the best of intentions, but who could not deliver the goods.

In mid-October 1987, Peres met again with Shultz—this time in Jerusalem. As long as others were in the room, Peres did not hear anything from his guest that he had not heard before in one form or another. But about an hour after the meeting between the two foreign ministers began, Shultz asked his aides and advisers to leave the room and made a new suggestion: the leaders of the United States and the Soviet Union would invite the governments of Jordan, Israel, Syria, and Lebanon to a meeting that would be the opening of the international conference—a sort of miniconference, under the auspices of the two leaders.

When would they issue the call? At their summit meeting, which was scheduled to be held in Washington at the end of the year, when they were due to sign an unprecedented agreement on the limitation of medium-range missiles. The idea had been the brainchild of the president himself, and at first, Shultz admitted, it had seemed laughable, "but the more you think about it, it is a great idea."

The secretary of state's enthusiasm for the idea was boundless. "We need something like the Sadat visit, a sort of central event. A meeting in Washington will be a tremendous thing. The world will catch its breath." He also thought the idea had a good chance of being accepted because it would enable Shamir to say that it was not an international conference, while King Hussein would be able to say—maybe even to feel—that this was the conference he wanted.

Just before setting out for London to meet with King Hussein, Shultz discovered that he had not been wrong about Shamir. The Israeli prime minister gave his consent to a miniconference on the following conditions: Soviet agreement to an immediate renewal of relations with Israel, a declaration on the right of every Jew in the Soviet Union to repatriation (to return to the homeland), and finally—a bonus to Shamir—an invitation to visit Moscow.

But after he landed in London, Shultz found he had been less right about Hussein. "Check with the Russians before you ask about my response," said the king cynically. "Let's also see the reactions of the Syrians and the PLO." It was the Russians who knocked the last nail into the coffin of Reagan's idea, when Shultz went to Moscow to prepare for the summit. They were not willing to mix the two topics and, in any case, thought that before going ahead with the idea, its prospect of success should be investigated.

And so another idea went down the road of no return, as had dozens before it. The only thing to distinguish it from the others was perhaps that any ideas coming afterward would find a new political reality, which Israel did not predict and for which it was not ready.

The Intifada

In the early part of December 1987, a Palestinian saboteur managed to infiltrate, by means of a hang glider, the outskirts of the Galilee town of Kiryat Shmona. He entered an army camp and, before he was shot, managed to kill six confused soldiers of the Nahal Brigade of the IDF. The success of the lone saboteur fired the imagination of the Palestinians and badly damaged the image of the IDF. At any rate, after his deed, only a spark was needed to set off a nationalist explosion all over the occupied territories.

The spark was provided a few days later, when a truck driven by a Jew fatally injured several Palestinian pedestrians in Gaza. The rumor quickly spread that the driver was the brother of a Jew who had been stabbed to death in Gaza a few days earlier, and that the occurrence had not been an accident but an act of revenge. The rumor was entirely spurious, but it did not need established facts to inflame passions, and the same day, mass demonstrations erupted all over the territories, with stones being thrown at Israeli vehicles.

The general impression in both public and political circles was that these were temporary disturbances that would quickly die down, as had happened in the past. Peres thought differently. On December 8, the eve of his departure for a long trip to the United States and Latin America, he met with Ambassador Pickering.

"We have received a serious warning from the territories," he said sadly. "When they see that Jordan has also not brought a solution, why shouldn't they prefer the PLO position?"

The disorders spread until they had taken on the character of an uprising—the *intifada,* as it was called by the Palestinians. The name caught on with the Israelis, also. The papers were full of gigantic headlines on the disturbances, and pictures of wounded children and women giving the V-for-victory sign. The IDF soldiers found themselves in a tragic confrontation with women and children.

American television networks flooded TV screens with horror pictures of Israeli soldiers beating unarmed youths. As a consequence, the Reagan administration found itself under pressure to do something. That something was the "Shultz Plan," which was as follows:

GENERAL:

1. The statement of principles is based on an interlocking timetable, including the letter to the U.N. Secretary General asking him to call the conference.

2. The purposes of negotiation are peace and security for all the states of the region, and a just solution to the Palestinian problem in all its aspects.

3. The peace negotiations will be based on U.N. Security Council Resolutions 242 and 338 in all their parts and will be held without threat, or terrorist acts, or settlement in the territories.

BASIS OF THE NEGOTIATIONS:

4. The future of the West Bank and Gaza will be determined as follows:

a. Agreement on an arrangement/interim period, during which the IDF and the civil administration will be withdrawn from the territories, and authority will be transferred to Palestinians.

b. The transition regime will last three years (instead of the five years laid down in the Camp David Accords).

c. During the second two years of the interim regime, the final agreement will start being implemented.

d. The negotiations on the final agreement will start no more than seven months after the start of negotiations on an interim accord.

5. The future of the Golan Heights will be discussed in parallel negotiations to those on the future of the West Bank and Gaza, including checking the idea of an interim accord on this front also.

6. Future relations with Lebanon will be discussed in parallel negotiations to those on the interim accords.

7. The final agreement will be a fulfillment of Resolutions 242 and 338, under appropriate auspices, and utilizing the good offices of the U.N. Secretary General.

CONDUCT OF NEGOTIATIONS:

8. The negotiations will be conducted as follows:

a. The negotiation will be in bilateral geographic committees.

b. Each committee will negotiate without reference to the other committees.

c. An agreement will not be imposed, and any agreement reached between the parties will not be vetoed.

d. The Palestinians will be represented in a Jordanian-Palestinian delegation, which will negotiate the Palestinian issue with the Israeli delegation.

e. The international sponsorship for negotiation will include representatives of the five permanent members of the Security Council, and the U.N. Secretary General, who will provide assistance. Other invitees will be determined by the parties, on the basis of mutual agreement.

WORKING PLAN:

9. The suggested timetable is as follows:

a. April 15, 1988: International conference.

b. May 1: Start of negotiation in bilateral committees for interim accords. This negotiation is scheduled to last seven months.

c. December 1: Start of negotiation for a final agreement. This date is not flexible, and is not connected to the progress made in the negotiations for interim accords.

d. February 1, 1989: Start of implementation of the interim accords (assuming that the negotiations are completed according to plan).

After getting a green light from King Hussein via Philip Habib, who visited Amman, Shultz decided to come on a shuttle to the region. Having learned from experience, Shultz made it clear that he was not prepared to compromise and that the plan was a "package that could not be unwrapped." He hoped thereby to prevent the destruction of the plan by endless arguments on this or that point, but he was quickly to learn that a simple statement not backed by determination would not get him far.

Shultz received his first lesson in this particular course when he landed with his plan on February 26, 1988. If the plan was a single package, so was Shamir's response, who gave the secretary a series of *nos*—no to the speeded-up timetable; no to starting negotiations on a final settlement before implementing autonomy according to Camp David; no to the international opening; no to a permanent agreement based on territories or peace.

This was an opportunity for Peres to settle accounts with the secretary of state on his modus operandi. "What did you gain by waiting ten months without doing anything? (He meant Shultz's withdrawal of support for the London agreement.) Democracy in the Soviet Union? Mass emigration of Jews? Arab moderation? The Egyptians are concerned that the demonstrations that started in Gaza could end in Cairo, and demonstrations beginning on the West Bank could end up in Amman. And it is not fanciful. We cannot achieve today what we could have achieved ten months ago, and in ten months' time it will be far more difficult to achieve what we might manage now. I saw a comment of yours with which I do not agree: that peace can only be made if there is broad agreement in Israel. I dispute that. We have arrived at the point where we must choose between unity and decision. I prefer a decision by a small majority to unity without a decision."

Peres recalled an old story. "When I was a young man of twenty-three, I worked with Ben-Gurion, and Moshe Dayan and I were sent as the young representatives of Mapai (Labor) to the Zionist Congress in Basel in 1946. We were sitting there in Basel, when suddenly, Mrs. Ben-Gurion came rushing in excitedly and told us, 'The man (Ben-Gurion) has gone crazy.' We asked her what had happened, and she replied: 'He walked out of the conference.' We went to his room but he did not answer our knocking. We opened the door, and he was standing with his back to us, packing his bags. We greeted him, but he did not answer. We sensed he was boiling with anger. Suddenly, he turned around and asked, 'Are you coming or not?' We asked, 'Where?' He replied, 'I'm leaving. Nothing will come of this congress. They are divided. We have to decide on establishing a state, on partition, on fighting the British. I know the structure of the congress, and there is no chance. I am going to found a new movement.' We tried to argue with him, but he wouldn't listen. We told him, 'We are prepared to come with you, but first we'll appeal to the party. If we are in the majority, we'll stay; if not, we'll leave.' We returned to the discussions. I do not remember a more furious session. The arguments were fierce, but in the morning there was a vote, and we won by a very narrow majority.

"What would have happened if Ben-Gurion had preferred unity to decision? The State of Israel would never have been established. I feel we are facing the same dilemma today; but instead of talking about establishing a state in part of the land of Israel, we are talking about peace, and it is clear there will not be peace without concessions."

Peres's comment about Shultz's wish for a broad agreement versus the need to make a decision worried the secretary. He often thought about this dilemma, he said, but "you have learned from your experience and I have learned from mine. During World War II, President Roosevelt won a decision for America to enter the war on one vote in Congress, but he actually went to war only after the Japanese attack on Pearl Harbor had crated national unity. I am thinking about the Reagan administration and our efforts in Central America. When I started my job (as secretary of state) six years ago, Costa Rica was the 'good boy,' which everyone supported; Honduras was going toward democracy; El Salvador was trying to hold elections, with murders every day; Guatemala—you couldn't mention it in Congress. And today Congress is ready to discuss everything on a bipartisan basis. We got the necessary funding for El Salvador and we have elections there. Afterward, there was broad support. So I don't disagree that you have to argue about the issues, and in a democracy there is ultimately a vote; however, if you start negotiations that lead to a result, and by then you don't have broad support . . . you cannot lead a nation to war or peace unless the majority of the population goes along."

Shultz continued with enthusiasm. "We have been working for this thing (the peace process) since you became prime minister, and we have achieved a great deal. I feel the change is coming now—a new page is opening in Israel's history and we must push ahead. To get there we will have to face traumas, and the wider the basis for support the better.

"I learned from September 1982 (the Reagan plan). If I had

known then what I know now, I would have done it differently. It was
a good proposal, but it did not take off because we did not do the
groundwork. This time we have talked to Jewish leaders, to the
Congress, to your representatives, Shamir's people, the Egyptians,
the Jordanians. We even sent Dick Murphy to [Syrian President]
Assad. We did our homework; that's what I mean when I say broad
support."

Peres disagreed with his guest's remarks. He pointed out that
Roosevelt had started with his policy of "lend-lease" without support.
After giving Shultz a lesson in American history, he went on to talk
about Israel. He recalled the dispute with Begin about German
reparations, the Rhodes agreements, the return of Sinai—both the
first and second times—and Camp David. "In my opinion, if one side
believes that nothing will happen without unity, there is no unity.
That is also true now. It was also true regarding Lebanon and the
economy."

As interesting as the exchanges were, it was clear that Shultz
was not about to change his ideas and his modus operandi, and he
continued with great dynamism to try to enlist the widest possible
support for the plan he had brought with him. Hussein was not
particularly enthusiastic, but he made it clear that he would not raise
obstacles if Israel accepted the plan. Shamir, who was due to visit
Washington in mid-March, was asked to convey his decision to the
Americans before his visit—at least, this was Shultz's understanding
and that of his advisers. Peres and his advisers—everyone connected
with the process—all understood this except Shamir. The prime
minister did not give any answer, claiming all the time he had never
been asked to.

Reagan gave his reaction to this on the White House lawn in his
speech summing up the visit. To Shamir, standing next to him—and
to the whole world—he condemned leaders who said no, who would
have to give an account to their peoples about missing chances for
peace. It was not very pleasant, but not so bad. They were harsh
words, but only words.

Against this, influential American newspaper columnists such as
George Will and William Safire wrote articles in support of Shamir's
stand. A letter condemning Shamir's stand that thirty senators sent
Shultz only encouraged American Jewish leaders to rally to Shamir's
support. Several of the senators hastened to apologize to Shamir for

what they had done, so he was able to return to Israel with the feeling that the U.S. tiger was only a paper tiger.

The riots in the territories continued and became increasingly violent. Jordan began to distance itself from the London agreement. Shultz was coming to realize that the uprising in the territories was creating a new situation that threatened the peace of the Middle East and America's position in the region. At the beginning of April, he came to the region in another attempt to sell his product. At dinner in Shamir's residence, he repeated his stand that his plan was a single package that could not be dismantled. He then took up knife and fork and listened to the prime minister's reply.

He was still digesting his hors d'oeuvres when his brain started to absorb the fact that his attitude toward Shamir was based far more on wishful thinking than on intelligent assessment. His host was telling him that, as far as he was concerned, Resolution 242 had completed its task. The withdrawal that was talked about in the resolution had been carried out in Sinai, and therefore, there would be no further territorial compromise.

Shultz left for Jordan in a rage, asking his advisers to prepare a structured crisis scenario to shock public opinion in Israel; he would leave the region that same night. His team rebelled, maintaining that there was no point in doing this without placing the blame clearly on Shamir; otherwise, it would be a victory for the extremists. Charles Hill, the head of Shultz's bureau, threatened to change the team if it did not carry out the instructions.

In the end it was King Hussein who got Shultz to desist from the idea, explaining it would strengthen the PLO's position. As a substitute, Shultz decided to appeal directly to public opinion in Israel and Jordan through news conferences and television appearances, and to content himself with trying to reassure those who were worried about his plan. He was careful not to blame any of the leaders, even indirectly.

Meanwhile, the PLO's control over the *intifada* increased. Information reaching Israel indicated that the PLO's chief of operations, Abu-Jihad, was guiding the civil insurrection, which embraced all sectors of the Palestinian population of the territories, from his house in Tunis. A force that reached his villa riddled his body with bullets and left rented cars on the beach nearby. NBC reported that it was an Israeli operation. If anyone thought that the killing of

Abu-Jihad would take the wind out of the *intifada*'s sails, he quickly discovered his error. The uprising continued with renewed vigor and, in fact, became part of the reality of Israeli life.

Peres again traveled to Washington, only to discover once more that peace would not be created from there. He found an abundance of goodwill, both from the president and Shultz, but reading between the lines, he saw that apart from lip service, they could not achieve much when the prime minister of Israel refused to allow the peace process to advance.

Peace was not going to be achieved by a broad-based agreement; therefore, there was no avoiding placing the decision in the hands of the Israeli voters at the general election that was due in a few months' time—November 1988. Would the electorate deliver a clear decision against the peace process by giving a majority to the Likud? Or would Israel's citizens grant Shimon Peres the necessary parliamentary tools to permit him to make a serious and effective effort to bring the peace wagon to its destination?

AFTERWORD

THE LABOR PARTY'S election campaign was based on the international conference and the personality of Shimon Peres. In television propaganda, public meetings, and newspaper advertisements, the party reminded the voters how Peres had received a nation in a terrible situation and returned it after two years in good condition. At the same time, Peres was presented as the architect of the international conference, the creator of the only possibility of achieving peace with Jordan and the Palestinians.

Once again, however, the public did not buy. The Likud managed to convince the majority of the people that, aside from Peres and his party, not many on the international scene were keen on the international conference. The Soviet Union didn't want it; the United States spoke of it unenthusiastically and uncertainly. Finally, a few weeks before the elections, King Hussein announced that he was no longer a supporter of the idea.

In addition, the public did not buy Shimon Peres. The message that came from the ballot boxes was: we value your abilities; we are full of admiration for your achievements as prime minister for two years; but we simply don't like you and your way of doing things, your drive to succeed at any price, and (maybe more than anything else) the fact that you want so much to be liked.

The Likud won 40 Knesset seats; Labor, 39. But when the votes of the other parties were calculated, it became clear that the Likud, the religious parties, and the extreme right could form a government based on 61 of the 120 Knesset seats unless the religious parties changed their stand and preferred Labor to the Likud.

Apart from Peres and a small coterie of close advisers, no one believed that this was possible, and this fact caused Peres to act in the very manner that makes the public see him as a man incapable of taking the straight path. After recovering from the disappointment, Peres made an attempt to form a narrow coalition with the religious parties. He did this despite the fact that the president had charged Yitzhak Shamir with forming the government, and despite the fact that he had publicly promised not to do so. As a result, he not only seemed deceitful but pathetic. He was totally obstinate in refusing to recognize the reality that everyone else could see: that the religious parties were using him to squeeze more concessions from the Likud and had no intention of joining a government under his leadership.

In the end it was Shamir who routed the religious parties and started negotiations with the Labor party. By then, Peres and his party had been so weakened in public esteem that they were forced to accept almost everything that Shamir proposed. Peres tried to save something, asking to be foreign minister, this time without being prime minister by rotation. Shamir vetoed the idea. He made it clear that he was not prepared to repeat the experience of serving as prime minister with a foreign minister pursuing his own independent policy. Peres had no alternative but to accept the difficult and unrewarding task of finance minister.

In the Labor party, voices were heard saying that they had had enough of Peres's leadership. He himself appeared angry and depressed, profoundly dissatisfied in the long corridors of the Finance Ministry. It was difficult for him to start the day when the morning papers reported on the meetings of Shamir and Moshe Arens, the new foreign minister, with world leaders, when he was scheduled to meet with the economic and business leaders of Israel. Most observers agreed that Peres's days as leader of the Labor party were numbered and that he would not lead the party into the next elections.

However, anyone who knows Shimon Peres—his stamina, his resilience even in the most difficult situations—is not prepared to bet on that.

INDEX